THE JAPANESE EXPERIENCE IN INDONESIA

THE JAPANESE EXPERIENCE IN INDONESIA:

SELECTED MEMOIRS OF 1942 – 1945

edited by

Anthony Reid and Oki Akira

with assistance from

Jennifer Brewster and Jean Carruthers

Ohio University Center for International Studies
Center for Southeast Asian Studies

Monographs in International Studies
Southeast Asia Series Number 72

Athens, Ohio 1986

© Copyright 1986 by the
Center for International Studies
Ohio University

Library of Congress Cataloging-in-Publication Data
Main entry under title:

The Japanese experience in Indonesia.

   (Monographs in international studies. Southeast Asia
series ; no. 72)
   Selected translations from Japanese.
   Bibliography: p.
   1. Indonesia--History--Japanese occupation, 1942-
1945. 2. World War, 1939-1945--Personal narratives,
Japanese. 3. World War, 1939-1945--Indonesia.
4. Japan. Rikugun--Civic action. I. Reid,
Anthony, 1939-   . II. Ōki, Akira, 1945-
III. Series.
DS643.5.J37 1986   940.54'82'52   85-26886
ISBN 0-89680-132-2

ISBN: 0-89680-132-2

CONTENTS

Page No

List of Illustrations   vii
Glossary   ix
Preface   xiii
Introduction   1

Conquest and Pacification, 1941–1942   7

Fujiwara Iwaichi   Fifth-column Work in Sumatra   9
Imamura Hitoshi   Java in 1942   31
Inoue Tetsuro   I) Suppressing the Aron Rebellion
                          in East Sumatra   79

Administration and Mobilization, 1942–1945   111

Miyoshi Shunkichiro   Problems of Administration in
                          Java, 1942–1943   113
Okada Fumihide   Civil Administration in Celebes,
                          1942–1944   127
Suzuki Seihei   Education in Bali, 1943–1944   159
Otsuka Tadashi   Education in Sumatra   173
Aoki Eigoro   Law Reform in Aceh, 1943   177
Inoue Tetsuro   II) Rural Mobilization in
                          East Sumatra   191
Miyamoto Shizuo   I) Economic and Military Mobil-
                          ization in Java, 1944–1945   217
Nishijima Shigetada   I) The Nationalists in Java,
                          1943–1945   251
Shibata Yaichiro   I) Nationalist Propaganda in the
                          Navy Area, 1945   277
Hirano Sakae   Policy for Sumatra   289

Japanese Surrender and Indonesian Independence   297

Nishijima Shigetada   II) The Independence Proclamation
                          in Jakarta   299
Miyamoto Shizuo   II) Army Problems in Java after
                          the Surrender   325
Shibata Yaichiro   II) Surabaya after the Surrender   341
Ushiyama Mitsuo   Conflict in Aceh after
                          Independence   375

Select Bibliography of Relevant Books in English   397
Index   399

LIST OF ILLUSTRATIONS

1. *Fujiwara Iwaichi in 1942*
2. *Painting of General Imamura by Basuki Abdullah*
3. *Wall painting by Japanese artists in Serang*
4. *Susuhunan of Surakarta visiting Imamura*
5. *General Imamura visiting an Indonesian school*

          ...   **between p.70 and p.71**

6. *Okada Fumihide, in retirement*
7. *General Staff of 16th Army, April 1945*
8. *Sukarno farewelling Sato Nobuhide*
9. *Ceremony to inaugurate PETA battalions*
10. *Sukarno arriving at Makasar, April 1945*

          ...   **between p.250 and p.251**

11. *Nishijima in 1943*
12. *Admiral Shibata in 1945*
13. *Sukarno's party in Makasar, April 1945*
14. *Sukarno celebrating the independence promise*
15. *Javanese rulers welcome independence*

          ...   **between p.280 and p.281**

16. *The Proclamation of Independence*
17. *Admiral Maeda's Jakarta house*
18. *19 September 1945 Rally in Jakarta*
19. *Jakarta slogans, October 1945*
20. *Surabaya fighting, November 1945*

          ...   **between p.300 and p.301**

Maps

Indonesia Under the Japanese Occupation   6

Sigli, Aceh: 'The first day of the PUSA-Uleebalang Conflict'   386

GLOSSARY

Words are Japanese unless otherwise indicated

adat (Ind.)	customary law
aron (Karo)	harvesting collective. Used of 1942 movement among Karos to cultivate estate land illegally
Banzai	'Hurrah', 'Three cheers'
bapak (Ind.)	father
Beppan	Special Task Team
Buchō	head of a department
Bukanfu	[Navy] Liaison Office
bundan	squad in Giyūgun
Bunken Kanrikan	Sub-prefectural head
Bunshū	Sub-Residency; **Afdeeling**
Bunshūchō	equivalent to Dutch Assistant-Resident
Chihō Sangi-in	Local Advisory Council
chō	the head, the chief; often used as suffix, e.g. **Keimubuchō**
Chōkan	Resident [Army]
chū	medium, middle (prefix)
chūdan	company in Giyūgun
Chūō Sangi-in	Central Advisory Council
Chū-sonchō	equivalent of **perbapaan** [head of parent village of a group of villages] in Karo area
dai	large (prefix)
daidan	battalion in Giyūgun
Daihon'ei	Imperial Headquarters
Dai-sonchō	equivalent of **Datuk** in Karo areas
daitai	battalion in Japanese Army
Datuk (Malay)	noble title; chief of an **urung** (Deli)
Dokuritsu Juku	School for Independent Indonesia

F Kikan	Fujiwara Kikan, a group of intelligence agents and language specialists assembled in Aceh in Sept. 1942 by Fujiwara Iwaichi
Fuku-bunshū	Sub-district, **Onderafdeeling**
Fuku-bunshūchō	Sub-district head
genjūmin	natives
Giyūgun	Volunteer Corps
Gummukyoku	Military Affairs Bureau
Gunchō	District Head
Gun Hōin	District Court
Gunseibu	Military Administration Department
Gunseikambu	Military Administration Headquarters
Gunseikan	Chief of Military Administration
Gunshireibu	Army Headquarters
Gun Shireikan	Army Commander
Haji (Ind.)	title given Muslim who has visited the holy places of Islam
Heiho	auxiliary soldiers; Auxiliary Corps
Hi-no-maru	the Rising Sun, often refers to the Rising Sun Flag
--- bentō	lunch box containing rice and pickled plums
Horas (Toba Batak)	'Long life!'
huis **arrestatie** (Dutch)	house arrest
Kaigun	Navy
Kaigun Bukanfu	Navy Liaison Office
Kaijō	abbrev. of Tōkaigan Shū Kaijō Jikeidan; East Sumatra Self-Defence Marine Corps
Kaikyō Hōin	Religious Court; highest religious court in Aceh
kebaya (Ind.)	women's upper garment
Keimubu	Police Affairs Department
Keimubuchō	Chief of Police
Kempei	military policeman

Kempeitai	military police
Kenchō	equivalent of **bupati**
Kō	Prince (Japanese title)
Kōchi	Princely Territory
Kōchi Jimukyoku	Bureau for Princely Territories; **Vorstenlanden** bureau
kōmin	Emperor's subjects
ladang (Ind.)	unirrigated field, especially in shifting cultivation
Minseibu	Civil Administration Department [Navy]
Minseibu Chōkan	Head of the Civil Administration Office
Minseifu	Naval Civil Administration Office
Minseifu Sōkan	Chief Civil Administrator in Naval Civil Administration Office
Nampō Seimubu	Southern Area Administration Office
palawija (Ind.)	secondary crops
parang (Ind.)	short sword; machete
pasar (Ind.)	market
pemuda (Ind.)	youth
penghulu (Ind.)	village headman (Sumatra)
perbapaan (Malay)	head of the parent village of a group of villages (Deli)
rōmusha	requisitioned labour/labourers
ryōminshō	certificate of good citizenship
sarong (Ind.)	wrap-around lower garment
sawah (Ind.)	wet-rice fields
sayyid (Ind.)	descendant of the Prophet
Seichō	Residency Administration
Seiji Sanyo	Political Participation
Seimubu	Political Affairs Department
Sendembu	Propaganda Section
Sendenhan	Propaganda Unit
Shibuchō	head of a branch office
Shichō	Mayor
Shihōbu	Judiciary Department

Shijun-in	Advisory Council
Shisei Chōkan	Chief Civil Administrator
Shiseikan	Civil Administrator
shō	small (prefix)
shōdan	platoon in Giyūgun
Shū	administrative division, formerly Residency
Shū Chiji	Regional Governors
Shū Chōkan	Resident [Army]
Shū Keimubuchō	Head of the Residency Police
Shū Sangikai	Residency Advisory Council
Shūkyō Hōin	Religious High Court
sirih (Ind.)	betel
Sōkan	Chief Civil Administrator (Navy)
Sōmubu	General Affairs Department of the Gunseikambu
Sōmubuchō	Head of the General Affairs Department
Sōmukyokuchō	Head of the General Affiars Bureau
Sonchō	Village Head
Son Hōin	Village Court
Susuhunan/Sunan (Ind.)	Title of ruler of Surakarta
Teuku (Ind.)	title carried by members of **uleebalang** families
Teungku (Ind.)	Acehnese honorific used especially for **ulama**
Tokubetsushi Sangikai	Special City Advisory Council
Tokumu-han	Special Task Team
Tuan (Ind.)	form of address, generally used for foreigners especially in the colonial era
Tuan besar (Ind.)	Chief
ulama (Arab.)	Islamic teachers; learned men
uleebalang (Aceh)	territorial aristocracy of Aceh
urung (Malay)	district (Deli)
wedana (Jav.)	local official

PREFACE

Most of those interested in the history of Indonesia find
the Japanese occupation a period of extraordinary importance
but very difficult to access. Japanese is not part of the
standard equipment of Indonesians or Indonesianists, and most
researchers must therefore seek assistance in consulting even
the most standard of Japanese sources. This book aims to ease
that problem in a small degree, while demonstrating how much
more material is available to those willing and able to
overcome the language problem.

Translation from Japanese is difficult - more difficult
than we appreciated in planning this venture. This has had to
be a team effort, requiring extensive consultation and revision
at every stage. Anthony Reid and Oki Akira planned the volume,
selected the extracts, interviewed some of the authors and took
final responsibility for the product. Jean Carruthers located
and translated the Japanese texts of Okada Fumihide, Suzuki
Seihei, and Shibata Yaichiro. Oki Akira translated the
remaining Japanese texts. Jennifer Brewster and Anthony Reid
edited all the translations with frequent consultation back to
the original translator.

With the exception of Imamura, Inoue, Miyoshi and Shibata,
the authors of the texts chosen for translation were still
alive and able to cooperate with the preparation of this book.
We thank them all for their assistance and their permission to
publish these translations.

We are also grateful to Nakamura Mitsuo for much expert
advice and assistance, and to Shimizu Hajime for his assistance
at many points.

We thank Robyn Walker, Judy Poulos, Rosemary Taylor, Julie
Gordon and Karen Haines for typing the book, and Lio Pancino of
the Department of Human Geography, ANU, for preparing the maps.
For permission to reproduce illustrations we thank Mr Fujiwara
Iwaichi (1), the Imperial War Museum, London (19, 20), Mr
Miyamoto Shizuo (7, 14, 15), Mr Nishijima Shigetada (8, 11,
13), Professor Nugroho Notosusanto (9), Mr Okada Fumihide (6),
Photo Ipphos (18), and Mr Saito Shizuo (3, 4, 5).

In romanizing Japanese words we have followed the Hepburn
system as used in Nelson's **The Modern Reader's Japanese-English
Character Dictionary** (Tokyo, 1962), though for technical
reasons diacritic marks are used only in the Glossary and
Index. We have retained the original order of Japanese names,
with the family name first. Square brackets represent
interpolations by the editors, who also provided all footnotes
unless otherwise stated. Asterisks indicate that a passage has
been omitted.

INTRODUCTION

The three and half years during which the Japanese military ruled Indonesia were critical for the country's development. Many of the structures and values of the European colonial era were turned on their head. Unlike other parts of Southeast Asia, the colonial restoration after the Japanese surrender was abortive in Indonesia. 1942 therefore marked in many respects the beginning of the revolutionary upheaval of the 1940s. The army, Sukarno and Hatta, the Muslim Masjumi, the anti-Western nationalist ethos, all moved to centre stage during the traumatic years of Japanese rule – virtually all the values and forces which would dominate modern Indonesia, in fact, with the exception of the Marxist left, which is singularly absent from our authors' purview.

Despite its importance, the period is poorly documented. The records of the Japanese military administrations in each area of Indonesia appear to have been destroyed in the interval between the surrender and the arrival of the Allies. In terms of contemporary records, we are obliged to rely principally on the tightly controlled press, both Indonesian and Japanese, and collections of documents sent back to Tokyo or originally recorded there, most of which refer to policy only at the highest and driest level. Many of the key policy decisions about Indonesia at the Tokyo level were published as appendices to a thorough study by a Waseda University team led by Nishijima Shigetada and K. Kishi in 1959. A translation of the study itself was published in Washington in 1963, while the documents were more professionally translated by Harry Benda and others in 1965 (see bibliography).

Given this paucity of archival material, we are dependent for a richer sense of the nature of the encounter between Indonesians and Japanese on the personal memories of those involved. Fortunately an increasing number of memoirs have been written and published, particularly in the 1960s and 1970s as the political passions of the time have receded. On the Indonesian side we now have the memoirs of Sukarno (1966), Sjahrir (1949), Hatta (1978), Ali Sastroamidjojo (1974), Margono Djojohadikusumo(1969), Subardjo (1977), Hamka (1966) and Abu Hanifah (1972), to name only the most important, all of which give prominent attention to the years of Japanese dominance.

Those years also had a dramatic effect on the hundreds of thousands of Japanese who were transported to the South for shorter or longer periods. Uprooted from their crowded, homogeneous, socially constrained islands to an 'exotic' tropical world, they enjoyed power and privilege undreamed of at home. Some reacted with real sympathy for the poor and

*exploited population for whom they had suddenly become
responsible; others recoiled from any real contact with the
seemingly backward 'natives'. The experience remained,
however, a vivid and dramatic part of their lives, about which
an increasing number would write once it became possible to do
so.*

*In selecting the passages below for translation from
thirteen Japanese authors, we have been guided by a number of
considerations. Firstly we have sought memoirs with a personal
flavour, shedding some light on the motives and reactions of
individual Japanese. Secondly we have focused on policy issues
which were important for the subsequent history of Indonesia -
education, military training, the relationship to nationalism
and Islam, and the crisis following the surrender in August
1945. Thirdly we have attempted to do justice to all three
major regions into which the Japanese divided Indonesia.*

*The most fundamental divide was that between Java and
Sumatra, which were administered by different units of the
Japanese Army, and the remainder of Indonesia which was
allocated in pre-war bargaining to the control of the Navy. In
no sense was Indonesia seen as a single unit with a single
destiny, and most of our writers long afterward continued to
avoid even using that term except when discussing nationalism.*

*The principal reason for the positioning of the Army/Navy
dividing line was that Borneo and the eastern islands were seen
as 'sparsely populated primitive areas' (Benda et al., 1965,
p.7), appropriate for the policy of 'permanent possession'
which was to be fundamental to administration there. Okada at
the highest level, and Suzuki as one of the educational
'shock-troops' in Bali, both reflect this policy aimed at the
long-term Japanization of the area. Okada is at pains to show
the very high calibre of the Japanese administrative personnel
with whom he hoped to make eastern Indonesia as bureau-
cratically efficient as any part of Japan. Suzuki well
reflects the missionary enthusiasm of many of the young
teachers sent to the South, an enthusiasm seemingly unqualified
by any concern for Indonesian identity and culture. In the
eyes of blinkered idealists of this sort the Indonesians
appeared as long-lost if primitive cousins, spoiled by the
disastrous effects of Western colonialism, but still capable of
being reborn through the energizing spirit of militant Japan.
Naive as their political ideas may have been, we know that the
dedication and sincerity of many of these young teachers made
an enormous impact on young Indonesians.*

*Such teachers also existed in Java and Sumatra, but were
confronted more quickly with the realities of Indonesian
distinctiveness. Java, administered by the Japanese 16th Army,
was accepted from the beginning as having some claim on the
kind of independence which Burma and the Philippines were
granted in 1943. The 'soft' policy described by Imamura, the*

2

first Java commander, manifested the relative indulgence
towards nationalism in that island. Those leading Indonesian
nationalists not already in Java were brought there by the
Japanese (Sukarno from Sumatra, Iwa Kusuma Sumantri from
Celebes). The Army sent all the Islamic experts available to
it to Java, seemingly because it did not take equally seriously
the indigenous institutions of Sumatra (or Malaya). Similarly
the Japanese civilians with the most extensive pre-war
experience in Indonesia tended to be sent to Java. Nishijima
and Miyoshi were both in this category, and their memoirs leave
no doubt about the close personal and even ideological sympathy
they developed with the Indonesian nationalists. There is an
enormous difference between these men who had close Indonesian
friends, and the high-level military officers, of whom Imamura
and Miyamoto are good examples. The latter spoke virtually no
Indonesian, moved among their Japanese peers, and tended to see
Indonesians as the relatively undifferentiated 'natives'
(**genjumin**) for whom they had assumed responsibility. Unlike
Okada and the Navy administration, these men were not pursuing
a deliberate policy of Japanization - it was simply, as
Miyamoto apologetically puts it, that 'the only ways we knew
were the ways of Japan'.

In Sumatra, the 25th Army adopted neither a full-blooded
Japanization policy nor one of accommodation with nationalism.
The most marked feature of its policy was the extreme autonomy
given to each of the ten **Shu** (formerly Residency), each under a
Shu Chokan. Unlike Java, Sumatra was permitted no island-wide
consultative organizations until the last six months of the
war. Within this **ad hoc** decentralized structure individual
Japanese could achieve quite extraordinary results by taking
some local initiative, with or without the support of their
Chokan. The roles played by Aoki in Aceh and Inoue in East
Sumatra altered the history of these regions very signifi-
cantly, even though neither of these men had either high rank
or Indonesian experience.

Eventually, in the last year of the war, both Sumatra and
the Navy area were forced by Tokyo to accept a policy of
independence for Indonesia as a whole, in the hope of obtaining
Indonesian support in the final stand against the Allies. As
explained by Nishijima and Shibata, the Navy accepted this new
line in late 1944 with surprisingly little resistance, despite
the totally different course on which they had led eastern
Indonesia up to that point. Sukarno and Hatta were even
permitted to tour the Navy areas from April 1945, as Shibata
relates. The 25th Army in Sumatra, even though it had followed
Java in setting up consultative bodies and Indonesian military
units (**Giyugun/PETA**) at the Shu level, was more stubbornly
opposed to any influence from Indonesian nationalists in Java.
Hirano explains how the 25th Army quietly prepared for a

separately independent Sumatra until finally forced into line at the eleventh hour.

The translation of Japanese into English involves not only linguistic problems but also cultural ones. Certain Japanese phrases are virtually untranslatable because there are no corresponding English expressions, or because their logic follows a specifically Japanese thought or sentiment. We are conscious that there is much that appears cryptic, puzzling or improbable to English ears especially when deeper emotions are described. The original phrases occur within a Japanese context where much can be taken for granted - for example when our writers touch on their reactions to the Japanese surrender; protest their sincerity in the face of seemingly disastrous consequences; or describe an intimate relationship (like Inoue's with 'Murni'). The importance of bonds of obligation (**on**) towards patrons, clients or those from whom a trust has been received, has to be assumed in reading all the discussions of political motivations - not least the curious 'test' which Miyamoto imposed on the Blitar rebels.

An example of the problem is the word **makoto**, which several of our writers invoke to show the purity of their intentions. The word has to be translated as 'sincerity', but as Ruth Benedict and others have pointed out, it means 'both far less and far more' than the word in English ears. Far from implying conformity between emotion and action, **makoto** suggests that emotion, especially self-seeking emotion of any sort, has been subordinated to a higher good. Considered the central moral quality in Shinto thought, it might more appropriately be explained in an essay than in a single English word.

Nevertheless such cultural boundaries lie at the heart of this project. The authors represented below all wrote not for a Western or Indonesian audience, but for a Japanese one. They could therefore be relatively honest about the values and hopes which motivated them at the time, however puzzling these might seem to outsiders in translation.

Needless to say a memoir by its very nature reflects its author's personal perceptions of events, and tends to avoid unpleasant memories. The darker side of the Japanese administration understandably remains in the shadows of this book. We have no spokesman for the **Kempeitai** (military police), though something of the chill it inspired even in Japanese is evident in Miyoshi and Nishijima. Some of our authors are clearly proud of the role they played - notably in assisting Indonesian independence; some accept a measure of responsibility for the terrible hardship inflicted by rice and labour requisitioning; still others see themselves as simple chroniclers of a drama far beyond their control.

These memoirs do not tell the whole story of the Japanese occupation of Indonesia, or even perhaps a balanced story. As sources, however, they are an indispensable complement to the

Indonesian and Dutch accounts which are so much more accessible to most Indonesians and Indonesianists. We hope that they demonstrate once again that governments are made up of individuals, whose hopes, fears and foibles need to be appreciated if a period as traumatic as this is to be understood.

Anthony Reid   *Oki Akira*

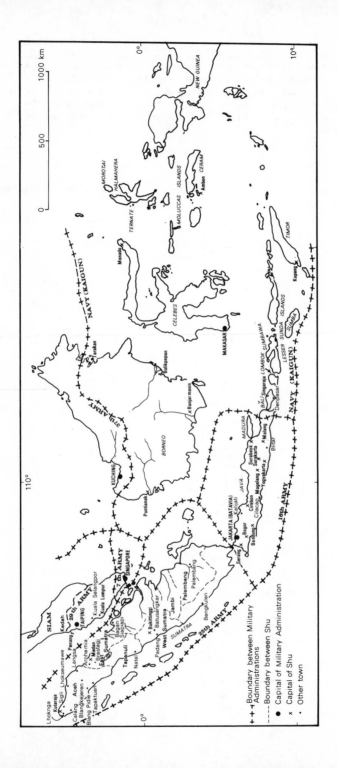

Indonesia Under the Japanese Occupation.

CONQUEST AND PACIFICATION

1941 – 1942

FUJIWARA IWAICHI

Fifth-column Work in Sumatra

The spirit of resistance to the Dutch conquerors always burned brightest in Aceh, an Islamic stronghold in the northwest corner of Sumatra. The ancient Sultanate, known as 'the verandah of Mecca' because it had been the departure point for Indonesian pilgrims, had only been conquered after a bloody Dutch campaign of almost half a century. When from about 1912 the Dutch alliance with the territorial aristocracy of **uleebalang** brought a tenuous peace, it was the **ulama** (religious teachers) who remained as the potential focus for resistance. On the eve of the Japanese invasion in March 1942 the Dutch had to retreat before a popular rebellion aiming to rid Aceh forever of Dutch rule.

Fujiwara Iwaichi tells the story of this revolt from the viewpoint of the Japanese agent responsible for fifth-column activity in the region. As is obvious from his account, however, the Japanese had no idea how explosive the situation in Aceh was, and no plans to make use of it until they were surprised by the overtures of Acehnese agents.

Fujiwara Iwaichi was born in Hyogo Prefecture, near Osaka, in 1908, and graduated from the Army Officer's School in 1931. He saw some action in China as a staff officer of the 21st Army, but by 1940 he was at Imperial Headquarters with the rank of Major, working in the 8th Section concerned with intelligence and propaganda. He was sent twice to Bangkok, in March and October 1941, to contact anti-British elements in the Malay Peninsula - particularly Indians who might be influential in undermining the morale of British Indian troops. In September 1942 he assembled a dozen intelligence agents and language specialists to pursue these tasks, giving the group the name **Fujiwara Kikan** or **F Kikan**. In December 1941 the group flew from Bangkok to accompany the Japanese invasion of Malaya, where it enjoyed the cooperation not only of anti-British Indians but also of the small but militant Malay nationalist organization, Kesatuan Melayu Muda. Responsibility for fifth-column operations in Sumatra appears to have been given to Fujiwara virtually by default, since the matter had been given no real thought until Acehnese agents made contact with the Japanese conquerors in Penang. Fujiwara meanwhile was moving his F Kikan headquarters progressively further south with the advancing Japanese army. He was in Taiping (Perak) when our narrative begins on 31 December 1941.

Throughout the war Fujiwara devoted most of his attention to relations with the anti-British Indian groups. Apart from the one-day visit to Medan mentioned below he never set foot in Indonesia, yet through the F Kikan his name has become an important part of Acehnese history. Most of the information he gives about the revolt in Sumatra appears to derive from the report drawn up in Aceh in 1943 for the purposes described by Aoki Eigoro in the extract below (p.180). It therefore tends to exaggerate the role of PUSA in the revolt.

Fujiwara's book is suffused with his romantic, paternalistic commitment to Asian 'liberation'. Unlike Nishijima (below), however, Fujiwara's sense of mission arose from a conservative political position. He wrote the first draft of his book in 1947-48 while a member of the war history section of military headquarters, under American supervision, and in 1955 he joined the Japanese Defense Agency. Since retirement he has headed a series of agencies to promote Japanese contacts with leaders of Southern Asia. The vision presented here of Japan's mission in Asia has had its echoes in post-war Japan, where his book has been reprinted at least seven times since 1966. The quixotic right-wing novelist Mishima Yukio wrote of it on the dust-jacket of later editions:

> I am greatly encouraged to find in this book a strong, pure sense of mission, which is like a stream of pure spring water in contrast with the degeneration which was taking place in the sense of mission of the Imperial Army; the fading of the old **bushido** ideal. This book is the record of how the trust and friendship of the people of Asia was won; the record of a great spiritual victory.

While this book was in press, a translation by Akashi Yoji of the whole of Fujiwara's memoir was published (**F. Kikan**, Hong Kong, Heinemann, 1983). While those wishing to understand the broader aims of Fujiwara may now consult that, the extracts more fully treated here form an integral part of the whole Indonesian picture.

Fujiwara Iwaichi

FUJIWARA (F) KIKAN: INDO DOKURITSU NO HAHA

[Fujiwara (F) Kikan: the Mother of India's Independence]
(Tokyo, Hara-shobō, 1966), pp. 149-87, 200-203, 273-80, 303-15.

On 31 December [1941] Masubuchi* came unexpectedly into my room, accompanied by a Sumatran named Mohammad Salleh who turned out to be an Islamic priest from Aceh.

The Acehnese, inspired by the example of the Malays and Indians who were already, in the wake of the rapid Japanese occupation of northern Malaya, cooperating with the Japanese army through the F Kikan to achieve freedom and the liberation of their peoples, had decided on a revolt in the name of Aceh and Islam. The Islamic priest had come to propose cooperation with the F Kikan. Following this visit by Salleh, Lt. Nakamiya and Tashiro, both of whom were working in Penang, brought along two more Sumatran youths. Both were from Aceh - the taller one was Said Abu Bakar, an Islamic teacher from Yen in Kedah state, and the smaller one was Teungku Hasbi.† Masubuchi explained the circumstances leading to the two youths being introduced to me. Said Abu Bakar's dream was the liberation of his people and the freedom of Islam, and on hearing the news of the Japanese invasion of Malaya, he had resolved to obtain help

---

* Masubuchi Sahei had spent more than twenty years in the Malaysia-Indonesia region, many of them as a rubber planter in Siak, East Sumatra, before returning to Japan in 1938. There he had published a few articles on the region and in 1941 a Malay-Japanese dictionary. Together with Lt. Nakamiya Goro and Tashiro, mentioned in the next paragraph, he had been recruited in Japan to join the F Kikan. He was to play a crucial role in the Japanese administration of Aceh.

† Said Abu Bakar was an Acehnese **sayyid** (descendant of the Prophet) who had studied at the modernist Islamic Thawalib School in Padang Panjang (West Sumatra) in 1930-32, and thereafter taught at one of the Acehnese Islamic schools most open to the new methods - that of Teungku Abdul Wahab in Seulimeum. In late 1940, after having attended the first PUSA Conference, he had accepted an invitation from the Acehnese community of Yen in South Kedah (Malaysia), to be their religious teacher. Teungku Hasbi was a young Acehnese from Lhoksukon working for a foreign company in Penang. **Teungku** is an Acehnese honorific used especially for ulama.

11

secretly from the Japanese army and realize his long-cherished ambition of fomenting action.

He had made use of the Islamic **Haj** holiday* to travel to Penang, where he had made plans in the company of the like-minded Teungku Hasbi. They had decided to try and make contact with the Japanese Army which, as it happened, had just landed at Penang, and gain entry to the Japanese Propaganda Unit's Penang broadcasting station. However, these plans had been unsuccessful. After several setbacks, they had heard a rumour that Lt. Nakamiya and Tashiro had been dispatched by the F Kikan to try and contact Indians and Chinese in Penang, and had finally succeeded in locating their office. They had been accosted by Lt. Nakamiya as they stood at the doorway, peering hesitantly into the interior, and had seized the opportunity to make known their hopes.

As the F Kikan had been actively seeking an opportunity to initiate special projects in Sumatra, Lt. Nakamiya had accompanied them to the head office of the F Kikan [then at Taiping].

I urged the two youths to be seated, and confirmed for myself their hopes and their determination. Then I said, 'I must point out the enormous difficulties you would face in crossing the Straits of Melaka - which are still under the control of the British fleet - and raising support for an anti-Dutch movement in Aceh. You would have to live under the constant threat of death. Are you both aware of the situation and prepared to face it?'

The Muslim, Said Abu Bakar, answered immediately, 'Our aims are to liberate ourselves from Dutch rule for the freedom of our people and the happiness of Muslims. We believe that the Japanese Army is a righteous army which can help us achieve our aspirations. We wish to follow the Japanese Army for the sake of our people and our religion. This is our one desire, and the reason why we have for some time been awaiting the assistance of the Japanese Army. This is also the desire of the Acehnese as a whole'. His face flushed red with passion as he spoke, I judged him to be 22 or 23 years old.

After expressing admiration for their determination and enthusiasm, I said, 'I believe that those who devote themselves to the nationalist movement and revolution must be prepared to let themselves be broken as the foundation stones of the nation and the people. You must be prepared to sacrifice your lives if necessary'.

Surprise at my unexpected words flickered briefly over Said Abu Bakar's face, before he replied proudly, 'We would not regret whatever fate might befall us, as long as it was on

---

* **Hari Raya Haji** (Arabic **Id al-Hajj**) fell on 29 December 1941.

behalf of the people and Islam. I hereby swear my determination before God. All Acehnese feel the same'.

'I must appreciate your determination and conviction. Can you rally Sumatran sympathizers in northern Malaya?' I replied.

'There are determined young Sumatrans along the Perak River and around Penang', he answered.

'Well then, why not first hurry and rally any sympathizers - not only those from Aceh, but also Minangkabaus and Bataks', I suggested.

'I will rally them immediately. And I trust that you will forthwith make us members of the F Kikan. I swear my complete allegiance to the Japanese Army.'

I granted the pair's request, and it was thus that they and Salleh became the first three members of the F Kikan. I placed Masubuchi in charge of contacting and backing the Sumatran youth groups.

*   *   *

Beyond the Straits of Melaka

After consulting with Lt.-Col. [Ozeki], I spent the night [7 January 1942] making another attempt at drawing up a plan for the Sumatra operation.

The Sumatran youths, watching the preparations of the IIL, INA and YMA* coming daily closer to completion, were ablaze with enthusiasm and rearing for action. It was my intention to finalize the plan, based on the advice of Abu Bakar, and, provided permission was granted by the Staff Officer, Lt.-Col. Sugita, and the Chief of General Staff, Maj.-Gen. Suzuki, to commence the operation for crossing the Melaka Straits that very day - 8 January. The essence of my plan for Sumatra was to create a pro-Japan and cooperative atmosphere among the inhabitants of Sumatra, in particular of North Sumatra; and to rally the population against the Dutch; then, once having landed in Sumatra, to seek the cooperation of the people in protecting transportation and communication facilities, oil refining and drilling facilities, bridges and so forth, from destruction by the Dutch; and to obtain the cooperation of the inhabitants in providing information, supplying food and water to the Japanese, and collecting arms and weapons abandoned by the Dutch so that the Japanese could use them at the time of their landing in Sumatra.

To achieve these aims, I divided the Sumatran youths into several teams, which were to leave the east coast of Malaya for Sumatra, crossing the Melaka Straits. I expected these youths

* IIL = Indian Independence League; INA = Indian National Army; YMA = Young Malays Association, or Kesatuan Melayu Muda.

to spread the word of the decisive Japanese victory in Malaya, the intention of the Japanese to liberate the Sumatrans, and the Japanese anticipation of the cooperation of the population. On the commencement of the Japanese landing, the mark 'F' was to signify cooperation and friendship towards the Japanese. Simultaneously, the Japanese Propaganda Unit was to provide a back-up through Radio Penang. Having obtained Abu Bakar's approval of this plan, I submitted it to Lt. Col. Sugita for his approval in the early hours of the morning [of 8 January].

So the last frenetic day at Ipoh came to an end. That night, after arranging the transfer of the head office [of F Kikan] to Kuala Lumpur, I attended a farewell party given by the Hayashi family.

*   *   *

Said Abu Bakar

With the Japanese control of central Malaya, the greater part of the Melaka Straits was liberated from British control. The training of the Sumatran youths, under the guidance of Said Abu Bakar, was also complete. The morale of the youths was at a peak. All were between 20 and 27 years old, with the exceptions of Kusa [Musa] who was 40, and Usman Basjah who was 18. They looked upon Masubuchi and Lt. Nakamiya as a father and elder brother, on account of their kindness and enthusiasm.

On 14 January I had an opportunity to talk with Abu Bakar and Hasbi concerning future activities. First, I asked them to give me a detailed account of the situation in Aceh. Abu Bakar provided the following account:

> The Acehnese are strongly antagonistic towards the Dutch and the uleebalang. As the uleebalang have been working as the right-hand men of the Dutch, the majority of the population distrust and hate them. The Acehnese are pious Muslims, and they are ready to embark on any difficult struggle as long as it is in the Islamic cause. The Acehnese are not afraid of death, if it is for the sake of Islam. All organizations in Aceh are based on Islam, and of them PUSA is the strongest. PUSA means Association of Acehnese Ulama, and its President is Teungku Mohammad Beureu'eh of Sigli.* He is an Islamic scholar and

* The Persatuan Ulama Seluruh Aceh (PUSA) had been founded in May 1939 on a programme of standardizing and improving Islamic education. It was led by Teungku Mohammad Daud Beureu'eh of Keumangan, near Sigli - a very charismatic ulama then aged 40. It embraced most Acehnese ulama except the more conservative on one side, and the Indonesia-oriented Muhammadiah elements on the other.

teacher, and is the acknowledged leader of the
Muslims. In Aceh, Islamic scholars and teachers
have great influence over the population.

Listening to this account, I thought I detected a
promising avenue for our future work. I questioned Abu Bakar
further , 'I believe that the most important thing is to
establish mutual communication between the Japanese army and
PUSA. How do you feel about this?' Abu Bakar responded
immediately, 'Yes, that's exactly right'.

So I asked him, 'Can your comrades sneak into Sumatra and
contact PUSA leaders?' Abu Bakar replied as if he had been
waiting for that question, 'Of course we can. As a matter of
fact I was intending to raise that with you today. All of us
want to carry out the task. I feel I should enter Sumatra
first, as soon as possible'.

While admiring his noble sentiments, I had to warn,
'Nevertheless, I fear this project is very difficult and
dangerous'.

This served only to produce an earnest entreaty from Abu
Bakar, who said, his eyes burning with intensity, 'I am well
aware of the difficulties, but perhaps they are not as bad as
you think. We must surely succeed since we know the situation
so well. We would be content to die carrying out the mission,
as long as we knew that what we were doing was going to bring
happiness to the people and to Islam. Please let us perform
the task'.

Deeply impressed by his enthusiasm, I proposed, 'I believe
that the Japanese will certainly respect the religion and
welfare of the Acehnese after their landing in Sumatra. I
would like to do my best towards this end. Do you wish to
become members of the F Kikan, which symbolizes freedom and
friendship?'

Abu Bakar replied, 'All of us regard membership of the F
Kikan as a great honour'.

This conversation set the stage for a full-scale operation
by the F Kikan in Sumatra.

I made the following points to Abu Bakar. They concerned
Sumatrans in general and PUSA in particular, and reflected our
great desire to encourage the cooperation of the Sumatrans with
the Japanese.

1. Enter Sumatra and there spread word of the
   Japanese victory in Malaya and the harmonious
   relations the Japanese have with the Indians and
   Malays. In addition, do all you can to undermine
   Dutch morale.
2. Foster among the Acehnese an atmosphere of
   friendly cooperation towards the Japanese, and
   prepare the population to help the Japanese at
   the time of their landing.

3. Prevent Dutch destruction of public and private facilities and properties, especially bridges, airfields, oil wells, oil refineries, oil depots, factories, railways, communication and transportation facilities, ports, ships, and so forth.

4. Be prepared to supply the Japanese with basic food-stuffs and drinking water when they arrive. Guide the Japanese and give them information. Cooperate with the Japanese in collecting abandoned arms, automobiles and bicycles.

Said Abu Bakar swore confidently that he, on behalf of the Acehnese, would do his best to meet the desires of the head of the F Kikan. After a series of discussions we decided to send two teams initially (including six Sumatrans from Minangkabau, the Batakland and Natal) to Sumatra from Kuala Selangor on 16 [February 1942]. Abu Bakar was to lead the teams.

On 16 February I went to [Kuala] Selangor to see off Abu Bakar and his party, and arrived there about noon. The teams had gone on ahead to [Kuala] Selangor with Masubuchi and Lt. Nakamiya, and had been organizing the boats. Masubuchi was preparing a farewell party for them with the cooperation of a nearby village head. The party began shortly after noon. The village head had generously provided the best Malay cuisine. We raised our glasses in a toast to success.

Abu Bakar, reponding to my speech, expressed his determination on behalf of the teams. I was unable to see them off that night as I had to attend an IIL conference. I entrusted the final arrangements to Masubuchi and Lt. Nakamiya and took my leave, after shaking hands with each team member.

So it was that the teams set out that night in two boats across the Melaka Straits to Sumatra, with the Southern Cross as their guide.

*   *   *

The Emergency in Aceh

At the beginning of March [1942], a telephone call came from Army Headquarters [**Gunshireibu**]: 'An important secret mission from Aceh has arrived in Penang to contact the Japanese. The military authorities there have sent them to us. Could you send an escort to Headquarters immediately so that they can be handed over to the Fujiwara Kikan'. I felt like jumping for joy when I heard this report from Lt. Yamaguchi, for I knew intuitively that it concerned the teams which had set out from Malaya and which had succeeded in infiltrating, and that moreover the people of Aceh were prepared to respond to a Japanese call to revolt.

The missions arrived at the F Kikan office escorted by Lt. Nakamiya. One mission consisted of Teuku Muda and three others, who had been sent by PUSA on 13 February.* The other consisted of Teungku Abdul Hamid and three others, who had been sent by PUSA on 20 February. Both missions had risked coming here in order to report on Acehnese resistance against the Dutch, to swear their loyalty to the Japanese, and to request immediate Japanese support. The second mission led by Teungku Abdul Hamid had limped into Penang after being adrift for 13 days. The reports of these missions were the first indications we had had of the surprising situation in Aceh. In addition, they were able to give us detailed and up-to-date information concerning the Dutch forces. According to these reports, the situation in Sumatra was as follows.

Beginning in May 1940, when the Netherlands was occupied by Germany, there was an upsurge of nationalism among the Acehnese. Since the signing of the Alliance between Germany, Italy and Japan, the Dutch government, in response to increasing tensions in the Pacific region, had been trying to mobilize the Indonesians for self-defence by introducing various wartime legislation. However, this policy had served only to arouse antagonism towards the Dutch. At the news of the Japanese invasion of Malaya on 8 December, the leaders of PUSA and PUSA Youth began to proclaim through all their branches: 'Whenever and wherever you see Japanese, you must immediately welcome them, and you must give any assistance that the Japanese Army might require'. The campaign was led by Hanri Masaki and Teuku Njak Arif.† In the middle of December a secret meeting was held at the home of Teuku Njak Arif, at which five people entered into a solemn covenant, among them the president of PUSA, Teungku Mohammad Daud Beureu'eh. The essence of the covenant was: to be loyal to Islam, the people and the homeland; to do one's loyal duty to the Japanese government; and to resist the Dutch in the name of PUSA. Arif was appointed general adviser/consultant. Meanwhile the president of PUSA Youth, Teungku Amir [Hoesain] Almujahid, made a tour of all PUSA branches, secretly advocating loyalty to Japan, extensive cooperation with the Japanese at the time of the Japanese landing, and preparations for fighting the Dutch.

* Teuku is the title carried by members of uleebalang families. This mission, from Lhoksukon, was not in fact a PUSA one - Acehnese of various persuasions were by now attempting to contact the Japanese.

† Teuku Njak Arif (1899-1946) was a leading uleebalang of Aceh Besar, and the leading spokesman for Aceh ever since his period as a member of the colonial Volksraad (1927-30). He was a nationalist, but not a member of PUSA.

The news of the Japanese seizure of Penang served to heighten anti-Dutch sentiment among the population. The Japanese broadcasts from Tokyo and Penang, especially those messages read by Acehnese and Malays, and in particular by Tengku Abdul Rahman of Kedah,* played upon such sentiments. As a reaction to this increasing unrest in Aceh, Dutch oppression of the population increased day by day, which in turn worsened the situation for the Dutch by stimulating further antagonism.

The two boatloads of members of the F Kikan who had set out from Selangor on 16 January under the leadership of Said Abu Bakar arrived in Sungai Sembilan and Bagan Siapiapi respectively. They had thrown all the arms given by the F Kikan into the sea and pretended to be refugees. On landing, all of them were arrested and transferred to the police station at Medan after rigorous interrogation. During ten days of questioning, none of them disclosed the truth, but kept to their story that they were simply refugees. The head of the mission, Said Abu Bakar, had sent a secret letter from prison to his friend Ali Hasjmy, who was a teacher at the Keunaloi Islamic school in Seulimeum district, a member of PUSA Youth and leader of the PUSA Scouts.

As a result of discussion between the leaders of PUSA in Great Aceh [Aceh Besar], it had been decided to dispatch a youth named Ahmad Abdullah to Medan to contact Said Abu Bakar. On 1 March the Japanese made their first air raid on Medan. The police and prison staff, terrified by the raid, fled, and this stroke of good fortune enabled the two [Abdullah and Abu Bakar] to meet. The instructions I had given Said Abu Bakar were immediately passed on to the PUSA leaders in Great Aceh. The leaders were enormously encouraged by the contact with the Japanese, and PUSA members launched a full-scale campaign as I had instructed. As a result of skilful negotiations, whereby PUSA obtained letters of guarantee from the local police stations, all the members of the mission were transferred to the police station in their home district. Finally all were released after re-examination. People from Aceh, Minangkabau, the Batakland and Natal thus returned to their homelands and initiated their activities. Said Abu Bakar was released from police detention in Kutaraja [Banda Aceh] on 13 February. His first move was to visit his friend [Joenoes] Djamil, an Islamic teacher.

The two of them then visited Teungku Mohammad Nur, a

* Tengku Abdul Rahman, later Prime Minister of Malaya/Malaysia (1957-70), had been among the first prominent Malay aristocrats to contact Fujiwara and the Japanese, having earlier 'kidnapped' his father the Sultan of Kedah to prevent his being evacuated by the retreating British.

former classmate of Abu Bakar's.* The three talked secretly in the Taman Pelajaran school building about the messages brought by the mission.

Djamil, grateful for Abu Bakar's patriotism, said, 'The Acehnese antagonism towards the Dutch has been growing every day. The people are preparing for revolt. The orders from the Fujiwara Kikan can surely be carried out. You are the bridge between the Japanese Army and the Acehnese. You are an envoy sent by God. However, the Dutch intelligence surveillance of the Acehnese is pervasive and shrewd. We must avoid communication by letter. Let us use reliable messengers. Each of us must swear to die if arrested, for the sake of the other members and the ultimate good of all. You should now visit the Tunong region (Seulimeum and Inderapuri) and so rally our able comrades. I will be in charge of the Kutaraja area. Before you persuade people to become F-members, ask them to take this oath: "I swear that I am loyal to Islam, to our country, and to the Japanese government. I will carry out my responsibility sincerely and never betray it. We must not divulge the names of F-members and must carry out our tasks to the end"'.

After this meeting Abu Bakar went to the Seulimeum and Inderapuri regions in search of comrades. In Seulimeum he gave instructions to Teungku Abdul Wahab, Ahmad Abdullah and Ali Hasjmy and in Inderapuri to Teungku Haji Ahmad Hasballah, a famous religious scholar and teacher. All pledged themselves to carry out his instructions. Abu Bakar next moved to Piyeueng, where he met the president of the Peramiindo Association† and succeeded in recruiting influential local people. All of the new members took the oath that they would carry out the orders from the F Kikan, and immediately began to make preparations to this end. Abu Bakar also dispatched missions to West Aceh and Tapaktuan to convey the instructions of the F Kikan to Ce' Amat, a wealthy and influential person in that area. Ce' Amat joyfully accepted the instructions. The mission also succeeded in recruiting as F-members influential persons in Mangeng, Hage [Labohan Aji?] and Tapaktuan.

Simultaneous with these activities of Abu Bakar, 20 F-members from Malaya initiated similar activities in central and north Sumatra. By the end of February, less than ten days after the release of the two missions from Selangor, all the

---

* Teungku M. Nur had studied with Abu Bakar in Padang Panjang. Joenoes Djamil was a son-in-law of Nur, and taught with him at the Taman Pelajaran private school in Kutaraja.

† Pergerakan Angkatan Muda Islam Indonesia (Peramiindo) linked students and graduates of Islamic schools, especially in the Seulimeum area. It was older than PUSA but became associated with it.

Acehnese were in a position to respond to instructions from the F Kikan as F-members. The propaganda was also spreading rapidly and secretly among Minangkabaus and Bataks in central Sumatra.

Dutch suspicion and oppression of the Acehnese intensified at that time. The Dutch were about to start destroying rice stocks, rice fields, communication facilities and oil wells in anticipation of a Japanese invasion. These measures by the Dutch authorities fuelled the antagonism of the population and heightened their determination to prevent such destruction. The situation in Aceh was critical, with the prospect of an outright clash at any minute between unarmed Acehnese and the Dutch military and police forces. It seemed that any delay in the arrival of the Japanese Army in Aceh would result in serious loss of Acehnese life and property. This was the reason why the Acehnese sent two missions to the F Kikan, to try to impress the Japanese with the urgency of the situation and to ask for Japanese support.

On the Japanese side, the Army was preparing a landing in Sumatra, and the Konoe Division, which had participated in the capture of Singapore, was ready to leave Singapore to carry out the Sumatra operation. The invasion date was fixed for 13 March - the major force on the Kutaraja coast, the remainder on the coat near Medan. I was anxious to move to Sumatra to check on the activities of my comrades there, to facilitate cooperation between Japanese and Sumatrans, and to work in the interests of the Sumatrans. However, I was obliged to return to a region opposite Sumatra.

I was busy at that time. At the request of Imperial Headquarters [**Daihon'ei**], I had to attend an IIL meeting to be held in Tokyo in a few days' time. In addition, I had to perform a difficult job in Singapore, looking after 50,000 Indian soldiers who were to become the core of the Indian National Army, and commencing a serious study of how that Army should be organized. I visited the Chief of Staff of the General Southern Army and discussed this problem. We decided to send Masubuchi, who had the greatest understanding of the Sumatrans and who was respected by F-members, to Sumatra with the Konoe Division, so that he could serve as a 'benevolent father' to the Sumatrans over a long term. To this end I asked to have Masubuchi made a senior official in the **Gunseibu** [Military Administration Department]. Eventually Masubuchi was placed temporarily under the command of the head of the Konoe Division, in the hope that the authorities of the Division would enthusiastically support him.

On my return to the head office of the F Kikan, I immediately entrusted my responsibilities to Masubuchi. I also asked him to stay in Sumatra for a long time in the interest of the Sumatrans and of those comrades who were regarded as F-members, and to help protect them.

Masubuchi expressed his resolve thus: 'I have deeply
appreciated your great favour to me and your enthusiasm for the
establishment of friendship among peoples.   I am determined to
devote myself to whatever task you give me.   All my life I
shall have a special love for the Sumatran people.   It is my
greatest desire to devote the rest of my life to my Sumatran
brothers.   I will endeavour to fulfill my duties on your behalf
to the best of my ability.   This may be our final parting.   We
have only known each other since last October, but in that
short period I have known greater kindness and nobility of
spirit than I have experienced in all my fifty years.   I would
be happy to reciprocate by fulfilling these responsibilities in
Sumatra'.

Masubuchi was a man of deep sensibilities, and tears were
streaming down his cheeks.   I appointed Hashimoto and
Saruwatari to go to Sumatra as his assistants.   The four of us
called on the commander of the Konoe Division, Lt.-Gen.
Nishimura, and the Chief of Staff, Col. Obata.   We explained
the Sumatran situation and the activities of F-members fully,
and asked for support and cooperation from the Army.   So it was
that Masubuchi and about 20 Sumatran sympathizers, including
the envoys sent by PUSA and Sumatran F-members, left the head
office of the F Kikan on 5 March to board ships of the
transport division for the crossing to Sumatra.

The activities of the F Kikan had now been expanded to
incorporate a wide region, centring on Singapore and including
Malaya, Thailand, Burma and Sumatra.

*   *   *

The Uprising in Aceh

After the return to Sumatra of Said Abu Bakar and twenty
F-members, the propaganda of the F Kikan literally spread like
wildfire throughout Aceh, and evoked a sympathetic response
from PUSA members.   The Acehnese antagonism towards the Dutch
reached a peak in the wake of the latter's preparation for
destroying important public facilities.   The Penang broadcasts
relating the success of the PUSA missions in contacting the
Japanese Army, together with the Tokyo broadcasts of the fall
of Singapore, further encouraged the population.

The uprising began with an attack on the night of 23
February, led by Teungku Abdul Wahab, on a Dutch-controlled
post office in Seulimeum.   By that time native Indonesian
members of the Dutch armed forces had already become agents of
the F Kikan.   The following morning the insurgents began
interfering with the Dutch destruction of bridges.   The
population set about removing dynamite set by the Dutch on 20
bridges, starting with the Keumiroe bridge between Lam Leupong

and Lampaku.*   Orders for such action had been out since the 21st.   Three hundred armed suicide troops wearing F-armbands took part in the operation and succeeded admirably in their task.   In addition they blockaded narrow paths at various places, they cut telephone cables, and in Inderapuri they destroyed railway lines and secured the town.   On the morning of the 24th, severe clashes occurred between the Dutch forces and the insurgents, resulting in more than ten casualties altogether on both sides.   On the night of 7 March some 800 F-members attacked the Dutch barracks at the Krueng Jreue bridge.   This attack led to the arrest of several comrades, who were imprisoned in Kutaraja.

In concert with the uprising in Seulimeum on the night of 22 February, a revolt was also planned at the big North Sumatran airforce base at Lhoknga.   Said Abu Bakar, acting on orders from the head of the F Kikan, had resolved to try and protect the facilities of this airforce base from destruction by the Dutch.   Said Abu Bakar dispatched 20 reliable F-members to take part in this uprising, and succeeded in recruiting to the cause 80 Indonesian soldiers who were in charge of the maintenance of the base.   Among the leaders of these native soldiers were two Menadonese, Melo and Walangintan, and a Batak, Pangsitorus.   The plan was to launch a simultaneous attack on the barracks from within and without during the night of the 23rd.   However, the Dutch were tipped off by an informer and captured Melo, who was to have struck the first blow against them.   Despite harsh interrogation by the Dutch, he steadfastly refused to answer.   Finally Melo was sentenced to be shot, the sentence to be carried out at the back of Sigli prison in the early hours of 12 March.   Fortunately the firing squad were F-members.   Although Melo fell down when the shots rang out, the bullets did not hit him.   Thus his life was narrowly saved thanks to the resourcefulness of his comrades. The growing antagonism of the population prompted the Dutch to strengthen their forces in the Kutaraja area.

As a result of this move by the Dutch, a conference of delegates from every district in Aceh was called on 4 March at Lubok, and a decision reached to launch a united uprising throughout Aceh.   Furthermore the following resolutions were adopted on oath according to Islamic ritual:

* This makes the Acehnese action conform more closely to Fujiwara's instructions than was the case.   In reality it was the Acehnese rebels who were attempting to destroy bridges and communications at this point, notably the Keumiroe bridge on 23 February, and the Dutch who were endeavouring to keep communications open until their withdrawal on 12 March.

In the name of God, in the name of God, in the name of God,* I pledge my loyalty to Islam, to the people and to the fatherland, and agree to resist the Dutch without breaching this three-fold pledge.

A. All Acehnese will unite and rise up simultaneously against the oppressors.
B. Such action derives from the need to protect Islam, the people and the fatherland, and is a pledge of our loyalty to Dai Nippon.
C. A manifesto will be sent to branch leaders in every district of Aceh.
D. A manifesto accompanied by demands will be sent to the Dutch.
E. A united attack on the Dutch barracks will be launched during the night.

On 6 March these resolutions were dispatched to all regions of Aceh. At the same time native colonial officials were warned that they would be regarded as Dutch unless they resigned from their positions. These manifestos were sent to the Dutch administrative authorities and the police, and were plastered in the streets and even on Dutch tanks. On 7 March, members of the self-defence force in towns and cities went on strike and began defecting to join the F Kikan. F-members were placed at all those public facilities, such as bridges, oil refineries, oil depots and transportation facilities, which were to be destroyed by the Dutch, and the dynamite removed. On the same day Teuku Njak Arif sent an ultimatum to the Dutch Resident: 'Administration in Aceh must be returned to the people. If this is not done the Acehnese will declare war on the Dutch'. From this time onwards telephone cables were cut and roads were blockaded by trees everywhere in Aceh. Meanwhile the Dutch forces and officials around Kutaraja gathered in the barracks.

On the evening of 11 March a plan was drafted for the coordination of all uprisings in Aceh. To counter Dutch attacks, villages were to be protected by barricades and fortifications, and counter-attacks planned. Near Kutaraja a clash with the Dutch occurred at the Lamnyong bridge about 11 p.m. on 11 March, and the Dutch were repelled. At about 2 a.m. on 12 March a fight occurred at Lhoknga between the Dutch and members of the F Kikan, who had taken the firing of oil depots at the airfield by the Dutch Army as an indication that the Dutch were about to destroy the airfield. At 4 a.m. that morning, thousands of shouting F-members descended on Kutaraja city, attacked administration offices and launched an offensive against the army barracks. At about 7 a.m., at the height of

* Arabic: **Wallahi, Billahi, Tallwani.**

23

the fighting, the Japanese Army entered the city, and was given a tumultuous welcome by **Banzai**-shouting Acehnese.

In the Lamno district the population had been preparing for an attack on the Dutch forces since 1 March, and at 8 a.m. on 11 March the offensive was launched at the Lamno market. F-members also ambushed the retreating Dutch Army at a crossing-point at Kuala Lambesu. As a result of this fighting the insurgents suffered a dozen or so casualties.

In the Calang area, during the night of 9 March, an attack was launched by F-members under the command of Teuku Pulo* on the Dutch forces which were stationed at Calang. The fighting continued until the 11th with dozens of casualties. The Japanese army arrived in the area on 19 March.

In the Tapaktuan district, the entire population banded together under the leadership of Bulanpitieh† just as had been directed by Said Abu Bakar, formed an association called GAFI, and began preparing for an uprising. The name GAFI comes from Gabungan Fucheyama Indonesia (The Indonesia Fujiyama Alliance).

When Said Abu Bakar had briefed this district, he had not explained that 'F' stood for Fujiwara Kikan, and so the people had taken it to stand for Fujiyama [Mt Fuji]. This is how the name GAFI had come about. Teuku Rasjid had assumed the position of chairman. The aims of GAFI included:

A. To carry out orders and instructions from the F
     Kikan.
B. To resist the Dutch government.
C. To be loyal to the Japanese government.
D. To organize a unified uprising against the Dutch
     in the Tapaktuan district.

On 15 March this organization immediately started an anti-Dutch uprising at the news of Dutch destruction of important public facilities and resources. The uprising began with an attack on the Dutch barracks at Blang Pidië. The Dutch forces had the advantage of mobility because of several dozen vehicles, and a bloody battle ensued during which over 30 GAFI members were killed.

---

* Teuku Pulo was younger brother of the uleebalang of Lageuen,
  Teuku Sabi, the dominant figure of the Calang area. Teuku
  Sabi was one of the few uleebalang who led the rebellion in
  his district instead of simply tolerating it.

† Fujiwara writes as if this 'Mr Bulanpitieh' were a person.
  It seems almost certain that this results from a confusion,
  somewhere along the line of transmission from Acehnese
  informants to Fujiwara's book, with the sub-district of Blang
  Pidië in South Aceh (Tapaktuan) district.

On 17 March a Dutch barracks at Apaan [Labohan Aji?] was attacked, and during 18 and 19 March the uprising spread to other areas. The fighting in this area resulted in more than 100 Acehnese killed and ten wounded. Owing to the courageous fighting here, the town of Tapaktuan escaped being burnt, and the oil depots, trading companies and military barracks were all handed over safely to the Japanese Army when it subsequently arrived.

In the Sigli region, revolts occurred under the leadership of Sab Cut,* in response to the general uprising in Great Aceh [Aceh Besar]. On the night of 11 March, at a signal beaten out on the big drum in the mosque by one of the comrades, Nairuddin, thousands of F-members descended on Sigli city. A simultaneous attack was launched on the military barracks, the prison, the residence of the Assistant Resident and other strategic places in the city. Within the space of half an hour the attack had successfully achieved all its goals. The Japanese Army entered the city on 13 March, at the critical moment when a full-scale battle was about to erupt between the Dutch forces and thousands of F-members. With the cooperation of F-members most of the Dutch were arrested, and the Japanese Army was welcomed by the cheering population. In other areas too the explosives set by the Dutch were removed, and consequently the Japanese Army was able to avoid the difficulties it had encountered in Malaya where the British had destroyed bridges, and was able to secure important facilities and resources.

While the Dutch defence forces were thus on the point of collapse due to the Acehnese resistance instigated by Said Abu Bakar, the Konoe Division of the Japanese Army began to land in the three districts of Peureulak, Krueng Raya Durueng and Sabang. Masubuchi arrived in Sumatra together with 24 comrades.

The major part of the Dutch forces was in retreat to the mountain districts. The rejoicing spread from the coastal people, the first to see the transport ships of the Japanese Army, to the whole of Sumatra. The inhabitants gave a flag-waving welcome to the Japanese, and provided water, fruit, food, drinks and chicken as they had been instructed by the F Kikan. All the villages and towns of Aceh prepared food, water and fruit in order to welcome the Japanese. Bicycles and automobiles were collected for the use of the Japanese. The roads were cleared and the bridges were guarded. Important resources were safely preserved and preparations were made for handing them over to the Japanese.

* The youngest of three Sab brothers from Gigiëng, near Sigli, all of whom were prominent in small trade, in PUSA, and in revolutionary activity.

Hurried repairs were made to damaged railways and telegraph wires. Hundreds of thousands of F-members collected the arms and weapons abandoned by the Dutch, and began rounding up remaining Dutch soldiers. Information concerning the retreating Dutch forces was clearly and openly given to the Japanese Army. Owing to the activities of F-members, Aceh returned to normal and order was restored within three days of the Japanese invasion.

All Aceh was ringing with shouts of **Banzai**. The PUSA Youth troops were temporarily put in charge of the maintenance of order in Sigli and other towns. On 15 March Masubuchi arrived in Sigli* to meet Said Abu Bakar. After a dramatic meeting between Masubuchi of the F Kikan and Teungku Mohammad Daud Beureu'eh, the chairman of PUSA, Masubuchi sped on towards Kutaraja, accompanied by Said Abu Bakar and other F-members. That night he shook hands warmly with the PUSA leaders in Seulimeum who had rendered such meritorious service.

At 11 a.m. on 15 March, Masubuchi and the other F-members arrived in Kutaraja. They immediately set up a head office for an F-committee, which was to comprise leaders such as Teungku Mohammad Joenoes [Djamil] and Teuku Njak Arif. Following the instructions of this committee, branches of the Chian Iji Kai (Association for the Maintenance of Order) were opened throughout Aceh. Aceh was to all intents and purposes an 'F-kingdom'. There were instances of some Acehnese pretending to be F-members and plundering the houses and properties of Dutchmen, Chinese and Menadonese. Many uleebalang who had been cooperating with the Dutch ran away for fear of attacks by villagers, while the remainder failed to display a cooperative attitude towards the Japanese Army by such things as joining the committee.†

The accidental contact between Said Abu Bakar and the F Kikan at Taiping airport had resulted in this truly remarkable success within the short space of 75 days. However, as the Japanese administration became more established and it was decided to follow in the footsteps of the old government administration, the uleebalang who had previously cooperated with the Dutch were reinstated. The uleebalang, becoming jealous of the increasing influence of F-members and fearing that they might disclose the hitherto anti-Japanese sentiments of the uleebalang, tried to eliminate F-members. They directed the main thrust of their criticism and acrimony against Said Abu Bakar and PUSA.

* By road from Medan, where he had addressed a meeting on 14 March.

† While not untrue, this comment reflects the influence on Fujiwara's view of Aceh of the anti-uleebalang PUSA elements described in Aoki's report below.

The Japanese **Kempeitai** [Military Police] and the staff of the Gunseibu were ignorant of the true situation, and were beguiled by the skilful propaganda of the uleebalang. Moreover, the plundering and violence committed by those pretending to be F-members provided the uleebalang with splendid ammunition.

In due course, officers of the Kempeitai and the **Gunseikambu** [Military Administration Headquarters] came to believe the vicious slander of the uleebalang and began clamping down on F-members. Reports critical of F-members were sent to the headquarters of the 25th Army in Singapore, and these eventually came to my ears. The sad news greeted me on my return to Singapore from Tokyo.

I was distressed to find that the Japanese authorities had failed to appreciate the genuine and enthusiastic loyalty of PUSA members to Islam and to their fatherland, their great service to the Japanese, and their noble self-sacrifice. Moreover, the time of the dissolution of the F Kikan was impending, which meant that it was nearly time for the hand-over of political, religious and cultural movements to the military administration. Furthermore, the army was going to take the perverse course of repressing these popular organizations. I called on Maj.-Gen. Manaki* again and explained in detail the great contribution of the Sumatrans, the unjust suppression of PUSA by the Japanese, and the possible frightening outcome of the present repressive policy. The result was that he promised me that the army would halt its repressive policy and re-evaluate those who belonged officially to the F Kikan. In return I promised him that I would dissolve the F Kikan and concentrate my activities on encouraging the people to work towards their religious and nationalist goals through the sole organization of PUSA. I immediately chose Lt. Nakamiya as an envoy and sent him to Sumatra. His task was to consult with the authorities of the Sumatran military administration and with Masubuchi, Said Abu Bakar and PUSA leaders on such subjects as the investigation of the real situation in Sumatra, the consolation of people who had sacrificed their life and family, the dissolution of the F Kikan, and the entrusting of the leadership of PUSA to Masubuchi. Nakamiya returned in two weeks, having accomplished his task. He had held a big memorial service for those who had died at the Keumiroe bridge, and brought photographs of the service back with him. He made a report on the magnificent achievements of the comrades in Sumatra, while at the same time complaining bitterly about the unsympathetic attitude of the

---

* Maj.-Gen. Manaki was Vice-Chief of Staff of the 25th Army in Singapore, which during 1942 had responsibility for both Malaya and Sumatra.

authorities towards those Sumatran comrades.

Although I was very busy winding things up prior to my departure from Singapore, I felt I should spare a day to show my warmest gratitude to the Sumatran comrades and to express my regret at parting. Accordingly, at the end of April [1942] I flew to Medan. Masubuchi kindly met me at the airport. His appearance bespoke the efforts he had been putting into protecting F-members from the oppression of the aggressive military.

First I called on the Chief of Staff of the Konoe Division, Col. Obata, at his headquarters in Medan. I begged him to protect F-members, just as I had done in my earlier talk with Manaki.

Col. Obata had been one of my supervisors at the Military Academy, and until five weeks earlier he had been director of the second division in the staff office of the General Southern Army. He was thus my senior. I was disappointed by his lack of understanding of our tasks. However, as a result of my attempts to change his attitude by explaining the situation, he finally accepted my recommendations. Had it not been for our relationship as a teacher-student and senior-junior I would probably have been unable to persuade him. After this talk Masubuchi took me to a hotel in Medan where Said Abu Bakar and a few of his comrades were waiting for me.

My meeting with Said Abu Bakar came 100 days after he had left Singapore with high hopes on 16 December [1941] to cross the Melaka Straits. He behaved like a dutiful son before his benevolent father, at once modest yet full of familiarity. No one would have believed that this was the man who had performed such an historic undertaking. We shook hands in silence, choked by deep emotion. Tears glistened in Said Abu Bakar's eyes. Masubuchi, who was looking on and a tender-hearted man, was also moved to tears. Striving to control my emotions, I finally managed to say, 'Thank you very much for everything. I am sorry to have had to ask you to perform so many difficult tasks'. Even after being seated he neither spoke of his great achievement and the tremendous difficulties it involved, nor did he voice any dissatisfaction over the cool attitude of the Japanese military authorities. Knowing the situation from the reports I had received, I sincerely praised his efforts and achievement. He nodded his head at everything I said, and accepted my sincerity.

Then I explained the details of my successful attempts at persuading the military authorities to change their attitude towards F-members. He was very appreciative of my efforts. When I told him of my scheduled return to Saigon a few days after dissolving the F Kikan, he stood up with surprise. He seemed disappointed and sorry at my departure. I tried to encourage him by saying consolingly, 'We have decided that Masubuchi is to stay in Sumatra over a long term as a "benevolent father" and friend of all Sumatrans. Please don't worry about the F Kikan, because the military authorities and I have already reached an agreement that all problems concerning F Kikan members will be dealt with through Masubuchi. I want him to contribute to the building up of Sumatra and to take on the permanent role of a "father" of Sumatra'.

Although he was very keen to accompany me to Kutaraja and introduce me to the population as a friend of all Aceh, I was unable to accept his kindness because of my scheduled return flight to Singapore that same day. After asking him to give my regards to the comrades, I regretfully boarded the aircraft. During the flight I prayed for the happiness of F-members, for the prosperity of Sumatra, and that Japanese would appreciate the selfless devotion of the Acehnese.

The realities of Japanese administration in Malaya, Sumatra, Java and Burma differed in many respects from the ideals and aims expressed in the Emperor's declaration of war and the statements of Premier Tojo in parliament in January. This resulted in first disappointment and later antagonism among the population towards the Japanese, since the people had been longing for freedom and independence, and had welcomed the Japanese and cooperated with them in the hope of achieving their ambitions. There were some unavoidable factors which made the Japanese unpopular, such as military demands for strategic purposes and urgent requisitions for war materials. Nevertheless, it cannot be denied that the Japanese, intoxicated with the initial victories of the war and the welcome and cooperation of the population, which far exceeded Japanese expectations, underestimated and misunderstood the real desires of the people. It must also be admitted that various propaganda and special task forces, such as the F Kikan and Minami Kikan (operating in Burma), deliberately manipulated nationalist sentiment and gave the population false expectations.

Most of the unfortunate incidents which occurred, such as the tragedy of the Chinese massacres in Malaya, the Acehnese anti-Japanese revolt in Sumatra (which did not come to much due to the frantic mediating efforts of first Masubuchi and then F-members),* and the uprisings of the Burma National Army at the end of the war, were the direct outcome of these Japanese errors. Had the Japanese implemented their plans for the New Order in Asia and the Greater East Asia Co-Prosperity Sphere, met the aspirations of the people for independence and freedom,

---

* This may refer either to the Bayu (Lhokseumawe) rebellion of November 1942, or the still more bloody Pandraih (Samalanga) rebellion of May 1945. Both were led by ulama unconnected with PUSA.

and clarified the reasons for the war, the course of the war would have been very different.

Be that as it may, it seems to be the fate of all who are involved in special task forces, at whatever time and in whatever land, that they face enormous difficulties through being caught in a dilemma between the policies of the military authorities of their own countries and the hopes and aspirations of the local people. A good example is provided by the case of Lawrence of Arabia, who was never understood by the British authorities.

Masubuchi, who remained in Sumatra throughout the war as the 'benevolent father' of the comrades, shot himself at the time of the Japanese surrender, thus making himself part of Sumatra forever.

IMAMURA HITOSHI

Java in 1942

General Imamura Hitoshi, a full general by 1943, was one of the highest-ranking active Japanese officers to escape execution at the end of the war, and his detailed four-volume memoir is a unique source.

Imamura was born in Sendai City in 1886, and joined the Army at the age of 19. After graduating from the elite Army Staff college in 1915, he had a formative period as military attache in London (1918-21). He also visited Germany and Italy, and was sent to India for a period in the late 1920s. The importance of the rule of law regardless of personal status impressed him greatly in British democracy. On the other hand he took a cynical view of British foreign policy, which he saw as designed to keep France and Germany in conflict in Europe, and China and Japan in Asia.

Throughout the 1930s Imamura was deeply involved in Army relations with China and Korea. As a colonel in the Army's Operations Department he had considerable influence in shaping Army policy towards Manchuria. He is generally considered a member of the 'Control Faction' (**Tosei-ha**) which came to dominate the Army in the late 1930s, but his stance was typically to oppose factionalism and excessive military involvement in politics. He was one of the officers who took a stand against the attempted coup of March 1931.

As Lieutenant-General, Imamura commanded Japanese troops in South China in 1937-38. His memoirs reveal a belief that Japan had been driven ineluctably to invade China by Anglo-American obstructionism over Japan's basic need for markets and materials. Nevertheless he began to doubt the legitimacy of the China operation as he witnessed the determination of the Chinese, including women volunteers, to resist.

By contrast, as can be seen in the following translation, the warm welcome given his troops in Java struck Imamura very forcibly. Imamura was given command of the 16th Army formed for one of the vital assignments of the Southern campaign - the conquest of Java. This was completed much more quickly than expected, not least because of the support of what Imamura calls the 'native' population. Their apparent cooperativeness encouraged Imamura and his principal advisers in what was regarded in Japanese circles as a 'soft' administrative policy. In essence this meant pragmatism towards the Dutch population, who were kept on at their jobs wherever they were useful, and paternalism towards the Javanese, who were believed by Imamura to be distant relatives of the Japanese, capable of adopting their virtues if correctly guided.

Such paternalism did not, of course, rule out the violent suppression of the anti-Japanese underground led by Amir Sjarifuddin, which is not discussed here. Nevertheless the Japanese impact is probably remembered less unfavourably in Java than in any other occupied territory, and its harshest aspects began after the departure of Imamura. Sukarno's appreciation of Imamura is apparent in both their memoirs. Imamura also quotes an incident in 1948 (not translated here), when over a thousand Indonesian fellow-prisoners of the Dutch sang the Japanese song **Yaeshio** (The Vastness of the Sea), which had been composed at Imamura's suggestion to celebrate Japanese-Indonesian friendship, as a tribute to the Japanese commander and a mark of defiance of the Dutch.

In November 1942, Imamura was transferred to command the 8th Area Army based in Rabaul. Although he left Java reluctantly, his new command was one of the most vital war theatres of 1943-45. After the war he was held initially in Rabaul by the Australians, and then transferred to Jakarta (Batavia) in May 1948. There, isolated from other Japanese, he began work on his memoir. This was encouraged by Allied authorities, who had the memoir translated into poor English by another Japanese under the title **A Tapir in Prison**. A tapir, according to Japanese tradition, lives upon its own dreams. The English translation is retained in the Rijksinstituut voor Oorlogsdocumentatie, Amsterdam (I.C. 002457). The Japanese original was later returned to Imamura, who used it as the basis for a much fuller autobiography in four volumes, which is also more frank in its treatment of questions sensitive to the Allies. The fourth volume of this autobiography contains his description of the occupation of Java, most of which is translated below.

Imamura Hitoshi

IMAMURA HITOSHI TAISHŌ KAISŌROKU

[Memoirs of General Imamura], Vol. 4 **Tatakai Owaru** [Cessation
of Hostilities] (Tokyo, Jiyū Ajia-sha, 1960), pp.104-95.

*The invasion forces which Imamura commanded had begun to
disembark near Merak, 60 km west of Jakarta, on the night of 28
February 1942. Two Allied cruisers, HMAS* **Perth** *and USS*
Houston, *attempting to withdraw through the Sunda Strait to
Cilacap and safety, accidentally came upon the invasion fleet
at 11 p.m. Before being sunk by Japanese torpedoes, the Allied
ships sank at least two Japanese transports, one of which
contained Imamura and his 16th Army Headquarters. We take up
his story of the invasion after he had scrambled ashore.*

Our Attack and the Enemy's Surrender

1 March 1942, about noon: hundreds of soldiers who had
been forced to swim naked managed to obtain uniforms and other
clothes, as reserve clothing was taken from a transport ship.
However, they were forced to march without arms after landing
behind the vanguard troops because there were no reserve arms.
The soldiers seemed to be very embarrassed by this situation,
even though arms might soon be obtained from wounded Japanese
soldiers and Dutch soldiers captured in battle.
According to information sent that evening, part of the
Second Division [of the 16th Army] was advancing towards
Serang, a town 16 or 17 kilometres east of the landing point,
pursuing the enemy. However, no information was available on
the state of the war in other areas because all radio
facilities had been sunk at sea. Thus, I was unable to command
the troops until radio facilities arrived later from the
Headquarters of the General Southern Army, after being
requested by one of the ships' radios and carried by an
airforce plane stationed in Singapore. As far as landing
troops were concerned, I could know only that the Shoji
Regiment, the Sakaguchi Brigade, and the Tsuchihashi Division
had completed landing.
The Staff Officers [of the 16th Army] camped in a coconut
plantation of a kampong in Banten that night. I, together with
Chief of Staff Okazaki* and Vice-Chief of Staff Harada

* Maj.-Gen. Okazaki Seizaburo, the 16th Army Chief of Staff,
  was at the same time Gunseikan or head of the military
  administration in Java. Okazaki had formerly studied in

Yoshikazu, slept in a blanket on the floor of a room of about two square metres, in a peasant house. Although I usually woke five or six times a night to relieve myself, I managed to sleep through the night until next morning. This was perhaps because I had not slept at all the night before, and I was tired by the two hours of swimming.

Morning, 2 March: I had dried bread and a coconut for breakfast. This was the first time I had drunk coconut juice. I emptied the coconut at a gulp from a hole made by a soldier. I was impressed how nature blesses the people of the tropics with such delicious water.

The Headquarters was moved forward to Serang after breakfast. The road system was worthy of admiration, though it had been completed as a result of 300 years of Dutch oppression. Big roads for automobiles stretched in all directions. On each side of the road or in the middle were planted tamarind trees - tall, evergreen trees belonging to the family **leguminosae** (pea) - so that pedestrians could walk in the shade during the day. Some of the trees were used for telegraph poles. When Allied forces, comprising Dutch, American, British and Australian troops, retreated, they blew up the roadside with explosives inserted at the foot of the trees. As a result, automobiles and horses could not pass, and the soldiers had to straddle huge trunks. This was not easy at all, as the trunks were often as much as one metre in diameter. All the Staff Officers including myself walked on in this way, allowing us to march at most one kilometre an hour.

To our surprise, natives along the way began running towards the road with long knives in their hands. They did not seem to be planning to attack us. On reaching the road they began to cut off branches and remove trees. As hundreds of people joined in the work, after 20 or 30 minutes the road became easier to walk along. I became worried: 'I wonder how many months this operation will take to complete if all the roads in Java are in this condition'.

When we had marched about three kilometres in three hours owing to the cooperation of the natives, we suddenly found that there were no more fallen trees on the way ahead, although explosives were placed in the trees. Anyway, we took a long rest while about 200 officers and men of the Headquarters Unit passed through. Many natives gathered around us from far and near, the way country people in Japan run to the road when soldiers are marching during manoeuvres. The natives - including even the aged and children, though there were few women - brought coconuts, bananas and papayas to the Japanese. They were saying something, but I could not understand it at

* Footnote continued from previous page:
  England (1925-27), and been a delegate to the Geneva Disarmament Conference (1931-32).

all. Some soldiers were giving them cigarettes, dried bread,
chocolate and so forth. Many of the natives were cheerfully
raising their hands with their thumbs up.
   I asked an interpreter, 'They are saying **tuan** something.
But what does that mean?'
   'That means "thank you master". Usually, **terimakasih** is
enough, but they add **tuan** out of respect for you.'
   Some Japanese officers took from their pockets the
Japanese-Indonesian conversation dictionaries which had been
given them at the time of embarkation, and began talking with
the adults and children with the help of gestures. I wondered:
'Is this really a battlefield?'
   Spontaneously I said to Maj.-Gen. Okazaki, 'Chief of
Staff! We have already won the battle, since even the population in this enemy area are offering cooperation and showing
goodwill to us'.
   An old man, perhaps a notable of the village and wearing a
somewhat better sarong, came to us and said something, also
sticking up his thumb. I told the interpreter to ask him what
he wanted to say.
   The interpreter began to talk with the old man, and told
me, 'The thumbs-up sign means "good". It seems that the
population are saying "welcome" to us. The old man is saying,
"In Indonesia, a prophecy has been passed on for hundreds of
years that people of the same race would come some day to
restore the freedom of Indonesia.* Are you **tuan** the same
people as us? Though your language is different from ours, you
look like us". This is what he is asking us'.
   I replied, 'Interpreter! Tell him this. "Some ancestors
of the Japanese came from these islands in boats.† You and the

---

* At least since the late 18th century there had been
  prophecies in Java attributed to the 12th century King of
  Kediri, Jayabaya, predicting that the rule of the Europeans
  over Java would be short-lived. It would be ended by another
  foreign power, variously identified as Kling (India), Rum
  (Turkey), or in the 20th century, Japan, which would then
  withdraw after a period of five years or after the time taken
  for corn to ripen. Java would then be reunited and free, and
  an age of righteousness would dawn. Such prophecies were
  particularly rife in the years before the Pacific War.

† Some physical, cultural and linguistic differences between
  Japanese and other East Asian people were popularly
  explained, particularly during the 1930s and 1940s, by
  Austronesian migrations from Southeast Asia to Japan.
  Archaeological and linguistic opinion now tends to prefer a
  theory of common dispersal, east and southeast, from the
  Asiatic mainland.

35

Japanese are brothers. We are fighting the Dutch so that you can recover your freedom"'.

The interpreter told the old man exactly what I said. The old man said **'Terimakasih tuan besar'** again, occasionally sticking up his thumb.

'Ask the man one more thing. Why did the Dutch run away without blowing up the trees around here?'

The interpreter again began to talk with the old man, who replied, 'Explosives were put into the trees by Dutch soldiers, but it was the village head who was responsible for ordering the villagers to light the fuses. When we set off the charges up to this point, the soldiers went away satisfied, ordering us to continue in the same way. However, we stopped lighting the fuses because the villagers would have had trouble walking if we had continued. If we were accused by the Dutch afterwards, we had decided to say that the Japanese soldiers reached here by using the ridges between the rice fields, so we had no time to light the fuses. As this village did not blow up the trees, the next village did not either, I think'.

While walking after our rest, we found that explosives were put in every tree as the old man had said. However, no tree was actually blown up. I understood why some units of the Second Division had been able to advance far ahead. That night I heard that thousands of natives helped to remove the trees that had been felled, so that the artillery corps could catch up with the infantry, arriving in Serang by evening with their vehicles.

Since the evening of 3 March, a total of only 3,000 officers and men of the 16th Infantry Regiment of the Second Division had been attacking about 7,000 Australian troops* around the city of Buitenzorg (Bogor) - a place 20 kilometres [40 km - ed.] south of Batavia and the site of the palace of the Governor-General of the Dutch East Indies and of the largest tropical botanical garden in the world. But the attack was making little headway due to vigorous enemy resistance, and the Japanese troops were having difficulty in crossing two rivers with high cliffs to the west of the city. Finally, however, on 5 March, Maruyama, the Commander of the Second Division, reported that the Australian troops had begun to retreat eastward towards the Bandung stronghold, and that the Second Division had occupied the city of Buitenzorg and was moving in pursuit of the enemy. However, the advance had been

---

* Although the Japanese widely believed there was a whole Australian Division in Java, there were in fact only about 3,000 men. The total of British and Australian troops was about 7,000. Gavin Long, **The Six Years War: A Concise History of Australia in the 1939-45 War** (Canberra, Australian War Memorial, 1973), p.166.

slowed down as the retreating enemy had destroyed a bridge over a precipitous river.*

The 29th Infantry Regiment (from Aizu Wakamatsu district), which had been advancing along the coast towards Batavia [Jakarta], occupied the city on 6 March, after crushing enemy resistance on the way. To avoid possible confusion I prohibited the Regiment from entering the city, with the exceptions of the Headquarters' Propaganda Unit [**Sendenhan**] (headed by Lt.-Col. Machida Keiji) and the staff of the **Gunseibu** [Military Administration Department] (headed by Maj.-Gen. Harada Yoshikazu), and ordered the Regiment to set up camp outside the city. In this way I tried to maintain peace and order in the city. By that time another infantry regiment of the Second Division, the 4th Infantry Regiment, had been transformed into a reserve corps of the Division.

Headquarters' telegraphic equipment was delivered from Singapore by air on 5 March, thus enabling us to communicate with distant corps. However, we had already learned the following from a communication cylinder dropped by plane:

1. The Tsuchihashi Division had succeeded in landing and was advancing towards the port of Surabaya, about 100 kilometres to its east.
2. The Sakaguchi Mixed Brigade had occupied the royal capitals of Solo and Yogyakarta on 3 March. Leaving behind part of the Regiment, the major force was moving towards the port of Cilacap, located behind the stronghold of Bandung.
3. The Shoji Mixed Regiment had endured an air raid immediately after its landing on 1 March, but had suffered little damage. In the afternoon of the same day, it had seized Kalijati airport, routing the defending Dutch-Australian forces.
4. Part of the Sugawara Airforce Unit under the direct command of the General Southern Army - a few dozen airplanes led by Maj.-Gen. Endo Saburo - had been heading for Kalijati airport since the

* The first two rivers mentioned here seem to include the River Cianten at Leeuwiliang, 20 km west of Buitenzorg, where the Allied troops eventually gave up their attempt to cross. S. Woodburn, **The War Against Japan. I: The Loss of Singapore** (London, HMSO, 1957), pp.446-7. Lionel Wigmore, **The Japanese Thrust. Australia in the War of 1939-1945** (Canberra, Australian War Memorial, 1957), pp.499-502. For detailed official documentation of these and other battles by the Japanese side, see Bōeicho Bōei Kenshūjo Senshi-shitsu, **Senshi Sōsho**, Volume III; **Ran-in Kōryaku Sakusen** (Tokyo, Shinonome Shimbun-sha, 1967).

37

afternoon of 2 March and was assisting the 16th
Army in its military operations.

As can be seen from the above my troops had steadfastly
performed their duties since the departure of the transport
ships, in accordance with the strategy mapped out beforehand,
even while I, the supreme commander of the whole Army, was
unable to contact the troops due to the sinking of our
transceiver and telegraph equipment in the sea. There is no
doubt that this success was made possible through the efforts
and sense of responsibility of the leaders, the hard fighting
of both officers and men and the cooperation of the 50 million
Indonesian people who had anti-Dutch and pro-Japanese
sentiments.

On the night of 5 March, at our Headquarters which was
temporarily located in the municipal building of Serang city, I
received the following telegraph report from Regimental
Commander Shoji:

> 3 [March]: A tank unit consisting of dozens of tanks
> suddenly appeared from the Bandung stronghold.
> However, it was repelled with heavy losses by a
> concerted counter-attack from our infantry and
> airforce and retreated to the stronghold, abandoning
> several tanks. Since 5 March the Regiment has been
> planning to mount an attack on the stronghold, and
> has been encouraging the frontline troops to action.

How splendid! What brave determination! And this even though
he had been informed that the Allied Dutch, British and
Australian forces - about 50,000 in total - were concentrated
in the stronghold under the protection of impregnable batteries
and fortifications.

Col. Shoji was born in Sendai as I was. When I took up
the position of captain of the 10th Company in that prefecture,
after graduating from the Military Academy, he was a platoon
leader under my command. He experienced my rigorous training,
as I was a Spartan in those days. Shoji was an upright and
kind man, but I thought him 'too gentle'. When I arrived at
my post as commander of the Area Army in Kwangtung, South
China, he commanded one of my regiments. I visited his
regiment twice and found that his followers were faithful to
him. Once I ordered him to charge deep into the midst of a
nearby Chiang [Kai Shek] force. As he won a great victory in
that battle, I formed a high opinion of him. I thought, 'He
has become a good captain during this long period I have not
seen him'.

Shoji's courage and boldness from the first day of landing
[in Java] was beyond my expectation, even taking account of his
experience in China. I speculated that Shoji might be
intending to make a surprise attack as he had done in the

north-west of Kwangtung five months earlier when he charged the Chinese enemy. That had been an ordinary field battle, but now he was facing the enemy stronghold. Accordingly I would not allow him to make a raid into the enemy zone, where 50,000 soldiers were deploying, with only a little more than 2,000 soldiers. I immediately ordered a telegram sent to Shoji as follows:

> I applaud the courage of your regiment. In view of the topographical difficulties of the Bandung stronghold, I have decided to change the plan of attack and move the major forces of the Second Division in front of yours. They will arrive on 8 March, and on 9 March, under my command, will storm the stronghold and destroy the enemy. The Shoji Regiment should secure the strategic point at the peak of the mountain facing the stronghold, and protect the concentration and operations of the major forces at the same time, but should not charge the stronghold in only regimental strength.

In the early morning of 7 March, I ordered Chief of Staff Okazaki to convey the following instructions to the Commander of the Second Division, Maruyama:

1. The Army is changing its plan of attack. You approach towards the forefront of the stronghold, which has been broken through by the Shoji Regiment, and then commence an attack.
2. Part of the Second Division will launch an attack upon the west side of the outer perimeter of the stronghold. While it is holding the enemy in check, more than two major regiments will march quickly to the north side of the stronghold, detouring 40 kilometres. Await instructions to be issued in the morning of the 8th, while deploying along the line already broken through.
3. The Commander moves to a suburb of Batavia on the afternoon of the 7th.

It was decided that the Headquarters staff were to leave Serang in the morning of the 7th, arrive at a southern suburb of Batavia about 4 p.m., and spend the night in Dutch barracks now evacuated. I heard that order was being maintained in Batavia city by the Gunseibu, and that the electricity system there was working.

In the meantime, Chief of Staff Okazaki returned and reported that the Second Division had ordered the advancing troops to stop where they were while Maj.-Gen. Nasu continued an attack with one regiment (minus one battalion), and that other troops had been concentrated in Buitenzorg by the evening of the 7th, and had started preparing for their advance to the

designated line on the morning of the 8th. It was about 11
p.m. when I went to bed that night.

   After I had slept for a while, the Chief of Staff and Oda,
a Staff Officer in charge of strategy, came to my room to wake
me. As I was sleeping in my uniform, I got up quickly and sat
down on a chair by the desk nearby. My wrist watch showed
12.30 a.m. Lt.-Col. Oda read a telegram report:

> This afternoon [7 March], an enemy mission visited
> the front line of the Shoji Regiment (What a
> surprise! The Regiment had reached the vicinity of
> Lembang, a bit more than 10 kilometres north of
> Bandung, by itself!) and stated: Please convey to
> the Commander-in-Chief of the Japanese Army the
> message that the Commander-in-Chief of the Allied
> Forces in the Dutch East Indies, Lt.-Gen. ter
> Poorten, intends to propose the cessation of
> hostilities. We await an immediate reply from you
> as to how we should answer.

   'Please be seated. Oda, take down what I am about to say.
Chief of Staff, back me up and tell me if I have left out
anything', I said, and then dictated:

1. Instructions to the Commander of the Shoji
    Regiment. Report the following as the answer of
    the Commander of the Japanese Forces: The
    Governor-General of the Dutch East Indies and the
    Commander-in-Chief of Allied forces in the Dutch
    East Indies should come to the Kalijati airport
    at 2 p.m. on 8 March, together with the Staff
    Officers concerned, in order to meet the Japanese
    Commander. The proposal for a cessation of
    hostilities will be answered at the meeting.
    Your passage from your stronghold to Kalijati is
    guaranteed by Japanese guards.
2. Order to the Commander of the Second Division.
    The enemy has lost his fighting spirit and is
    proposing the cessation of hostilities. Taking
    advantage of this situation, we must strongly
    display our fighting spirit. Your Division must
    advance to the areas where the Shoji Regiment has
    broken through.
3. Measures to be taken by Headquarters. An
    immediate assembly of its staff. The Chief of
    Staff, the Staff Officers concerned, and Diplomat
    Miyoshi* - seconded from the Ministry of Foreign

* For Miyoshi Shunkichiro, see the extract below. He had been
  Vice-Consul in Batavia, 1936-39, following periods of
  consular service in the Hague and Surabaya.

Affairs (he had served in Java and the Netherlands for a long time and was the best Dutch linguist among the Japanese forces in Java) - are to accompany the Commander. Arrange so that a Japanese party for the meeting can arrive at Kalijati airport by 2 o'clock. The remaining Headquarters Staff Officers should advance together with the Second Division under the command of Sen. Adj. Inoue.

These instructions were immediately carried out. I left the bedroom and moved to the next room which was used as an office of Headquarters.

I wondered why the enemy had given up before any substantial fighting had taken place, despite the fact that he could potentially mobilize 50,000 soldiers in the Bandung area alone, in contrast to the 40,000 total Japanese forces which had landed in Java, and only 25,000 of this number who were advancing on the stronghold.* I suspected that the enemy General Staff might be sending the mission in order to investigate the size of the Japanese forces. With this in mind, I had instructed the advance of the Headquarters and Second Divisions, in order on the one hand to conceal from the eyes of the Allied delegates the smallness of the Shoji Regiment which was attacking the stronghold, and on the other to reduce their morale. After the cessation of hostilities, however, I discovered the truth from the enemy staff and officers. The enemy had speculated the Japanese forces totalled as many as 200,000 soldiers, which became the main factor behind the enemy surrender.

The commander of the Shoji Regiment at one point decided to make a charge into the stronghold, on the advice of Staff Officer Yamashita, who had been assigned to assist the Regiment's commander. Although he changed the plan after my telegram, and then ordered the battalions under his command to suspend attack after the seizure of the peak of the mountain facing the north side of the stronghold, this order was not conveyed smoothly in the battlefield. As a result, the battalion under the command of Maj. Wakamatsu Mitsunori crossed over the peak down to the major defence line of the stronghold in pursuit of the enemy.

The enemy staff, who had imagined the Japanese force to be twice as big as theirs, judged that the Shoji Regiment, with only 2,000 men according to their calculation, would not dare

* The total regular Dutch Army (KL and KNIL) in Java was only 25,000 strong, though as many as 40,000 more were formed into a ineffective home guard (**landwacht** and **stadswacht**). Kirby, p.432.

41

to launch such a bold action by itself. They thought that a
total of 100,000 Japanese soldiers must have been approaching
the north side of the stronghold under the direct leadership of
the commander. These judgements led most of the Allied General
Staff to favour a cease-fire and drove the enemy commander,
Lt.-Gen. ter Poorten, to propose one in view of the difficulty
of centralized command of the Allied Dutch, American, British
and Australian forces, and the impossibility of winning.

It seems that the enemy gave up the battle in the face of
a Japanese battalion of about 500 soldiers who continued
attacking them simply because the order to suspend operations
had not reached them. After the cessation of hostilities,
Staff Officer Yamashita came back to headquarters and said, 'I
am very much ashamed to have been ordered to stop an attack.
It was youthful passion which caused me to launch an attack
with a single regiment'.

I answered, 'Your action was certainly not correct. But
there is a saying: "Good results from incorrect behaviour".
God himself might be amazed by such success'.

Later on, I gave a letter of commendation to Col. Shoji
and Capt. Yamashita, which was addressed to all the members of
the Regiment.

As I had summoned the Headquarters staff quite early, I
thought we could leave Headquarters at about 3 a.m. However,
things did not proceed as I had expected. I asked my adjutant,
Capt. Tanaka, 'What is going on? When can we start?'

'The men have to have breakfast now. In addition, lunch
must be prepared', he replied.

'This is a very important time, you know. Can't we
dispense with one or two meals?'

'If we are hungry, our arrival will only be delayed.'
Tanaka smiled at me. He had been working with me for three
yeas since I had been commander of the Fifth Division, and
therefore he knew that I was apt to be impatient. His smile
had an air of amusement. 'You should not be the hasty one,
since you are the commander.' I had to wait, however
impatiently. It was only at 6 a.m. that we could finally
depart.

When we arrived at Kurakan [Krawang] about 9 p.m., having
quickly overtaken soldiers of the Second Division on foot, we
found that an iron bridge about 150 metres long, over a river
running through the east of the town, had been blown up.
Engineers were busy replacing it by a wooden bridge. In spite
of their efforts, we were told that some more hours of work
were needed before automobiles could cross the new bridge. We
had to cross the bridge on foot and borrow an automobile from a
kampong nearby. I rested in the shade of a tree beside the
bridge while some people were looking for an automobile. As
several Japanese with epaulettes were standing in front of me,
two or three Chinese, perhaps regarding me as a high-ranking

42

person, spoke to me volubly after saluting politely several times. The language did not sound Chinese. Diplomat Miyoshi translated, 'Immediately after all the public servants, police, and so forth retreated into the stronghold with the Dutch, Indonesians plundered more than ten Chinese shops and took all the property, even glass windows. Could the Japanese army please recover them?'

[The Chinese] had fawned upon the Dutch and promoted a boycott of Japanese commodities until the very day before the outbreak of war. Despite the antagonistic attitude of the Chinese to the Japanese before the war, I told these Chinese, 'As you can see, we are fighting the Dutch. We have no time to search for stolen goods. When we win this war, which is sure to be soon, an order will be issued for the police to search for them and recover them. Whenever your lives are threatened by the natives, you can come to the Japanese who will certainly protect you'. These Chinese seemed to be satisfied. They went away saying **'Terimakasih tuan besar'**. The damage suffered by the Chinese seemed to be quite serious, seeing that all the houses demolished in towns along our way were Chinese ones.

At about 1 p.m. a soldier brought a car, which he had found with difficulty, driven by a native. I, Chief of Staff Okazaki, Col. Takashima, Lt. Oda, and Diplomat Miyoshi left for the airport in this car. Later, another car was found. The remaining Staff Officers, my adjutant Tanaka, and Lt.-Col. Okamura Masayoshi, a liaison officer sent from General Headquarters in Tokyo, arrived at Kalijati airport at 2.30 p.m., having caught up with us in the second car.

The Dutch representatives consisted of Governor-General Tjarda; Lt.-Gen. ter Poorten, Commander of Allied Forces in Java; the Chief of Staff of the Dutch East Indies Army; the Commander of the Bandung stronghold; the secretary of the Governor-General; and an interpreter. (He had been working in the Dutch Embassy in Tokyo and knew Japanese well, though his knowledge of Japanese was far inferior to Miyoshi's knowledge of Dutch.)

They arrived at 1.54 p.m. and waited in a room of the Japanese Headquarters building arranged by Maj.-Gen. Endo Saburo of the Sugawara Airforce Unit and belonging to the Headquarters of the General Southern Army. I and the Japanese party were also led to the room. The room was about 5.4 metres wide and 7.2 metres long, with a table in the centre 1.5 by 3.5 metres. Chairs were arranged so that the Japanese were to sit on the right side of the table seen from the entrance, and the Dutch party on the left. The interpreters of each side were to sit at opposite ends of the table for convenience. There were about ten Japanese altogether: I was in the middle; Maj.-Gen. Okazaki on my right; Maj.-Gen. Endo on my left; and flanking them Okamura, a Staff Officer from General Headquarters, two Staff Officers [of the 16th Army], and my adjutants.

I initiated the meeting, 'I am Lt.-Gen. Imamura, Commander of Japanese operations in the Dutch East Indies. Dutch interpreter! Explain my status to your party and let us know the names and positions of the representatives of the Allied Forces'.

The Dutch interpreter did what I said, and introduced their representatives to the Japanese.

'Well, Diplomat Miyoshi! Introduce the Japanese side.' Miyoshi did what I said.

First, I spoke to Commander ter Poorten. 'Did you order one of your staff yesterday to go to the Japanese advance unit to convey your message that you wanted to suspend hostilities?'

'Yes, I did.'

'Was that because you thought you were unable to continue the war?'

'Because I did not want to extend the horror of war any further.'

Turning to Governor-General Tjarda, I asked, 'Governor-General, do you accept an unconditional surrender?'

'No, I don't.'

'If you would not accept an unconditional surrender, why did you come here?'

'I came here to discuss with the Japanese Commander how to deal with civil administration in the Dutch East Indies.'

'We, the Japanese Army, were not sent here to administer the Dutch East Indies, but to eliminate all Dutch forces. Was not the proposal made yesterday for a cease-fire the result of your decision?'

'I have no intention of accepting an unconditional surrender.'

'Then, why did you come to this meeting?'

'Because I was informed by the Commander of the Dutch East Indies Army that the Japanese Commander wanted me to come.'

'If you had no intention of accepting a cease-fire, why didn't you prohibit such a proposal by your Commander? I understood that the Governor-General is given the authority of Supreme Commander in the Dutch East Indies by the Dutch Constitution, with overall responsibility for the army.'

'Before the war, I had that authority. However, it was transferred to Gen. Wavell of Britain from the time of his arrival in Java, as a result of an agreement between the Allied countries.'*

* Gen. Sir Archibald Wavell (later Field Marshall Earl Wavell) was appointed Allied Supreme Commander for the Southwest Pacific Area on 4 January 1942, without the prior approval of the Netherlands Government (in exile). This was a source of considerable resentment. He left Java on 25 February, to resume his appointment as Commander-in-Chief in India.

'Commander ter Poorten. You said that you wanted to suspend hostilities to avoid extending the horrors of war. Do you accept an unconditional surrender?'

'[I meant] a cessation of hostilities only in Bandung.'

'Do you not care if the horrors of war are extended to areas beyond Bandung?'

Ter Poorten meditated for a while. 'All channels of communication are now broken, and I can order the cessation of hostilities only in Bandung.'

'Japanese radios at this airfield have been intercepting communications between Dutch East Indies troops. We also monitored Bandung radio broadcasts this morning. It must, therefore, be possible for you to order your troops in the Dutch East Indies as a whole to cease hostilities. We demand the total and unconditional surrender of the Dutch East Indies Army.'

The Dutch representatives looked at each other, apparently reluctant to answer immediately. I continued, 'You have only two alternatives: unconditional surrender or continuation of the war. As you have seen while passing this airfield, dozens of Japanese bombers laden with bombs are ready to fly. If you go back to Bandung without accepting surrender, we will ensure your personal safety up to the Japanese forward line. But I will order bombing to begin immediately after you cross that line. I will give you ten minutes to think it over. Please discuss the matter and make your choice'.

I and the Japanese party moved to the next room leaving the Dutch representatives where they were. Ten minutes later we returned to the room. I asked the Governor-General and the Commander, 'Although the Governor-General said that you came here to discuss administrative matters, we do not comply with that intention. What we want to hear is whether you surrender or continue the war. What have you decided, Commander?'

The Commander said dejectedly, 'We think there is no use resisting any longer'.

After exchanging a few words with the Commander, the Governor-General spoke. 'I am prepared to ask the Queen for permission to surrender. However, this meeting is no further concern of mine, since it involves purely military matters. I wish to leave this room.'

'Well, you may rest in the garden until the meeting ends and all of you go back to Bandung.' The Governor-General went out of the room with his secretary.

'Do you, Commander ter Poorten, want to suspend

* Footnote continued from previous page:
  According to the British War History, he then formally returned the command of all forces in Netherlands India to the Governor-General. Kirby, pp.263-8, 429-30. Long, p.137.

45

hostilities in spite of the disagreement of the Governor-General?'

'Yes, I do.'

'Well, I will conclude a cease-fire agreement with you if you take the following measures, regarding your answer as the expression of your willingness to accept total and unconditional surrender. The measures are:

1. to send a message from yourself to the whole of the Dutch East Indies from the Bandung broadcasting station at 8 a.m. tomorrow morning saying, "After 8 a.m. you must stop all hostilities against the Japanese Army, and surrender unconditionally to the Japanese troops in your respective areas";

2. to return here by 1 p.m. tomorrow, accompanied by the appropriate members of your staff and bringing lists of the number of commissioned officers, noncommissioned officers and men who will surrender, and the horses, automobiles and military equipment to be delivered.'

Miyoshi's word-for-word translation seemed to be well understood.

'If you agree with my demands, this meeting will be closed. I would like to emphasize that bombing, now temporarily suspended, will begin again if we do not hear your message from Bandung at 8 a.m. tomorrow morning. Your return journey to the [Bandung] stronghold will be quite safe.'

The Governor-General was taken from the garden to the gate and rode in a car together with the other Dutch representatives.

Officers of the Airforce Unit were going to blindfold with white cloth all the Dutch representatives except the driver. Blind-folding was stipulated by a military manual, allowing any country to conceal its inner defences from a military messenger. However, I stopped this practice, since they were not messengers but the highest enemy authorities. Moreover, I thought it useful to let them see the imposing scene of dozens of loaded bombers in the spacious airfield, in order to display our strong fighting spirit and to discourage the Dutch from changing their minds about suspending hostilities - the bombers ready to fly at any time at the command of Endo, the Airforce Unit commander, whenever the situation of the Second Division troops required.

The outline of the meeting has been described above. As the negotiation was carried on through interpreters for Japanese and Dutch, it took almost two hours. It was not until 5 p.m. that the Dutch representatives departed under guard of our motorized corps.

In the evening, the commander of the Second Division,

Lt.-Gen. Maruyama, returned to report that most of two infantry regiments had already advanced very close to the front line of the stronghold, although cavalry and motorized corps were delayed by the damage to bridges. A slight suspicion occurred to me that Governor-General Tjarda might send a telegram to the Dutch government in Europe to retract the surrender agreement concluded by Commander ter Poorten. But I had great confidence that I could break into the stronghold at a stroke, after hearing of the arrival of the Tohoku Division*, whose men showed so much fight. I thanked Maruyama for the tough march of his officers and men in the tropical heat, told him about the cease-fire meeting, and ordered him to launch an attack, including the Shoji Regiment (a mixed regiment), if there was no message from the Bandung broadcasting station at 8 a.m. next morning. Throughout the night I prepared plans for capturing the stronghold, just in case.

At about 8.10 a.m. on 9 March 1942, Diplomat Miyoshi came into my room smiling. 'Congratulations! General ter Poorten has just ordered all troops in the Dutch East Indies to suspend hostilities and declared an unconditional surrender over the radio.'

At last we were sure of avoiding a bloody battle like the one in South China two years earlier when I was divisional commander. I prayed for divine blessing: 'God! Let us end the Great East Asia War now'.

*   *   *

Imamura then describes his final surrender talks with ter Poorten, from 1 p.m. to 3 p.m. on 9 March. Ter Poorten presented details of the 80,000 Dutch troops and the military equipment he was surrendering into Japanese hands. At the time of the talks the British and American commanders in Java had already told ter Poorten they would surrender, although the Australians were preparing a guerrilla struggle in the mountains. Imamura conceded ter Poorten's request for senior Dutch officers to carry pistols as well as swords in the transition period, 'to protect ourselves from outrages on the part of some Indonesians hostile to us'.

*   *   *

The Dutch representatives left for Bandung by car at about 3 p.m. At almost the same time the headquarters staff of

---

* The Second Division. Imamura stresses the name Tohoku, in Northeastern Japan, since this was his own birthplace.

the Maruyama Division entered Bandung. The Shoji Regiment and troops of the Second Division began to march in grand order into the fortress city from the west and north sides.

I entered the Cecil Hotel building in the city at noon on 10 March, together with the principal Headquarters staff. As a matter of principle I never held a triumphal entry into the city or any such ceremony.

Prior to the entry into Bandung, the Tsuchihashi Division made one enemy division surrender in Surabaya on 7 [March], and captured that important East Java city which was the largest naval base in Java. The Sakaguchi Combined Regiment also captured Cilacap on the 7th, and cut communications between Allied forces there on the one hand, and Australia and MacArthur's headquarters on the other. These two events were also important factors in the surrender of the Dutch East Indies Army. I granted a letter of commendation to the Sakaguchi Regiment.

On the night of the 9th, I sent a telegram announcing the unconditional surrender of the Dutch East Indies Army to General Headquarters in Tokyo. At noon on the 10th, a telegram of Imperial congratulation was sent from Tokyo to the army and navy corps involved in the operations. I expressed deep gratitude for it.

I still admire the attitude Governor-General Tjarda showed at the surrender talks at Kalijati airfield, even though he was an enemy. Nevertheless, I think he should have consulted the Dutch government in Europe and should have ordered the Commander not to accept surrender, as communication was still possible at that time. He might have consulted [Europe] but still have been ordered to surrender. The greatest mistake of the Dutch government (though it had already been driven out by Germany and had only a nominal office in London) concerning the defence of the East Indies seemed to be that it transferred supreme command in the Dutch East Indies from the Governor-General to Gen. Wavell of Britain, who commanded only 10,000 British and Australian forces altogether. In fact, Gen. Wavell fled to India by air when the Japanese troops began to land and move forward in East and West Java, leaving the Allied forces behind. As a result, the remaining Allied forces did not follow the lead of Commander ter Poorten at all, making it very difficult for him to carry out his strategy. I think it was natural that the commander lost the will to fight. Had the Allied forces in Java been commanded by the Governor-General, the Japanese army would have had to face a tough battle. In contrast to the Governor-General, the attitude of the Commander as a military man was questionable. This might be the reason Tjarda was appointed Ambassador to France after he was released from detention in August 1945 and returned to the Netherlands,

while the Commander was immediately enlisted in the reserve
army after the war.*

       *   *   *

    On 10 March, the day after the formal conclusion of
unconditional surrender by the Dutch East Indies Army, I
entered Bandung, and on the next day I instructed Col. Nakayama
Yasuto, who was in charge of military administration, and
Vice-Chief of Staff Harada, about measures to be taken for the
military administration [of Java].
    On the 12th, Headquarters was moved from Bandung to the
capital city, Batavia. After giving orders for the necessary
facilities to be organized, I myself began to make inspection
trips to various divisions on the 12th, accompanied by Chief of
Staff Okazaki and Staff Officer Takashima. On the morning of
the 12th, we left Bandung by air to visit the Sano Division
which occupied the oilfield areas of Palembang in Sumatra. On
the 13th, we discussed means to repair the oil facilities,
after investigating the magnitude of the damage. On the 14th,
we left Sumatra for Surabaya and Malang, where we stayed for
two days visiting troops of the Tsuchihashi Division. Less
than a week after the occupation was complete, I noticed
everywhere that the population showed goodwill and was willing
to cooperate with the Japanese, which convinced me that peace
and order were secure. On the 16th we flew from Malang to
Batavia.
    I myself wanted a simple life. However, there was the
possibility that many Japanese might lose their sense of
simplicity unless they were carefully directed. For there were
many Dutch private and public facilities, accumulated as a
result of their exploitation of the Indonesians for 300 years,
as well as Chinese houses, available everywhere in Java.
Despite my preference for simplicity, I was unable to refuse a
request from the Gunseibu to use the official residences of the
Governor-General in order to maintain the dignity of the man
who was to govern 50 million people in Java. For this reason I
felt obliged to use them, although I was determined not to use
the official residence in Buitenzorg, which was constructed
like a palace.

       *   *   *

* Jhr. Mr A.W.L. Tjarda van Starkenborgh Stachouwer (b. 1888)
  became Governor-General in 1936, and still held that office
  when released from Japanese internment in September 1945.
  His rigid national pride proved a mixed blessing, however,
  and he was relieved of his duties on 17 October 1945 after
  rejecting the Netherlands Government's policy of working with
  acceptable Indonesian nationalists. He was Ambassador to
  Paris from 1946 to 1948, and from 1950 Netherlands
  representative to the North Atlantic Pact.

*Imamura here recounts three incidents where published
reports of his actions differed from his own
down-to-earth interpretation of them. He rebuts a
friend's criticism of his impetuosity and
foolhardiness in swimming ashore fully clad during
the Java invasion - a criticism prompted by
spectacular headlines in Japan - by explaining that
in reality he clung desperately to a raft until
picked up by a landing-craft. At the capture of
Nanning, Imamura had declined to use a fine rosewood
bed, not as reported because he refused to set
himself above his men, but simply because the bed was
infested with bed bugs. Finally, a report that on
the way back from the surrender talks at Kalijati,
Imamura leaped from his car during a torrential
downpour and pushed from behind to prevent it
slipping over the edge, is dismissed as an act of
panic rather than bravery.*

*   *   *

Farsightedness of a Superior

Once I had settled down in the former Governor-General's
official residence in Batavia I had dozens of visitors every
day, including the division commanders under my authority, and
those who came from Singapore, Saigon, Tokyo, and so forth by
boat and aeroplane. One day my orderly, L/Cpl. Kono Yoshitada,
brought me two namecards which had been brought in by the
soldier in charge of the guard post beside the official
residence. He said, 'The man whose namecard is on top has come
from Tokyo by air, bringing the second namecard. He wants to
meet you. What shall I tell the guard?'
    Although I did not know the name on the first namecard,
the other was my former superior, Gen. Ugaki Kazushige,* who

---

* Ugaki Kazushige (1869-1956) was trained in Germany after
  graduation from the Army War College. In 1924 he became the
  first Army Minister to break the monopoly of this post by the
  Choshu faction of generals from Yamaguchi prefecture. During
  the 1920s Ugaki became himself the epitome of the Army
  establishment, identified with a policy of mechanization and
  rationalization popular with many younger officers. In March
  1931, still as Army Minister, he quashed an ultra-nationalist
  coup which had intended to inaugurate a military government
  with himself as premier. (Then Col.) Imamura was reportedly
  one of those whose opposition to the plot dissuaded Ugaki
  from supporting it. Ugaki's action nevertheless further
  alienated the younger faction which came to dominate the Army

lived in Kunitachi, a suburb of Tokyo. On the reverse of the namecard was written in pen, 'Ask the bearer for my views'.

'Tell the guard that I will see him, and show him in here.'

The man who appeared in my study was a youth who did not seem to be much more than 30. His appearance gave me the impression of sincerity. He was wearing a dull suit, but I intuitively felt that this person was reliable.

'How could you get a seat on an aeroplane, when so many people are coming from Tokyo?'

'Fortunately, Gen. Ugaki asked somebody in the Army Ministry.'

'Does this trip have a special purpose? Have you visited other occupied areas on the way to Java?'

'Of course I was able to see the places where the plane landed, but the major purpose of this trip is to hear your views about this war, as I was instructed by Gen. Ugaki.'

'I wonder why such a knowledgeable person as Gen. Ugaki wants to know my opinions.'

'Gen. Ugaki is very worried about the war, saying, "I might have to wind up this war like Marshall Pétain did in France". He is concerned that Japan might lose the war, even though she can win battles, due to her inferior overall strength. But he realizes this is only how it seems to him in Japan. Thus, he wants to know how the Japanese in occupied areas, based on their own observation of the enemy's war potential and morale, are judging the question of whether Japan can carry this war through successfully. This is the reason he ordered me to ask you opinions in Java, and why I am here now.'

Since Japan lost the Greater East Asia War, I feel very much ashamed [of my own shortsightedness] whenever I recall this episode. At that time, I was one of those who overestimated the initial Japanese victory, and accordingly I was unable to see the point of Gen. Ugaki's anxiety. I therefore answered, 'I am very grateful that Gen. Ugaki is concerned about the war situation in the occupied regions. It is very difficult for me to judge the outcome of this war, since my view is limited to a narrow perspective without being able to see the general situation. The impression I have now is that we should bring our offensive to a close with the Java operation, and begin to strengthen a defence build-up. Otherwise the nation will find itself in a perilous situation. But after completion of the Java operation, two thirds of army

* Footnote continued from previous page:
  in the 1930s, and the Army blocked his appointment as premier in January 1937 by refusing to appoint anyone to fill the Army Ministry. He also served as Governor-General of Korea (1931-36) and Foreign Minister (1938).

51

strength in Java was moved elsewhere. It seems that the battlefield is going to be expanded, which I am afraid may lead to a situation beyond our control as happened in China.'

My perspective was still limited to worrying about the expansion of battlefields, whereas Gen. Ugaki had already been thinking of defeat at the initial stage of the war.

*   *   *

Had Ugaki Kazushige been Prime Minister, the Greater East Asia War would not have occurred; or if it had occurred, he would not have misjudged the timing of retreat.

Criticisms of the Military Administration

When I entered Bandung on 10 March, I established my Headquarters in the Cecil Hotel, and held a meeting of my staff at 2 p.m. in order to hear their frank opinions about future policies for the administration. Twelve staff members, including the Chief of Staff, attended the meeting. Many of the young officers insisted, 'Although the administration may gradually be altered to a "soft" one in the course of time, we must adopt an iron-handed policy at the initial stage to demonstrate the authority of the Japanese Army'.

However, Col. Nakayama, who was in charge of the administration, opposed this opinion. 'The military administration should be directed, as is clearly prescribed in the **Outline of Military Administration in Occupied Regions,*** towards the acquisition of the hearts and minds of the people through a fair policy of virtue and dignity, the quick restoration of damaged military resources, the requisitioning of all military resources and an increase in their production.'

The chief of the strategy section, Col. Takashima, Vice-Chief of Staff Harada, and Chief of Staff Okazaki agreed with Nakayama's opinion.

Then I presented my resolution. 'Military administration will be handled by the Vice-Chief of Staff and Col. Nakayama.

* Imamura's title for this document, **Senryōchi Tōchi Yōkō,** appears to be an abbreviation of **Nampō Senryōchi Gyōsei Tōchi Yōkō** - Outline of the Military Administration in Occupied Regions of the Southern Area. This was a policy document ratified by a liaison conference of the Government and Imperial Military Headquarters in Tokyo on 2 November 1941. See Nishijima, Kishi et al., **Japanese Military Administration in Indonesia** (Washington, 1963). A similar document dated 20 November 1941 and included in Benda, Irikura and Kishi, pp. 1-3, distinctly subordinates winning hearts and minds to Japanese military and economic needs.

As commander I have resolved to implement a military administration congruent with the instructions of "the Centre".* The
term **hakkō ichiu**† originally means familism and brotherhood,
but it is often misunderstood as something expansionist. The
Army is strong enough to put pressure upon the population
whenever necessary. Since we are strong, the administration is
to be implemented as softly as possible.'

In the middle of April, Kodama Hideo (a former Minister of
the Interior),# Hayashi Kyujiro (a former ambassador to
Brazil),+ and Kitajima Kenjiro (a former Vice-Minister of
Colonization) flew to Batavia as political advisers of the 16th
Army by order of the Minister of the Army. They came to my
official residence to notify me of their arrival at their
posts. While we were having dinner together, I said, 'The
administration of Java is now primarily being conducted by

---

* Imamura's term **chūō** (centre) refers to the nucleus of
  military power in Tokyo. This covers the dominant figures in
  the Cabinet, the Army and Navy Ministries, and Imperial
  Headquarters, but refers more particularly to a clique of
  generals in the Army General Staff and the Military Affairs
  Bureau of the Army Ministry.

† **Hakkō ichiu** literally means 'Whole world under one rule', and
  was often used to refer to Japanese leadership of Greater
  East Asia.

Kodama Hideo (1876-1947) inherited the title Count from his
  father Kodama Gentaro, a distinguished military figure who
  obtained the title posthumously. Kodama Hideo graduated in
  law from Tokyo Imperial University and made a successful
  career as an administrator concerned with Korean affairs. He
  eventually reached Cabinet rank, holding the Ministries of
  Colonization (1934-36), Communications (1937), Interior
  (January-July 1940), and later Education (1944-45). He was
  the most senior civilian adviser to the 16th Army until his
  return to Japan in April 1943, but appears to have exerted
  little real influence.

+ Hayashi Kyujiro (1882-1964) was a diplomat in Britain, China
  and Thailand before assuming the critical post of Consul-
  General in Mukden (1928-31), where he attempted in vain to
  find a peaceful solution to the Manchurian Incident
  (September 1931). After his period as Ambassador to Brazil
  (1932-36), he took up commercial interests in Tokyo and
  became Director of the Nanyo Kyokai (Southern Ocean Association). He toured the Netherlands Indies in 1940, and was
  alleged by the Dutch to have coordinated espionage activities
  there.

Vice-Chief of Staff Harada and Col. Nakayama, both of whom you saw at the airport. As we have no experience of politics and administration, we need your guidance'.

Count Kodama spoke on behalf of the three. 'It may be discourteous to say this at this dinner you have arranged for us, but I think I should say it at the beginning. To tell the truth, there is criticism of the military administration in Java from Tokyo, Saigon, and especially from Singapore, which claims: "The dignity of Japan and the Japanese Army is not in evidence at all [in Java]. The whites are behaving as though they were not defeated. A forceful administration like that in Singapore is the way to make the coloured people obey us".'

'Is that so? There may be many views. I imagine that the administration in Singapore has had to face serious resistance from millions of Chinese, and therefore an iron-handed policy is necessary. However, such a policy is not necessary in Java. To begin with, I have been convinced since the second day of our landing that the Indonesians are truly our "brothers" of the same race. If not, how could those who are not our brothers cooperate with us and favour us? Our victory is partly due to their cooperation. Secondly, concerning the Dutch, those who resisted us are all now interned as prisoners of war. As the **Senjinkun*** says, it is not permitted to take measures against the families of war prisoners and ordinary citizens. Thirdly, although many Chinese in Java certainly participated in the boycott of Japanese commodities, commerce in Java was totally in the hands of the Dutch and Chinese. If, therefore, we oppress and detain them in a spirit of revenge, as happened in some other occupied regions, we will be unable to exploit all resources, especially oil, nor to make use of the munitions produced here for the Japanese army as a whole. I request the three of you to make a tour of inspection separately to the appropriate areas for two or three weeks. If you perceive that my understanding of the situation is incorrect, or that Chinese and Dutch people are thinking lightly of the Japanese Army, please report to me frankly.'

One week after this dinner, the three political advisers left for a tour of inspection all over Java, and returned in three weeks one by one. They reported their impressions. 'We were able to feel as relaxed as if we had been travelling in Japan, without a sense of insecurity anywhere. The natives are very friendly to the Japanese, and the Dutch seem to have given up their hositility. As for the Chinese, they are eager to

---

* The **Senjinkun** (Code for the Conduct of Soldiers in Wartime) was written by Imamura himself in 1940, when he was super-intendent of Military Education in the Army. After the war Imamura regretted that it was in too abstract a style to have much effect on individual soldiers.

please the Japanese. Under these circumstances, the full recovery of industry may be achieved earlier than expected. We saw that there is no necessity for an iron-handed policy in Java. Those who criticize the Java administration do not know the reality here. The criticisms are nothing but superficial theorizing.'

There is a saying in one of Mencius' writings: 'If I am convinced that I am right after examining myself, I will go even against ten million people'. To such a person as myself, who is very cautious and seriously reconsiders his position on the advice of a thousand, a hundred, or even of one person, not to mention ten million, the reports of these advisers gave considerable encouragement.

Shortly after the arrival of the advisers, the chief of the General Staff, Gen. Sugiyama Hajime,* came to Java with such members of his staff as Cols. Hattori and Takeda. The Staff Officers stayed at a hotel in Batavia, but the Chief and his adjutant stayed at my official residence (the official residence of the former Dutch Governor-General), which enabled me to talk with him for two days.

'Imperial Headquarters calls the 16th Army the "Osamu Troop" [osamu means 'to end something', 'to pacify']. A member of my staff has told me that the 16th Army is called "Osamu" to indicate the general policy of Imperial Headquarters to end the Greater East Asia War with the Java Operation. Is this true?'

'Yes, that was the case. However, Japan will implement a Burma operation because of the strong recommendation of the General Southern Army. On the other hand, there is no intention of launching the so-called India operation or the Australia operation, both of which have been insisted on in some quarters. If the battlefield were expanded to such an extent, the war would become too great to be managed with the national power of Japan.'

I thought this quite right. Nevertheless, as far as I could see, the measures 'the Centre' had so far taken gave rise to some suspicion. 'Although Imperial Headquarters says it will end the war with the Java operation, it has already reduced the Japanese forces in Java to one third. Does Headquarters think it possible to defend Java with this small force? It would be understandable if part of the forces in Java had been shifted to the Philippines whose occupation has not been completed. But the troop movement was in fact to expand

---

* The senior position in the Japanese Army was Chief of the General Staff, a post occupied by General (from 1943, Field Marshall) Sugiyama Hajime from October 1940 until Tojo himself assumed the post in February 1944. Sugiyama had been deputy Army Minister in 1931-32 and Minister in 1937-38. He committed suicide in September 1945.

the field of battle, which is what I am most afraid of.'

'We may have to reconsider the defence of Java if circumstances change. However, the shift was caused by the need to adjust the balance of forces within the Southern Army because of our limited shipping ability. In any case, you should draw up defence plans as quickly as possible.'

When Gen. Sugiyama spoke of the policy not to expand the area of battle, he must have meant it seriously and not as a perfunctory part of the conversation. I can say this because we had come to understand each other as a result of a long-standing relationship, as I had worked under him in each of his four periods: as Director of the Military Bureau, as Vice-Minister, as Minister, and as Commander of the North China Army. Because I believed in the genuineness of his words, I could only wonder why Japanese operations were in fact expanding from Rabaul to Australia, while the so-called Burma operation was extending to eastern India. What circumstances had led to the Japanese Army being scattered over such a broad front for which supply was difficult?

On the morning of the day Gen. Sugiyama was to leave Java at the conclusion of his tour of inspection, he told me, '"The Centre" is satisfied with the results of the Java operations, but there is a lot of criticism of your administration. Muto (Director of the Military Affairs Bureau) and Tominaga (Director of the Personnel Bureau)* are scheduled to come here soon. You might be well advised to take heed of the opinions of "the Centre"!'

These words were meant as a kind expression of concern about my future career. I answered, 'I also have heard of criticisms of my administration raised in Tokyo and other places. However, I am convinced that my policy is adapted to the reality of this place. This was the approach instructed by "the Centre" when I left Japan. If "the Centre" now orders me to alter my policy, I must do so. However, I have no intention of changing my policy simply because it is unpopular. On the one hand, my conscience tells me that the iron-handed policy suggested by Tokyo is unsuitable as far as Java is concerned. On the other hand, I do believe that armies in the field should follow a uniform central policy. Since I cannot harmonize these two beliefs, please discharge me and send somebody else to Java after consulting Prime Minister Tojo'.

As Gen. Sugiyama had said, the two directors of the

---

* Generals Muto Akira and Tominaga Kyoji were both very much at 'the Centre', particularly Muto who was among the five men executed with Tojo in December 1948. Before moving to the key Military Affairs Bureau, Muto had pressed effectively for a more forceful Army role as a young major and colonel in the Operations Division of the General Staff (1931-37).

Ministry of the Army, Muto and Tominaga, with some of their staff, came to Java before long. After an inspection tour of strategic places, they visited members of my staff at Headquarters prior to meeting me. Although I could not hear clearly what they were saying, as my room was separated from the adjacent meeting room by a thick wall, the discussion seemed to be getting bogged down, to judge from the steadily rising voices which could be heard periodically, particularly of my Staff Officer Takashima.

The two directors came into my room and said, 'We should like to convey the advice of "the Centre" about the administration [of Java], and ask you to think it over'.

'It is already past 4 p.m. If I remain here late into the evening, my subordinates may be inconvenienced. My plan is that we should all return to our private residences and have dinner together at my place after having a bath. Please come one or two hours before dinner. Then we can talk satisfactorily without being heard by anybody.'

A little after 5 p.m., both of the directors arrived at my study. The Director of the Military Affairs Bureau, Muto Akira, explained that their discussions with my Staff Officers had been fruitless, and stressed the necessity for adopting an iron-handed policy in Java as in Singapore.

'Are you saying that "the Centre" has modified the contents of the **Outline of Military Administration in Occupied Regions**?', I asked.

'No, the **Outline** has not been changed. However, we do not need to stick to it now that circumstances have changed.'

'I understand that the **Outline** became the basis of Army policy after receiving the sanction of the Emperor. Has the change of policy also received this sanction?'

'No, it has not. We are intending to ask for [Imperial] sanction only after "the Centre" has proposed the new policy to the Emperor, and the whole of the Army is ready to implement it.'

'You said that we need not stick to the **Outline**, since circumstances have changed. But how have they changed?'

'The Japanese troops defeated the enemy [in Java] more quickly than we expected. Now we are free from any serious concern about resistance from the natives. We therefore have to keep a tight control over the natives, and mobilize them to facilitate military activities and the acquisition of military resources.'

'I think the situation has not changed at all. If we oppress the natives, it will in the end create a situation like the Sino-Japanese War. Under such circumstances we cannot expect industry to develop. It is incorrect to judge the situation on the basis of a superficial impression obtained just one month after the occupation.'

'We were deeply impressed with the situation in Singapore

where we certainly felt Japanese power had established itself. In contrast to this, we feel that in Java the prestige of the Dutch has not yet been wiped out. As a consequence of this the natives may even come to follow the Dutch lead once again.'

'Different people may have different opinions. I am not saying that your impressions and opinions are mistaken, but that we have different ideas. In any case, as long as the iron-handed policy you refer to is instructed by the Minister [of the Army] as the basic policy of "the Centre", we have to obey it. For to reject instructions is to breach military discipline.

'But as you may know, the **Senjinkun**, which was delivered to every soldier, was mainly drawn up by me and promulgated in the name of the Minister. I cannot tolerate any breach of the **Senjinkun**. Accordingly I request you, Director of the Personnel Bureau Tominaga, to discharge me after consultation with the Minister, and then to issue a modified **Outline of Military Administration**. This is the only solution. Even though you have come all this way, I have not changed my policy for the administration of Java.'

We were unable to reach a mutual understanding. The directors' party made another inspection tour of various places in Java for one or two days, and publicly said afterwards: 'Administrative policy here is not in conformity with the intentions of "the Centre". It should be more forceful'.

As a result, I understand that some young officers - even in the Kempeitai - came to be suspicious of my policy. Nevertheless, I continued to demand respect for my policy at every monthly meeting of commanders.

The Director of the Ordnance Bureau of the Ministry of the Army, who came on an inspection tour of Java at the end of May, told me during a conversation, 'I hear that you had a lot of arguments with the Directors of the Military and Personnel Bureaux. At a meeting of directors of the Ministry, immediately after the two directors returned to Tokyo, Muto reported to the Minister: "The military administration in Java contrasts markedly with that in Singapore, and there are many criticisms of the former. I myself was influenced by these voices, regarding the Java administration as too mild. On proper consideration, however, it appears natural that the nature of the administration in each of these regions should be different, since the administration is directed towards Indonesians and Dutchmen in Java, as against Chinese and British in Singapore. The Java administration has been implemented for less than two months. I think we must allow it to run for at least half a year before judging its propriety. I feel that 'the Centre' should avoid intervening or demanding modifications at this stage". Muto's opinion was endorsed by the Minister'.

Lt.-Gen. Muto was soon moved to Sumatra as the commander

of the Konoe Division. Sumatra formed part of the Dutch East
Indies, and it was my troops that captured southern parts of
Sumatra. Nevertheless, Imperial Headquarters surprisingly
transferred the Sumatra administration and my divisions there
to the jurisdiction of Gen. Yamashita in Singapore, perhaps
judging that the total area under my command would become too
large, as large as the whole of Europe except Russia, and that
Sumatra could not be maintained by one or two divisions.*

Lt.-Gen. Muto made an inspection tour of Sumatra for one
or two months after taking up his position. After this trip,
he sent a Staff Officer of his Division to me with a long
private letter, which said:

> It is much to be regretted that, when I visited you
> in Java this April, I used impolite language about
> the Java administration on the basis of a superficial
> observation, without understanding the real situation
> in Java nor the substance of the administration
> there. Since I have taken charge of the Sumatra
> administration under Gen. Yamashita, I have observed
> the flexibility of the Indonesians and the passivity
> of the Dutch.
>
> In view of these conditions, it has become clear
> that your policy in Java is perfectly justifiable. I
> have reported my opinion to the [General Southern]
> Army and the 'Centre' that the administration in
> Sumatra should be modified to follow the example of
> Java. Once again, I am sorry for my previous
> impoliteness.

Lt.-Gen. Muto and I knew each other quite well, as he was
one of my subordinates while I was a section chief in General
Headquarters in Tokyo and the Vice-Chief of Staff of the
Kwangtung Army, and he was one of my good partners at
go-playing.† In spite of this good relationship, we had heated

---

* The principal reason for uniting the administrations of
 Sumatra and Malaya under the control of Singapore appears to
 have been that these areas were 'the nuclear zone of the
 Empire's plans for the Southern Area', of much greater
 strategic interest than Java. Gen. Muto, whose Konoe
 Division command comprised the northern third of Sumatra,
 reportedly favoured a policy of making Sumatra as well as
 Malaya direct colonies of Japan. Any such plans were
 abandoned in April 1943 with the separation of Sumatra, then
 under the 25th Army, from Malaya. Benda, Irikura and Kishi,
 p.169. Kanahele, p.39 and pp.264-5.

† **Go** is an ancient, elaborate Japanese form of chess, especially popular among military officers.

arguments about the administration of Java as already described, because we had made it a rule to set aside personal sentiments in public matters.

In June, the Commander-in-Chief of the General Southern Army, Gen. Terauchi, came to Java on a tour of inspection after visiting the Homma Army of the Philippines and the Maeda Army of North Borneo. On the last day of his six-day visit to Java, he summoned me, Chief of Staff Okazaki, and Vice-Chief of Staff Harada to his hotel in order, we expected, to state his opinions and give us instructions. In reality, however, he merely said: 'The strategy of the 16th Army, its plan for successive defence, the military administration, and its implementation are going quite well. So I have no demands to make'. Then he invited us for tea and we began to chat.

I had many visitors who came to Java on inspection tours from Tokyo and the Headquarters of the General Southern Army, including a political adviser of the Army, Nagata Hidejiro.* From the comments of these people I knew that Gen. Terauchi and Staff Officers of the General Southern Army were critical of my administration. As I thought that Gen. Terauchi was sure to refer to this, his brief and uncritical comment was unexpected. I wondered why he did not mention his reservations. I came to understand the reason that night when Col. Ishii Akiho, a Staff Officer and Section Chief of the General Southern Army, explained.

Col. Ishi, born in Yamaguchi Prefecture, was an honours graduate of the Military Academy. He served in the Military Bureau of the Ministry of the Army for a long time. Immediately after the outbreak of the Greater East Asia War, he became Chief of the Third Section of the General Southern Army, in charge of inspecting and guiding the military administration in occupied regions. However, I had not talked with him until that night. He called on me the evening before he left Java, and said very earnestly, 'I have toured various places in Java, accompanying the Commander-in-Chief everywhere for six days. Although I wanted to talk to you, I have not found an opportunity. This is the reason why I visited you tonight. Presumptuous as it seems to say so, the **Outline of Military Administration in Occupied Regions** distributed to every unit by the Minister was initially drafted by me on instructions, when I was a member of the Military Bureau of the Ministry of the Army. The draft was approved by the Director, Muto, and was

---

* Nagata Hidejiro (1876-1943) was Minister of Colonization in 1936-37, having previously been twice Mayor of Tokyo. He was also President of Takushoku University, and a well-known broadcaster and **haiku** poet (going by the name Seiran). He died in the Philippines while serving as an adviser to the military.

completed by adding the opinions of the Staff Office of Army Headquarters, the Ministry of the Navy, and the Ministry of Foreign Affairs.

'Being elated with their initial success, the armies in the field have tended to ignore the **Outline** under the pretext of "the change in circumstances", and to determine their own policies arbitrarily. This tendency has affected officers in Tokyo. Unfortunately, most leaders of the General Southern Army would not listen to my arguments for maintaining the direction of the **Outline**. I am very pleased to find that the **Outline** is respected in Java.

'The Commander-in-Chief himself investigated Java this time more carefully than any other region, and he realized that what he had been told by many people was mistaken. He seemed to feel: "Military administration should be like it is here". Please do not change your policy in the future.'

'This is the first time I have heard that you were the one who drafted the **Outline**. As men are weak in nature, the more we try to stem the tide of public criticism, the more we are depressed. However, the dark clouds around me are now dispelled, for I have learned from your words why the Commander-in-Chief changed his evaluation of the Java administration to a positive one. Thank you very much', I replied.

I told the story of Col. Ishii to the leading administrative officials, including the Chief of Staff and department heads. Although my staff remained calm, they seemed still to hear the accusation from the North of 'Weak! Weak!' against the Java administration. The Kempeitai also reported to me that visitors from Tokyo and other occupied regions were criticizing the Java administration loudly in the dining room of the Hotel des Indes, which had been used for accommodation and dining facilities for such people and officers in Batavia.

One night in July, I ordered a blackout as part of air defence drill. The next morning, Col. Nakayama reported an occurrence to me. Incidentally, he was born in Kumamoto. In spite of his childish face, he was a man of strong will. He would not be swayed by criticism. Even when I planned to concentrate Dutch civilians in one area in order to protect them while keeping an eye on them, Col. Nakayama was reluctant to consent to the plan because of the troubles the Dutch would suffer in moving house. When the plan was at last implemented, he ordered his subordinates to assist the move, using most of the Army's automobiles. I entirely trusted him. Even Indonesian leaders put faith in him. He was a good friend of Sukarno (the President of the present Republic of Indonesia). He reported, 'Last night, a drunken Japanese captain rushed into the residence of Sukarno. The captain hit Sukarno, railing at him that light was escaping from a window contrary to the blackout regulations. I hear Sukarno is very angry about that. An investigation proved that the captain belongs to the Military Accounting Department'.

I replied, 'Some young officers seem to have been mislead by those who say that the policy of the Java administration is too mild or that the Gunseibu makes too much of Indonesian leaders, and consequently cannot understand the present situation. But since the captain concerned belongs to Headquarters staff, we cannot overlook the incident. Explain to the Director of the Accounting Department, Mukai, what sort of person Sukarno is and how he has been cooperating with the Japanese. If the captain realizes his fault, take him to Sukarno to make an apology. If he does not reconsider his action, I, as Commander, will punish him'.

I heard that the captain felt very much ashamed after the remonstrations of Col. Nakayama, and that he visited Sukarno to apologize, accompanied by Col. Nakayama.*

The day after the captain apologized to Sukarno, the latter came to my office, asking for an interview through Col. Nakayama. We talked through an interpreter, a 17-year-old boy called Shogenji (he was born in Java and speaks Indonesian as well as a native speaker).

Sukarno began, 'The night before last, an officer suddenly rushed into my house and slapped me, pointing at a window and a light. Although I got angry at this action then, I realized my fault only later when I was told that the blackout order was in effect. Moreover, I felt ashamed when the captain visited me accompanied by Col. Nakayama, and apologized to me politely. I also expressed regret for my mistake. In this way we became very friendly, shaking hands with each other. After the captain left, I heard from Col. Nakayama that the Commander had regretted the deed of this captain. I came here today to acknowledge my fault and thank you for your concern over me'.

I replied, 'It is clear that the captain resorted to this rude behaviour to admonish someone violating the blackout order, without knowing the house was yours. In the Japanese Army, it was conventional to slap and hit a person who committed a fault without punishing him by law. Army authorities have tried to discard this unfortuante convention for 30 years, but in vain. In fact, there are such officers even in my Headquarters. There may be soldiers who slap and hit Indonesians. At the next meeting of commanders I will instruct them to put a stop to such bad habits. Please inform us without hesitation if Japanese officers and men show bad

* Sukarno's account of this incident is in **Sukarno. An Autobiography as told to Cindy Adams** (Hong Kong, Gunung Agung, 1966), p.180. He does not mention the following meeting with Imamura.

manners to Indonesians again. Anyway, it is good that you are reconciled'.

As was usual, Sukarno retired after chatting for an hour or so.

Mid-July: The Commander-in-Chief, Gen. Terauchi, summoned seven commanders under his jurisdiction, from Thailand, Indo-China, the Philippines, Borneo, Java, Malaya and Burma for a three-day meeting in Singapore, where the Headquarters of the General Southern Army had been located. I found that the Chief of Staff [of the General Southern Army] had been changed from Lt.-Gen. Tsukada to Lt.-Gen. Kuroda, and the Vice-Chief of Staff from Lt.-Gen. Aoki to Maj.-Gen. Takahashi, while the commanders of the Philippines and Malaya had also been replaced by different people only seven months after the outbreak of the war.

It was good that there was no address by some high-ranking officer, an Army tradition at such meetings, thanks to the new Chief of Staff Kuroda, and that the meeting started by discussing the opinions of each participant in turn. I was asked to speak first, on the ground that I had been in the position of Commander longer than the others present. I began, 'As I made a detailed report to the Commander-in-Chief when he made an inspection trip to Java last month, I should like to raise only two points here, concerning an instruction and a suggestion from the General Southern Army. Firstly, when the new Vice-Chief of Staff visited Java, he said to my subordinates: :"Although the 16th Army is planning to expend money and energy to restore and develop school education for youth, this will contribute only to the encouragement of a desire for independence among the natives, and nothing to the expansion of Japanese power. This will lead to the same error as we made in Korea". I want to ask you whether that was based on the thinking of the Commander-in-Chief?'

Kuroda answered emphatically, 'It was a personal opinion of the Vice-Chief of Staff. I agree with the education policy you explained during Terauchi's tour of investigation'.

I continued, 'Secondly, it is quite reasonable that an office for the control of oil should have been established at Headquarters. The first instruction of this office was to equalize the price of oil for the population in regions under the jurisdiction of the General Southern Army, and it also suggested the price. When the oil facilities destroyed by the enemy had almost been restored, I issued an order to reduce the price of oil in Java itself to half what it had been in the Dutch period. This was reported to Headquarters at that time.

'According to the latest instruction, however, the price of oil has been raised to four times the level I fixed, and two times that in the Dutch period. When I asked the reason, I was told that only Java could benefit from the existing system as an oil-producing region, but the population of non oil-

63

producing regions had to use expensive oil, which was undesirable for the unified administration of the General Southern Army as a whole.

'Fifty million Indonesians will come to distrust the Japanese if they are notified of this price rise, double the price in the Dutch period and four times that which I fixed two or three weeks ago, since they have been cooperating with the Japanese in the hope of obtaining oil as early as possible. Such an instruction will be made use of by the enemy for anti-Japanese propaganda. Although it grieves me not to implement the instruction from Headquarters, please consider Java as an exceptional case because of the reason mentioned above.'

Terauchi inquired, 'Chief of Staff Kuroda! When did you issue such an instruction without consulting me?'

Kuroda replied, 'I know nothing about it, as I have just arrived at my post'.

Gen. Terauchi ordered, 'This instruction is really thoughtless. Chief of Staff Kuroda, withdraw it immediately'. He was just such an open-hearted warrior.

Otsuka Isei, a political adviser of the Singapore Army [29th Army?], flew to Java on a liaison mission. He was married to the eldest daughter of Field Marshall Uehara*, and I had come to know him during the four years when I, then a major, was serving as adjutant to the Field Marshall. We had remained on good terms ever since, and now he said to me, 'To be frank, the "soft" administration in Java contrasts too sharply with the forceful policy in the Malayan region. As a result, the inhabitants of the latter are beginning to complain: "Why must we alone suffer from a repressive administration?" Moveover, the British side is intensifying anti-Japanese propaganda, taking advantage of this popular dissatisfaction. In fact, the administration is quite difficult to carry out there. Once I asked the Headquarters of the General Southern Army to adjust the administrative policy in the two regions to conform to each other. Initially Headquarters seemed to be doing this. However, Headquarters has recently been losing its conviction, saying that it is inevitable that we should have different policies in different regions because of the special circumstances of each region. How about adjusting the extent to which policies are "soft" or "hard" by mutual consultation [between Java and Malaya], to

* Field Marshall Uehara Yusaku (1856-1933) was Chief of the Army General Staff from 1915 to 1923. His son-in-law Otsuka Isei (1884-1945) had been an official in the Ministry of Home Affairs before the war, rising to become commissioner (**Sokan**) for the Hiroshima area.

ease the task of military administration in Malaya, the nucleus of the Southern Areas'.

A month prior to this proposal, the highest political adviser of the General Southern Army, Nagata Hidejiro (a former Minister of Colonization), who was an authority on colonial policy, had come to Java and advised me to adopt a policy midway between a 'soft' and a repressive one. As I did not feel inclined to change my policy, I told Otsuka I would continue the existing policy. At that time, the three political advisers of the 16th Army also supported me. One of the three, Kodama, went to Tokyo and Singapore to explain the substance and the results of policies in Java.

In October, my Chief of Staff, Okazaki, received a telegram from Tokyo ordering him to report there immediately. I thought that 'the Centre' would now finally modify the **Outline of Military Administration in Occupied Regions** and order the implementation of a new repressive policy. I had already made up my mind to resign, under the pretext of being 'unable to carry out my present responsibilities and to keep my present position', if 'the Centre' were to order me to implement such a different policy without discharging me, since the matter concerned not military strategy but politics.

About the time I was expecting Maj.-Gen. Okazaki to arrive in Tokyo, I received this telegram from him:

> Arrived in Tokyo. In response to my report to 'the Centre', the [Army] Minister and the Chief of the General Staff both agreed that there was no need to change the policy of the Java administration. The administration is permitted to continue with the present policy. Details will be reported on my return.

Okazaki came back by air after staying in Tokyo for five days or so, and reported, 'The value has been proven of a consistent soft-line policy. "The Centre" has been comparing the law and order situation, the recovery of industry and the acquisition of munitions in all occupied regions over the past six months. It has accepted "to some extent" that the results obtained by the Java administration have been excellent. But it was disagreeable to find myself being flattered and offered criticisms of other administrations by some of those who had previously spoken ill of the Java administration'.

Since the Chief of Staff reported on this in detail, even those who had been wondering whether it was right to pursue a policy different from 'the Centre' gained new confidence in the existing policy on Java. The same applied to officers in each division, making the administration run more smoothly.

Six and a half years after the event mentioned above, I faced trial by the Dutch East Indies war tribunal. Mr Smit, a judicial captain and an examining prosecutor of the Public

Prosecutor's Office, examined me about 20 times in three months, using Morita Shoji as interpreter. One day he said, 'Among those who were questioned in Tokyo by other Dutch prosecutors, Takashima Tatsuhiko, a major-general and former staff officer in Java, testified: "There was a considerable difference of opinion concerning the military administration in Java between Tokyo and Java. This placed the Commander in a difficult position". Perhaps because of this, you may have yielded to Tokyo, changing your policy to a repressive one and inflicting hardship upon the population as a result'. As he said this, the prosecutor showed me a copy of Takashima's testimony. Of course the testimony of Takashima was intended to protect me.

The war tribunal followed the general policy that the person giving an order and the one who implemented it were equally to blame. Thus, if I said that I was forced to adopt a repressive policy, although it contradicted my belief, the prosecutor could make me a war criminal. He attempted this ruse. I defended myself by telling the truth, as follows, 'Since Staff Officer Takashima was of entirely the same opinion as myself, he was concerned about the conflict at the initial state of the administration. However, as he was transferred from Java to another region in August, he was not aware of the change of policy in Tokyo thereafter. The Minister [of the Army] and the Chief of the General Staff summoned my Chief of Staff [Okazaki] from Java to Tokyo and instructed him that there was no need to alter existing administrative policy in Java. He informed me of the instruction by telegram. The criticisms of me in Tokyo were nothing but irresponsible attacks by lower-ranking officials'.

Smit intervened, 'However, former Chief of Staff Okazaki, now being summoned to Java and on trial in another tribunal, testified, "Most of the Headquarters staff were saying that Commander Imamura was relegated from Java to Rabaul because he did not follow the instructions of Tokyo". On this point, your statement is inconsistent with Okazaki's'.

I replied, 'Of course, not all leading figures approved of the administrative policy in Java. There may have been some who were still criticizing it. Okazaki presumably speculated that I was relegated to Rabaul by General Headquarters, on the basis of these criticisms by some people. But it is a total misunderstanding. I was moved to Rabaul because the American and Australian forces were launching an attack on this region, which was therefore becoming very important from the strategic point of view. In fact, the official designation of the military force under my command was upgraded from an Army to an Area Army, and the military forces of the latter were many times larger than those of the former. It is obvious that my transfer was quite the reverse of a relegation'.

The young judicial officer, about 30 years old, seemed to accept my statement.

Indonesian Children

My official residence, the former palace of the Governor-General, and the building occupied by Headquarters faced each other across the largest square in Batavia called Koningsplein, 600-700 metres square; one was on the west and the other on the east side of the square. To go to the office I used a car, but when I retired at 4 p.m. I rode a horse on an avenue around the square, together with three cavalry guard soldiers. I would either exercise the horse for 30 minutes or look around the city. Although I do not know when it started, six or seven boys of primary school age used to wait for me, standing in line on one side of the avenue holding bamboo sticks in their hands as if they were rifles. When I reached where they were, they put the sticks forward at the command by one of them, **'Sasage tsutsu** [Present arms]', and saluted me, just like Japanese soldiers.

Children of any country are fascinated by soldiers and seem to yearn to sit astride a horse. The Indonesian children were no exception, and approached the Japanese soldiers, with whom they felt a kinship because of the similarity of our skin colour to theirs. I did not know who initiated it, but the salute of these Indonesian children to me was performed every day except when it rained. In the course of time, the number of children increased to 14 or 15 altogether. When I saluted in return by raising my hand, they smiled and appeared to be really pleased with my response. In time they came to follow me in a double column after the salute, watching my riding exercise.

One of my guard soldiers recommended, 'Let us stop the children following you'.

'Why ...? They are cute, aren't they?'

'But it looks somewhat funny, and it is undesirable in terms of your dignity.'

'Is that so. Well then, if the children follow tomorrow, I will tell them to stop through an interpreter at the official residence.'

I asked a man at my residence to prepare 14 or 15 bags of candy and to let the children come inside the gate on the following day. I told them the following via the interpreter, Shogenji Teiji (17 years old), 'All of you are good boys. You should become soldiers to defend Java when you are grown up. From tomorrow I shall be taking a different way home every day, in order to have a look round the city and suburbs. As I may pass the avenue only occasionally, you need not wait for me any more'.

The boy, Shogenji, was born in Java and spoke Indonesian

better than Japanese. It seemed that the children understood what I said. They went home with a bag of candy each.

The Headquarters Propaganda Team comprised Lt.-Col. Machida Keiji, the leader of the team and the only military officer, and ten or more civilians who are now active in writing and the other arts. The propaganda team endeavoured to foster harmony between the Japanese and Indonesian peoples, with remarkable success. I had dinner and chatted with them two or three times. One of them once asked me, 'Would you mind visiting a Japanese language school run by the propaganda team? The children are very quick to learn Japanese and Japanese songs. They are cute and innocent'.

One day I visited the school with my adjutant at about 10 a.m. I was told that, although there were many applicants for the school, the number of pupils was limited to about 150 because it was difficult to recruit Japanese staff who had been teaching in primary schools before the war. They said that many of the pupils came from wealthy families. The pupils were divided into four grades and eight classes altogether. They were not yet taught Japanese mixed with Chinese characters, but Japanese in **kana moji** [a simpler script]. The education there was focused on Japanese reading and writing as well as arithmetic and singing. The pupils understood Japanese so well that I was deeply impressed, saying to myself: 'It is surprising that the children have mastered Japanese like this in three or four months!' Because their voice and tone were so good, we could believe it was Japanese chidren singing if we listened with our eyes closed. After looking around eight classes I was asked to say something to the children. Standing in the midst of the children clustered in the playground, I addressed them, 'You are all very sweet. You know Japanese writing and songs well. Your singing is especially good. You must continue to study earnestly, following your teachers. If you have understood me, raise your hands'.

When I said this slowly, they raised their hands saying, 'Yes! We've understood', in unison.

Then I said again, 'As you are all good children I will send cakes to the school by noon. You can get them from the teachers'.

They again raised their hands, laughing, and shouted, 'Great! Great!' Somewhat to my surprise, a photograph of me surrounded by the children appeared in a Tokyo newspaper.

As I was leaving the Japanese language school, I spoke to a member of the propaganda team - I believe it was Oki Atsuo, a poet, but I may be mistaken - 'There are five Japanese boys at my residence who graduated from middle school. I want to put two Indonesian boys among them. If possible I plan to let the Indonesian boys live in my residence and attend school from my house. Could you select such boys from among those who are willing and have their parents' approval'.

In four or five days, a member of the propaganda team in charge of the school visited me bringing four Indonesian boys. Supposing that I had to choose two out of the four boys, I said to him, 'I don't mind which ones come. Please select two of these boys'.

The man replied with a troubled look, 'Could you allow all of these four boys to stay at your residence? In the Dutch period no Indonesian was allowed to enter the palace except for those who cleaned the premises. Because of the curiosity of parents who thought, "Now there is no Dutchman here, and our children can live in that house", there were a great many applicants, leading to a keen competition. It was really difficult to limit the number to four. If we choose only two and ask the rest to go back, the parents of the boys who are not accepted, as well as the boys themselves, will be very disappointed'.

'Is that so. I was thinking that there might be only one or two boys out of the 150 in the school who would be willing to come, since I expected that most would feel queer living in such a grand house as this. If that is not the case, I will accept all of the four. I will let them go home after school every Saturday, stay at their parents' place until Monday, attend school from the parents' place on Monday, and come back here after school in order not to worry the parents. Their rooms will be fixed beside the guards', and they are to take meals together with soldiers. As for home discipline, please tell the parents that Kono, a model youth from a peasant family, will be in charge, and I will tell him not to slap the boys. When the parents want to see their children, they can see them at any time via Kono.'

'If you could do that, the parents would be free from anxiety.' And so the four Indonesian children were handed over to Kono.

*   *   *

The four Indonesian boys already spoke Japanese freely, and they soon became good friends of the orderlies with whom they practised sumō [Japanese wrestling] before dinner at the sumo ring at the corner of the garden. After dinner the Japanese and Indonesian boys, nine altogether, sat on the lawn forming a circle, with Kono in the centre. The sight of them singing Japanese military and popular songs in this way looked harmonious and gave me much consolation. When I took meals with visitors, the Indonesian boys served us, dressed in white aprons and knee trousers given by the Japanese. Most visitors were pleased with their service.

National Pride

As part of my task of superintending the administration in Java, I tried to restore railways, communications and oil facilities. To this end I employed, under Japanese supervision, private Dutch citizens who had been engaged in these fields in Java, and those Dutch prisoners-of-war who had been engineers before joining the army. These Dutchmen, a few hundred altogether, enjoyed security for themselves and their families, and were provided with accommodation and wages. I am sure that such a policy contributed to the maintenance of order in Java and the recovery of industry. Japanese coming from Tokyo and elsewhere, seeing numerous Dutchmen on the way to their place of work or taking a walk after dinner, were indignant at the sight. Why was it necessary to leave the Dutch so free? This was one of the reasons for criticism of my administration. However, I did not stop making use of the Dutch.

Whenever I asked Japanese officers who were supervising Dutch workers at railway centres and electricity installations how these Dutchmen worked and what their attitude was, the officers replied almost without exception: 'It is rather surprising that the whites work for us Japanese, their enemy, without conducting any sabotage behind our backs. They never fawn or make any attempt to win our good opinion. They express their position clearly, which is to work purely in proportion to their wages. Although they are not impolite to us, they do not try to ingratiate themselves'.

*   *   *

Sukarno

Sukarno had been a student of engineering. He had devoted himself exclusively to the independence of Indonesia for the ten years since leaving the Bandung School of Engineering where he had been a professor at the age of 27. He experienced all sorts of hardships, including imprisonment in New Guinea.* When I landed in Java, he was imprisoned in Bengkulen, Sumatra. I heard that he was about 40 years old at that time.

When the Java operation was largely completed, many petitions were sent to the Gunseibu from students and youth

---

* Sukarno graduated from the **Technisch Hogeschool** (School of Engineering) in 1926, at the age of 25, but never taught there. His only teaching experience appears to have been in history, at the secondary-level **Ksatriya Instituut**. He was exiled in Flores and Bengkulen, but was never sent to the notorious detention camp in Boven Digul, New Guinea.

1. *Fujiwara Iwaichi in 1942.*

2. *Painting of General Imamura by the Indonesian artist Basuki Abdullah (see pages 74-5).*

3. Wall painting by the Japanese cartoonists Ono Saseo and
   Yokoyama Ryuichi on a house in Serang, West Java, 1942.
   The slogan proclaims: 'People of Asia unite. A friend has
   come'.

4. The Susuhunan of Surakarta with Imamura after his formal
   appointment as *Ko*, 30 July 1942 (see page 118). Front row
   from left: Machida (Head of Propaganda), Okazaki (Chief of
   Staff), unidentified, Imamura, Susuhunan, Hayashi
   (political adviser), Nakayama (Head of General Affairs).
   Second row on left: Miyoshi Shunkichiro.

5. *General Imamura visiting an Indonesian school (see page 68).*

groups appealing: 'Please release Sukarno, who is an object of worship for the Indonesian people'. Staff Officer Nakayama explained to me that the Headquarters Propaganda Unit had arranged the release of Sukarno in view of the importance of obtaining his cooperation in the smooth running of the administration, and that one of the team members, Shimizu Hitoshi,* had taken him to Batavia. Offices of the General Southern Army Headquarters, then located in Saigon, bantered that 'The Imamura [16th] Army, will certainly have its fingers burned if it allows fanatic nationalists like Sukarno in Java'. However, I was not concerned.

One day in May,† Sukarno asked to meet me through Col. Nakayama, to pay his respects on returning to Java. Since there was no reason to refuse his request, I accepted. In contrast to his reputation as a man of passion, he was a mild person with elegant featues, and he talked calmly. Nevertheless, his wrinkled brow, furrowed by the agony of a long imprisonment, showed the fight he had been through. I invited Sukarno to my study instead of the parlour, to be more relaxed. I offered him a chair directly facing mine, without putting a desk between us.

There were many interpreters at Headquarters. Among them were two sons of Shogenji. While working as a newsman in Fukuoka Prefecture, Shogenji had made up his mind to go abroad. He moved first to China, next to Singapore and finally to the Dutch East Indies. There he lived in Surabaya for a while, and then successfully set up coconut and rubber plantations and diamond mining in South Borneo. Japanese enterprises there, including the Nomura Trading Company, were greatly assisted by him. At the outbreak of war he was seconded to the Navy, and was appointed to assist the Mayor of Banjarmasin, the capital of the region.

The first son of Shogenji, called Kan-chan (then 18 years old) - born in Banjarmasin and educated in Dutch primary and secondary schools - and his second son called Tei-chan (16 years old), were employed as interpreters, attached respectively to Army Headquarters and to my official residence. The

---

* Shimizu Hitoshi was a flamboyant hyper-nationalist who became notorious through his leadership of the 'Triple-A' movement to mobilize popular support for Japan in the early months of the occupation. He was frequently regarded as a nuisance by the army, which expelled him from Java in 1945.

† Sukarno did not in fact return to Java until 9 July 1942, although he began his journey from West Sumatra in May and was delayed in Palembang. **Sukarno. An autobiography,** pp.175-6, gives his version of this initial meeting, which he placed the day after his arrival in Jakarta.

elder brother looked fairly mature, but the younger one had the look of a child. I asked, 'Adjutant Tanaka, can that boy really function as an interpreter? He looks childish, but ...'

'Certainly he can. In fact we have been using the older one in Headquarters for complicated matters. Anyway, translation is not a matter of appearance but of language', replied Capt. Tanaka Minoru, and would not replace Tei-chan by an adult interpreter.

Sukarno visited and talked with me six or seven times altogether, through Tei-chan every time. He was always satisfied with Tei-chan's translation, commenting, 'We can discuss any complicated question as long as the boy interprets'.

For our first meeting only, Sukarno and I were joined in our talks by Col. Nakayama. At this first meeting I welcomed Sukarno on his return to Java. Then I made the following proposal: 'Mr Sukarno! As a result of reading about Java and hearing of you since my landing in Java, I know you well: the kinds of ideas you have, the actions you have taken in the past, the hardships you have suffered. I would not order you to do this or do that, since I know that you do not obey orders if they are not in accordance with your own ideas. I cannot say anything about whether Indonesia is to achieve complete independence, to become an ally or a confederate of Japan, or to become a highly autonomous state under Japanese military protection. These are matters the Japanese government is to decide through negotiations with Indonesian leaders, and I am not given any authority to intervene in such matters.

'The only thing I can promise the 60 million people of Indonesia publicly is that my administration will definitely result in greater political participation by the people and greater welfare than in the Dutch period. You are free to choose either to cooperate with us or to watch the situation from the sidelines. In the latter case the Army will fully protect your honour and your property.

'However, I will not allow you to obstruct the Japanese administration and objectives through your behaviour or in the press. Even if you were to do so, I do not intend to put you in prison as the Dutch did. You need not hasten to answer. Please let me know through Col. Nakayama after consulting your comrades thoroughly.'

'I understand clearly what the Commander has said. I will think it over and tell you my decision before long', replied Sukarno.

It took one hour even for this discussion, as it took place through an interpreter. Sukarno went back soon after the above conversation.

Four days after the first meeting, Sukarno sent a reply through Col. Nakayama: 'I and my comrades will cooperate with the Japanese administration, since you have promised to improve the welfare of the Indonesian people above the level of the Dutch period. However, I clearly state here that I retain my freedom of action after the end of this war'.

As a result of negotiations between Sukarno and Col. Nakayama, it was agreed that the Japanese would establish an organization and provide an office, staff, automobiles and the financial resources necessary for the cooperation of the Indonesians in the administration. In this way, Sukarno came to visit me frequently.

One day, I suggested the following to Sukarno: 'Firstly, I promised before to replace most Japanese officials in high positions by able Indonesians, in order to promote the welfare of the people. However, the Japanese government in Tokyo has notified me that they are sending dozens of high-ranking officials, such as **Shisei Chokan** [Chief Civil Administrator] and **Shiseikan** [Civil Administrator], to fill offices such as those of **Shu Chokan** [Resident] and **Shicho** [Mayor] of the larger cities. This procedure is to be applied not only in Java but in all occupied regions, for cooperation between the military and civilians is indispensable if we are to prepare for an enemy counter-attack against the regions.

'Nevertheless, I intend to pursue the idea of administering through native officials, and to appoint them to positions of **Kencho [bupati]** rank and below as early as possible. I am also planning even to replace Japanese by able Indonesians at the level of **Shu** [Residency] administration when such Indonesians become available.

'Secondly, I am going to establish a **Shijun-in** [Advisory Council] for the administration. Under present wartime conditions it may be impossible for its members to be elected by the whole population. The Council is intended to be an agency to investigate the demands and grievances of the people, the chairmanship alternating between you, Mr Sukarno, and Count Kodama.

'Apart from the chairman, the number of Japanese members may be five or six, and of Indonesians about ten. In addition, day-to-day administration will be in the hands of Col. Nakayama and one you recommend. I hope you can cooperate with us, investigating both the expectations and the hardships of the people, so that the administration can be made to conform to reality. The three Japanese political advisers have endorsed this idea. What do you think of it?'

'It is desirable to establish such an organization. I am in agreement', replied Sukarno.

'In that case, please recommend ten Indonesian members. We do not want to burden you with any financial loss over expenses for travel, research, and so forth. If you can accept the idea, please begin tomorrow working out a concrete plan in consultation with Col. Nakayama.'

The final blueprint was completed in one month, and the

personnel were also decided. (The Japanese members included the three political advisers, and the Chief and Vice-Chief of Staff, five altogether. Among the Indonesian members were the present President and Vice-President [Sukarno and Hatta], and many Ministers at the time of independence.)*

During my term in Java, the Council met three or four times. The Gunseibu implemented many sound policies proposed in the Council. I hear that the Council continued to function until the end of the war.

One Sunday, Sukarno telephoned my adjutant, Capt. Tanaka Minoru, to ask whether he could visit my official residence on personal business. As I agreed, he came in bringing a young man about 30 years old. This time, too, we talked through Shogenji Tei-chan as translator.

'This young man is my nephew, Basuki Abdullah,† who is our best painter in the Western style. He pressed me to ask permission for him to paint a portrait of the commander. Is that acceptable?' asked Sukarno.

'My face is hardly an object of art. I don't mind if you

---

* In **A Tapir in Prison** III, p.125, Imamura names Sukarno, Hatta, Soedjono, Soetardjo, 'and other three' as the 'native' members of this Council. Soedjono had taught Malay at the Tokyo School of Foreign Languages from 1938 until brought back to Java in Nakayama's staff in 1942. Soetardjo Kartohadikoesoemo was the leading pre-war spokesman for progessively-inclined Indonesian officials, a prominent member of the Volksraad (1931-42) and one of the first Indonesians appointed **Shu Chokan** by the Japanese. This **Shijun-in** can only be the Komisi Menjelidiki Adat-istiadat dan Tatanegara (Committee for the Study of Customs and Administrative Institutions) mentioned by G.S. Kanahele, **The Japanese Occupation of Indonesia: Prelude to Independence** (Ann Arbor, University Microfilms, 1967), pp.66-7, and Mohammad Hatta, **Memoir** (Jakarta, Tintamas, 1979), pp.418-19, even though the latter appears to have had a slightly different membership and a different Japanese title from those mentioned by Imamura. This Committee was announced by Imamura in late September, and inaugurated just before his departure, on 8 November.

† Basuki Abdullah was a favourite and protégé of Sukarno, but no relation. Born in 1915, he studied at the Academy of Arts in The Hague and had already become established before the war as Indonesia's leading portrait painter. He spent some time outside Indonesia in the 1960s because his academic naturalist style was not approved by the Left. Basuki's father, Abdullah Surio Subroto, had also been a prominent painter.

want to use me for practice, but I couldn't bear to sit still for a long time as a model', I replied.

'No, it is not necessary to be still. You can just be talking with me.'

They both came to my place four times at intervals of two or three days. At the last visit, Lt.-Col. Machida (the head of the Propaganda Unit) and Shimizu, together with Sukarno, Abdullah and Hatta, gave me the painting set in a fine frame, saying that it was a present from Sukarno to me. My offer to buy the painting from the young man was refused. I finally accepted this favour from Sukarno, in order not to give the impression by refusing it that I thought it inferior. Later, however, I sent an adequate present to Abdullah in return for the painting. I learnt only much later that the affair of the portrait had been arranged by Shimizu so that I and Sukarno could meet more frequently. I was happy to be able to become familiar with Sukarno in this way.

The youth of Indonesia seemed to place an absolute trust in Sukarno. It seemed as though almost all youths were prepared to devote their lives to Indonesian independence under the leadership of Sukarno. Consequently his cooperation contributed greatly to the smooth running of the administration. It was said he was an eloquent speaker. As I had never heard one of his speeches, I was rather sceptical: 'Could this mild-looking person...?'

While I was chatting with one of the political advisers, Hayashi Kyujiro, he told this story: 'The other day, when I was approaching a public square by car, I met a huge crowd of people which made it impossible for me to pass. Stepping out of the car, I asked people what was going on. It turned out to be one of Sukarno's mass rallies. I listened to the speech in the crowd. Unfortunately I was unable to understand the content because it was in Javanese. But I could observe the fascination of the crowd with his excellent voice, tone and enthusiasm. The audience responded ecstatically to each change of tone in the speech. I was deeply impressed: "Indeed, he is as outstanding a speaker as he is reputed to be". I realized then that the Dutch authorities abhorred him, repeatedly interned him in remote places, and separated him from the people, because of his influence in arousing a desire for independence'.

Postscript I

Seven years after these events [i.e. 1949], I was in the Cipinang prison as an [alleged] war criminal. During detention pending trial, I was given a cell in the block for [Indonesian] political prisoners, where living conditions were relatively easy. The cell was opened for two or three hours each morning and afternoon, and I was allowed to walk about, to play cards, and to go into the cells of other detainees to chat.

There were 120-130 prisoners in that block. Of course some of them had been detained because of their political activity in the cause of independence. But I heard that more than half of the prisoners were ordinary criminals who were being treated as political prisoners because of bribes from their family to the prison authorities. Among the political prisoners were two officers in the Indonesian Independence Army, one being a captain and company commander and the other a second lieutenant and platoon leader. Both were attached to the Military Academy in Yogyakarta. The captain saluted me politely when we met while walking, but did not enter my cell. The second lieutenant, with features similar to those of a Japanese, told me that he was 22 years old and was born of a noble family. As he had been enrolled during the war in a youth training centre under Japanese supervision, he knew some Japanese. He often came to my cell and spoke to me in imperfect Japanese and English. One day, the captain and second lieutenant visited my cell together, and said, 'We have a very important thing to discuss today. Could you ask Mr Yamazaki, in the cell opposite yours, to translate, as our English is not good enough.'

Yamazaki was a graduate of Hosei University. At university, his surname had been Sumiya and he had played baseball in the league of the six major Tokyo universities. By the time he was conscripted for military service and came to Java, he had been adopted by the Yamazaki family. After the war, he was sentenced as a war criminal due to an event in which he was involved while serving in the Kempeitai. He spoke Indonesian very well and was liked well by many natives. By order of the prison authorities, he was one of the intermediaries between the authorities and the 700 Japanese war criminals.

As Yamazaki kindly came to my cell almost immediately, we started to converse using him as interpreter. The Indonesians began, 'As you may know, more than half of the native warders of this jail support the Republican Government. In this block for political prisoners, there are three or four reliable spies on the Republican side who are in contact with the Government. One of them gave us an instruction from the Government'.

'What does this instruction have to do with me?' I asked.

'The instruction concerns you, General. According to information from spies of the Republican Government, General Imamura will probably be sentenced to death, judging from the fact that Division Commander Maruyama and Regiment Commander Shoji, both of whom were formerly your subordinates, have been sentenced to death.

'Although it cannot be certain what verdict the judge will bring, if both Maruyama and Shoji are executed, you will face the same fate. A plan is therefore being made to rescue you on the way to the execution ground, after making secret enquiries of the date beforehand. The Republicans will send a car, and you should jump into it [as it passes yours]. We are instructed to tell you this.'

I did not know the captain well. But from the appearance of the second lieutenant this did not seem to be empty talk. In any case, I could not reply carelessly, since I had heard that there were Republican spies among the warders who were at the same time bribed to work as Dutch agents. Because, among other things, I disliked the idea of escaping in itself, I asked Yamazaki to translate the following as my reply: 'Please convey my answer to the Government through the warder who delivered the instruction to you.

'From the point of view of Japanese **bushido***, it would be considered shameful to save one's life by such a rescue. Moreover, we must at all cost avoid having Indonesian rescue forces and Dutch soldiers exchanging fire with each other and suffering casualties.

'Of course, I would not refuse to be taken from this jail to another place in the event that Cipinang jail fell into the hands of the Independence Army as a result of a struggle before I was executed. I am very grateful for the concern of the Sukarno Government. But please understand that I do not agree with the recapture plan under consideration.'

For a time the two officers of the Military Academy looked as though the reasons for my refusal were incomprehensible to them. Only after repeated explanations by Yamazaki did they say, 'We will give your answer to the warder who is an agent'. They went out, still looking doubtful.†

Unexpectedly, the Prosecutor's demand for the death penalty was dismissed by the Judge and I was declared not guilty, owing to the intervention of the then Governor-General of the Dutch East Indies. As a result, the plan to rescue me on the way to the execution ground became fortunately unnecessary.

* **Bushido** is the way of the **samurai** or warrior, the chivalric code which should guide the military officer.

† This incident is also described in **Sukarno. An Autobiography**, pp.244-5. Sukarno makes it appear as though it occurred in 1946 or 1947, though it was not until May 1948 that Imamura was even transferred to Jakarta from Rabaul.

INOUE TETSURO

I) Suppressing the Aron Rebellion in East Sumatra

In the eyes of the Allies who reoccupied Sumatra in 1945, and of most Indonesians in the area, Captain Inoue was the epitome of the mysteriously powerful Japanese committed to mobilizing a dangerous Indonesian terrorist force for obscure but sinister purposes. He is the only representative in this book of those who chose to join their former proteges among the Indonesian nationalists after the Japanese surrender, rather than face arrest and possible execution by the Allies.

Inoue was born in Fukuoka, northern Kyushu, probably around 1910-12. He studied at the Agricultural Faculty of Hokkaido Imperial University, a school famous for inculcating a pioneering, ambitious spirit. After graduation he went to Brazil, where he founded and led for two years an agricultural training school for (Japanese migrant?) farmers, in San Paulo. He returned to Japan in 1934 by way of a lengthy tour in the 'Southern Regions', and established his own farm. In 1937 he was conscripted into the army and sent to China on intelligence duties. With the outbreak of the Pacific War he appealed directly to General Yamashita in Singapore to be allowed to go to Indonesia to develop training institutions for farmers.

Inoue arrived in Medan at about the same time as the Chokan, General Nakashima, in August 1942, and immediately gained his confidence - perhaps because he combined an unusually good education with a dynamic, confident manner. For a time Inoue acted as Nakashima's secretary, in addition to being simultaneously police chief and administrator of the key Deli-Serdang district. When he withdrew from these functions in May 1943 to concentrate on his original idea of developing an agricultural training school (Talapeta), he by no means withdrew from the limelight. Readers of the Japanese-controlled press could have been in no doubt that his project was seen by its founder and by Nakashima as the front line in implanting Japanese patriotic ideals among the widest possible group of Indonesians.

Undoubtedly Inoue was influenced in his youth by the romantic ultra-nationalism of the twenties, with its slogan of **Nampō Yūhi** (Flying Courageously to the South). He also appears to have had an almost mystical belief that regeneration had to begin with the peasantry, by inculcating in them a sense of their own worth. Even if in practice many of those who went through Talapeta were not peasants at all but urban political activists, they all bear testimony to the remarkable effect- iveness of the training in hardening them to rigid discipline and back-breaking physical labour. In Inoue's eyes nothing could be achieved without complete and sacrificial commitment.

As his memoir reveals, however, Inoue's extraordinary sense of mission became increasingly difficult to separate from his own charismatic, almost messianic, role. In a speech to Talapeta graduates he proclaimed that 'I, your father, will always be at your side, like your shadow. When you encounter obstacles in the course of your duty, remember ... the name of your father [bapak] and your spirit will rise'.* He appears to have been well equipped to occupy the centre stage - a tall, handsome figure, with the highly unusual distinction of a beard ('more like a European', according to one Indonesian). By 1944 he was fully master of Indonesian, and used it to remarkable emotive effect. Though no one would have dared use his Indonesian nickname, Bapak Janggut (Mr Beard), to his face, he was evidently pleased enough by it to use it as the title of his memoir.

Inoue appears to have had no particular sympathy with Indonesian nationalism initially, and came into contact with the radical-nationalist Gerindo group only through suppressing them. His relationship with Jacub Siregar's wife must have helped him come to understand the nationalist position. Historically, his principal significance was the mass base, the tough training and the readiness for violence which he was able to bestow on the Gerindo group through Talapeta and the KTT. These factors became important in the struggle against the Dutch, but still more in the fratricidal infighting on the Indonesian side, particularly the toppling of the Sultans and Rajas of East Sumatra in the so-called 'Social Revolution' of March 1946. Inoue himself (p.140) describes with as much pride as shame the bestialities committed by his proteges against the Malay and Simalungan aristocracy at this time.

As this memoir shows, Inoue took no account of the extent to which his remarkable charisma was due to the seemingly unlimited power he could wield as the trusted right hand of Nakashima. The Japanese surrender must therefore have been a doubly cruel blow for him, since he now became dependent on the man he had cuckolded when their roles had been reversed. Not surprisingly, the psychological pressure which Jacub Siregar appears to have suffered during the occupation was now transferred to Inoue, who suffered some kind of a breakdown during the revolution, according to some informants.

While some more left-wing Japanese, like Yoshizumi Tomegoro in Java, undoubtedly joined the post-surrender independence struggle out of real commitment to it, Indonesians tended to be unconvinced that Inoue's motives were so pure. He

* Cited in Reid, **The Blood of the People**, p.132; see also p.146 n78.

would probably have faced execution had he remained in Medan, and he himself claimed (p.141) that the Allied price on his head in 1946 was 50,000 guilders. Nevertheless Jacub Siregar and Saleh Oemar ('Iwan' and 'Suleiman' in this memoir) did attempt to protect him, even though they did not altogether trust him. In 1947 the Republican Military Police arrested him after some particularly nasty murders by his former KTT proteges, though he was later released. He returned to Japan about 1951, and died in the 1960s.

Inoue explains that he began this memoir in response to a request by Siregar's wife Chadidjah ('Murni') that a record should be made of the struggle of the Gerindo/KTT radical nationalist group. Since he claims (pp.49-50) that the request was brought to him in his jungle hideout by 'Abdi', Chadidjah's child whom he appears to have fathered in 1943, it may not have been written until he had been in hiding for some years - perhaps in 1949 or 1950.

Inoue Tetsuro

BAPA JANGO: BAPA DJANGGUT

(Tokyo, Kōdan-sha, 1953), pp.50-80

Chapter 5:   REMINISCENCES

From early in the morning I was busy writing my memoirs in
my 'palace' [jungle hideout], having changed my routine in
response to a request which Abdi had brought me from Murni
[Chadidjah].

Living in hiding in the jungle I naturally had no desk,
but I managed to write by sitting on the ground between the
entrance and the sunken hearth, and facing the bed. This
position made the height of the bamboo matting bed just right
for writing, which I did by the light of a lamp. While I told
myself that my motive in writing was simply to fulfil Murni's
request, and that one never knows where or when one's end will
come, in reality her request reinforced what I had been wanting
to do myself.   I had been thinking already about writing a
memoir to give to some reliable Indonesian.

Before and After the Aron

A night in early August 1942. The setting is the official
residence of the **Shu Chokan** [Resident] of East Sumatra, Jalan
Sukamulia, Medan. It was an unusually sultry night, and I was
having difficulty in sleeping. Shortly after the cuckoo clock
struck 1 a.m., I was suddenly roused by the insistent ringing
of the telephone.

'Hallo. Hallo. Rumah Gouverneur disitu? (Hello. Hello.
Is that the Chokan's residence?).' The voice of the Indonesian
on the telephone seemed very agitated. Moreover I was aware of
some commotion in the background behind the speaker, and
guessed that something must have happened.

'Ah, **Tuan Keimubucho*** is it? This is the switchboard at
the Arnhemia† Police Station. I will convey an emergency

---

* **Tuan** is an Indonesian form of address, generally used for
foreigners especially in the colonial era. **Keimubucho** is
Chief of Police (for East Sumatra), Inoue's principal
function at the time.

† Since 1943 named Pancur Batu, Arnhemia was the chief town of
Upper Deli.

82

report from the **Fuku-bunshucho** [Sub-district head], Tashiro:

> Arnhem. 6 August. 1 a.m.
>
> Report of Fuku-bunshucho Tashiro of Upper Deli. Some members of the **aron*** from the region around Arnhemia, who have been staging demonstrations to demand the unconditional release of farmers detained on the charge of illegal cultivation, suddenly launched as assault on the police office here at 12.30 a.m. Casualties so far confirmed: on the aron side, two dead, five seriously wounded, an unknown number of minor injuries; on the police side, two seriously wounded, two slightly injured. After trying to placate the aron insurgents, I am now with the leaders...

The telephone was suddenly disconnected at that point, and I could get no response thereafter, even though I called back repeatedly. While I was wondering what had happened, the telephone rang again. It was from Lt. H., head of the Medan Kempeitai.

'We have received a report from the police in Arnhemia ... Ah, you know about it already. The Kempeitai here is preparing the immediate dispatch of a squad commanded by a certain sergeant-major. What is the view of the Gunseibu on this?'

'Ah, yes,' I replied. 'Thank you very much for your trouble. When we received the report this morning, we planned to deal with the aron incident ourselves. However, since our police forces are inadequate and you have already begun preparing a force, we would like you to settle the incident however you wish, though I am sorry to ask it of you. I must stress that the Gunseibu still adheres to the policy that a peaceful solution must be found to the aron problem, and that you should bear this in mind at all times.'

I put down the telephone, went out of the room and awoke Chokan N [Nakashima], who was asleep in his room directly opposite mine. I briefly reported the sequence of events. The Chokan looked troubled and pondered for some time. Then he abruptly told me to call up the Divisional Chief of Staff. When I had got the Chief of Staff on the phone, the Chokan outlined the Arnhemia developments to him. The Chief of Staff must have been giving his opinion, to judge from the Chokan's responses - 'It would be good if you could do that... I am most appreciative... Thank you very much.'

* The Karo Batak word **aron** normally refers to a group of villagers who harvest collectively, moving through the fields of each in turn. It was the only term by which the 1942 movement among Karos to cultivate estate land illegally was known.

However, the conversation ended with the Chokan saying, 'In any event, please leave the matter in our hands for a while longer. If we reach a deadlock, we will certainly call on your ample military forces.' He hung up and went back to his bedroom, saying to me, 'I want to think this over lying down. Let me know if there are any important developments.'

I waited for the next developments, but no further reports came in from either the Kempeitai or the police. Thinking that the disturbance must have been put down, I began to relax and fell asleep. Before I knew it, it was dawn. Feeling heavy in the head, I gulped down a strong cup of coffee, and as usual I got to the **Seicho** [Residency Administration] office before the Chokan. At the time, I was holding three positions at once: in the morning I was **Shu Keimubucho** [Head of the Residency Police], working in the police section of the Seicho; in the afternoon I was **Bunshucho** [equivalent to Dutch Assistant-Resident] of Deli-Serdang, working in the office assigned to that post; and all the time I was secretary to the Chokan, whether I was in the Seicho or the Deli-Serdang office.

Immediately, I contacted the Fuku-bunshucho and the Chief of Police at Arnhemia by phone. I was told, 'The casualties are the same as have been reported already. The aron rioters, who had been insisting on the release of the detainees, were persuaded to withdraw temporarily by the kempei who came to help, leaving the question of the aron movement unresolved. The Arnhemia area appears to have now returned to normal. As Fuku-bunshucho I consider we had better release the detainees. What do you think?'

I ended the conversation by instructing, 'Don't be in too great a hurry. Watch the movements of the aron closely from all angles, and at the same time take all precautions against another possible attack by the aron.'

While I was still thinking over possible means of settling the problem, the bell suddenly rang above my head. The indicator showed that it was the Chokan's room. I went quickly up to this room on the second floor where I found Flora, a blue-eyed maid attached to the Seicho, who said, 'His Excellency is waiting for you in the secret meeting room.' The Chokan told me, 'On my way here to assume my post as fourth **Shibucho** [head] of the East Sumatra branch of the Military Administration and first Shu Chokan* of the region, I talked over many things with the [25th] Army Commander. The thing he

---

* Until August 1942 a provisional administration was conducted by the senior military officer in each **Shu**, who had the title **Shibucho**, and acted for the Military Administration of the 25th Army with its headquarters in Singapore. Nakashima and Inoue both arrived in August to begin a more permanent administration.

emphasized most was: "Uprisings caused by the aron secret society are a cancer in the law and order situation in North Sumatra. The situation has now reached a critical point. I must ask you to make a special effort to solve the problem."

'As you well know, after the Kempeitai confessed itself beaten by this problem, the civil administration of East Sumatra, from the time of the first Shibucho to myself, the fourth, has tried every method and every combination of people that might reasonably be expected to prove effective in solving this problem. Unfortunately, we have still not found even the glimmer of a solution. Meanwhile, as we can see from the incident last night, the aron are becoming more and more violent. Moreover, the same trend is spreading with every passing day into Tanah Karo and Upper Serdang.* As Chokan I am extremely worried by the situation. Last night the Divisional Chief of Staff recommended that I mobilize his units to provide a military solution. Since I am basically a military man myself,† I am tempted to use such methods. However, not only would it leave an indelible stain on the history of our military administration, but it might also prove a serious source of political trouble in the future.'

'I thoroughly agree with you,' I replied.

'Right. Well then, I am going to have one last try, win or lose, at a political solution. I have neither a clear plan nor any real confidence of success. I have thought about it a great deal since last night, and reached the conclusion that I must pin all my hopes on you this time. I feel there is no alternative but to entrust both the planning and implementation of a solution to you. Do you think you could do it?' The old Shogun repeated, 'How about it? Will you do it for me?'

At the time I had no more idea how to pacify the aron movement than the Chokan did, and no more confidence that it could be done. Nevertheless, I immediately answered, 'I will do my best to live up to your expectations.' Inwardly I came

---

* The Karo Batak population of East Sumatra live predominantly in the highlands known as Tanah Karo or Karoland, but also extend to the adjacent upland areas of the Malay-ruled sultanates of Langkat, Deli and Serdang. Because large areas of these Sultanates had been alienated to Western plantations by the Malay rulers, movements of resistance such as the aron were more likely to begin there than in Tanah Karo itself.

† All Chokan in Sumatra were military men. Lt.-Gen. Nakashima Tetsuro was unusually senior, having been brought out of retirement for this prize post. He had earlier been a military attaché in Paris and an instructor at the Imperial Military Academy. He was held responsible for excesses in East Sumatra and executed by the Allies.

to the simple conclusion that I would be prepared to die for this Chokan, and would atone with my life in the event that I failed. That very afternoon I received my official orders:

> East Sumatra Policy No. 1. Operation Order to Captain Inoue Tetsuro of the Army:
> You are to proceed to Upper Deli district as quickly as possible, and to bring about a settlement of the aron incident. Fuku-bunshucho Tashiro of Arnhemia will be ready to provide immediate support to you in any emergency.

After dinner [on August 6] I managed to escape from the Chokan, as he seemed about to begin his customary eulogy of Bismarck. Back in my own room I leafed through a thick file of documents on the aron which I had brought from the Seicho. I hoped that the sources on the history of the movement would provide a basis for developing an appropriate policy. The following Kempeitai report was the first document to draw my attention.*

> ... During the disturbed time when the Japanese were landing in Sumatra, one or two members of the **Fujiyama** [i.e. Fujiwara] **Kikan**† made propaganda among the people, especially those of Upper Deli (Batak and Karo people)# hoping to win their favour. They told them, 'When the Japanese come, the native chiefs will be thrown out, and you can own whatever land you like.' The people believed them and expected to have their hopes realized, but a month after the Japanese landing the native chiefs still held power and the people had to obey the existing land laws. They became increasingly dissatisfied with the Japanese military administration. It was only to be expected that ambitious leaders of political parties would realize the opportunity presented by the frame of

* A translation of the two following reports, differing very slightly, appeared in A. Reid & S. Shiraishi, 'Rural Unrest in Sumatra, 1942: A Japanese Report', **Indonesia** 21 (April 1976), pp.118-19.

† For the **Fujiwara Kikan** or **F Kikan**, the Japanese fifth-column organization for India, Malaya and Sumatra, see Fujiwara Iwaichi, above. Inoue's memory failed strangely in calling it Fujiyama.

Batak by itself usually refers to the Toba Batak, some of whom did join the Fujiwara Kikan. The farming population of Upper Deli, however, was overwhelmingly Karo Batak.

mind of these ignorant people and distort the rash
promises of the Fujiyama Kikan members to mean the
Japanese Army's recognition of their demands. They
instigated innocent people to cultivate land
illegally and to become members of the aron secret
society. Then, native leaders such as the **Dai-soncho**
and **Chu-soncho,*** and their retainers, were frequently
assassinated, injured, robbed and assaulted. If
possible, they tried to cut down the chiefs and
replace them; or failing this, they aimed to
strengthen their own power by such actions.
    ... The aron problem was created by the land
problem. As long as the authorities maintained the
existing one-sided land law which was based on a
secret contract between the traditional aristocrats
and the Dutch planters, the prospect of a return of
public order in Upper Deli was unlikely ...

I also found the following in a written report by the
Fuku-bunshucho of Arnhemia:

1. The major incidents caused by the aron in June
   (leaving aside the question of illegal
   cultivation):

3 June [1942]	The Soncho of Sumba [Sembahe?] was killed.
5 June	The banana plantation of the Soncho of Tangkahan was seized.
8 June	The Dai-soncho [Datuk] of Gunung Mulia [Suka Mulia?] was terrorized.
14 June	The Soncho of Sibolangit and his wife were both killed.
20 June	The house of the Soncho of Lau Cih was plundered and burned.
25 June	The wife and children of the Soncho of Namo Mungkuru [Namokamura?] were killed.
27 June	Twenty pigs belonging to the Soncho of Puneng [Penungkiren?] were stolen.

---

* **Soncho** (lit. village head) appears to have been applied in
East Sumatra primarily to the **penghulu** (headman) of a village
- a smaller unit than the **son** of Aceh or West Sumatra, or of
course Japan. The heads of larger units in East Sumatra
appear to have been distinguished by the prefixes **dai** (big)
and **chu** (medium). **Dai-soncho** and **Chu-soncho** in Karo areas
may have been equivalent respectively to **Datuk** (chief of an
urung) and **perbapaan** (head of the parent village of a group
of villages).

2. Initiation procedures for the aron and number of aron members by the end of June:

New members had to bring a white chicken to the aron leader. Its neck was wrung, and all drank the blood. Uncooked rice was put in front of the new member, who had to swear his loyalty to the aron and promise secrecy. Then the new member had to insert the grains of rice sideways into his mouth one by one, and swallow them.

There appear to be about 15,000 members of the aron initiated in this way.

3. Attitude of the general population towards the aron:

The clever concealment and strange doings of the aron had brought it a series of successes, but the majority of the population were as terrified of the aron as they were of phantoms and ghosts, and after 6 p.m. everyone shut their doors and dared not put a foot outside.

The next report to attract my attention was written by Police Superintendent Arifin,* who was at the time my right-hand man in the Police Affairs Department (he was a notable figure in the native chiefs' group and a relative of the raja of Serdang).

... Based on the above observations and many reports from spies, I venture the following opinion on the question, 'Who are the leaders of the aron?'

1. The top leader is Iwan Siregar,† chairman of the Gerindo party in East Sumatra during the Dutch period.

---

* Tengku Arifin Tobo was a pre-war police **wedana** in charge of surveillance of political activities in the province, and was therefore an old antagonist of the nationalist movement, particularly Gerindo.

† 'Iwan Siregar' is Inoue's soubriquet throughout his memoir for Mohammed Jacub Siregar (1912-1960?), the son of a well-to-do businessman and publisher of Mandailing origin. Jacub had a good Dutch education to MULO level, but directed most of his energies to the nationalist movement after joining Partindo in 1932. He led the East Sumatran Gerindo, the strongest political movement of the area, from August 1939.

2. Although the role of Suleiman,* vice-chairman of
    Gerindo, in the aron movement is not clear, there
    is no doubt of his important role.

3. The remaining leaders of the aron all live in
    Upper Deli and are followers of Iwan Siregar.
    Kitei Karo-Karo, Gumba Karo-Karo,† Hussein
    Surbakti and Keras Tarigan are prominent.

Although there were a variety of other reports and
opinions about the aron, I thought it unnecessary to check all
of them. Right at the end, however, I came across some which
looked like petitions. When I read them I found they were all
from nobles connected with the Sultan of Deli, with the titles
Tengku and Datuk.# Every petition complained, 'Because of the
influence of the aron we cannot attend the office and therefore
we cannot collect taxes. We beg that it be suppressed as
quickly as possible.'
After checking through the aron file, I went out on the
balcony in search of the fresh night air of the tropics, and to
ponder the question how to fulfil the Chokan's expectations and
shoulder the burden of pacifying the aron.

By the morning of the following day [7 August] I was
already busy with important preparatory measures for the Upper
Deli business. While carrying out the suppression of the aron
in the area, to ensure that my work would not meet any
uncalled-for obstacles and that the people of the area would
not be influenced, I arrested those regarded as influential
among the local leaders, as well as the mysterious Iwan
[Siregar]. To begin with I managed to assemble tactfully about

* Suleiman is Inoue's soubriquet for Mohammed Saleh Oemar (born
  Pengkalan Brandan, 1909). He was active as a writer and
  journalist as well as a Gerindo leader, and used the pen name
  Surapati.

† Kitei and Gumba Karo-Karo were both from Lau Cih, mentioned
  above in connection with an aron attack in June 1942. Both
  had been arrested by the Dutch in December 1938 in connection
  with their leadership of the predecessor of the aron - a
  Gerindo-inspired farmers' organization of Upper Deli known as
  Setia.

Although given considerable autonomy in the Dutch colonial
  structure, the Karo area of Upper Deli remained part of the
  Deli Sultanate, administered through four **urung** each headed
  by a Datak of Malay-ized Karo lineage.

60 popular leaders at the Seicho, of whom 40 were allowed to go home with a warning, while the other 20, whom I sensed might be important, were detained there. Next I had to deal with Iwan Siregar. With the secret consent of the Chokan, I drove out without using a chauffeur or wearing a military uniform. I expected Iwan Siregar, who was at that time an adviser to the mayor of Medan,* to be at home because it was the time of the siesta. When I got out of the car and knocked at the door, a tall slim woman, who had the look of a Eurasian, came out. In answer to my enquiry whether her husband was at home, she replied, as expected, that he was sleeping. 'I am the Keimubucho of this Residency,' I said. 'I have come here by order of the Chokan to collect your husband. Please tell him to get ready immediately'.

The woman frowned slightly, but walked into the back of the house calmly, saying, 'Is that so? Just a moment, please.'

Iwan, who soon emerged, was an extremely ugly man, quite the opposite of his beautiful wife. He had frizzy hair like a Papuan, large bulging eyes, thick lips and a black face. He was dressed simply, and clutched a shabby hat. On seeing me he bowed and murmured something, but his words were inaudible, perhaps because he was anticipating the worst. I put Iwan in the back seat of the car, and as I grasped the handle I said to his wife, 'Sorry to have disturbed you.' She answered, 'Selamat jalan (Take care),' and forced a smile, but her face was emotionless.

In no time I was at the gate of Medan's second prison. I summoned the director and explained the circumstances to him. Then, saying, 'It'll probably be dull, but be patient,' I drove off, leaving the bemused Iwan there.

Back at the Seicho office, I gave a brief report of this to the Chokan. Then a sudden thought occurred to me and I called Superintendent Arifin to my office. 'Arifin, I'll come to the point at once,' I said. 'I have locked up Iwan in the Second Prison.'

'Really? You've got Iwan at last! Bagus tuan, bagus tuan (Well done, well done, sir).' Arifin's oily features expressed astonishment.

'I have something I want to say to you - that it will be the **Bucho** (myself) who is in charge of Iwan while he is in prison. In other words, nobody except myself is allowed to intervene in any matter whatsoever concerning Iwan. Is that clear?'

'Yes,' he replied.

* The mayor of Medan was Hayasaki, pre-war Japanese Consul in the city, who had used his contacts to assemble a group of prominent Indonesian politicians as 'advisers'.

'I am going to leave the office at about 9 p.m. and make a house search at Iwan's. You may come with me.'

'Yes, I will be there,' answered Arifin cheerfully. In contrast to him, I could only feel gloom.

When Arifin and I knocked at the door of Iwan's house at 9 p.m. that night, the lights were off, perhaps as a deterrent to us. A woman in a long nightgown came out from the back, holding a candle in her hand, her hair still damp from being washed. It was the same woman I had met earlier. I apologized for disturbing her at night, and explained politely the purpose of our visit. This time she reacted very calmly to my visit and said, 'Please feel free to search anywhere.' She held the candle to guide us to Iwan's study.

Superintendent Arifin, like a hunting dog showing the way to his master, began to pull out drawers and search energetically through documents. However, the woman appeared completely unperturbed. I lost interest when I realized that there could not be any important documents left as long as a woman like this was in charge of the house. I asked her, 'What were the aims of the Gerindo party which you led during the Dutch period?'

'The annihilation of the Dutch Government! The expulsion of the Dutch!' was her bold reply.

'Well, why weren't you exiled to Boven Digul, then?' I teased her.

She smiled and replied quickly, 'Because the manifesto of Gerindo stated that the aim of the party was the improvement of the living standards of the Indonesian people.' When she smiled she was extremely attractive.

Arifin reappeared carrying a bulging bag and reported that he had finished the search. His oily features were puffed with triumph. What a disgusting fellow!

I said, 'Well, ma'am, I am very sorry to have troubled you. You need have no misgivings on this question, as we have found nothing suspicious in our search. Although I say so from my own personal feelings, the Chokan is particularly concerned about you over this business, and has telephoned the mayor of Medan to order that Iwan's salary be paid as usual. Furthermore, I intend to take personal care of your husband while he is in prison in the matter of meals, entertainment and so on. Please don't worry on account of these matters.'

The woman, who had been standing erect like a statue, suddenly collapsed on the floor and burst into tears. Feeling that clumsy attempts at consolation would be out of place, I beckoned Arifin, and we quietly left the house.

The next day or the day after, I was hard at work on the preparations for my departure. I was impatient because my orders had stated 'as early as possible', but day after day my departure was delayed by all the things to be prepared - studying the itinerary, selecting the attendants, communicating with the relevant local rulers, contacting the families of the detainees, and procuring the necessary supplies such as medicine, cakes and provisions.

It was about noon when the Eurasian maidservant Elly came into my office with a namecard which read, 'Murni Iwan Siregar'.* I said, 'Please show her in, and call the interpreter, Yoshida.'

The woman who was shown in by Elly a moment later was without doubt Iwan's wife. But today she was dressed magnificently in pure Indonesian style. Her choice of **kebaya** and **sarong** bespoke her highly cultivated personality, and hinted at hidden depths. She had probably been expecting to talk to me in English, as she was carrying a small Dutch-English dictionary. However, we did not have long to wait before the interpreter arrived.

She began, 'I think you are fully aware of the important role my husband played as one of the top leaders of the F [Kikan] when the Japanese landed in Sumatra, and what great service he has since rendered to the Kempeitai and to the Medan municipality. Iwan is of course anti-Sultanate, but sensible enough to know that he cannot eliminate the authority of the sultans through reckless measures like those of the aron. Iwan is indeed the "father" of the people of Upper Deli, but certainly not a leader of the aron. I came here today to ask a favour of you on these grounds. I beg you - please find a way to release Iwan.'

'Your husband's arrest was based on purely political requirements,' I replied, 'as declared by the Chokan himself. His arrest has nothing at all to do with his being a leader of the aron. I should like to tell you in confidence that although we have gathered all sorts of evidence relating to the relations between Iwan and the aron, there is nothing that proves any definite involvement. Thus we must ask both you and your husband to be patient with us until the "political requirements" no longer apply.'

Murni cried, 'Oh, poor Iwan! That he should be so rewarded for serving the Japanese Army at the risk of his life! I came to you, trusting in your competence as Keimubucho. I beg you - release him and pardon him.'

'No,' I replied, 'whatever you say, this matter lies

---

* 'Murni' (lit. pure) was Inoue's soubriquet for Chadidjah, the beautiful Eurasian singer and political activist who married Jacub Siregar about 1936.

outside my jurisdiction, and there is nothing I can do. I
should like you to accept this and go home.' Her face became
wet with tears as I spoke. I decided to say no more. After a
long silence, she apologized for having taken my time, and
despondently took her leave.

However, she was back at my office the following day. She
appealed, 'Isn't there some way you could get Iwan released.
I don't mind how you manage it - even in the form of **huis
arrestatie.**'

'I am terribly sorry, but as I told you yesterday, it is
beyond my competence, and there is nothing I can do.'

She suddenly began to show some spirit. 'Well then, could
you please introduce me to the Chokan. I would like to appeal
to him directly.'

'No,' I replied. 'It would be pointless, at least as long
as the "political requirements" remain.'

'Well then, when will the "political requirements" no
longer apply?'

'That depends for one thing on the progress of the aron
affair,' I replied. 'I am planning to go there myself in two
or three days' time.'

'In order to subjugate the aron?'

'You may suppose what you like.'

'I am sorry to have to say it,' she said, 'but have you
even begun to understand Indonesian politics? If you are
really hoping to solve the aron problem, you must definitely
release Iwan at once.'

'No,' I replied, 'I have quite the opposite opinion.'

Again an awkward silence hung between us. Abruptly she
broke it. 'Are you aware that many members of the party are
ready to swing into action in that district as soon as I give
the word?'

I reacted angrily. 'Be careful what you say! I am not
foolish enough to arrest a woman like you. If you are planning
to obstruct my work - fine! You give any orders you want. Let
us see which of us will prevail. However, by way of warning, I
want to make it clear to you that if you make out to be a
defender of the people, I will appear before the people of
Upper Deli with much more sincerity than you.'

Breakdown! The charged atmosphere eventually forced her
to withdraw. I felt that the situation was becoming more
difficult.

On the evening of 10 August, I was talking with the
Chokan over a cup of tea after dinner. I announced, 'I want to
leave tomorrow, since everything is ready at last.'

'Really? You have a very difficult task this time. I

93

hope you will do your best. How long are you planning to be there?'

'If it all goes smoothly, I should be back in two weeks.'

'Ah yes,' he said. 'Well then, I am going to appear an old fuss-pot, but I think you should take at least one squad of soldiers. You are venturing into a remote area of which even the Kempei are afraid. If you want I will ring the Divisional Chief of Staff and ask...'

'Thanks very much,' I replied, 'but I am hoping if at all possible to avoid anything that will provoke the people, so I am restricting my party to two interpreters.'

'You may feel it's all right, but I still feel uneasy,' he said.

'Ha...'

The Chokan continued, 'How about cracking a bottle of Bordeaux to celebrate your departure?'

'No thanks,' I said, 'I still have a few things left to do tonight.'

Back in my room, I went straight to my desk and took up my pen. I wrote two letters, put them in envelopes, and addressed them. On both I wrote 'testament' in red down the side. One was to the Chokan and the other to my family in Japan.

With this, my preparations for departure were complete. Just as I began to relax, the servant Tjokro suddenly appeared and said, 'Dari, Chokan kakka [From the Chokan]'. He handed me a bundle of bottles of sherry, on which I found a handwritten note, 'I pray for your success. Nakashima.'

Memoir on the Suppression of the Aron in Upper Deli

11 August

At 10 a.m. all the members of my pacification team gathered at the residence of the Fuku-bunshucho in Arnhemia, the capital of Upper Deli, about 17 kilometres south of Medan. The team consisted of 44 persons in all - myself, interpreter F (Indonesian language), interpreter S (Karo language), Teguh (a Karo Batak **sawah** [wet-rice] expert) as guide, ten Indonesian policemen whom the Chokan had forced on me as a guard, and 30 coolies (for the transport of provisions, cakes and medicines). In addition, we had a horse called Marco for me (an Anglo-Norman breed), and two horses (Batak breed) for the inter-preters. Before we set out, I instructed the following order of march (with the head at the left):

police	guide	me	F	police superin -tendent	police	coolies	S	police

At 11 a.m. the big square of Arnhemia, the first place to be pacified, was packed with Karo people, milling around the assembly hall roofed with **ijo** [rice straw]. Teguh, who had a reputation as a humorous speaker, gave an eloquent opening address in Karo, after which it was my turn to address the crowd. As I had to use the interpreter, and the translation was far from smooth, I became irritated, though there was nothing to be done about it. I made an effort to control my seething emotions, and proceeded sentence by sentence, very clearly. In reality the speech presented no problems, as all I had to do was to state honestly that the Japanese were giving serious consideration to improvements in the peoples' welfare, particularly in the area of agricultural land.

In response to my speech, various members of the audience raised their hands. I listened patiently to each appeal, to each lament, and to each entreaty:

'Give us more **ladang** [unirrigated land].'

'Let us prepare more **sawah** [wet-rice] fields.'

'Allow us to cultivate **palawija** [secondary crops] if we wish.'*

'Increase the distribution of **garam** [salt].'

I answered those demands I could; the rest had to be content with promises that we would do our best, giving our decision at a later date. I do not know why, but after we had spoken, many members of the aron who were there opted openly to leave the aron, and came forward to ask for a **ryominsho** [certificate of good citizenship]. The number of converts was about 60. At this unexpected victory the members of our pacification team began to relax. Even the policemen began to smile, though they had been tense with strain up to that point. There is nothing so pleasant as to be touched by the goodwill of a fellow human being.

Our trial run in Arnhemia had been most satisfactory. The next destination for our pacification team was Namo Rambei village in Serbanyaman district [**urung**].† Traversing hills and

---

* The point about these requests was that the area was dominated by Western-owned tobacco and rubber estates. The rights of the peasant cultivators to work land leased to the estates was carefully regulated by negotiations between the colonial government, the estates and the Malay sultans. Pressure on land in the 1930s, and the desire of the estates to limit peasant claims to land, had made the issue particularly sensitive.

† Upper Deli was divided into four **urung** - Serbanyaman (also called Sunggal), Duabelas Kota (Hamperan Perak), Sukapiring and Senembah. Serbanyaman was the most seriously affected by the aron, though Namo Rambei in reality lies in Sukapiring.

swiftly flowing streams, with the **Hi-no-maru** flag above us, the team advanced in high spirits.

We arrived at the village of Namo Rambei at 5 p.m. and decided to spend the night at the house of the village head, in preparation for our pacification campaign the following morning. The elderly village head and his wife, both formally dressed, came and sat down near the hearth in front of me in order to pay their respects. The old woman first offered me **sirih** (a quid made up of betel leaf, tobacco, lime, areca nut and gambir). Then offerings of rice, fruit, chicken and so on were brought out and arranged before me. These rituals signified the highest respect according to Karo custom.

Then the old village head came forward on his knees, and began slowly. 'Welcome. I am really glad to see you. Last night I had a strange dream. As my ladang field had turned golden, my wife and I set off for the harvest. When we reached the ladang we were astonished to find a crowd of aron people already there, busily harvesting. I was furious and began to upbraid them without thinking. They rushed upon me and beat me up, and finally they tied both my wife and myself to coconut trees in a corner of the ladang. Before long the aron people were off, carrying their bundles of harvested paddy. I was so upset I could not stop myself from weeping. Suddenly a **tuan besar** (chief), dressed in a red mantle and riding a white horse, appeared from somewhere and quietly released us both. He opened the palm of my hand and put something in it, then promptly disappeared. After consulting my wife I fearfully opened my hand, and what was our surprise to find a shining gold ring set with precious jewels, the like of which we had never seen before...

'A strange dream indeed! We talked it over and decided that the dream must be a good omen. And just then you arrived unexpectedly. My heart is full of joy.'

The old village head spluttered over this speech as if he were being overcome by smoke from the fireplace. His wife nodded agreement. 'You are most welcome with us. The villagers too will be very pleased.'

I replied, 'Well, I feel that our visit to this village will be very rewarding. Your account of your dream is most interesting. I will write it down in my notebook before I forget it.'

The dinner menu that evening was newly harvested red rice, chicken in Karo style, fried carp, banana and papaya. After dinner I summoned about ten local dignitaries and talked with them around the fireplace. Their demands were similar to those of the Arnhemia people the day before – a minimum allocation of 6,000 square metres of ladang* for each married couple. The

* For Footnote see following page.

96

discussion ended at 2 a.m., but those present did not go home for fear of the aron, spending the night instead in nearby houses.

12 August

At 8 a.m. we began our pacification campaign in the village square of Namo Rambei, where about 500 villagers were gathered. We followed the same procedure as the day before. Thirty-five people came forward to renounce their affiliation with the aron. We gave candies to the children, and continued to offer free medical treatment to the new converts. This was highly appreciated. The major complaints were asthma, malaria, malnutrition, beriberi, trachoma, **bonggol** (growths on the neck), framboesia (tropical boils), ringworm and scabies.

At 11 a.m. we left the village to shouts of farewell from the village head and the other villagers - **'Horas** [Long life]!' **'Mejuwah-juwah!'**† Although the path climbed ever more steeply, we felt even more invigorated. It was pleasant for me to see the big Hi-no-maru flag as I rode along on Marco. Fields newly opened by the aron could be seen here and there on the steep slopes on both sides of the path. In some of the fields peasants were already harvesting their first crops. I spoke to one of them, an honest-looking fellow, 'How did you get this ladang?'

He replied, 'Iwan Siregar gave it to me.'

'What is that man to you?' I asked. 'Is he a **pemimpin** (leader) of the aron?'

'Yes. He is our **bapak** (father),' was the reply.

'Is the rice ripening well?'

'Because the villagers did not all plant rice at the same time, we have had serious damage from birds.'

'Are you also a member of the aron?' I asked.

'Well,' he replied, 'if I refused, I would be killed.'

---

* Footnote from previous page:

This demand relates to the allocation to peasants of prepared strips of farm land, called **jaluran**, by tobacco estates for the year between the harvesting of the tobacco crop and the five-year fallow period before the next tobacco planting. Up until the late 1930s the allocation had been fixed at 6,000 square metres [0.6 ha.], and the Karos of Upper Deli had been particularly incensed by estate attempts to reduce this amount.

† **Horas** in Toba Batak and **mejuwah-juwah** in Karo Batak are the greetings used both for meeting and parting. Each is taken to be the characteristic expression of Toba and Karo respectively.

At about 3 p.m. we arrived at Namo Ukuru [Namourat?] village, the place for our third campaign. The Dai-soncho and notables from neighbouring areas warmly greeted us in the village square. Women in formal dress, who had been waiting for us, began scattering rice grains in time with the shouts of 'Horas! Horas!' Then the Dai-soncho and some other notables, with their wives, respectfully lined up in a row facing us. Shortly, a very slow melody, similar to the **charamela*** began, quiet and beautiful, and played on hand drum, gong and pipes. Pii... hyuru, hyuru, hyuru, pii hyuru, pii hyuru, pii... Boon pokopoko pokopoko, pii... The tone of the music reminded me somewhat of the Japanese **Okagurabayashi** [ceremonial music offered to spirits and gods].

Their hands and heads were slowly moving, but the legs and body were almost still except when leaning left or right. As they danced, their eyes were always downcast. At each beat of the gong they bent their knees, and bowed at the waist as if saluting. It was truly an elegant and meaningful dance, and I was entirely absorbed in watching it. Teguh advised me, 'Please join the dance, tuan, just doing what the others do. Otherwise you infringe Karo custom.' I was thus compelled to dance, following the moves of the Dai-soncho in front of me, even though I was in military uniform. The audience burst out clapping. At the last beat of the gong they stopped dancing and quietly withdrew, saluting me by joining their hands together.

After ceremoniously receiving the usual sirih and presents, we began a propaganda campaign according to our previous formula. About 1500 villagers attended, of whom 30 proposed to leave the aron. The propaganda rally was concluded, and we later attended a dinner at the Dai-soncho's. The meeting with local elders proceeded in the same way as before, without any notable petitions except a strong complaint against the tyranny of the aron.

13 August

At 8 a.m., with the hearty farewells of the Dai-soncho and villagers ringing in our ears, we left Namo Ukuru for our fourth destination, Gunung Mulia. The path became steeper, and the swift streams and cliffs we encountered caused great trouble to the horses and team members. When we had marched eight kilometres or so, we suddenly heard behind us a call to stop. It came from a Karo messenger, who had come at speed on horseback. He turned out to have brought a letter from

* The **charamela**, though probably of Portuguese origin, became widespread in Japan, especially as the characteristic sound of an itinerant noodle-seller.

Tashiro, Fuku-bunshucho of Arnhemia, warning us, 'There is a plot to murder you along the way. Please be careful.' I replied through interpreter F, 'Many thanks for your warning. I am confident of success, so please don't worry.'

After two hours' walk we reached a savannah of **page page** (a kind of cogon grass), and saw a wooden bridge which was not particularly long but lay across a deep valley. After taking in the bridge and its surroundings, I spurred on my horse and caught up with Teguh who was in front. I ordered him with my eyes to stop. Immediately understanding the meaning of the sign, the guide ran back to alert the police inspector. Soon seven of the guards took up a position beside the bridge. They used their rifles first against the clump of page page just across the bridge, then divided into two parties, one comprising four and the other three riflemen, to fire at the page page on the right and left side of the bridge respectively. The calmness of the Serbanyaman plateau was abruptly shattered. Water fowl flew away here and there, and monkeys began to gibber.

After the firing, the police inspector and eight of his men carefully crossed the bridge one at a time. Once across, they re-formed and ran into the page page. An examination proved, as expected, that the bridge had been sabotaged so that it would collapse as soon as a substantial weight was put on it. Consequently all the members of our party, except a few like myself who were lightly dressed, had to take a round-about route across the river. In the meantime the policemen captured a half-witted looking young man. He must have stopped a bullet in the firing just before. As his knee was bleeding, I ordered through interpreter F that he be given first aid. After untying him and giving him a cigarette, I began questioning.

'Which is your village?'

'Lau Kerumat.'

'How many were there in your band?'

'About ten.'

'Who is your leader and which village does he belong to?'

'Paken of Gunung Mulia.'

'What were you trying to do here?'

'First of all we were planning to kill tuan together with your horse by making the bridge collapse, and then if possible kill other members of your party with our **parang** [short swords].'

Although I was full of gloomy forebodings about this Paken's village, I ordered that we continue the march toward Gunung Mulia. Except for putting our young captive at the head, we did not change our order of march, and the Hi-no-maru flag still fluttered gaily above Teguh's head.

We arrived at the entrance to Gunung Mulia after two hours' difficult march across steep slopes, dangerous cliffs and swift rivers. The village was fortified with a bamboo fence.

There was no movement; an unnatural stillness. 'Suspicious,' I thought. In spite of my order to investigate the village, the policemen were too frightened to move. 'Follow me', I said, and walked into the village, only to find it an empty shell, occupied by half-starved dogs and pigs running loose...

(As I had expected, we experienced several incidents there, the most dangerous of which was an impending attack by the aron. It is a pity that I cannot relate the details now. But the reader should understand that my wisdom and courage, at the risk of my life, forestalled the aron's attack.)

I put a stop to the medical treatment of the sick as there seemed no end to the demand. By the time I could relax, the **pepe** [bird] had already ceased its warbling and the mountain village was sinking into the calm of an evening twilight. I thought it better to stay there the night in order to accept aron converts, and if possible to talk with the villagers, which seemed particularly necessary in that turbulent village. However, because all the policemen and coolies were really frightened of staying there and wanted only to leave the village as quickly as possible, I had to commit us to a night march to our next destination, Tanjung Beringin eight kilometres away.

Before we left the village, I summoned the local head of the aron, Nichoh, and the Dai-soncho, and made them shake hands with each other. I did not forget to give them this final message, 'If we cooperate with each other, you two and I, we can give the villagers all the happiness they hope for. To this end I am planning to come here again, by which time you must have begun to improve the living standard of the villagers. I am sure you will not betray me. By the way, tell Paken, the man who tried to kill me, when he comes back, that I am not angry with him now, so he has no need to worry.'

It was already pitch dark when we left Gunung Mulia and entered a forest path which crossed a ravine and river. Since the effectiveness of the only light we had, a pine torch, was limited to the few people walking at the head, the rest had to be very careful not to lose the path and slide down the bank. There seemed to be terraces for growing gambir (a liane plant). The air was full of woolly caterpillars radiating a fluorescent light. This frightening, bewildering atmosphere spurred on our party, which had fallen silent due to hunger and fatigue.

Just as I began to feel the journey would never end, we suddenly heard a noise in front of us. I could see some pine torches approaching, and from the same direction a call, 'Hoy, hoy,' seemed to come. It was evidently a hearty welcome arranged by the representatives of Tanjung Beringin, which lay a few hundred metres ahead. The moon was rising when, at 10 p.m., we reached the village. Music of the unique Karo type began as if at a sign from the rising moon. Before we realized it an elegant dance by older couples, similar to the one at

Namo Ukuru, had begun. When this dance had finished and various gifts had been presented, music in quicker tempo began so the 'girls and boys' dance could take place. The blazing fires and the dinner provided for the policemen and coolies seemed to represent the warmth of the villagers' welcome. What an enormous difference in atmosphere was created by the eight kilometres' distance! The aged village head roused me from my reverie by asking if I would like some **arak**. The villagers went on dancing until late at night.

At 9 a.m. [on 14 August], we began our propaganda campaign by the riverside. About 400 villagers attended. There were no aron members. I praised before the villagers the good administration of the old village head.

(I shall abbreviate the description of our subsequent campaign.)

After finishing the pacification campaign in the Serbanyaman district as described above, I immediately left for the Duabelas [Kota] and Sukapiring districts. Although the physical conditions for walking became much easier, I was given no chance to relax because of a continuous string of incidents arising from the aron's obstructionist tactics. Some of these incidents were very dramatic, but this is no place for all these stories.

Thus, my pacification tour came to an end after many incidents and episodes. On my return to Medan I immediately wrote a report for submission to the Chokan. I did not forget to attach my recommendations in roughly the following form:

1. To deal with the population in all sincerity, and to implement completely what has been promised.
2. To satisfy the most important of the popular demands:

   a. Lease of 6,000 square metres of unirrigated [ladang] land for each family.
   b. Complete freedom for growing palawija.
   c. Permission for new sawah wherever this can be done without disruption to the irrigation plans of the estates.
   d. A tripling of the salt ration.

3. To establish an agricultural training centre in Arnhemia in order to provide the people of Upper Deli with agricultural guidance in every field.
4. To open an office within the Police Department in Medan for the provision of ryominsho to converted aron members.

As a result of my report, the Chokan of East Sumatra

forthwith summoned a meeting consisting of four departmental chiefs - those of General Affairs, Industry, Treasury and Police. Happily the meeting decided to implement all my suggestions immediately. I was as excited by the decision as if it affected me personally, and hurried to Arnhemia by car, where I summoned the most influential village heads of the region. When I told them the good news they went wild with joy, shouting 'Horas'.

It was decided that Jalil, a graduate of an agricultural school in Java, would become head of the planned agricultural training centre in Arnhemia, with his first concern to assist in the expansion of new irrigated rice fields. Meanwhile, the number of aron converts coming to the administration office increased considerably. As a result, the area around the office became alive with Karo colour, and the staff were kept busy issuing ryominsho. As a result, not only did murders and assaults by the aron virtually cease, but so also did incendiarism and robbery, although such minor incidents as illegal cultivation, coercing labour, and stealing occasionally took place. The Upper Deli region was gradually returning to peace. It was at this time that people began saying, 'We will follow whatever that tuan says.'

Suddenly, an unexpected event occurred which led to the total collapse of the aron. One day at the beginning of October, as Bunshucho of Deli-Serdang, I was studying a plan entitled 'The Leasing of Estate Land (approximately 180,000 hectares) formerly owned by Dutch tobacco estates, to the population, with the aim of increasing food production and preventing a repetition of the aron incident', when I was surprised by a telephone call from the newly appointed Fuku-bunshucho of Arnhemia.

'A short time ago a police corps led by Roti encountered men and women of the aron (300 in total) who were cooperating to engage in illegal cultivation near Ujung Labuhan, 15 kilometres east of Arnhemia. These aron people are now interned in a **bangsal** [hut for drying tobacco leaves] under police guard. What are your instructions?'

Intuitively I realized that the people in question had to be the core of the aron. I told him that I would go there myself, and that the **status quo** should be maintained by a strict watch. I then went straight to the Chokan to receive his instructions. After thinking the issue over for a while, the Chokan simply said, 'Unfortunate as it is, if some of the conspirators are found to be guilty of staging violent resistance, both anti-military and anti-Japanese, they must be punished on the spot as sacrifices for the sake of peace for the whole of the population.'

As soon as I had completed preparations, I left for the spot at full speed, accompanied by three non-commissioned officers - Sergeants O and M and Corporal I, who were university graduates working in the Seicho as members of a support team sent by the Division.

I found an indescribable, extraordinary scene when I arrived. In a rice field, half of which had already been harvested, there was a big nipa-roofed bangsal, into which were jammed armed people who had the definite look of core leaders of the aron. A platoon of police surrounded the bangsal at a distance, training their guns on the buildng but trembling as they did so because of the extreme tension. 'Very dangerous. A touch-and-go situation,' I thought.

I went into the bangsal with the non-commissioned officers and interpreter, taking no notice of Fuku-bunshucho M who was trying to waylay me to say something. With the eyes of the aron members in the bangsal upon me, I shouted in Karo, 'Kundul kerina! (Sit down all of you!).' The aron people sat down obediently, and I ordered them through the interpreter, 'I will take charge of your parang until this matter is settled.' Before they knew what they were doing, the aron members followed my order, disarming themselves with surprising passivity. Consequently we soon had a truckful of parang.

Seizing the favourable moment when the aron became calm, I began to talk. Although the content of my talk was much the same as on previous occasions, it naturally took a long time because I gave it all the energy and sincerity I could. When I had finished talking I ordered the Fuku-bunshucho, the police chief and the interpreter to pick out influential aron leaders and most wanted criminals. They brought forward eight men from the 300 aron members there. Since three of these eight men had been identified as known criminals, we were obliged to handcuff them to take them to Medan. The other five had to be sacrificed for the peace of the people of Upper Deli, for they were, in the Chokan's words, 'manifestly guilty of staging violent resistance and antimilitarism'. After meditating a while my mind was made up. The non-commissioned officers made the preparations. The five young men were forced to sit down a little apart, facing their 300 friends. Water was brought. Japanese swords glittered in the hands of the non-commissioned officers ...

'Eih,' shouted Corporal I suddenly, as if to harden himself against pity. And 'Yah,' cried Sergeant O.

The several hundred 'spectators' - aron, police, locals - had all thought that we were bluffing, but retribution had been swift and tragic, and the results were now spread out before their startled eyes. Whether out of fear or sadness, all 300 of the aron members threw themselves on the ground. Only the sobbing of women could be heard from the silent bangsal. I allowed the people a reasonable time to grieve, and then I addressed them quietly, drying my own tears: 'The precious lives of these five young men have ben sacrificed in the interest of the happiness of the people of Upper Deli, and to give you an opportunity for self-examination. Now we must express our unbounded gratitude to them. We must endeavour to give peace to their spirits and to help their families. I beg you not to make their deaths meaningless. Return once more to being good and diligent villagers. On my sole responsibility I will take the risk of discharging all of you and returning your parang. To you, the village head of Ujung Labuhan, I present this money I have brought with me. As chief of this tragic village, please use it to arrange a memorial service.'

I ordered the Fuku-bunshucho to investigate the circumstances of the families of the victims and to work out ways to support them. After praising the police chief, Roti, for his services I went back to Medan, farewelled by the grief-stricken aron.

Within two days of this event, the news of the Ujung Labuhan affair had spread all over Upper Deli through the unique communication system of the Karo people, bringing real terror to the remaining aron. This was the immediate reason for the complete collapse of the secret society, the aron.

About a week had passed since the Ujung Labuhan affair. One day I was having lunch with the Chokan at his official residence, when a servant brought us a letter from Murni addressed to the Chokan. I said to him, 'Here is a letter for you from Iwan's wife. As it is written in English, shall I read it for you?' The letter read roughly as follows:

Your Excellency, Governor of East Sumatra,

Please forgive my writing to you like this. As you know better than anybody, two months have already passed since my husband Iwan was imprisoned in Medan. The 'political necessities' which required Iwan to stay in prison, the excuse the Keimubucho [Inoue] once gave me, seem not to have been removed in this time.

I should say that, as the family of the detainee, we have had no difficulty mantaining ourselves, thanks to Your Excellency's special concern. I should like to express my sincere gratitude to you.

I have now a new problem, however, Your Excellency. It seems that I am the type of woman who cannot be satisfied with merely making salads, tatting lace, and looking after the garden. To be honest, I want to have a worthwhile job. When my husband was at home, I used to spend most of my time as his secretary or adviser rather than his wife. Your Excellency may well understand how much the empty life of these months has tortured me. Nobody

104

could safely predict that I would not go mad if I have to go on like this.

Please give me some worthwhile job - for my own development and for the benefit of others. I should be very grateful if you could kindly find something related either to the newspaper or the Seicho.

In anticipation of your reply, Murni.

'What do you think of that?' asked the Chokan.

'How about the branch office of Domei Tsushin [a Japanese news agency]? She cannot be trusted altogether, though,' I replied.

The Chokan commented, 'Moreover, I hear that she is an extremely beautiful woman. If she gets into trouble on the job we will not be able to show our face to Iwan in prison.'

'I agree with you. When we find her a job we had better get permission from Iwan.'

'How about employing her for a while, on a trial basis, in your office in the Police Department? She shouldn't give you any trouble.'

'She doesn't seem to like anything to do with the police, but I will discuss it with her tomorrow,' I answered.

Five days after this discussion between the Chokan and myself, Murni was already at work in the office of the Police Department. She was particularly good at Dutch, her English was fair, and her typewriting was remarkable. To begin with I asked her to submit 'a life history' in order to test her typewriting ability and keep her from feeling bored.

She always came to the office in modest and purely Indonesian clothes, spreading a heliotrope perfume around the room. She added colour to the office, where there had previously been only the Eurasian servant girl, Elly. I introduced her to Salmiah, who was working as a typist in the Transportation Department, and who I thought might be a companion for Murni. They got on amazingly well together. Salmiah was of noble birth - a daughter of the youngest brother of the Sultan of Deli.

Murni came to the office punctually every day and seemed to be typing enthusiastically. In a few days she had completed her life story.

Life History of Murni (Outline)

Murnie was of Eurasian birth, from the union of D, the Dutch deputy manager of a tobacco estate near Binjai in Langkat Bunshu, and a Javanese woman Saniam. When she was about three years old, the Dutchman D returned to Holland, leaving Saniam behind. Although D tried to take the child with him, Saniam managed to prevent this by her rigorous opposition. Consequently Murni was left in the hands of Saniam. Later a Dutch businessman, H, happened to notice Murni's beauty and talent, and proposed bringing her up. Murni thus came to be looked after by H; it was a happy time and she lacked for nothing. Murni came to love H as if he were her real father. However, during her first year at the MULO Girls' School, H died suddenly in a tragic car accident. Murni had to return to her mother's house near Binjai, but money for her education throughout high school had been guaranteed by a verbal will H made to his relatives on his deathbed.

In the meantime, her mother Saniam had become intimate with a Javanese man called Hassan. One day the mother said to Murni, hoping for her agreement, 'I am thinking of living with Hassan. How do you like the idea?' Murni at first opposed the plan because she did not like the man at all and because she sensed that he had his eye on her education fund. However, Murni had to agree in the end, out of sympathy for Saniam's lonely life, as she had been a widow for a long time. Hassan came to live in the house, but as Murni had surmised, he lived an idle life. Belongings which represented her mother's savings were sold one by one. As the atmosphere at home was unpleasant, Murni tried to come home as late as possible each day, and also began to devote herself to music. She had musical talent and soon became popular among her classmates. They began to refer to her as 'Nightingale' or 'Nuri' (Parrot), nicknames which derived from her unusually beautiful voice.

After turning all the mother's property into cash and cunningly misappropriating Murni's education fund, Hassan at last ran away. Although the mother wailed about it, nothing could be done. Saniam was forced to earn money to support herself and her daughter and to provide for the latter's education, but her earnings were far from sufficient. Thus, Murni too had to work occasionally a a typist for a Dutch company when she could spare the time from her studies. Through her contacts with the Dutch and the many things she witnessed, Murni, as a sensitive girl, gradually inclined towards an anti-Dutch attitude.

Murni had jut managed to graduate from the MULO Girls' School in this way, when she by chance became acquainted with a young man called Iwan Siregar, who lived near her place. Iwan was tall and well built, but he had a sour face. Though Iwan's father was the richest man in his district, Iwan was then living on his own as a result of a sharp difference of opinion between them. He did not seem to have any regular job but was always busy studying, surrounded by piles of books. After finding that Murni and her mother were living in poverty, he began to provide them with financial support whenever the opportunity arose.

Through this association with Iwan, Murni was attracted to him on two grounds in particular. Firstly, Iwan was not only very knowledgeable - especially in politics, sociology and psychology - but was also deeply concerned about the rights of Indonesians and Indonesia's manifest destiny, putting these questions in an admirable perspective. Secondly, he was quite different from most young men who curried the favour of pretty girls and posed self-consciously in front of them. He was older than Murni by only five or six years, but he behaved as though he were her father or teacher and gave her lectures on practical sociology.

This friendship eventually led the two to marriage. The annoncement of their marriage surprised and disappointed many Dutch and Indonesian men who had been attracted by Murni's beauty and talent. After the marriage, Iwan was made head of the Gerindo party in the East Coast of Sumatra, and became involved in underground anti-Dutch activities. Murni, though a woman, supported Iwan by becoming leader of the Binjai branch of the party. The result of their activities inevitably manifested itself in relentless pressure upon them from both the Dutch and the sultan's party. They therefore had to face continuous difficulties.

When Japan began the total attack on Singapore in 1942, Iwan realized, through secretly listening to radio broadcasts from Malaya, that a Japanese landing in Sumatra was imminent. He immediately dispatched a mission to Penang and succeeded in contacting the Japanese Fujiyama Kikan.* Then he initiated underground activity by the name of the 'F Movement' throughout East Sumatra, aiming to support the expected Japanese landing. After this landing took place, he helped the Japanese Kempeitai in Medan considerably by finding Dutch troop remnants, enemy elements and hidden arms, by making propaganda, and by providing information. This was the time when Murni travelled about giving singing performances to solace the Japanese soldiers.

In the ten days since Murni had submitted her life history, she had come not only to handle difficult Police Department work, but also to show her unusual gifts in many areas. When dealing with petitions from poor people, she showed an extraordinary devotion. In the questioning of Dutch authorities, she played the role of a dignified interpreter. Her analysis of information was as good as a specialist's.

Moreover, as she was fond of arranging flowers, every room of the Police Department began to shed the perfume of flowers

* See p.86†.

put there by her. I do not know why, but red roses and white lilies were placed in regular rotation in my room.

As for Iwan, his health had improved markedly since he was first put in prison. He was given a special room with a bed and desk, he ate meals prepared by Murni, and he was allowed to exercise and to read newspapers and books freely. On my part, I did not forget to send cakes and so forth to him through a servant whenever we had some at home. At first he used to cry each time he saw me, but by now he had become quite cheerful.

One Sunday I went out for a ride on my beloved horse, Marco. The horse headed instinctively for the peaceful, beautiful district of Mangalaan. Before I knew it, I was passing in front of Murni's house. Murni's family was living modestly in a pavilion formerly owned by the Dutch, now rented to them by the Japanese administration. Somebody seemed to be playing a record in the house, as 'The Serenade of Dorigo' could be heard outside.

I was just wondering whether to pay a call when a pretty girl about five years old came running out gaily. On seeing me, however, she jumped back into the house in surprise. I could hear her voice calling, 'Sister!' After a while Murni came out in a simple house dress and gave me a smiling welcome.

Murni, the girl and I began to chat, sitting on the ground beside Marco, who was munching at the lawn. I said to Murni, 'I took this girl to be your child, but I see she is not.'

'No, we have not yet had any children,' she replied, in a somewhat sad tone. Then, abruptly, she pointed to the roof and asked me, 'Do you like doves? Look! Up there.' The doves were exchanging tender kisses.

Suddenly the sky became threatening, and black squall clouds began to sweep towards us with a swiftness like raging horses. Murni allowed the strong wind to tousle her black hair, and gazed raptly at the tumultous clouds. 'Of all the wonders of nature, this is my favourite moment', she murmured with a look which seemed at once exultant and sad...

A fortnight or so passed since the event described above. One day I was slightly reproved by the Chokan after dinner. 'You've been a bit peculiar recently, haven't you? Frankly I have been meaning to ask you why ... For instance, once when I came back from a walk with Chiro (the Chokan's pet dog), I found you in Chinese dress asleep on the garden lawn, getting soaked by the night dew. When I woke you up, you said you didn't remember what you had done the night before. This happened more than once or twice. Doctor A, whom I consulted, suggested that you might be suffering from somnambulism, perhaps influenced by some sort of illusion.'

At this point in the Chokan's conversation, I grew moody,

recalling the question, 'How did this Chinese robe come to shed a heliotrope perfume?' - a question which I myself was yet unable to answer.

The Chokan went on, 'Apart from this issue, I suspect that these incidents are related to mental stress and an immoderate use of your brain. You have worked intensively from the settlement of the aron affair to the release of 180,000 hectares of tobacco estate land. Why don't you take a rest at Brastagi? I believe we are not short of hands now in the office.'

'Let me think it over for a while.'

Following the Chokan's advice, by the end of November I was recuperating at Brastagi (70 kilometres south of Medan), a famous resort on the Karo plateau with an average altitude of 1,500 metres. The fields were ablaze with flowers - carnations, cannas, lilies, gladioli, chrysanthemums, roses and so on. The place was agreeably located with the green of the lawns of many gardens surrounding it, and Mt. Sibayak commanding the scene, issuing white smoke as it looked down on the town.

One Sunday morning while I was at Brastagi, Murni and Salmiah, both dressed formally, visited me without warning from far-away Medan. After greeting me, they explained that the reason for their visit was that they had heard nothing of me since I left Medan. We took tea on the terrace of the guest house and ate the cakes they had brought. The beautiful riding ground of a horse-riding club could be seen down below us, and a man was galloping about on a grey horse. Although Murni and Salmiah were making merry, exhilarated by the fresh air of the plateau and the beautiful flowers, I was becoming increasingly reticent. Eventually my irritation developed to a point where I felt I would roar at them if the situation continued any longer. Asking to be excused, I left the terrace and ran down the slope to the riding ground. I leapt on to a horse, whipped it fiercely and headed like a madman for a broad grassy field outside the riding ground. I rode from one end of the field to the other, forcing the horse to jump over every ditch, hillock and fence in its path. A voice inside me cried, 'If you are supposed to be a madman, why not act like one?' I whipped the horse again...

Somebody is calling me. Who is it?

It was night when I awoke and saw, beside my pillow, Murni and Salmiah gazing sadly and thoughtfully at me.

ADMINISTRATION AND MOBILIZATION

1942 – 1945

MIYOSHI SHUNKICHIRO

Problems of Administration in Java, 1942-1943

As we have seen in Imamura's account, Miyoshi Shunkichiro was invaluable to the Japanese conquerors for his knowledge of the languages and peoples of Indonesia. Born in Fukuoka Prefecture in 1896, Miyoshi graduated in Malay from the Tokyo Foreign Language School in 1919. He immediately joined the Ministry of Foreign Affairs, and spent most of the following 25 years in Indonesia. He also served as a consular official in the Hague (1921-25) and became fluent in Dutch as well as Malay/Indonesian. From there he was posted to the Japanese Consulates in Surabaya (1926-32) and Batavia, finally with the rank of Vice-Consul (1936-39). He was a member of the Kobayashi trade mission to Indonesia in 1940.

Miyoshi was withdrawn to Tokyo in 1941 in time to be seconded to the Java invasion force and the subsequent military administration. Remaining in Java throughout the occupation, he was official interpreter at most important discussions with Dutch (as in the surrender talks above) and Indonesian leaders. He was always the chief Japanese link with Hatta. In the delicate negotiations preceding the Indonesian independence proclamation he was once again a key intermediary.

Miyoshi initially set down his recollections of the occupation in 'Jawa Gunsei (Shuki)' [The Java Military Administration (Memoirs)] in January 1947. This manuscript, referred to as 'an indispensable source' by Nishijima (p.151), is held by the Institute of Social Sciences at Waseda University. An expanded version, from which our translation is taken, was published nearly 20 years later in serial form in **Kokusai Mondai** [Monthly Journal].

Miyoshi Shunkichiro

JAWA SENRYŌ GUNSEI KAIKOROKU

[Memoirs of Military Administration in Java], in **Kokusai Mondai**
(Tokyo, Kokusai Mondai Kenkyūjo, 1965-67), Vols 61-82

The Hatta Kikan
[Vol. 67 (October 1965) p.75]

     After releasing Hatta, who had been imprisoned in Sukabumi
by the Dutch since February 1942, the Japanese military
authorities asked him to become a popular leader in cooperation
with the Japanese. Since Hatta willingly promised to do his
best, the Japanese authorities decided to set up the **Hatta
Kikan** [Hatta Organization]* The Hatta Kikan was in charge of
keeping contact with Indonesian leaders of various circles,
promoting and guiding Japanese policies, and collecting
information and source material on political and economic
affairs, and customs in general, which were considered to be
useful for planning the military administration. As well as
reporting the above matters, the Hatta Kikan was also
responsible for publicizing Japanese policies and intentions
among the people on the one hand, and conveying the voice of
the people to the military authorities on the other,
functioning as an intermediary between the two. Being one of
the top nationalist leaders together with Sukarno, erudite, a
pious Muslim and a bold man, Hatta was highly respected by both
the masses and the intellectuals. For these reasons the
Japanese thought Hatta the most suitable person as a
cooperative leader.

[Vol. 69 (December 1965) p.60]

     Among prominent leaders who cooperated with the Hatta
Kikan were later Prime Minister Wilopo; the later president of
Partai Nasional Indonesia, Suwirjo; the later Minister of
Foreign Affairs, Subardjo; and the later Chief Secretary to the

* This office was established by May 1942, with the Indonesian
  title Kantor Penasehat Umum (General Advisory Bureau). Its
  centrality as a link with the nationalists was clearly
  diminished after Imamura's negotiatons with Sukarno.

President, Djamin.*   Many people, representing a variety of
circles and regions, gathered at the office of the Hatta Kikan
all day long.   The office laid petitions before the military
authorities, gathered information, and made reports which were
useful to the military administration.

Hatta was a man who fixed the independence of Indonesia as
his earnest, lifelong aspiration. He never breached his
resolution not to marry or pursue his personal desires until
independence was achieved. I heard from Hatta directly that,
after a thorough deliberation on the question of how he should
behave at the time of a Japanese landing, he reached the
conclusion that underground activities under the Japanese
military occupation would be altogether impossible, and would
only result in a stupid sacrifice of life. He therefore made
up his mind to cooperate with the Japanese within the limit set
by his conscience; to hold by this decision once it had been
firmly made; to function as a protector of the Indonesian
people; and to seize the appropriate opportunities to demand
that the Japanese implement the aspiration of the people, i.e.,
independence.

Being a pure and sincere person, Hatta did not adopt any
kind of stratagem or deviousness, but he never failed to carry
out what he had made up his mind to do, or to declare boldly
what was in his mind. He reported complaints from the people
straightforwardly to the Japanese authorities, and expressed
his opinions on the military administration.   However, this
attitude of Hatta's was misinterpreted by many Japanese as
criticism or protest against the military administration
itself. As a result Hatta came to be deliberately left out in
the cold on every occasion. Eventually he was labelled a
communist by the Japanese. This Japanese view developed into
an incident in which Hatta was nearly assassinated.   I was
assigned to supervise and communicate with the Hatta Kikan, and
Terada Kiichi was appointed to its full-time staff.

---

* For Mr Subardjo see Nishijima, below, p.254*.   Mr R. Wilipo
(1909-81) and Mr Dt. Djamin had both been in the last class
of the Batavia Law School to be given rushed degrees before
the Japanese invasion in 1942.   Wilopo had been active in
Taman Siswa, Partindo and Gerindo as a student, became a PNI
leader after the war, and was Prime Minister in 1952-53.
Raden Suwirjo (born Wonogiri, 1904) had entered   the   Law
School earlier, but became involved with the PNI in 1927 and
did not graduate.

Hatta, **Memoir**, p.414, describes how these and other young
law students offered their services to him because they had
no established position in the Dutch, and therefore Japanese,
administration.

The Japanese Policy towards the Sultans' Autonomous Regions [Vorstenlanden/Princely Territories]

[Vol. 69 (December 1965) p.60]

There were about 230 autonomous regions in Indonesia as a whole, and four in Java, of which the Sunan's autonomous territory of Surakarta and the Sultan's of Yogyakarta were the largest of all. The rulers of the four autonomous regions were the descendants of the Mataram dynasty which ruled the whole of Java and claimed hegemony not only over the archipelago but also over Malaya and the Philippines before the Dutch subjugated the dynasty. However, the dynasty's territory was [sucessively taken and] divided into four autonomous regions after 1755 by the Dutch along the lines of the 'divide and rule' policy.

Because the Javanese had regarded the dynasty as a divine authority for a long time and because it had great influence upon the population, the Dutch were unable to exterminate the dynasty completely. Instead they divided the territory into autonomous regions by treaties concluded as a result of their intervention in internal dynastic conflicts over the succession to the throne. The handling of the self-governing regions was a political issue which required the most careful consideration. If the Japanese were to mishandle the matter, there was a great danger of bringing about a serious situation. Accordingly it was not only the rulers but the Javanese people as a whole who were watching how the Japanese would treat the special regions. As the priority of the Japanese Army was overwhelmingly on the execution of war, the general guidelines of the administration were limited to making use of existing organizations and structures, respecting religion and customs, and in this way drawing support from the population, as long as such measures were not harmful to the administration. Although the policy of making use of the existing organizations and officials had been implemented, nothing had been done about the special regions since the beginning of the occupation.

The people concerned in the special regions entertained some apprehensions about the Japanese attitude, and they were making overtures to learn what Japanese intentions were. Speculations were rife among them about the matter. Since the Japanese authorities judged that it would cause undesirable results to leave these speculations to take their own course, they decided in June [1942], three months after the beginning of the occupation, to make detailed investigations into the regions in order to establish a policy. I was dispatched to the four self-governing regions in Central Java with the task of investigating and reporting on the past agreements between the Javanese rulers of Mataram and the Dutch, the existing state of the administration, the way religion affected the people, and their social customs. I invited ministers of each region to the office of the **Kochi Jimukyoku** [Bureau for Princely Territories] of the **Gunseikambu** and checked through documents of relevant Dutch treaties. I also made trips to the regions for further investigation and the collection of documents.

My reports were to be sent to the Japanese government in Tokyo via the Headquarters of the General Southern Army, and the final decision on this matter was to be made by the government in Tokyo. However, many complicated problems were involved in the process of decision-making and implementation. The General Southern Army was divided between the Army and the Navy, and Indonesia was divided into Army-controlled and Navy-controlled areas. Under these circumstances, the implementation of policy differed according to the characteristics of each area, even though the basic policy was shared. To make matters worse, there was much factionalism arising from the struggle for pre-eminence not only between the Army and the Navy but also between all kinds of groups. As far as the Indonesian area as a whole was concerned, Java was the political, economic and cultural centre with the largest population. In addition, most leaders from other islands had also concentrated in Java. For these reasons the administration in Java was considered a model for other parts of Indonesia. Because of that I was sure that the achievement and methods of the military administration in Java would become the object of envy, antipathy and criticism by Japanese in other areas. In this sense the decision how we should deal with the self-governing regions would have direct influence upon other areas.

Because I knew that even though the final decision was to be made by Tokyo, opinions and recommendations from Java had a crucial importance for the decision, and because I felt my report very important, I prepared two different reports. One recommended accepting the former status the self-governing regions had enjoyed. The other suggested the immediate abolition of their special status, if it was eventually to be abolished, on the ground that the General Southern Army and the military in charge of Malaya [the 25th Army] were not allowing any political privileges to the Sultan of Johor beyond the titles due to a distinguished family and the nominal position of Sultan.

There were different opinions on the issue of the self-governing regions in military circles in Java. Some insisted that if it was necessary to admit some kind of influential position and privilege to the ruler of a special region, this should be similar to that of the pope in the religious arena. Others insisted on abolition. As far as I was concerned, the idea of creating popes in Java was out of the question. In the Islamic world the Turkish ruler had once assumed the title of Caliph, the pope in Islam, but he was

117

deprived of the position of king and pope at the same time by Kemal Ataturk. The pilgrimage to the holy places of Islam, Mecca and Medina is an obligation for every Muslim, which should be made at least once in his life, endowing him with the highest, most desired title of **Haji**. However, Java could claim no historical significance in the Islamic world as a whole. The creation of the title of pope in Java would not only be meaningless but would evoke enormous opposition among Muslims throughout the world. Japan would inevitably be accused of a political and religious impropriety.

Just about the time I was preparing the reports, a meeting of representatives of all occupied areas under the control of the General Southern Army was held at its headquarters. After returning from the meeting, Col. Nakayama asked about my reports on the self-governing regions. When I explained my ideas, Nakayama said angrily that abolition would be stupid. I answered in my own defence that two reports, one for abolition and the other for continuation, had been drawn up as reference materials to serve for the final decision, taking account of the results obtained from my investigation and various views in the General Southern Army and the military authorities in Java. Nakayama's response to my explanation suggested that the atmosphere of the meeting had favoured adopting the policy of maintaining the **status quo** in order to avoid untoward incidents if the four special regions had been abolished.

After several rounds of negotiations between the General Southern Army and the government in Tokyo, it was at last decided to allow the existing autonomous status to the four regions, to make no distinction in rank among the four rulers, all of whom would be given the same title of **Ko** [Prince], and to appoint them formally to this status. Subsequently, ceremonies of appointment were held in Jakarta in the presence of the Commander-in-Chief [Imamura] on 30 July 1942 for the Surakarta ruler, on 1 August for Yokyakarta, and on 14 August for the Mangku Negara and Paku Alam.* The Commander-in-Chief handed over the appointment certificate and 'Order of the Army' and 'Instructions of the Gunseikan' to each of the four Princes in the same form. Those of the Surakarta Prince follow as an example:

Order of the Army

1. I, the Commander-in-Chief, appoint Susuhunan XI as the Prince of Surakarta.

---

* This order seems to belie the decision for strict equality, since it coincides with the seniority of the dynasties. Problems of protocol and seating in any joint ceremony for the four rulers may have proved too much for the Japanese.

2. The Prince is subordinate to the Japanese Commander-in-Chief and is responsible to the Commander-in-Chief for the administration of his **Kochi** [Princely Territory].
3. The privileges the Prince has enjoyed in the past will in general be maintained.
4. The Bureau for Princely Territories [Kochi Jimukyoku] is entrusted with the task of supervising the administration of the Prince.
5. The disciplines the Prince must observe in carrying out the administration are stipulated in the 'Instructions of the Gunseikan'.

Instructions of the Gunseikan

1. The Prince is required to conduct a good administration maintaining close contact with the Bureau for Princely Territories.
2. In regard to important administrative questions, the Prince must obtain the sanction of the Commander-in-Chief by way of the Chief of the Bureau.
3. The existing administrative apparatus may continue to function.
4. Police affairs in the Prince's Territory will be dealt with by the Chief of the Bureau.
5. The Prince is required to keep a reduced, sound budget by economizing on expenditure as much as possible.
6. The office of Chief of General Affairs is instituted to support the Prince's administration. Its occupant will be appointed by the Commander-in-Chief on the Prince's nomination from among Javanese officials.

The above Order and Instructions defined the relationship between the Prince and his territory on the one hand and the Japanese Army on the other, in a similar fashion to the treaties concluded during the Dutch period. It should be remembered, however, that the Order was issued in the name of the Commander-in-Chief and made no mention of any involvement of the Japanese Government. This was deliberately done by the Japanese with a view to the future. Furthermore, the Commander -in-Chief was authorized by the 5th clause of the Order to change the substance of mutual agreements [in the Order and Instructions] whenever necessary by an order to the Gunseikan. This stipulation was motivated by the same factor - the Japanese retained the right of issuing orders and instructions to the Prince so that we could readily respond to unexpected problems in the future. In contrast to the treaties concluded during the Dutch period, which could only be amended by negotiation between the Javanese rulers and the Dutch, the Order could be amended unilaterally by the Japanese.

Since the rulers were formally permitted to retain their position and former rights, they seemed to feel relieved for the time being. However, there remained one controversial issue, that all of them were given the same title regardless of historical background and the order of relative importance among them. The Susuhunan of Surakarta was the legitimate successor of the Mataram dynasty, while the Sultan of Yogyakarta became independent and separate from Surakarta as a result of a succession conflict, and the Mangku Negara and Paku Alam territories were created by Dutch intervention in dynastic disputes. Surakarta and Yogyakarta had been at loggerheads over the legitimate inheritance of Mataram. The territories of Mangku Negara and Paku Alam were much smaller than Surakarta and Yogyakarta. As for titles, the ruler of Surakarta bore the title of **Susuhunan** (Great King), and that of Yogyakarta, **Sultan**, while the rulers of both Mangku Negara and Paku Alam held the title of **Pangeran** (Prince). The rulers of the last two were very pleased to have the same title as the former two, feeling their relative position enhanced, but the former two rulers seemed quite disgruntled. I was several times at a loss for an answer when asked by the rulers of Surakarta and Yogyakarta, 'What does **Ko** mean?'

Apart from this difficulty over their titles, it was also a subtle problem for us to define the relationship between the Princes and top nationalist leaders such as Sukarno and Hatta. We were unable to find a reasonable answer to the question, which of the two parties should stand higher? Thus we had always to arrange ceremonies so that the Princes and the leaders did not sit side by side.

The Implementation of Seiji Sanyo [Political Participation]
[Vol. 72 (March 1966), p.70]

With an ordinance issued on 5 September [1943], **Chuo Sangi-in** [Central Advisory Council], **Shu Sangikai** [Residency Advisory Council] and **Tokubetsushi Sangikai** [Special City Advisory Council]* were to be instituted in October. The Shu Sangikai and Tokubetsushi Sangikai each consisted of 12 members, in part appointed by the Shu Chokan [Resident] or Mayor, and in part elected by the population of each Shu and Special City. The Council was to be summoned regularly by the Shu Chokan, and the Council was given the authority to discuss enquiries from the Chokan and report on them. In addition the Council could present its own proposals. The internal

* There was only one 'Special City', Jakarta.

organization and the way of management were similar to those of
the Chuo Sangi-in.

The Chuo Sangi-in was also authorized to discuss and
report on enquiries from the Commander-in-Chief and to present
its own proposals to the Commander-in-Chief through the
adoption of motions brought forward by members. The Council
was to be summoned by the Commander-in-Chief once every three
months, and extraordinary sessions could also be called when
necessary. As a rule the Council sat for five days. The
Council consisted of the members and the Secretariat. Of the
43 members, 23 (including three Chinese) were appointed by the
Commander-in-Chief selected from among distinguished persons of
various circles, 2 were appointed by the Commander-in-Chief on
the recommendation of the Princes, and 18 were elected from
among members of local councils [i.e., Shu Sangikai and
Tokubetsushi Sangikai]. The Chairman and two Vice-Chairmen
were to be decided in the following way: first, the members of
the Council would nominate two persons for each post by
election; then the Commander in Chief would appoint one of the
two nominees. The term of office for the Chairman, Vice-
Chairmen and members was one year. Among the 20 members
[excluding 3 Chinese representatives] appointed by the
Commander-in-Chief were 12 nationalist leaders such as Sukarno
and Hatta, 4 representatives from Islamic circles including
Hadikusumo and Mansoer,* and 2 representatives from the
self-governing regions.

Problems over the Election of the Chairman and Vice-Chairmen

For the post of the Chairman, the two top nationalist
leaders, Sukarno and Hatta, were nominated. For this position
of Chairman the military had no difficulty in choosing Sukarno.
However, there was a mysterious incident in the process of
electing the candidates for Vice-Chairmen, after Hatta was
overwhelmingly elected by the Council members. The military
authorities had mistakenly regarded Hatta as a communist, and a
dangerous person, and had planned beforehand to stop his
nomination by juggling the voting figures even if the votes
really favoured him. The Japanese planned this move because
they feared the serious consequences which might follow if the
Commander-in-Chief did not appoint Hatta a Vice-Chairman after
a public announcement that he had been nominated.

Although Hatta was actually elected by the members,
receiving a majority of votes, the Japanese juggled with the

* Ki Bagus Hadikusumo and Kiyai Haji Mas Mansoer were both
  prominent Muhammadiah leaders. The other two Muslim
  appointees were both traditionalists - K.H. Wachid Hasjim of
  N.U., and K.H. Abdul Halim.

voting figures as planned, and thereby caused his nomination to fail. Instead, the Japanese appointed Koesoemo Oetoyo and Buntaran as Vice-Chairmen.* The fact that Hatta was not appointed a Vice-Chairman evoked wide-spread suspicion and unpleasant feelings on the part of Indonesians. We therefore had to make a desperate effort to smooth away this suspicion, explaining that such a learned and able person as Hatta should play an active part in the Council as an ordinary member rather than being set up on a pedestal as Vice-Chairman.

The Hatta Affair - Plan for the Assassination of Hatta by the Kempeitai [Vol. 73 (April 1966), p.64]

Hatta was a man of calmness, sincerity and strong will, saying only what was necessary and never seeking to ingratiate himself with his superiors. These characteristics often caused misunderstandings among those who did not know him well. In fact, the military authorities had labelled him a communist since the early stages of the occupation. From the viewpoint of the Japanese military with its bitter experiences in many occupied areas, the maintenance of order was one of the most vital problems in the military administration. It was, therefore, quite natural for the military to keep stringent controls on Hatta if such a significant leader as he was really a communist. Being in a position to supervise and utilize Hatta directly, I often sensed the wariness and suspicion directed towards him from military circles.

After about July 1943 the military authorities intensified their criticism of information and reports from the Hatta Kikan, and even rejected them outright. Almost all reports were now returned with negative comments and marks of censure in red ink. Although I knew we had to observe the military discipline of absolute subordination to our superiors, I took the view that it would be a breach of my duty to allow such inordinate misunderstanding and criticism to continue. About that time I heard from someone of a plot which involved my life.† According to him the Kempeitai was planning to

---

* Kanahele, p.102, states that the voting order had been Hatta, Ki Hadjar Dewantara, Koesoemo Oetoyo, Buntaran. R.M.T. Koesoemo Oetoyo (1871-1953), Regent of Japara (1905-26) and Volksraad member (1918-39), was among the best-educated regents of pre-war Java. Dr. R. Buntaran Martoatmodjo was born near Purworejo in 1896 and took his medical degree from Leiden in 1930. He had not been politically active before the war, but became prominent during the Japanese Occupation.

† Because Miyoshi would have been killed in the same car as Hatta.

assassinate Hatta secretly, on the grounds that he was a dangerous person. The military feared that not only Sukarno and other nationalist leaders, but also the masses, would surely realize that Hatta had been killed if he suddenly disappeared, and this was likely to cause an unpredictable spirit of rebellion. As the Japanese trick at the Chuo Sangi-in election had already left an unpleasant taste with Indonesian leaders, the disappearance of Hatta would immediately have been interpreted as an assassination by the military, and might have given rise to a serious incident. If such a crisis were to arise, not only the military administration but Japanese military strategy as a whole might be seriously jeopardized. In view of these harmful possibilities, my informant told me, the Kempeitai was planning to kill Hatta by staging an automobile accident.* What an inhuman plot this was! Learning of this dreadful plan, I was gravely troubled.

Fearless of the possible alarming consequences, I had the courage to visit the **Somubucho** [Head of the General Affairs Department] and protest against his rejection of reports from the Hatta Kikan. Furthermore, I frankly demanded an explanation of the report [of the plot]. As the issue was very sensitive, the Chief ordered the people in his office to leave. After listening to my explanation for two hours, he began to tell the truth. According to him, the Kempeitai had submitted a detailed report to the Commander-in-Chief, which stated in black and white that Hatta was a communist and a dangerous person, so that in the interests of maintaining order he should not be allowed to behave freely. Even the Commander-in-Chief could do nothing about a report of the Kempeitai Chief once it was submitted. The Chief of General Affairs added that the military authorities were also concerned about the report, and that he was condemned by the Chief of Staff and the Commander-in-Chief at lunch every day because the Gunseikambu was using this dangerous man Hatta. He finally told me I should at once meet the Chief of Staff asking for an explanation, if my information was correct.

After explaining what I had already told the Chief of General Affairs, I requested the Chief of Staff to correct the official misconception of Hatta and to take measures to resolve the problem. However, he too told me he could do nothing about it once the report was submitted, and suggested that I negotiate directly with the Deputy Chief of the Kempeitai, Lt.-Col. Murase. I immediately met Lt.-Col. Murase who, as

* In an interview with Kanahele (Kanahele pp.92 and 95), Hatta argued that the specific reason the Kempeitai had decided to get rid of him was the petition described by Nishijima, below pp.271-5, which (according to Hatta) Hatta had written on behalf of the **empat serangkai.**

well as Deputy Chief, was Chief of General Affairs of the Kempeitai and in practice its most influential officer. In addition to accusing him of responsibility for the matter, I asked him to what extent he knew Hatta and whether he had ever examined him. Lt.-Col. Murase replied that he had not met Hatta and that [his decision to assassinate him] was based on the reports of his men. I once again attacked him for his thoughtlessness in blindly sanctioning such an important move as this. After explaining that I had come to see him by order of the top military authorities, I asked him to re-investigate the matter and to agree to meet Hatta personally when I brought the Indonesian to him. Although Murase tried to avoid meeting Hatta under various pretexts, I refused to compromise and finally succeeded in arranging the meeting in the evening of the following day.

The following evening Hatta and I visited the official residence of Murase, where for three hours we discussed such issues as the suspicion cast upon Hatta, his career as a nationalist, his attitude towards communism and so forth. In contrast with Murase's preconception of Hatta as coldly calculating, Hatta answered every harsh question Murase put honestly and enthusiastically, always with a smile. Thus Murase was unable to produce any counter-argument. Moreover, he seemed to suffer from a sense of guilt for having thoughtlessly written the report in the name of the Kempeitai Chief, simply based on rumours and the distorted reports of his men. Murase asked me whether Hatta had displayed a different attitude from his usual one. I explained Hatta's character to Murase. Hatta is too cautious to make a hasty decision, but once he has made up his mind he executes the decision without regard to the obstacles. Although his appearance and attitude can change considerably, as if he has become a different person in these circumstances, sometimes even showing a countenance which strikes terror into peoples' hearts, normally he is a sincere and warm person. I again asked Murase to reconsider the question and take appropriate measures. Murase confessed that he felt dreadful and he looked shame-faced over his thoughtlessness.

The Settlement of the Hatta Affair

As long as the report of the Kempeitai Chief concluded that Hatta was a most dangerous man, Hatta had to be punished. On the other hand, however, the Japanese could not deal lightly with the matter because of Murase's meeting with Hatta, the military's notorious conduct at the election for the Vice-Chairmanship of the Chuo Sangi-in, and the fact that the Hatta affair was already known to Sukarno and other nationalist leaders and was a big issue among them. The military authorities therefore decided to include Hatta - who was the

obvious succesor to Sukarno as leader of the country - in a
mission which included Sukarno and was being sent to Tokyo as a
response to the grant of political participation to the
Indonesians. In this way Hatta, who needed to be kept under
surveillance as a dangerous character, could be sent for a year
to Yasuoka Masahiro's Kinkei Gakuin* in Tokyo, where he would
study the **Kōdō Seishin** [The Spirit of Benevolent Imperial
Rule]. Then, on the pretext that Hatta had been transformed
into an honest citizen as a result of having studied the
Japanese spirit, he could be used again as a leader of the
people.† This whole tragicomedy was enacted to enable the
Kempeitai to shake off the heavy responsibility it had to bear
as a result of its ill-considered report based on ignorance of
the native people.

---

* Yasuoka Masahiro (b.1898) was a right-wing intellectual who
  gave ideological support to the 'new bureaucrats' of the
  Saito and Okada (Navy) Cabinets of the 1930s. In 1927 he
  founded the Kinkei Gakuin (Golden Pheasant Academy) where he
  lectured military and civilian officials on the neo-Confucian
  philosophy of Wang Yang-ming.

† Hatta in fact avoided even this 'detention' in Japan.
  According to Nishijima (**Shōgen**, p.152), when Hatta and
  Sukarno met Prime Minister Tojo in Tokyo, 'Hatta proposed
  that although he was eager for the study leave it should be
  postponed so that he could better prepare for it. Sukarno
  also opposed study leave for Hatta in view of his need for
  Hatta's support. Consequently the Japanese plan for the
  'informal confinement' of Hatta in Japan under the pretext of
  study leave did not materialize'.
  Hatta, **Memoir**, pp.428-33, states that he was protected
  from Kempeitai machinations by the Emperor's warm reception
  of him, and implies that Tokyo throughout took a more benign
  view than the Gunseikan in Jakarta.

125

Civil Administration in Celebes, 1942-1944

Unlike Sumatra and Java, the eastern area of Indonesia occupied by the Japanese Navy was intended to remain a permanent part of Japanese territory. The Navy's plan was therefore to establish there an administration wholly Japanese in style, staffed by civilian bureaucrats of the highest level possible. While Army officers were in total control of Java and Sumatra, frequently without any Japanese civilians coming between them and subordinate Indonesian officials, professional Japanese administrators were intended to administer the other islands on the Navy's behalf. As the Navy's choice to head this administration, Okada Fumihide was the highest ranking civil official to serve in Indonesia. However, the realities of war, which impinged ever more directly on the Navy area as MacArthur's troops advanced from the east, made it increasingly difficult for civilian Japanese to resist the demands of the military. Okada's memoir illustrates the growing frustration of the civilians as they were pushed ever further from real power in the administration.

Okada Fumihide was born in Shimane Prefecture in 1892, as the third son of a middle-class family named Yoshioka. After gaining admission to the elite Tokyo high school, Dai-ichi Kōtō Gakkō, he was adopted by the Governor of Ibaragi Prefecture, Okada Unosuke, in 1913. He graduated from the Law School of Tokyo University in 1917, having passed the higher civil service examination the previous year. This ensured him a place in the elite administrative corps as **Kōtō Bunkan**, and he rose rapidly in the Ministry of Home Affairs. Most of his time was spent in the Ministry in Tokyo, with a concurrent appointment (1925-32) as lecturer in Tokyo University, but he had two periods as Prefectural Governor - in Chiba (1932-34) and Nagasaki (1937-38).

He joined the Hiranuma Cabinet as Vice-Minister of Public Welfare in January 1939, and retained this position through two successive cabinets until resigning in August 1940. Thereafter he appears to have cooperated with powerful Navy figures in an attempt to increase the influence of the Navy against that of the Army in Japanese politics. He was appointed adviser to the Navy Ministry in March 1942, and his selection by the Navy as their principal administrator in the South followed logically thereafter.

Okada was a strong believer in traditional Japanese values, as is clear from our extract. Although a highly educated and cultivated man, he had never been abroad until his posting to Makasar. He was a great admirer of the imperial system (*Tennō-sei*), and openly sceptical about the post-war changes in Japanese values. He published his autobiography in 1974 as a chronicle of Japanese political life in the first half of the century, but also in the hope of increasing appreciation for the emperor-centred legal and philosophical world he had known in his youth.

Okada Fumihide

DOTŌ NO NAKA NO KOSHŪ

[A Lone Boat on the High Seas], (Tokyo, privately published,
1974), pp.341-85

CHAPTER 8: NAVY MINSEIFU SOKAN
- MY ROLE IN THE GREATER EAST ASIA WAR

I was Commissioned as Adviser to the Navy Ministry,
then Appointed Sokan [Chief Civil Administrator] of the South
Western Fleet Minseifu [Civil Administration Office]

One day in February 1942 Yamazaki Iwao (after the war he
became Minister of Home Affairs in the Higashikuni Cabinet)
visited me at my home in Hatanodai, Shinagawa Ward, Tokyo.
Yamazaki had just that month been appointed Vice-Minister of
Home Affairs, due to the resignation of Tojo as Minister and
his replacement by the Vice-Minister, Yuzawa Michio. At the
time of his promotion Yamazaki was an adviser to the Navy
Ministry, and I was now recommended as his successor. It was
easy to see that Capt. Ishikawa and Capt. Takagi were
responsible for my selection (Takagi Sokichi, **An Autobiographic
Account of the Japanese Navy**, pp.199, 236). At that time both
of them were on friendly terms with me.* Takagi was close to
Harada Kumao who was Prince Saionji's secretary, and Harada in
turn was a good friend of Privy Councillor Ushio. It seems
that it was through this connection that Takagi's desire to
have me appointed as adviser was conveyed to Ushio. Yamazaki
suggested that I visit Ushio to discuss the issue of my
appointment directly with him. When I went to see Ushio I was
still not certain in my own mind whether I should accept the
position. It was in this manner that I became adviser to the
Navy Ministry.
I was appointed adviser to the Southern Area Administration Office [**Nampo Seimubu**], and my colleagues were the former

* Capt. Ishikawa Shingo and Capt. Takagi Sokichi were both
heads of sections in the Navy Ministry at this time.
Ishikawa was very well connected with Admiral Suetsugu, and
Takagi with the leader of the other principal faction in the
Navy, Admiral Okada Keisuke (no relation to the author).
Okada Fumihide had cooperated with these two rising young
Navy figures in attempts to unite the two Navy factions and
thereby increase Navy influence in the Cabinet.

Minister of Commerce and Industry, Fujiwara Ginjiro; the former Vice-Minister of Commerce and Industry, Takeuchi Kakichi; and two businessmen, Fujiyama Aiichiro and the President of the South Seas Development Company, Matsue Haruji. Apart from occasional meetings and discussions with the Navy, we had no special duties. We were, however, given lectures by people with experience in the South on the races, culture, religion and industry in the Southern Occupied Territories.

We were very anxious to discuss the administrative organization in the Occupied Territories, and so on one occasion we held a meeting and listened to a lecture on this topic by Capt. Ishikawa, Head of the 2nd Section of the Military Affairs Bureau [**Gummukyoku**]. After the meeting adjourned, Ishikawa invited me to lunch at the **Suikosha** [Navy Club]. There was, however, an ulterior motive in this invitation. In an extremely nonchalant manner Ishikawa asked, 'Okada, how would you like to go to the South?' I was caught off my guard and inadvertently replied, 'Well, I wouldn't mind going for a little while'. We continued a little longer in this flippant tone, but then gradually the conversation became more serious. Ever since I had accepted the position of adviser, I had in my heart been prepared to go to the South if approached. When Yamazaki first came to me about the job, he explained that, as in his own case, there was a stipulation that it was not necessary to go to the South. However, since I didn't think that I should impose such a condition, I took no notice of him. Even when I assumed the position of adviser, I did not attach any such proviso. Thus, when Ishikawa mentioned the possibility to me, I wasn't particularly surprised.

When I heard that Oka Keijun, Head of the Military Affairs Bureau, wanted to meet me immediately, I rushed straight to his office, and there, quite out of the blue, he said 'Thank you' and congratulated me on agreeing to go to the South. I was stunned by the cleverness of the Navy clique. It had been a pre-emptive tactic. After meeting the Minister of the Navy, Shimada Shigetaro, and the Vice-Minister, Sawamoto Yorio, it was formally decided that I would go. The Navy Minister greeted me politely and said, 'Since the military men in the Navy are not well acquainted with administration, I will leave the civil administration of the Southern Territories completely in your hands'. In the case of the Army, the natives were ruled by a purely military administration, and the Chief of Staff in each territory was placed in charge of this administration. In the Navy Territories on the other hand, the Commander of the Base Force in the area helped maintain law and order from the flanks, while the administration of the natives was the task of the **Minseifu Sokan** (a Chief Civil Administrator [**Shisei Chokan**], personally appointed by the Emperor), who was a civilian official. The Commander-in-Chief of the South Western Fleet, the top man in the area, held the position of Governor-

General only as a formality, for it was the Navy Ministry in Tokyo which had complete command.

For the purpose of liaison with the Navy, a Rear Admiral was appointed Head of the General Affairs Bureau within the **Minseifu*** organization. Underneath him, a Navy Captain was assigned as Head of the Political Affairs Section, and a Navy Accounting Captain as Head of the Accounts Section. In the plan of the Minseifu organization which I received from the Military Affairs Bureau, in addition to the above, a Secretariat Director of the rank of Civil Administrator [**Shiseikan**] was appointed to the Sokan's Secretariat. However, due to the importance of this position as the agent for inter--departmental liaison, I requested successfully that this position be changed to Chief Secretary with the rank of Chief Civil Administrator. In addition to the Head of the General Affairs Bureau, there were heads for each of the following Bureaux: Finance; Industry; Transportation and Public Works; Health; and later on, Judicial Affairs. The position of Bureau Head carried the rank of Chief Civil Administrator.

The Minseifu was the central administration office in the Occupied Territories, and beneath it, regional administration offices, called **Minseibu**, were established in Borneo (South Borneo), Celebes and Ceram. Each Minseibu was headed by a **Minseibu Chokan**, of the rank of Chief Civil Administrator [**Shisei Chokan**]. The Head of the Political Affairs Department [**Seimubucho**] in each Minseibu was a Navy Captain. It was a fundamental policy that the Minseibu was to have direct contact with the natives, and to perform the civil administration. When Yamamoto Isoroku became Commander-in-Chief of the Combined Fleet, the official residence of the Navy Vice-Minister, which was the former American Embassy in Akasaka, was temporarily converted into the office of the Minseifu organization. There I arranged the appointment of important Minseifu and Minseibu personnel and other preparatory business.

Before I had accepted the job of adviser to the Navy Ministry, I was asked by Gen. Honjo whether I would like to work under Lt.-Gen. Isoya Hirosuke who was then Governor-General of the Occupied Territory of Hong Kong. Isoya (formerly Chief of Staff of the Kanto Army) wanted to discuss the matter with me, but I declined. I had no desire to work with the Army. The Vice-Minister of the Army, Anami, with whom I was on friendly terms, mentioned to me that he would find me a position in Manchuria if I went there. However, I refused without bothering to find out what the position would have

---

* The **Minseifu** was the Naval Civil Administration Office for the southwestern area, in Makasar. It comprised a Secretariat and five bureaux, the most important of which was the General Affairs Bureau.

been. Goto Takanosuke offered me a similar position, but I refused this too. Seri Takeji, former Head of the Transportation Bureau in the Taiwan Government-General, went to the Hong Kong position and Takabe Rokuzo to Manchuria. Takabe became Director-General, and died there from illness after the war. It was extremely unfortunate because he was a man of great talent who had begun his career in the Ministry of Home Affairs. The reason I chose to work only for the Navy was because I was under the impression that the Navy, unlike the Army, was sensible and wise. However, when I went to the south, I was surprised to find that even in the Navy, the number of sensible military officials employed in the occupation administration was indeed small. It dawned on me that perhaps this was caused by the fact that the civilian Sokan system had been planned by Takagi and others in the Research Section of the Military Affairs Bureau. It gradually became apparent that this in fact was where the problem lay. I will deal with this aspect of the problems of the Occupation Administration later.

The Selection of Personnel, Collecting
Highly Talented Men from each Ministry

I selected as Chief Secretary Mizuike Ryo, who was at that time Head of the Archives and Documents Section of the Ministry of Home Affairs. (He later became Head of the Police Bureau of the Suzuki Kantaro cabinet.* As a man with great promise, he was extremely popular amongst the staff of the Police Bureau.) I approached Furui Yoshimi, Head of the Personnel Section (after the war a Member of the House of Representatives, and Minister of Health and Welfare) about Mizuike's appointment, and obtained his approval. I thus started with Mizuike as my adviser and chief personnel officer. The Navy had told me that it was anxious to select personnel for the Minseifu and the three Minseibu from a wide variety of Ministries. In regard to the selection of the Head of the Finance Bureau, I first turned to Sakomizu Hisatsune (who later became Chief Secretary of the Suzuki cabinet, and son-in-law of Admiral Okada Keisuke) on Capt. Takagi's recommendation. Thinking that he was indeed the most appropriate choice, I was keen to discuss the matter of his appointment.

Sakomizu was an extremely talented man, and had served as Prime Minister Okada's private secretary.† By way of an introduction from Councillor Izuwa, I visited the private residence

* The Navy-led Cabinet of April-August 1945.

† Admiral Okada Keisuke had been Prime Minister from July 1934 to March 1936.

of Admiral Okada Keisuke and discussed Sakomizu's appointment with him directly. However, the Admiral replied that it would cause difficulties because Sakomizu had various important things to do in Japan. I was forced to abandon any idea of selecting Sakomizu. At that time he was working for the Cabinet Planning Board, and according to Admiral Okada he was responsible for investigating the supply of war commodities. In view of the general war situation, I had no alternative but to look for someone else. I then consulted with the former Finance Minister, Ikeda Seihin. He in turn sought the advice of the Finance Minister, Kaya Okinori, and together they decided upon Secretary Nakamura Kenjo (after the war President of the Japan Real Estate Bank).

Since the prevention of epidemics was of the utmost importance in the Occupied Territories, I felt that Katsumata Minoru from the Ministry of Health and Welfare (after the war a Member of both the House of Representatives and House of Councillors, as well as Vice-President of the Tuberculosis Prevention Society) would be the most appropriate choice as Head of the Health Bureau. However, because I too was from the Ministry of Health and Welfare, I temporarily set him aside as an applicant upon whom I could fall back. I then discussed the matter with Ushio. I told Ushio that since it was the Navy's wish to select personnel from as many different Ministries as possible, personnel from the Ministry of Health and Welfare would have to be chosen only as a last resort. I asked him if he had any ideas about who would be suitable for the job. He asked me what I thought of Professor Azuma Ryutaro from the Medical Department of Tokyo University (after the war Governor of Tokyo city and President of the Japanese Red Cross). I discussed this suggestion with the Navy and they agreed whole-heartedly. I visited the University President, Ariga, and the Head of the Medical Department, Takahashi Akira, and obtained their approval. However, because Azuma's speciality was not epidemic prevention, I sought the advice of Professor Tamiya Takeo. Tamiya discussed the matter with Katsumata, who said he knew of an epidemiology specialist. Since Katsumata was friendly with Tamiya, he introduced one of his subordinates, Abe Toshio, to him. Abe, however, would not accept the position. I decided therefore to negotiate directly with Abe, and by cleverly promising him the position of Civil Administrator appointed by the Emperor, I was able to obtain his acceptance.

With regard to the Head of the Industry Bureau, I first consulted the Ministry of Agriculture and Forestry, and they picked out Yugawa Mototake who was Chief of the Food Agency and who was particularly knowledgeable about the matter of rice, and Shigemasa Masayuki, Head of the General Affairs Bureau (after the war he became a member of the House of Represent-atives, and Minister for Agriculture and Forestry), as

133

candidates. However, they both declined the offer. In the end, Okamoto Naoto was decided upon.

Samejima Shigeru, an expert on harbour technology in the Ministry of Home Affairs, agreed to become Head of the Transportation and Public Works Bureau.

Regarding the selection of the Celebes Minseibu Chokan, as distinct from the Borneo and Ceram Minseibu Chokan, it was essential that this person be on friendly terms with me. If not, the relationship between the Minseifu and the Celebes Minseibu would not be smooth because both administrative bodies were located in the same city, Makasar. For this reason I decided to appont Sudo Tetsuomi (at that time Governor of Gifu Prefecture, and later Vice-President of the Military Rehabilitation Institute) who was my junior at Middle School. As the Ceram Minseibu Chokan I appointed Shimizu Shigeo (formerly Governor of Wakayama Prefecture, and later Governor of Saitama Prefecture) on the recommendation of Councillor Izuwa. The Navy was anxious that I appoint someone from Foreign Affairs to the position of Borneo Minseibu Chokan, so I selected Inoue Kojiro (formerly Head of the Europe and Asia Bureau, and Japanese Minister to Hungary).

With the exception of the military men, I made it a policy to select each Bureau Head and each Minseibu Chokan myself, and to decide upon the Civil Administrator personnel who were to be Section Heads and administration officials after hearing the recommendation of the respective Bureau Heads and Minseibu Chokan. It was my opinion that in foreign countries, especially in occupied territories, it was of the utmost importance to establish harmony amongst one's personnel, and to create an organization in which everyone was unified as if with ties of blood. Those selected to serve under Chief Secretary Mizuike included Eguchi Mitoru, administrative official in the Ministry of Home Affairs (after the war, Chief of the Metropolitan Police, and Vice-Minister of Labour); Nishimura Naoki (after the war a member of the House of Representatives, Head of the Defence Agency, and Minister of Agriculture and Forestry); Kaiho Yoshio; and Omori Hiroshi (after the war, President of the Defence University). Nishimura, Kaiho, Omori and their colleagues had gone on ahead of the rest of us to Makasar, and were already engaged in civil administration.

Maoe Shigesaburo, administrative official in the Ministry of Finance (after the war a Member of the House of Representatives, Finance Minister, Chief Cabinet Secretary, and Speaker of the House of Representatives), was appointed to work directly under Nakamura, Head of the Finance Bureau. Those chosen to work for the Head of the General Affairs Bureau were Kobayashi Yukio, administrative official in the Ministry of Education (after the war Vice-Minister of Education); Maeda Ryuichi, a school inspector (after the war President of the Osaka Publishing Company); Kubota Yoshimaro (after the war

Secretary General of the House of Councillors and President of
the Diet Library); Ohara Bunshichi (after the war President of
Shiga University); and Eguchi Toshio, administrative official
in the Ministry of Home Affairs (after the war Head of the
National Police Agency). As Public Relations Officer, Yugawa
Morio from the Ministry of Foreign Affairs (after the war
Ambassador to Britain and Grand Master of Court Ceremonies in
the Imperial Household Agency) was selected on the recommendation of Capt. Takagi. Mori Naoki (after the war Vice-Minister
of Foreign Affairs and Ambassador to Britain) was also
appointed as a Public Relations Officer. Athough I have only a
slight memory of these men nowadays, they did indeed form a
group of extremely talented men.

Furthermore, among the young civil administrators there
were many who became Vice-Ministers and who were selected for
important jobs: Nagano Shiro (after the war Vice-Minister of
Home Affairs and Governor of Okayama Prefecture); Sumida Tomo
(after the war, Vice-Minister of Finance and President of the
Japan Export Import Bank); and Osawa Toru (after the war Vice-
Minister of Agriculture and Forestry and Chairman of the
Central Turf Club). Many of these young men were later also
appointed to important positions in non-governmental bodies.
For instance, Imai Hidebumi became President of the New
International Aviation Corporation.

The Army complained when they discovered that I had
appointed such a large number of extremely talented men. The
Navy, though, interceded on my behalf and told me not to
withdraw any of the personnel I had already selected. After I
had taken up my position in the South, the Army and Navy left
the selection of new appointments up to the various Ministries.
This naturally resulted in the appointment of both good and bad
personnel.

There was great difficulty in deciding upon the very
important position of **Somukyokucho** [Head of the General Affairs
Bureau]. Finally, Oka, Head of the Military Affairs Bureau,
selected Rear-Admiral Ito Kenzo, though this decision gave rise
to a great deal of opposition within the Military Affairs
Bureau. Although Ito had a pleasant disposition, he tended to
be an exhibitionist, and consequently, once the decision to
appoint him had been made, he frequently told people that he in
fact was the Sokan. When, on occasion, Capt. Ishikawa reminded
Oka of this fact, Oka merely reprimanded the Captain for
behaving indiscreetly. Since exhibitionism was a fundamental
part of Ito's personality, it soon became evident when we
boarded the **Kamakura Maru**. I tried to make him more
considerate by indicating my displeasure. In order to offset
Ito's weaknesses, Oka appointed Capt. Sasagi Takanobu as Head
of the Political Affairs Section. This post was initially
designed to assist the Head of the General Affairs Bureau.
However, although Sasagi was a capable man he had an unpleasant

135

character, and in this regard he was the direct opposite of Ito. By making Ito look a fool he would come to dominate him. His scheming nature equalled Ito's exhibitionism.

From the beginning I doubted whether these two military men would ever be of help to the civilian Sokan, and I regarded them as being extremely disruptive elements in the Minseifu. Within the Military Affairs Bureau they both had very poor reputations, and the opposition movement against their appointment was led by the two Section Heads, Ishikawa and Takagi. Takagi, Head of the Research Section, and the person at the centre of the planning of the Minseifu, was hoping to go to the South himself, and if either he or Ishikawa had been appointed as Head of the General Affairs Bureau, I would have been very fortunate indeed. However, because Takagi had not entirely recovered from a chest infection, the Medical Affairs Bureau advised against him working in the South. It just didn't work out as I had hoped. With this personnel problem I set out for the South.

Directly after the Midway Naval Battle, I led the first group of Civil Administration personnel aboard the KAMAKURA MARU, and we set sail for Makasar

So that we could commence work immediately we arrived in the South, we had made arrangements for the appointment of not only the important personnel of the Minseifu and the three Minseibu, but also for such people as cooks, drivers, typists and servants. However, despite these detailed preparations, the Navy authorities continued to postpone the announcement of our departure. I began to become exasperated with waiting. Initially the Navy had planned to send the Minseifu and Minseibu personnel by the **Kamakura Maru**, but later they altered it to the effect that Bureau Heads and above would fly to the Occupied Territories. After discussing this change with Chief Secretary Mizuike, we decided to oppose the move, and proposed that all personnel go by ship as originally planned. Our objection was based on the view that it would lead to unnecessary problems with regard to the overseeing of personnel once we had arrived in the South. The Navy then came up with a new plan by which all Civil Administrators and above would go by the Navy warship **Ashigara**, after it had been repaired at the Sasebo Naval Base. I opposed this also. Rear-Admiral Ito requested that he be permitted to go ahead by plane, but I refused him permission and he went with the rest of us aboard the **Kamakura Maru**. Only Capt. Sasagi and Accountant Capt. Iwasaki Takehiko went ahead by plane. This was so that they could make arrangements for my official residence.

I later discovered that the Midway Naval Battle had taken place on 5 June 1942, and that as a result the seas had become extremely dangerous. The Navy kept it a top secret that they had lost the battle at Midway, and we were consequently not informed. The Navy did, however, display extreme anxiety over our sea voyage. On one day towards the end of June we sailed secretly from Yokohama, and spent that evening in the waters just outside the port. We then advanced on a southerly course. We were guarded by a spectacular array of Navy ships and planes. In front of us and behind us, to the left and right, there were destroyers escorting us, and above flew several fighter planes keeping a look out. When we passed out of territorial waters, and on to the high seas, we had a Navy destroyer continually at our side. This strict Naval surveillance was in part sparked off by the recent sinking by enemy attack of a transport vessel carrying important administrative personnel. All those aboard had been killed.

We were in high spirits as we sailed towards the South. The sky was clear and the sea blue. The Pacific Ocean stretched for miles around us, and as far as the eye could see there was no-one else. Occasionally we would catch sight of the beautiful coral reefs unique to the Pacific Ocean. Sometimes there were squalls. Finally we crossed the equator, and when we looked up at the Southern Cross we were all overcome with emotion. Although we frequently practised putting on life jackets there was never any danger, and we arrived safely at Makasar on 7 July 1942.

My Peaceful Life at the Sokan's Residence

When we arrived at the port of Makasar we were greeted by the two Civil Administrators, Nishimura Naoki and Kaiho Yoshio. They had left for Celebes before us and had been performing civil administration duties under the command of Mori, Commander of the Base Force, and his senior staff officer, Noji Munesuke. On the evening of our arrival, a banquet was held at the Suikosha by Vice-Admiral Ibo, Commander-in-Chief of the Southwestern Fleet. At that time there were still plenty of provisions available in the South, and so the Navy was able to provide a splendid assortment of food at the banquet. The quality of the food surpassed anything available in Japan. We returned that night to the ship, and it was not until the next day that we were allocated our accommodation. Commander Mori was an extremely charitable person, and it is very unfortunate that despite the fact that he treated his prisoners of war with kindness, he was hanged as a war criminal.

I will describe my life at the Sokan's residence. The residence was built on a 33,000 square metre site, and was the Dutch Governor's residence before the war. It is still standing today, and is used as an official residence. I lived in this large residence together with Iizuka Choichi (after the war he changed his name to Iizuka Takahisa) who was my private secretary's office boy, a driver and a cook. There were also

137

several male servants (**jongos**), who wore the uniform they had received from the Dutch. Their duties included cleaning the rooms, gardening, washing and ironing, and setting the table. Their monthly salary was three yen at first, then it was increased to ten yen. This is an indication of the degree to which prices rose during the war. They were able to support a family on this salary. For a short time there was also a young native who had been appointed on the recommendation of Yamazaki Guntaro, Mayor of Makasar City. However, she was not competent and left. My private secretary was Yamamoto Seiji. He was selected on Capt. Takagi's recommendation, and was the adopted grandchild of the Navy Admiral, Yamamoto Gombei. A female employee who was a friend of Yamamoto lived in the official residence and looked after me. She was like a lone flower in the wilderness, and was able to make my life a little more enjoyable. I have forgotten her name, and never found out for certain what happened to her afterwards. It was rumoured that she died in Manchuria towards the closing stages of the war. Yamamoto, who was just a young man then, is now dead. Iizuka was a government clerk in the Ministry of Home Affairs, and became Prime Minister Ashida's private secretary after the war. He was an extremely active person, who later became manager of the Mainichi Baseball Club and an employee of the Japanese Telecommunication Company. He too is now dead.

I ate my meals three times a day in the company of the native servants and Iizuka. It was very lonely eating in the large dining room on the second floor. At that time I didn't have much of a liking for sake, and Iizuka, with whom I ate, was shocked by the fact that I only drank two or three cupfuls. After dinner I would quickly leave the table, and sit down-stairs on the verandah where there was a cool breeze. There I would drink beer with the secretaries of each Bureau Head and discuss the local customs. Sometimes I would be woken up late at night by the sound of a car returning to the official residence, and I knew that that meant they had remained drinking on the verandah long after I had gone to bed.

Each day I made two return trips to the Minseifu office. I was driven there by a car flying the yellow Admiral's flag. Naturally I wore the uniform of a Navy Chief Civil Administrator. Considering it was war-time it was probably a little too showy. The Bureau Heads wore tropical dress (to protect them against the heat), but the Sokan was not permitted to dress so informally. I assure you that my uniform was extremely hot to wear. During my two hour midday break I returned to the official residence and had a nap. The busy Bureau Heads and their subordinates worked through this lunch-time break, but because I had nothing to do and I was interested in looking after my health, I never missed out on this midday sleep.

I Thought of Japan when I Looked up
at the Bright Moon Rising out of the Sea

The population of Makasar at that time was about 100,000. It has now developed into a big city of 800,000. During the war it was a pleasant town with a holiday atmosphere. A cool breeze blew in from the sea, and on the main street along which I passed from the official residence to the Minseifu office, spacious mansions with a holiday villa appearance were thinly scattered. These were the houses the Dutch had lived in. Now, though, they were occupied by the Minseifu and Minseibu personnel. Several employees lived together in each of these houses. The wide street was lined with big green trees, and there were beautiful flowers in the gardens of these mansions.

Every day I had nothing to do at home apart from reading and writing letters to people back in Japan. The book I read most often was **Shōhō Genzō** [Teachings of Buddha] by Dōgen Senji. It is concerned with the **rōnin** [lordless samurai] period of Japanese history. My life in the Southern Occupied Territories provided me a great opportunity to develop my education. Since my life at the official residence was rather uninteresting, at night, after the evening meal, I often used to hail a simple vehicle called a **tiga roda,** * which had a sort of box on the back for two passengers, and together with my secretary or a servant, I would go to the harbour. On these occasions, I would dress casually in white linen civilian clothes with short sleeves and short pants. We would stand on the seashore in the cool evening air, and stare at the beautiful setting sun. As I gazed at the waves breaking on the shore and remembered that this same water would wash the southern coast of Japan, I became extremely homesick. On clear evenings the moonlight shining through the trees was so bright that you could read large newspaper print by it. The air was really very clear, and you could often smell the indescribably beautiful fragrance of flowers wafting through the air. The South was abundant in nature.

1942 was a peaceful year, and welcome visitors often came to the South on inspection tours. Among such visitors were the Navy Ministry advisers Takeuchi Kakichi and Fujiyama Aiichiro. They stayed for several days at my official residence. Coincidentally, a crocodile had been sent to the residence, and so it was added to the feast held for my two visitors. The food was set out on Japanese-style tables. The crocodile meat did not prove a success, for they warned against eating such meat and refused to eat it themselves. It tasted like a cross between a fish and a chicken, but had the texture of rope.

---

* Literally 'three wheels'; a bicycle rickshaw known in Western Indonesia as **becak.**

Groups of advisers from the House of Representatives and the House of Councillors also came. Such Members of Parliament as Ogawa Gotaro and Hashimoto Kingoro came to visit Makasar too. When much-welcomed visitors like these arrived, the executive staff of the Minseifu and Celebes Minseibu would gather for a banquet at the Sokan's residence. Everyone at the banquet would appreciate the superb food. On one occasion Hirose Toyosaku, adviser to the Army Military Administration, came from Singapore and stayed several days at the official residence.

I was always very happy to have the opportunity to meet close friends from far-away Japan. The vocalist, Fujiyama Ichiro, also came to Celebes as a Navy-commissioned employee to entertain the Japanese abroad. Soldiers and officers alike were moved when they heard his voice, young, yet strong and beautiful, sing such songs as 'Oka o Koete'. Another visitor was the accomplished female author Morita. It was very enjoyable eating together in the evening with these welcome guests, and discussing affairs in the South with them. 1942 remained a peaceful year. My memories of my life at the official residence are endless. However, I will end here, and discuss the administration in the Southern Occupied Territories.

My Distress over the Conflict between the Japanese Military Officials and the Civilian Officials in the Occupation Administration

The most difficult problem in the Occupied Territories did not concern the natives, but rather involved the important Civil Administration personnel who had come out from Japan. I had given strict instructions to these people when they arrived in Celebes that they were to maintain their dignity as Japanese and be respectful and tolerant of the natives. However, among the lower class of employees attached to the administration like servants, there were a few who treated the natives violently and who were involved in incidents of theft. The Head of the General Affairs Bureau warned that those people who acted indiscreetly would be sent home. These kind of incidents tended to be motivated by sudden impulse and were, as such, not particularly troublesome. It was only natural that amongst both the **Kamakura Maru** group and the Occupation Forces group undesirable and unpleasant feelings would develop, and that these would eventually subside and disappear. It was also quite natural that any small incident would excite and aggravate male colleagues who were deprived of a sex life in the Occupied Territories. Without us being aware of it, this began to exert an influence over the management of public affairs.

This, though, was the sort of problem that would naturally

140

disappear once the female prostitutes arrived. Although this
rather trivial matter had the potential to develop into something rather serious, if a close watch was kept it could be
adequately controlled. A more serious and difficult problem
was the alienation which arose out of the struggle for
leadership between the civilian officials and the military
officials, and among the military officials themselves. No
matter when or where, this seems to be a fundamental trait of
man, and the more competent the men the more easily it occurs.
As this problem grew increasingly serious, it began to develop
grave implications from the point of view of the Civil
Administration of the Occupied Territories. Soon after I took
up my post, Commander Ogi of the Navy Ministry's Southern Area
Administration Office made an inspection tour of the area. He
asked me to give my honest opinion of the key personnel in the
Administration. I replied frankly that when Rear-Adm. Ito and
Capt. Sasagi were together they served to hinder the smooth
running of the Civil Administration. I told him that it would
be a good idea if Sasagi were transferred elsewhere because he
tended to overrule his superiors. The Commander then said that
he too had been worried about this problem, and that he would
speak to the Fleet Commander-in-Chief about the matter
immediately.

It had been my ambition to go to the most remote Occupied
Territories, and I had believed that the military and civilian
officials would work harmoniously together in their task of
governing the natives. I had believed that personal rivalries
would be no more of a problem than children's games. I began
to become extremely concerned that if things continued as they
were the Civil Administration would crumble. Soon after I
assumed my post I flew to Surabaya with my Chief Secretary,
Mizuike. I there paid my formal compliments to Takahashi, the
Fleet Commander-in-chief. Whether it was the strain of the
long sea trip or the excitement of my first air flight I don't
know, but that evening I was suddenly confined to my bed with a
high fever. The Naval doctor looked after me well, and
fortunately after a night's rest I recovered. The next day I
met Takahashi, his Chief of Staff, Nakamura Toshihisa, and
other staff officers. That night a feast of famous Surabaya
Chinese food was held on my behalf at the official residence of
the Commander-in-Chief. I was very impressed by the Chinese
cuisine. During this visit the Commander-in-Chief and the
Chief of Staff spoke to me about the situation with regard to
the key military personnel. Their words were to this effect.
'Please discuss matters with us frankly, because we will
arrange things in accordance with your wishes.' As it turned
out, however, it would have been better had I not confided in
them, for, before anything could be done, Capt. Sasagi got wind
of this discussion. It seemed that a certain Commander who was
a Communications Staff Officer leaked the story. As a result,

an extremely dangerous and disquieting atmosphere began to affect the Minseifu, and from that day on a strange whirlwind blew up. I will discuss this in detail later.

The Basic Policy of the Civil Administration, and the Implementation of the Occupation's Political Measures

The basic policy which the Minseifu was responsible for carrying out had been laid down for us by the Navy Minister, Shimada, at the time of our departure. In addition, the Naval authorities informed us of the agreement between the Army and Navy Military Administrations regarding the fundamental principles of government in the Occupied Territories. According to this, the basic policy of the Civil Administration in the Navy Territory was no more and no less than **eikyū senryō** [permanent occupation]. This was a military secret, and only a small number of people in the executive division were informed of it. Later, after I had returned to Japan, the basic policy was reversed to one of **Indoneshia dokuritsu** [Indonesian independence]. This alteration was made at a time when the war outlook was extremely pessimistic. Army adviser Kodama Hideo was at the centre of this policy change, and I also participated in the planning in my capacity as Navy adviser. Together we presented the new proposal for independence to the Government. Because the initial policy in the Navy area was **eikyū senryō**, our administration of the natives was not a temporary thing designed to operate only for the duration of the war. Rather, we were building an important basis for future administration. Included in the basic policy for the administration of the Occupied Territories were a variety of concrete policies spanning politics, economics, religion and education which had been mutually agreed upon by the Army and Navy authorities. By sending to the South talented men from each Ministry, and by appointing civilians as Sokan, Bureau Heads and Minseibu Chokan, the Navy was deliberately and carefully laying a foundation for the future. If the Administration had just been set up for the temporary convenience of prosecuting the war, then it would not have been necessary to have gone to such lengths.

As Civil Administration authorities, we regarded the basic Occupation policy as our Constitution, and devised concrete policies appropriate to the South. These administrative policies were decided upon by a conference of Bureau Heads which was held almost every day at my official residence. These decisions were not made arbitrarily by military officials. Each Bureau Head carried out his own respective duties. There were some military officials who claimed that they held all responsibility for decision making and that they controlled the administration, but they were not liked by the rest of us. The Head of the General Affairs Bureau was always

142

extremely careful when an incident looked like developing which would lead to a military official questioning who was in charge of the organization, and he would always accept my decision in the matter. At the time I didn't worry too much about these incidents, especially if there were no mistakes made. I did not know then to just what extent those who dabbled in underhand schemes had damaged the Civil Administration.

In order to assist the development of industry in the Occupied Territories, the Navy Ministry sent out from Japan a variety of businessmen representing a variety of industrial fields. These men were selected by the Navy Ministry, and we were not consulted. This, though, was only natural considering the severe war situation.

When I arrived in the Occupied Territories and actually took charge of the Civil Administration, I became aware of the fact that it was almost impossible to gain control of the natives in the interior with the existing administrative structure, relying entirely upon the three Minseibu. It was therefore essential that we establish a subordinate organization to the Minseibu in each area. The Navy Ministry had instructed us to follow their policy of utilizing the government system imposed by the Dutch. That was all very well, but it was a very vast area with no railways and only roads to rely upon. Moreover, there was an extremely limited number of vehicles. The demand for a subordinate organization to the Minseibu became more and more urgent as the Japanese businessmen became increasingly active in industrial development. It was deemed necessary to have about two Japanese officials in each district town. The natives also expressed a desire for such a system. In order to expand the regional administration, the Minseifu requested that a considerable number of Japanese officials be sent from Japan, and we devised a plan whereby Regional Governors [**Shu Chiji**] would be appointed to Menado, Bali, Balikpapan etc,* and a system of Sub-prefectural Heads [**Bunken Kanrikan**] would operate under them. When I received the Navy's approval for this plan, I made arrangements to return to Japan by the **Asama Maru** to

---

* Whereas in the Army-administered areas **Shu** coincided almost exactly with the Dutch Residency, and was the basic administrative unit headed by a Chokan, this role was taken in the Navy area by the Minseibu. The Shu was introduced to the Navy area only belatedly as a consequence of poor communications, and was somewhat smaller than the Dutch Residency had been.

Okada appears to be mistaken in mentioning a Bali Shu, as Bali remained directly under the Ceram Minseibu until the Lesser Sundas Minseibu was established with its capital in Singaraja (Bali) in 1944.

select these Governors. Nishimura Naoki, a Civil Administrator, accompanied me on the trip. Mori Katsuei, President
of the New Southern Industrial Company, and a unit of 'Sky-
borne Soldiers of the Gods'* who had participated in the Menado
invasion were also aboard the ship.

According to my plan to establish a subordinate local
organization, Japanese rule would extend right into the
hinterland of Celebes, South Borneo, Ceram, the Lesser Sundas
and Timor. As Regional Governors, I selected men like Endo
Naoto, Koshino Kikuo and Goto Masao from the Ministry of Home
Affairs.

My Inspection Tour of the Vast Area under Navy Jurisdiction

In order to inspect and establish contact with various
areas in the East Indies under Japanese control, I took a break
from deciding upon policy measures to conduct tours of both
Java and each Navy-administered region. I went to the holiday
resort of Malang on the occasion of my first visit to Surabaya,
to Bali, and also to Jakarta to visit my old acquaintance
Maj.-Gen. Okazaki Seizaburo (later promoted to Lt.-Gen.), who
was Chief of Staff of the Army Occupation Unit. Okazaki was an
old class-mate of mine at Matsue Middle School. One evening he
held a banquet on my behalf. I also contacted Capt. Maeda
Tadashi of the Java Navy Liaison Office, and discussed a
variety of matters with him. When I toured South Borneo, I
visited Inoue Kojiro, Minseibu Chokan in Pontianak, and
inspected the oil refinery at Balikpapan on the East Coast. I
also flew to Ceram to visit Shimizu Shigeo, the Minseibu
Chokan, and Shibata Yaichiro, the Comander of the local Base
Force. Unfortunately, I was unable to visit New Guinea, which
at that time was still under the command of the Ceram Minseibu.
On one occasion I toured South Celebes by car, and on another,
I flew to Menado to inspect the new battle front of the
Parachute Corps, and to discuss administrative matters. I also
had the opportunity to visit the homes of the rajas, and
thereby became familiar with the style of life of the native
upper class. In the reception room of one such raja I was
extremely pleased to see a newspaper supplement with pictures
of the Meiji Emperor decorating the wall. As a Sokan I had
many varied duties.

* This phrase, **Sora no Shimpei**, is derived from the title of a
popular wartime song written by the poet Saijō Yaso,
celebrating the deeds of paratroopers. It is a romantic way
of referring to paratroops.

Enemy Air-Raids Brought this Year of Peace and Serenity to an Abrupt End, and Turned the South into a Battlefield

At about the time of the anniversary of the Greater East Asia War on 8 December 1942, the Southern Occupied Territories were still free from war. Since one of the basic policies of our Administration was to make the Occupied Territories self-sufficient in essential commodities, we had planned the development of a variety of industries, which had quickly come to fruition. At that time it was even possible to make a direct telephone call from Makasar to Japan. Furthermore, the natives had a great deal of confidence in the Japanese, and our humanitarian treatment of them had prompted their cooperation with the Japanese Occupation Administration. Public security was good, and the diffusion of the Japanese language had advanced at a rapid pace. As we watched the day-by-day progress of the peacetime administration, we began to think that the 'permanent occupation' of the Southern Territories was not just a dream. However, this tranquility disappeared with the new year.

As 1943 opened, we would occasionally catch sight of an enemy reconnaissance plane in the sky above Makasar. The military defence facilities in Makasar at that time were completely inadequate. All we had was one anti-aircraft gun with a broken sighting instrument which had been left behind by the Dutch Army. We placed this in the middle of the parade ground and occasionally fired menacing shots, which fell far short of the high-altitude enemy planes. It was indeed a rather pathetic sight, reminding me very much of the old story of the Bakumatsu fort on the Shinagawa coast which, having no cannons, used temple bells to deceive the enemy. On my return from Surabaya, this anti-aircraft gun was the cause of a rather frightening incident. As my plane drew close to Makasar, it was mistaken for an enemy plane, and artillery shots were fired at us. Fortunately we were not hit. In Makasar at the time we did not have even one fighter plane, and the plane we used for training purposes was concealed at the critical moment when enemy planes attacked. The natives grew suspicious and asked why Japan's planes did not fly. Sometimes Japanese fighter planes which had stopped over at Makasar to refuel would attempt to resist any enemy air attack that occurred at the time, which tended to reassure the natives. However, we rarely conducted such counter-attacks. By showing the natives films of aeroplane construction in Japan we attempted to deceive them into thinking that our planes would definitely come to the South should an emergency situation arise.

My first close encounter with an air-raid was when a bomb exploded 50 metres from my official residence. There was only one air-raid shelter in my house, and it was a flimsy construction made by the Dutch. I occasionally took refuge there. Whenever I heard the warning siren, I would take a chair into the garden, sip a glass of brandy and keep a lookout. We civilian officials knew quite well that we were in the midst of a war, and were consequently not at all alarmed by these attacks. My secretary at that time was Shudo Koetsu. Iizuka had already returned to Japan. Shudo and I both came from the same town, Matsue. Before he arrived he had been a government clerk in the Military Rehabilitation Institute, and had also served at the front in North China as a Second Lieutenant in the Army. He was posted to the South as a Civil Administrator. Due to his first-hand experience at the front he was almost fearless, and whenever there was an air-raid, he would stand alone outside the air-raid shelter and scan the evening sky for enemy planes.

As the War Situation Worsened, a Sense of Alienation Developed between the Civilian and Military Officials

The military personnel changes that I describe above were not carried out satisfactorily. Vice-Admiral Takahashi Ibo, Fleet Commander-in-Chief, was succeeded by Vice-Admiral Takasu Shiro. Rear-Admiral Ota Takeo (later Head of the Military Affairs Bureau, then Navy Minister) was appinted as the new Chief of Staff. He was an old friend who had worked together with me at the Wounded Soldier Rehabilitation Centre. Capt. Ishikawa Shingo was promoted to Vice-Admiral and made the new Vice-Chief of Staff. When the new Fleet Commander-in-Chief arrived at Makasar aboard the warship **Ashigara**, both he and his Vice-Chief of Staff stayed at my residence. An extremely regrettable incident as far as the honour of the glorious Imperial Navy is concerned occurred at that time, and although I am rather reluctant to elaborate upon it here, I feel that if I do not, the real situation in the Occupied Territories will never be made known. With this intention, I will provide a brief account of it.

Commander-in-Chief Takasu and Vice-Chief of Staff Ishikawa were both absent from Makasar, having gone out on an inspection tour. Officials of the rank of Civil Administrator and above from the Minseifu and the Celebes Minseibu had gathered in the great hall of my official residence to watch a performance by a group of **gamelan** players and dancers from the Solo royal household in Java. As the dancing drew to an end, Sudo, the Minseibu Chokan, secretly whispered to me that some sort of underhand scheme had been organized to take place at the end of the performance, and in order to foil it I should quickly leave the hall. I thought nothing of it, but sure enough, as soon as the dancing ended, Capt. Sasagi stood up and ordered us to stay where we were because there was to be a meeting. Since I had received no information of such a meeting from either Mizuike, Chief Secretary, or Ito, Head of the General Affairs Bureau,

146

and because a Sokan does not follow arbitrary instructions from the Head of the Political Affairs Section, I immediately stood up, walked calmly across the great hall and retired to my room on the second floor. The rest of the party left after me. Only Sasagi and a certain Commander remained behind in the hall. My Chief Secretary Mizuike returned to the hall to confront these two military officials over the matter. A smart young servant boy reported their conversation in detail to me. When I asked Mizuike the next day what had happened, he told me that the Commander in question had had a great deal to drink and abused him profusely. Capt. Sasagi stood back and watched. That Commander was a dull-witted person who put on the scene at Sasagi's instigation.

I did not venture to ask Mizuike about the content of the discussion with the two men because it was obvious that he was reluctant to talk about it. At the time I did not think that the incident was all that important, but as it turned out, for a long time afterwards they attempted to provoke Mizuike by constantly abusing and insulting him. However, Mizuike endured all this without resisting. Had he reacted with force he would no doubt have won, for he was an expert in judo. However, he knew quite well that if he acted in such a fashion they would have made an issue of it and demanded that he take all the responsibility. On the evening of the performance, Rear-Admiral Ishikawa happened to return home from his tour in time to witness the strange incident involving Mizuike and the two military officials. Judging that the issue was no trivial matter, he immediately led that certain Commander to his room, locked the door and cross-examined him. The Commander thereupon cursed Ishikawa repeatedly, to which Ishikawa responded by reprimanding him physically. That evening I was oblivious to what was going on, and fell asleep while reading in my room.

Early the next morning Rear-Admiral Ishikawa asked to speak to me. We hurriedly met in the reception room and he related the above incident. He pointed out to me that he had acted completely out of consideration of us civilian officials, and that he had responded to the Commander's outrageous behaviour in such a manner because he was no longer able to suppress anger over the high-handed attitude of the military officials in the Occupied Territories. In his opinion it was essential that the Fleet Commander-in-Chief be told all the facts. When Takasu returned, I reported the above sequence of events to him, and requested that he treat the matter indulgently. I heard that Sasagi had appealed to Takasu that it was disgraceful for an Admiral to discipline a field officer physically, but Takasu ignored the incident completely.

I became acutely conscious that the administration of the Occupied Territories was by no means an easy task. A man like Inoue, Borneo Minseibu Chokan, suffered a nervous breakdown and was forced to return to Japan. Mizuike was reduced to tears one day as a result of such difficulties. He lamented that the Japanese were more difficult to control than the natives. I have already given various examples of the problems that cropped up in the South, but the fundamental cause of all these problems was the initial Navy policy of entrusting the Civil Administration of the Occupied Territories to civilian officials, and the dissatisfaction that generated amongst the military officials, especially as a result of my appointment to the top position of Sokan. The problem lay in the fact that I did not possess the type of nature which would submit meekly to the military men and be a slave to their whims. Furthermore, I admired greatly the Navy's unique policy of a Sokan/civilian official system which aimed at the permanent occupation of the Navy Territory, and thus fully endorsed the concept of a Sokan in the Occupied Territories. I had been very dissatisfied with the Army's policy of military as opposed to civil administration. I had disregarded my declining state of health to participate in the Navy's plan and, with the cooperation of a great many talented men from the Ministry of Home Affairs and other Ministries, it had been my ambition to see the Navy policy succeed. The planning, however, of this policy was confined to a mere handful of far-sighted men in the Navy, with the result that most of the military officials were not aware of the significance of these careful plans for the future. Imbued with a strong sense of bureaucratic sectionalism, they did not like the idea of civilian officials occupying the high administrative positions in the islands which they had occupied at great sacrifice.

Needless to say, the military officials attached to the Minseifu and the Minseibu had not participated in the invasion of the Occupied Territories. After we arrived, the Commander of the Invasion Force and his officers were transferred elsewhere. Nevertheless, the idea persisted that it was the Navy which had conquered and occupied the area, and this influenced the bureaucratic mentality of the military officials serving in the South. Thus, when the matter of [my dissatisfaction with] military personnel, which ought to have been kept a closely guarded secret, was leaked, the situation became exceedingly unpleasant. Under such conditions it was inevitable that underhand schemes would emerge in the Administration. Just at this time, Fleet Commander-in-Chief Takasu was transferred, and Vice-Admiral Mikawa Gunichi was appointed as his successor. Although the position of Chief of Staff remained unchanged, Vice-Chief of Staff Ishikawa was promoted to Commander of the Kendari Squadron and moved to the front line. When I requested that a plane be made available so that I could fly to Surabaya to pay my respects to the new Fleet Commander-in-chief, Sasagi, who was in charge of the organization of planes, refused to comply on the grounds that it was not opportune to fly at that time. In the meantime he flew to Surabaya on the plausible pretext of making preparations for my trip. I still believe his trip was unwarranted, and was part of some sort of scheme he was devising. However, I had no way of stopping him. He was in Surabaya a long time before he reported that preparations for my arrival were completed and that I was free to go whenever I pleased. Mizuike accompanied me on the flight. The mood in Surabaya had altered dramatically. The peaceful atmosphere that had prevailed immediately after the invasion had been changed by harsher realities as the war impinged directly. Our movements were restricted, though this was not the chief problem which was, as Mizuike observed, the coldness of the Fleet Staff Officers. At the time I did not sense this as strongly as Mizuike, and tended to believe that Sasagi's manoeuvring behind the scenes was a mere figment of my imagination. This was not the case.

Despite the despotic behaviour of Sasagi and his stupid machinations, the Civil Administration was well on the way to success. The war situation was still relatively peaceful in the South, public security amongst the native population was good, and industrial activity was progressing gradually. I will discuss this administrative situation later. Ishikawa's recall to Japan marked the long-awaited military personnel changes. It was indeed slow in coming about. Capt. Sasagi was ordered to go to Saigon contrary to his wishes. It was the Navy custom for officers to return once to Japan before being posted abroad again. In the case of Sasagi, though, he was not recalled to Japan, but ordered to proceed directly to his new post. It was a rather harsh move on the part of the Navy. His successor was Capt. Tominaga Shozo who rarely got out of his seat to work. His stay dragged on until finally he was posted elsewhere. It was impossible for us bureaucrats from the Ministry of Home Affairs to comprehend either the lethargic pace at which the Navy personnel worked or their indiscreet and wilful ways. In due couse Rear-Admiral Ito was transferred, while Tominaga was promoted to Rear-Admiral and took over the position of Head of the General Affairs Bureau. Tominaga had commenced his career in the Personnel Bureau and was apparently appointed on the recommendation of Rear-Admiral Takagi. He was an amicable and sensible man who was popular amongst the civilian officials. Relations in the Minseifu and the Minseibu gradually grew more harmonious, and I began to feel greatly relieved.

The Tragic News of the Withdrawal from Guadalcanal and the Death in Battle of Yamamoto, Commander-in-Chief of the Combined Fleet

After the withdrawal from Guadalcanal on 31 December

1943, the objective situation in the South worsened. The Civil Administrator, Yokoji Shun'ichi (later a lawyer), and other administrators who had been serving in New Guinea were withdrawn to Makasar. On 18 April 1943 Yamamoto Gombei, Commander-in-Chief of the Combined Fleet, died in battle, and from the end of that year Celebes began to receive heavy and repeated bombings by enemy planes. Eventually it became necessary to reinforce my air-raid shelter. Apparently, just after the Ogawa Unit (Ogawa later became a restaurant manager), accompanied by beautiful geisha from Shimbashi, Akasaka and Yoshimachi, arrived in Makasar, there was an air-raid which terrified the girls staying at the Suikosha. It seemed that it was their first experience of an enemy attack. At around about this time, the see-saw game between construction and destruction began. We Civil Administrators were not informed of the deterioration in the war situation, and so we carried on our work in accordance with original policy. Policy changes were not even suggested. We became, however, swept up in the objective situation. There were those amongst the natives who possessed ultra-shortwave radios and who were therefore able to perceive the serious changes in the war situation.

As the war outlook grew increasingly pessimistic, instability amongst the natives became gradually more serious, and by the end of 1943 the initial weaknesses of the Minseifu tended to grow into unmanageable problems. It was, however, precisely at this critical stage that it was imperative for we rulers to develop a sense of unity and a disciplined administrative posture. But, like a malignant cancer, the friction between the civilian and military officials spread further and further, with the result that the gap between the civilian officials centring around the Sokan and the military officials attached to the Minseifu and the Minseibu grew wider. When the war was going well and prospects looked bright, the Sokan/civilian official framework proved effective, but as the war situation became grave the relationship between the civilian officials who were ignorant of the deteriorating war situation, and the military officials who were directly affected by such an outlook, was bound to become confused. It was my belief that at this time of worsening conditions, in which a vast number of military officers were being killed in battle, it was simply no longer economical in human terms for military men to devote their energies to civil administration. Moreover, since there were a great number of brilliant civilian officials in the Occupied Territories, I truly felt that the Civil Administration should be left to them alone. With this in mind, I called to my residence all the military officials attached to the Civil Administration, as well as other senior executive officers in the Administration, and before them I stated my belief that in accordance with the Navy's original policy the Sokan was at the centre of the organization, and that it was their duty to cooperate in the Administration. It was obvious, though, from the atmosphere of the meeting that they were not of that opinion, and consequently my move failed.

When the meeting ended, even Rear-Admiral Tominaga, whom I had trusted, spoke out against me. He maintained that after I had retired from office he would propose to the heads in the Ministry of the Navy that they appoint a military officer as my successor. He explained that, 'It is my opinion that in the event of the Navy heads not approving such a proposal, then I must apologize for their indiscretion in deliberately pursuing a policy contrary to that of the Army, and for the time being there will be nothing we can do about it'. I was then convinced that it was impossible to obtain a sense of unity between my military and civilian officials. There was only one path left for me to take.

The Realization of my Resignation

Having made up my mind to resign, I requested the Fleet Commander-in-Chief's approval to go to Tokyo for important discussions. When I received notice that he had agreed, I telegraphed the Ministry of the Navy for permission to go to Japan. I received, however, no reply. As the days passed by with no word from them I grew increasingly anxious. I then decided to send Mizuike to Tokyo with instructions to hand a long letter I had written to Oka Keijun, Head of the Military Affairs Bureau, and to negotiate with the Navy in my place. The gist of the letter was as follows:

> I have shown great loyalty towards the fundamental
> Navy policy of entrusting the Civil Administration of
> the Occupied Territories to the civilian officials,
> and despite my weaknesses I have carried out the
> responsibilities of Sokan. I have gathered together
> here many brilliant men from various administrative
> fields, and I have witnessed the gradual success of
> their efforts. Now, however, as a result of the
> deteriorating war situation, it has become increas-
> ingly difficult to prevent the spread of unstable
> trends amongst the natives. I believe that it is
> absolutely essential to strengthen and unify our
> administrative organization. However, the fact of
> the matter is that at present this organization is on
> the verge of disintegration due to the military
> officials' dissatisfaction with the system by which
> civilian officials occupy the top positions in the
> Administration. Day by day the number of military
> officers killed in battle is increasing, and in the
> light of the subsequent shortage of such men, it is
> both irrational and wasteful to employ military

officials in the Civil Administration. It is my
opinion that we must now implement the drastic
measure of consigning all military officials to their
primary duty of conducting the war, and thereby leave
the operation of civil administration to the civilian
officials. I have devoted all my abilities to the
benefit of the Civil Administration of the Occupied
Territories, but if my above proposal is not approved
and implemented, I am not confident that I will be
able to remain here or produce the expected results.
In this event, I ask permission to resign.

As a result of Mizuike's negotiations with the Navy in Japan, I
finally obtained approval to go to Tokyo. I left immediately.
The Navy explained to me, however, that they were bound by
their honour, and could not possibly alter their original
policy by replacing a civilian Sokan with a military Sokan.
Once they had accepted my resignation it seems that it was not
an easy task to find a civilian Sokan to succeed me. I then
understood why the Navy had been so reluctant to agree to my
coming to Tokyo. Eventually, they turned to the ill-fated
Yamazaki Iwao.

Yamazaki was at that time adviser to the Navy, having
retired from the position of Vice-Minister of Home Affairs. He
had once come to Makasar in his capacity as Navy adviser to
inspect the Occupied Territories, and on that occasion I had
explained the situation there in detail to him. He was
therefore not surprisingly reluctant to accept the appointment
as Sokan. Eventually, however, the Navy laid down the
condition that it would just be a three month appointment.
Yamazaki apparently responded by saying that he would only make
a decision on the matter after he had had a chance to discuss
it with me in Tokyo. With this, approval for my return to
Tokyo was granted. On my arrival, I had an interview with
Vice-Minister Sawamoto, and it was he who granted approval for
my resignation. He begged me to assist him in persuading
Yamazaki to accept the position. Soon after this interview
Yamazaki visited me to discuss the matter.

I expressed my opinion that he should agree to the job.
It seemed that he had would accept the position. I then
returned to Makasar with Mizuike who had also resigned from his
position as Chief Secretary, and there welcomed Yamazaki to his
new post. Irie Seiichiro was appointed as the new Chief
Secretary. After greeting them both in Makasar, we held a
banquet to celebrate both their arrival and our departure.
Mizuike and I then flew to Surabaya. I have a great many
memories of the variety of experience I had on Celebes for the
period of one year and eight months.

*   *   *

OKADA'S REPORT ON HIS ADMINISTRATION, FEBRUARY 1944 (EXTRACTS)*

(4) The natives are fairly earnest in their cooperation with the Japanese. Take, for example, our 1943 cotton production drive. Cotton production had already been experimentally grown by Japanese cultivators in the Minahassa region of North Celebes before the war. The cotton produced as a result was of superior grade and variety. When we began a promotion drive of cotton production throughout all of Celebes and the Lesser Sundas, we received an enthusiastic response from all the native classes. Due to their cooperation we were able to produce the planned amount of superior ginned cotton. In the first half of this year we are expecting an even higher level of production due to improvements in the method of cultivation. The natives have also displayed a great deal of enthusiasm for our plans to increase rice production. We are therefore looking forwad to a successful harvest. Many more examples can be given of the natives' keenness to assist, especially in the area of air-raid defence. This enthusiasm can be further gauged by the facts that very few of the young men being trained at the Sailors Training Institute have dropped out, and that their first wish is to join a warship, and their second to join a transport vessel.

*   *   *

(5) I will elaborate firstly upon the rearrangement of the regional administrative system. We have established as a subordinate organization to the Minseibu and the State Governor's Office which form the military organization, a system of cities and prefectures, the latter of which are in turn divided into sub-prefectures. In each of these administrative divisions we have set up local governments which are run primarily by Japanese officials. These officials guide and control the self-governing territories which are ruled by rajas, district heads and village heads. In this way we aim to extend our administrative control to the very extremities of the region, and to thereby carry out our policies to perfection. The positions of City Mayor, Prefectural Governor and Sub-Prefectural Governor are front-line administrative jobs which involve direct contact with the natives, and as such are regarded as being extremely exciting. The posting of capable men to these positions has a direct and important bearing on

---

* As an official report designed for general circulation during the war, this document has in part a propaganda function. The author conceded in a postscript that he omitted from it any discussion of the weaknesses of the administration.

whether or not the Civil Administration will succeed in the area. Japanese Civil Administration employees who are now serving in remote areas and outlying islands are, by leading and instructing native officials, and by guiding employees in the self-governing territories, endeavouring to bring to fruition our various administrative policies. We must always keep in mind that, although the police system has been reorganized, law and order and the successful penetration of Japanese control is still very much dependent upon the presence of Japanese officials.

With regard to education, we examined the system the Dutch had adopted and introduced radical reforms eliminating undesirable elements. We established a Japanese style of education, revised text books, made the schools open to everyone, and laid down plans to improve the natives' spiritual, physical and technical abilities. At present there are 450,000 pupils attending government schools. The Middle Schools, such as the Boys/Girls Middle School, the Normal School, Industrial School, Agricultural School and the Sailors Training Institute, have been reorganized and newly established on the basis of the guidelines of the reformed education system. By appointing Japanese officials to the positions of headmaster, spiritual education teacher and technical training instructor, we are endeavouring to implement an education system which is Japanese in style.

We have set up and put into operation a new judicial system which both conforms with our Military Administration and preserves law and order, by respecting as much as possible the natives' moral principles and customs, and by refraining from implementing unnecessary civilian laws which only serve to disrupt the lives of the people.

Literally tens of thousands of native employees have been appointed to the Civil Administration. We have established a wage and appointment system, and are planning improvements in working conditions and job security. In addition, as the Japanese Military Administration is becoming more skilful, the way is being opened up for the gradual appointment of natives to high-ranking positions. As part of the political participation system, we have set up Municipal and Provincial Councils, and by way of the native intellectual class which participates in these Councils, we plan to both bring to perfection the Military Administration and to gain popular support. Since the opening of these Councils, we have achieved considerable success in this field.

(6) The East Indies is now passing through a period that could justly be called 'the Indonesian Restoration'. Japan has taken the place of Holland. The Indonesians who, as an ignorant, unhealthy and lethargic race became the victims of skilful Dutch tyranny, are now taking the opportunity of the Greater East Asia War to undertake a great political, economic

and spiritual restoration. This restoration is based on our power. We Japanese must awaken the Indonesians in a manner which conforms with our unsurpassed nation and ideals, in order to muster their strength under the Rising Sun to resist and defeat the British and Americans. If the Indonesians do this, they will for the first time experience real happiness. If the Indonesians believe that we Japanese are simply replacing the Dutch, then they will continue to suffer as a pathetic and eternally subjugated race. Under the Rising Sun and Japanese leadership, the Indonesians have been spiritually united with Japan, and as a result a glorious way of life has been opened up before them. It is the primary objective of all educational and cultural activities in the East Indies to imbue the Indonesians with a belief that the future will bring forth bright hopes and happiness.

Through our education programme in Borneo and Celebes, we are endeavouring to exalt the ideals of the Indonesian Restoration and to awaken the masses in such a way as to promote their cooperation with Japan. The school education system has advanced their knowledge of the Japanese language at a remarkably rapid rate. Our efforts, though, are not just confined to the diffusion of the Japanese language; we are also striving to make use of this knowledge so as to increase the natives' understanding of Japan and the Japanese people. This process of enlightenment is taking place not only in the schools but also wherever Japanese come into contact with Indonesians, be it in the company, factory, dormitory or plantation. The Eastern virtues which the people of Indonesia originally possessed disappeared during the long Dutch regime. We are, however, attempting to make the Indonesians once again conscious of these old virtues so that eventually they will be restored. If we can make them advance in this direction, then the impact of education will be enormous.

Generally speaking, the first Japanese to come to the East Indies looked upon natives with affection and regarded them as able workers. However, after a short time, they grew disappointed with the natives' lethargy and it became common belief that they had a low intellect. This, however, was due to a long history of oppression, and was not an original characteristic of the natives. The men who have guided and instructed this enthusiastic, sincere and unflagging race are now truly convinced of the power of education and of its necessity. One Japanese Middle School headmaster who had served for many years in the field of education in Japan made this comment to me: 'The power of education over the last year and a half has caused a visible improvement in the spirit and physique of the Indonesian youth'.

In the field of culture, we have introduced newspapers, films and radio. Films in particular have had a tremendous impact upon the general populace. Their success here outweighs anything achieved in Japan. A great number of people walk for 25 miles down from mountain redoubts to watch films put on by the travelling film groups in the towns. We have built cinemas at various localities throughout Celebes. The circulation of the Malay language newspaper is relatively small. This, though, is to be expected when you consider that the intellectual class in the area is not large. This paper, nevertheless, does play an important role in guiding and controlling the attitudes of the intellectual class. The manipulation of newspaper articles in such a way as to seize hold of and play up their typically Eastern desire for fame and prestige is proving to be of considerable success. It goes without saying that it is important to understand the psychology of the simple and innocent Indonesians in order to be able to encourage and guide them in the desired direction. From the outset we have placed a ban on professional teachers who simply inject knowledge from the rostrum. We have emphasized over and again that education means control and that educators are administrative officials.

(7) ...In the field of mineral exploration, a provisional mineral investigation team made up of academics and other experts was organized to accompany the Minseifu to the South. This team was divided into many groups which moved in to the hinterlands and rapidly began research. As a result, they discovered many valuable minerals which were not known to the Dutch. In Makasar we now have a permanent research body called the Makasar Research Institute which employs many expert academics who are engaged in fullscale investigations. By fullscale, I mean only those matters which are of direct relevance to the war effort. Although their efforts are modest, they play a very important role in the Civil Administration.

*   *   *

The construction of ships is now a top priority, and the wooden-shipbuilding factories we have established in various localities are well on the way to producing results. With regard to land transportation, our plans to enlarge the regional transportation network set up by the Dutch are progressing well. Despite the current shortage of both labour and materials, we have - as you may have seen in the papers - been able to complete rapidly the road running north-south through Celebes.

The rapid development of the mining and manufacturing industries has given rise to a serious shortage of labour. Fortunately Java, across the sea, has the highest population density in the world, and so it is just a matter of organization before we can obtain the necessary labour.

*   *   *

It is also imperative that we encourage the natives to work and to save. The upper class and the intellectual class have taken the lead in this field, to set an example for the rest of the population. In addition, I am happy to see the hitherto dormant female labour force emerging to take up front-line industrial positions.

*　　　*　　　*

(9) In conclusion, I will express my opinion on several matters relating to political control which I believe should be given due consideration.

Firstly, it is important to obtain a tight hold over the native upper and intellectual classes. Anyone who has had experience in the foundation of a colony is keenly aware of the fact that the success of the colonial regime is dependent upon the ability to control these classes. If the rulers immediately thrust upon the natives policies which emanate from the rulers' own distinct history, ideals and morality, then it will cause the natives to be unnecessarily confused and will give rise to unwanted discontent. The changing of customary practices and their replacement with new forms will cause the masses to be displeased with the regime. Such a policy will only lead to insecurity. If things are left as they are, the masses inevitably feel that their livelihood is secure and stable. It is therefore essential that the new rulers first curry the friendship of the upper and intellectual classes and then, having formed this basis, begin to open up the path of the new regime. If you turn these two classes into enemies, then there is no way your administration will succeed. There is, moreover, a tendency for the new rulers to overestimate their own power, and to underestimate the social power of these classes. It is also very easy to make the mistake of ignoring them completely in the exhibition of one's own power. For a short time it is probably possible to push the people in such a manner; however, it must be remembered that once the general situation turns against you, there will be no way to prevent the downfall of the regime. The secret of a successful colonial regime is for the government and people on the ruling side to prevent the alienation of the native upper and intellectual classes by establishing close personal friendships with them, and by protecting to the bitter end their economic and physical well-being. They will consider it strange if we Japanese officials draw a sharp distinction between our relationship with them in the work place and our relationship with them in our private social lives. What seems only too natural for we Japanese, is impossible for them. It is essential from the point of view of control that we do not be unfair in making a distinction between our relationships with them in private and public, and that we establish deep personal

157

as well as public ties with them. In the control of different races, it is taboo to rule through impersonal political relationships.

Secondly, we must pay attention to the fact that, due to the long Dutch regime, the native intellectual and upper classes have succumbed to a Western individualistic and materialistic lifestyle. If we do not recognize this fact, and consequently deal with them in the Japanese manner, we will in all probability fail. Furthermore, we must consider the fact that the younger generation will, on the other hand, rediscover their original Eastern values, and will come to feel respect and familiarity with things Japanese, and as a result there will develop an ideological generation gap between the young and old. We should bear in mind that it is important to give Japanese training to the young, and that this should be done by the Japanese themselves. We must not entrust the present native adult population with this.

Thirdly, we must find a way out of the present situation in which, in spite of the fact that Islam plays an extremely important role as the religion of the people of Greater East Asia, there are an exceedingly small number of talented Japanese leaders in this field.

Fourthly, it is important to consider policies which will, based on concrete examples, protect to a certain degree the economic position of the Chinese, and which will draw their interests in line with our economic construction. We must not let them feel that the economic position they have held in the East Indies up until now is on the decline. Japan's economic construction in the East Indies must not be so narrow as to do away with the small-scale Chinese businesses. We must pursue broadminded governmental policies.

Finally, I believe that the unfortunate and temporary change in the war situation will have a great impact upon the natives, and consequently we must plan a variety of bold and intelligent policies. In short, it is important that we make them believe in Japan's ultimate victory, and thus make them feel happy to be together with Japan. It is necessary to provide the upper and intellectual classes with a certain degree of material satisfaction so that they do not experience hardship. We must devise serious plans as to how to win the hearts of the people both physically and psychologically.

Education in Bali, 1943-1944

When Suzuki Seihei left Japan aboard the southward bound **Kamakura Maru** *on 18 June 1942, he was charged with the ambitious task of 'introducing culture and education to the South'. At 43, Suzuki considered it an honour to participate in the 'development of Asia', and viewed the establishment of the Greater East Asia Co-Prosperity Sphere as a 'noble achievement'. As a school teacher in Wakayama Prefecture he had held lectures and written pamphlets elaborating upon the experiences of educationalists in Greater East Asia, and advocating education as an integral part of the 'development of Asia'. Suzuki had also been secretary of a local study group formed by the Prefectural Governor around a nucleus of nationalistic young teachers eager to discuss Japanese thought and discipline. This Governor, Shimizu Shigeo, was appointed the first* **Chokan** *(Resident) of the Ceram* **Minseibu,** *and personally asked Suzuki to accompany him as education specialist.*

Suzuki arrived in Ambon, headquarters of the Ceram Minseibu, on 11 July 1942. The Ceram Minseibu, which administered the Moluccas and the old Residency of Timor en Onderhorigheden, was made up of three administrative Bureaus (Politics, Economics, and Health). Suzuki became Chief of the Education Section within the Politics Bureau. In February 1943 the Ceram Minseibu was abolished when it was feared that the area would become a war zone. Minseibu staff were evacuated to Singaraja, which became the headquarters of the new Lesser Sundas Minseibu, comprising Bali, Lombok, Sumbawa, Sumba, Flores and Timor. In February 1944 this area was reduced to Bali, Lombok and Sumbawa. Suzuki retained his position as Chief of the Education Section in the new Minseibu until he returned to Japan on 1 December 1944.

The section of Suzuki's autobiography describing his experiences in Bali is based on a voluminous collection of meticulously ordered letters, official reports, personal records and teaching materials. Fortunately, Suzuki was able to preserve these documents intact because he returned to Japan before the end of the war. Those who were still in Indonesia at the surrender destroyed their diaries, notes and official documents to avoid their confiscation by the Allies. The fact that Suzuki's autobiography is founded on papers he wrote at the time makes it uniquely vivid. Much of the extract below appears to have been originally in the form of letters, probably to his patron Shimizu. It conveys the confident spirit of the new masters of Bali.

Suzuki's anxiety to disseminate Japanese language and culture was not unusual in the Navy-occupied areas of Indonesia. Long after the Army in Java had become quite cynical of attempts at 'Japanization', the Navy continued the programme of indoctrination which we have seen outlined above by the first **Minseifu Sokan**, Okada Fumihide. As late as June 1944, Okada's successor, Yamazaki Iwao, stressed in a report:

> The object of education, based upon the fundamental policy of the Navy controlled areas, is to gradually Japanize the natives ... The diffusion of the Japanese language in towns and villages will result in the unwitting Japanization of their lives ...

The proselytizing attitude Suzuki displayed towards the Indonesians was, therefore, very much in line with official policy. His lengthy report on education in the Lesser Sundas written in September 1944 echoed the words of the Minseifu Sokan. 'Education should be concentrated upon Japanization', he explained, through 'the teaching of the Japanese language, Japanese traditions, Japanese gymnastics, Japanese singing, discipline, ceremonies and celebrations.' The aim of education was to 'tame' the natives' to 'think, feel and act like Japanese East Asians'.

In the long term Japanization was imperative if the Navy was to execute successfully its 'fundamental policy' of permanent possession. For someone like Suzuki, who believed in the ultimate righteousness of Imperial Japan, it was both necessary and right that education should be used to mould Indonesians into good subjects of the Emperor.

Suzuki Seihei

TOISHI NO UTA - ARU KYŌIKUJIN NO ARUITA MICHI

[A record of My Island-hopping - the path of a certain educationalist] (Yokohama, privately published, 1971), pp. 131-44

The Education Staff in the 'Decisive Battle'

Our Education Section is not an administrative body, but rather functions as a 'practical' section. Our field of battle is not the government office, but the schools, and our allies are the teachers and the natives. Our guiding principle aims at both developing the natives as people, and making them understand Japan and the true meaning of the Greater East Asia War.

For just over a year since I first arrived, there have only been three people in the Section, including myself, with teaching experience. Moreover, there has been no end to the work that has to be done. I have, therefore, not been able to afford to set aside people with no teaching experience. I mobilized the whole Section, from clerks to copy and typing girls, and sent them out to the actual places of education. Because they have been made to teach not just Japanese language, but also physical education and drill and how to lead one's daily life, the teaching has been amateurish, but the results these non-professionals have achieved are so remarkable that we professional teachers have been amazed. These non-professionals are Okuda Kiminobu, Ina Hirofusa, Takei Toshiyada and Ueda Mitsuko.

As a professional teacher I don't deny that teaching involves skill and professionalism, but I have seen in Bali that in fact the really essential qualities of teaching are enthusiasm and devotion.

Ina holds classes at the Japanese language school for ten hours each week and spares another six hours of his own time after leaving work to teach. Although I have advised him many times to include these outside classes in his regular working time, he does not listen at all and continues on in the same way. In addition, every night he goes to the Chief Librarian's home to study Balinese. (He has already mastered Malay).*

*   *   *

* For Footnote see following page.

*Suzuki here describes the qualities of Okuda, Takei,
and Ueda, before returning to his professional
teaching staff.*

Asari Seiichi - as you know, he arrived in Bali with me
and is my righthand man. He graduated from Wakayama Normal
School in 1930. He was a rough boy and has been known by the
pet name 'Benkei'† since his school years. Nevertheless, he is
very good-natured, obliging, gentle, sensitive and frank. Yet,
at the same time, when it comes to teaching, he is like a ball
of fire: 'The unit of education is ten years and nothing can be
achieved in two to three years. I will work on a plan of a
minimum of ten years and then you will see that a bronze statue
of me will be erected in Bali.'

Despite the fact that he left behind in Kumano an only
child who was born three months after his departure, he is so
possessed by the South that he tends to make these kind of
emphatic statements.

Believing that you cannot educate the natives without
understanding their language, as soon as he landed in Bali, he
decided to live with the translator who accompanied us, and
specially requested that he teach him the language. As a
result he has mastered Malay faster and more proficiently than
anyone else. He then travelled around Bali to learn Balinese,
and after obtaining special permission, often moves into the
homes of the Balinese (as a rule it is prohibited to lodge in
the natives' homes).

It seems that he came across problems learning the
language. Later I recalled that he once said, 'It is a lonely
and oppressive life not being able to speak the language, so
much so that I want to cry - I can't use Japanese or Malay at
all'. However, in about six months he mastered Balinese and
suddenly his whole world changed. He plunged into Balinese
society and at the same time, the Balinese flocked to him.

He is now Head of the Teacher Training Institute (the
Institute is marvellously run) in Denpasar (the Capital of
South Bali), and not only the teachers and pupils there but
also natives of all social classes in the area come and stay

* Footnote from previous page:
  As with many pre-war Dutchmen, Suzuki's persistence in
  calling the national language Malay is a conscious denial of
  the claims of the nationalist movement which had adopted an
  'Indonesian' language and identity.

† Benkei is a near legendary figure in Japanese history who has
  been likened to Little John of the 'Robin Hood' story. He
  was a priest with superhuman qualities, especially skilful at
  sword fighting.

with him - District Heads, Village Heads, the executive staff of the **Seinendan,** and even Chinese and Arabs who rarely have contact with foreigners. He has a continuous stream of people visiting him, who come appealing to his goodwill and to seek advice and guidance.

I would like to relate an incident concerning the District Head of Mengwi. On one occasion he came to discuss with Asari an affair involving a Japanese. However Asari was absent when he arrived. After waiting a little while, the District Head grew sleepy and finally dozed off in Asari's bed. When Asari returned he woke up. Don't you think that is incredible?

I am just giving an example of the extent to which the wall between Asari and the natives had been removed. Doesn't this demonstrate just how much mutual understanding and trust there can be between people? I haven't the space to relate the sort of activities Asari, who had won the hearts of the natives, was involved in, but I don't think it is an exaggeration to say that he has already carved a bronze statue of himself in the natives' hearts.

There is one more person among the professional teachers I would like to introduce. Tsuchiya Masanari - he arrived only a year beforehand and, belonging to the same generation as Asari, is in the prime of life with regard to work. As a genuine child of Gumma Prefecture, he works like a ball of fire.

* * *

His daily routine, in summary, is as follows. At 6.30 a.m., when it is still dark, he jumps out of bed with the other male students and begins work. He personally leads his male and female students in their morning duties and drill, and after eating breakfast together with them, when the sun is just appearing above the coconut groves, he goes to work at the schools in the city. There are three of these schools. They are Higher Grade Public Schools to which the female student teachers are consigned. It is a four-kilometre return trip to the three schools, and there are 29 student teachers assigned to them. So as not to miss one student, Tsuchiya rides around by motor-bike between the schools. He has surprising stamina. He has set a record of making the return trip five times in one day.

Just after 3 p.m., when he returns to teaching, he teaches drill and instructs work-operations to the male students, and after that teaches Japanese to the female students. After the evening meal he finishes off the work from the day - that is, giving individual guidance to the 29 student teachers, commenting upon the classes they held that day, and instructing them in class plans for the next day. Thus, by the time he returns to the male dormitories it is past 11 o'clock.

He surely must be some sort of superman to continue this

sort of life for the past 40 days since he began instructing
the student teachers. Headmaster Yano and myself have been
worried, but when we tell him to relax his tempo a little, he
replies, 'The job is so interesting, there is nothing I can do
about it. I'm alright. On the contrary if I stop, one or two
of my pupils may suffer. New history always demands compensa-
tions, doesn't it? I intend to look after myself, so don't
worry to much.'

Needless to say, the natives are as much astounded as we
are worried. I heard Miss Yasumin, one of the female teachers,
lament, 'Why do Japanese teachers work so hard?'

Whether we are working hard, or burning with a sense of
mission, or frolicking in a state of rapture, it is no exaggeration to say that we have developed a quite definite mental
attitude.

'Recently I have thoroughly forgotten everything - my
wife, my children and Japan. At the moment there is no room in
my mind for anything other than student teacher guidance and
Japanese language education... How could I go on living if I
came to this place and didn't find my job worth living for?'
Tsuchiya recently disclosed to me, and you can probably
understand what this mental state is like. I will add one more
example.

Tsuchiya graduated his pupils at the Normal School and
sent them to their positions. After only one month of rest, he
travelled into the deep mountain recesses to inspect the
reaction of the people and to guide his former pupils. Then he
reported to us on his inspection of the new graduates, and
surprised us with some first-class ideas. He relied on his
motor-bike, not using a push-bike once. In remote places where
his motor-bike could not be used he rode a horse. His plan was
to send relays of native teachers and young people from village
to village, to lodge at Sub-Prefecture offices, and homes of
District and Village Heads.

> It is not an easy job to educate the people in the
> mountains. On one occasion when I entered a kampong
> all the residents fled. The villager who first saw
> me misunderstood why I was there and signalled to the
> others. They all ran away into the mountains and
> would not come out. Finally I caught hold of the
> village head, and when I disclosed who I was and the
> purpose of my visit he relaxed and thereupon began
> preparations for a banquet. That was a real
> spectacle. Unhulled rice was taken out of the
> granary and they began to pound it. There were still
> husks on the rice. They made it into brown rice,
> then into white rice, cooked it and fed it to me.
> They even brought out a small low Japanese-style
> table for me to eat from. The feast continued for

four hours, and at the end, to show my sincerity, I
told them how delicious it was.

This was an unpretentious mountain village. It is
by no means easy to make such people understand the
meaning of the war. Since the beginning of the war,
clothing had become scarce. I tried to give a superficial explanation of the war but they could not
comprehend it. One village chief recalled that,
'When the Dutch left they took all their wealth',
and I felt as if he sensed a little what I meant. If
you know anything about the low standard of living of
the natives, you would understand why their understanding of the war was so limited. It is an
absolutely absurd idea for a Minseibu official to
ride around by bike trying to assess the reactions of
the people to the Japanese Occupation.

This is a section of the report he wrote on returning.
It captures well the situation of the natives living in remote
areas.

Japanese Language Education

Nowadays the slogan 'The Education Staff in the Decisive
Battle' conjures up a fighting spirit, but had we not sensed
this spirit at the time there would have been something wrong
with us. Furthermore, we all persisted in our work because we
felt as if we were part of the struggle. The people I have
mentioned in this book were of precisely this nature, but there
were other people too who were aroused in the same manner. In
such a short space of time we achieved brilliant results, but
what particularly surprised us was the success and popularity
of Japanese language education and physical education.
Since the basic objective of making the natives understand
both Japanese and the war could only be achieved through a
knowledge of the Japanese language, both the natives and
ourselves were enthusiastic about Japanese language education,
and in fact the enthusiasm of the natives greatly exceeded
ours. There is no end to the examples I could give to
illustrate this. The following account of the Singaraja
Japanese Language School is just one of these examples.
About 50 people came to this school for teachers, and of
those 50 about 12 or 13 commuted from places over ten kilometres away. They came in the evening from 5 to 7 p.m. when
they had finished their regular work. The classes were held
five days a week and they were rarely absent. In the case of
the class for younger people, similar situations occurred.
Amongst them there was a group from a mountain village who
insisted on riding their bikes for the ten kilometres return

trip. The fact that two others came from a place 22 kilometres away made a deep impression upon us.

After almost a year the majority of the pupils were able to make simple everyday conversation, and had passed the Japanese language teachers' licensing examination. There is no doubt that this success was due to the fact that they studied a great deal by themselves.

This trend was to be found not only in Singaraja, but almost everywhere. Why did the natives display such enthusiasm to learn Japanese? Some learnt because they were opportunists, others because they fawned upon the Japanese, and others because they were ambitious to have a successful career. Somehow, though, I don't think you can explain it in these terms alone.

According to the School Inspector's explanation, the Dutch opened the door to the study of Dutch only to a small and limited number of talented men. Moreover, the extraordinarily high monthly tuition fees acted as a deterrent to most people. In other words, study of Dutch was well and truly out of the reach of the common people. However, because Japan issued Japanese language text books and taught Japanese for free, the natives, while being a little mystified at first, gradually caught on to the idea of learning Japanese.

The Normal School which we opened at Singaraja was the most far-reaching aspect of Japanese language education in Bali. Mr. Yano, the Headmaster, persevered with the basic policy that Japanese only was to be spoken in the school grounds and in the dormitory. The Malay language was entirely prohibited. At first both the natives and ourselves thought it could prove to be inconvenient and inefficient, but on the contrary, it acted as an incentive to study. The students all worked hard, and in no time results began to appear. Within a few months the students were able to make themselves completely understood in Japanese.

When the students reached this stage, the atmosphere inside the school changed completely - when the school first opened we would freely comment upon and gossip about the pupils in front of of them, but this became impossible as they began to understand Japanese.

They became so good that they could understand our Japanese when it was spoken in whispers or even when we spoke about delicate topics.

Tsuchiya had mentioned, 'The Japanese language classes have begun to show improvement, so I would like you to come along and have a look'. So today, under his guidance, I inspected one by one the Japanese language classes of about ten student teachers in the female teachers department. What surprised me at first was the fact that nearly all

the classes were being held only in Japanese. I saw
two or three teachers translating into Malay on odd
occasions in places where they thought the children
were finding it difficult to understand. However,
the rest of the time they taught in Japanese only,
not even using a few words of Malay. The teachers
are encouraging the children so that the majority of
them are able to cope with this system. There is no
doubt that the children have improved through the
efforts of their class teachers, but, on the other
hand, I fully agree with Tsuchiya's explanation that
the success is ultimately due to the efforts of the
student teachers themselves.

On one occasion I could hear the students through
the walls of a neighbouring room, and their Japanese
was so much like standard Japanese, that I thought
that it was actually a classroom full of Japanese
children. The Japanese I heard was not sing-song,
slow or accentless - the type the ordinary teacher
hears from his pupils. The tone, speed, tempo,
accent and enunciation were so good that their
Japanese resembled the Standard Japanese spoken by
over 80% of native Japanese. It was particularly
similar to the Standard Japanese spoken by people
from Tohoku.* I respect and appreciate the ability
of these children to improve so much over one year
...

(A report on the Inspection of Japanese
Language Classes for Student Teachers -
12 July 1944.)

There is a great deal I would like to write about physical
education and drill in how to lead one's daily life, but
unfortunately I do not have the space.

The Flood of Pupils

If I was asked, 'What was the most pleasurable thing you
experienced in the South?', I would undoubtedly answer without
hesitation, 'The sudden increase in school children'. This
phenomenon was common throughout the areas of Military

___

* Tohoku was one of the seven traditional circuits of Japan,
and the term is still commonly used to refer to northern
Honshu. The Tohoku region has a distinctive dialect which
differs from Standard Japanese in terms of phonology, grammar
and vocabulary. Suzuki means that the Japanese of the
Indonesians was as good as the Standard Japanese spoken by
people who normally converse in Tohoku dialect.

Administration in the South, but I think it was particularly noticeable in the Navy area of occupation (the former Dutch East Indies Outer Territories). This was probably because it was an educationally backward region, and the natives' reaction was, without exaggeration, spectacular. The following table illustrates the situation in the area under our jurisdiction.

Throughout the world there are probably only a limited number of examples of this type. It seems that there were a number of criticisms concerning education by other administrative departments under the Military Administration, but, as you can see by the statistics, our education policy was unconditionally and extensively accepted by the natives.

I first noticed the increase in the number of pupils when I inspected schools between April and May 1943 soon after my transfer to Bali, but that was just the beginning. The real increase occurred with a bang in 1944.

> For a week I have been inspecting schools in the South of Bali, and everywhere there is a deluge of school children. At the Ordinary Public School in Abang village the number of pupils has increased from 95 to 194, in Rendang village from 106 to 216, at Gianjar Ordinary Higher Grades Public School there has been an increase from 119 pupils to 281, at Denpasar it is the same with an increase from 193 to 351, and at Tabanan from 234 to 341. The increase witnessed in the agricultural and mountain villages, which up till now have been culturally backward, greatly exceeds that in the towns and cities.

> (Diary – May 1944)

Why did the number of pupils increase so suddenly?

According to the native Inspector of Schools, 'The main reason is the abolition of school fees, but also the fact that if you go to school you receive tuition in physical education, and the fact that Japanese is taught for free, have contributed to this increase'. This was his frank answer. Setting aside the point about tuition fees and Japanese language instruction, the fact that physical education aroused such popularity is the best proof that in the schools up until then the children under the Dutch education administration were taught only how to hold their breath.

The system of school fees during the Dutch period was different from that in Japan. It was a complex system which grouped school children according to the income classification of each household. The problem with this system lay in the heavy burden it placed on the people.

In the case of Ordinary Public Schools (a village school of three years [**Volksschool**]), the first child of First Class households – those with a monthly income over 50 guilders –

AREA UNDER THE SUPERVISION OF THE LESSER SUNDAS MINSEIBU

TYPE OF SCHOOL	PERIOD	NUMBER OF SCHOOLS				NUMBER OF TEACHERS				NUMBER OF PUPILS			
		BALI	LOMBOK	SUMBAWA	TOTAL[1]	BALI	LOMBOK	SUMBAWA	TOTAL	BALI	LOMBOK	SUMBAWA	TOTAL
PUBLIC SCHOOL	a. Before the War	244	93	82	419	519	230	181	926	23,859	11,713	11,378	47,150
	b. 1943 School Year	244[2]	113	93	450	545	295	217	1,057	35,186	18,383	15,740	67,309
	c. 1944 School Year	256	136	107	499	636	411	264	1,308	50,987	25,063	17,483	93,533
	(c) minus (a)	12	43	25	80	117	181	83	382	27,128	13,350	6,105	46,383
	%age of the above									114%	114%	54%	98%
MIDDLE SCHOOL	a. Before the War	5	4	3	12	6	4	3	13	170	120	90	380
	b. 1943 School Year	7	7	4	18	18	12	6	36	411	216	106	733
	c. 1944 School Year	10	6	4	20	27	13	10	50	708	325	244	1,277
	(c) minus (a)	5	2	1	8	21	9	7	37	538	205	154	897
	%age of the above									316%	170%	171%	236%

1. The situation in the two other prefectures of Flores and Sumba is not known.

2. The fact that the increase is small compared to prewar figures, is due to the amalgamation of schools.

All figures are for the month of April, except for before the war when they are taken in September 1941.

paid a monthly fee of 50 cents. Similarly, in the case of Seventh Class households - those with a monthly income of 2.5 to 5 guilders - the first child paid 3 cents. Eighth Class households - those with a monthly income of less than 2.5 guilders - were exempt from paying fees. In this manner an extremely heavy tax was imposed upon the common people.

In the case of the Higher Grades Public School (a five-year system, comparable with the old Upper Primary School in Japan), fees ranged from 125 cents to 5 cents. At the seven-year Dutch schools (these were elite schools where Dutch was taught [i.e. H.I.S.], and there were only three of these schools in Bali), the monthly tuition fees were astoundingly high - from 18 to 2 guilders. If you consider that a perforated coin with the value of 1/10th cent was the coin most commonly used and that rice sold for about 6.7 cents a shō (1.8 litres), you can easily understand how heavy a burden the monthly tuition fee was, and how great an obstacle it was to school entrance.

In March 1943, immediately after the announcement that school fees had been abolished, I was in a store in Denpasar in South Bali when I was surprised by a young female shopkeeper who delivered a kind of speech to me praising the abolition of school fees. (Of course there was no reason she would have known that I was in charge of education at the time.) Even now, her flushed cheeks and earnest speech have remained deeply impressed upon my memory. The fact that there was a great increase in the number of pupils at the time, however, is not just a romantic recollection. It was a reality.

The flood of students necessitated numerous changes. Classrooms had to be hurriedly built, schools newly constructed, teachers trained, text books and school equipment supplied, and middle schools increased. It was the need for teacher training, though, that was by far our highest priority. The construction of classrooms and schools was not that much of a problem. We made classrooms in barrack-like fashion with bamboo pillars and coconut leaf roofs. There was no lack of building materials. Land was easily borrowed, and one classroom could be built for the cheap price of ¥ 300. We had no real financial problems. The above chart indicates how many schools were newly constructed during this period.

In Bali up until then teachers were trained at Teacher Training Institutes. There were three Institutes in Bali. These teachers were termed 'Ordinary Teachers' for they taught at the three-year Public Schools. There were no Normal Schools which trained Higher Grade Teachers (those teachers who taught at the five-year Public Schools). Normal Schools were only located in Java.

In the case of Ordinary Teachers, it was sufficient to enlarge the already existing Teacher Training Institutes. As for the Normal Schools, we decided to establish one in Bali.

The school was founded in Singaraja in September 1943, dormitories were added and it was completed in July 1944. The problem, however, was the four-year study course - the absurd thing was that we could not supply Higher Grade teachers for the next four years. Then we recalled the night school system in Japan whereby graduates of the old middle school were trained to be licensed regular teachers under a one-year education scheme. Our attention was particularly drawn towards the pupils of the Java Normal School who had returned home with the temporary closing of the school due to the war, and we thought of a scheme whereby a class would be formed combining these Higher Grade students and the young and bright amongst the Ordinary Teachers. Under this scheme they would graduate in one year. We opened this school, calling it the Temporary Higher Grade Teacher Training Institute, and ran it alongside the regular four-year course. The student teachers who Tsuchiya looked after and who graduated at the end of August 1944 took precisely this course.

In this way, we were able, with some difficulty, to solve the problems created by the flood of school children. However, the fact that a great number of educational personnel were sent over from Japan during this time also helped us to cope with the new situation.

I mentioned before that the sudden increase in school children was the greatest pleasure I experienced. If you look back on education in Bali from an historical viewpoint, it seems as though some sort of natural phenomenon occurred, as the collapse of a levee allows the dammed up water to gush out freely. We Japanese simply sponsored this process. Ultimately, it was the meritorious action of the Military Administration which caused this phenomenon to occur. I gain great pleasure, though, in recalling that the initial idea to abolish school fees was none other than my own. No doubt this would have given rise to similar results anywhere else in the world.

OTSUKA TADASHI

Education in Sumatra

Otsuka was born in 1915 in Shimane Prefecture, graduated from the local Teachers College in 1934, and began work as a primary teacher the same year. In 1944 he was conscripted, to become a teacher in the Southern Occupied Territories. He was placed in Batusangkar, West Sumatra, primarily as a teacher of Japanese language and music. He returned to Japan in 1947. His account appeared in a book produced 30 years after the war by the **Sekidokai** (Equator Association), the organization linking civilians who had served in Sumatra.

Otsuka Tadashi

SUMATORA JŌKYŪ GAKKŌ NO KOTODOMO

[Concerning the Higher Officials School in Sumatra], in
Sekidōhyō (Tokyo, Sekidokai, 1975), pp. 328-29

We reach Batusangkar after a forty minute drive from
Bukittinggi, passing Kayumanis and having a view of terraced
rice fields which make us feel as though we are in Japanese
countryside. However, palm trees again remind us that we are
in a tropical country.

Batusangkar is the cradle of the Minangkabau people.*
This was the place where the **Jōkyū Shikan Gakkō** [Higher
Officials School] was located. This school, at which I was
employed as a teacher, was the highest educational institution
in Sumatra, occupying a similar position to Tokyo University in
Japan. It might sound strange that the highest school was
located in such a country town as Batusangkar. We chose the
place because it was the cradle of the Minangkabau people, the
most intellectual people in Sumatra, and therefore the town was
considered to be the cultural centre of Sumatra.

The schoolhouses on a small hill were very simple, like
easily made barracks. They were roofed with bark and the
ground had to substitute for a floor. This simplicity should
be attributed to the war situation which made everything very
scarce. Despite the simplicity of the bottle, however, all of
us were enthusiastic about ensuring the quality of the wine.
Entrance to the school was limited to those who were
recommended by the **Chokan** [Resident] of each **Shu,** and all
students were sponsored by the Japanese. The students from all
over Sumatra were dressed in a uniform with knee-length shorts,
and strict discipline was maintained by the Japanese in a
school dormitory. Japanese teachers, who patrolled the
dormitory at night, sometimes caught students climbing over the

* Bukittinggi had been selected as the Sumatran Military
Administration headquarters primarily for strategic reasons,
but Japanese propagandists frequently stressed its
appropriateness as the 'cultural centre' of Sumatra. By the
'cradle of the Minangkabau people' Otsuka is presumably
referring to the Tanah Datar district, the centre of the
once-flourishing Minangkabau gold industry and therefore of
the major ancient capitals of Pagarruyung and Buo.
Batusangkar (Fort van der Capellen under the Dutch) was one
of the modern administrative centres of this district.

fence to try to buy condoms. Education was given in Japanese on subjects such as ethics, geography, history, the Japanese language, and physical training. The students seemed particularly impressed by the fact that they were able to cope with the pressure of physical training, including marching under the burning sun. This training excited the admiration of the girls who watched.

As there was no electricity network there, we installed a single generator and provided the school and town with electricity. The people of the town and the students were very pleased with this. The way we grew sweet potatoes and maize in newly opened gardens, and rice on fields which we borrowed, was greatly appreciated by the people of Batusangkar. They were surprised at the efficiency of the Japanese method of rice cultivation. Students went back to their respective Shu after three or six months of this type of education.

Our school management made a good impression on the natives. In due course, girls requested that they also get an education in the school, and I, the youngest of the Japanese teachers, came to look after them, mainly for the subjects of moral exhortation, music, physical exercise, and gymnastics. The girls enormously enjoyed the education because they had not experienced collective training. They voluntarily made uniforms for the male students when the latter were busy planting rice seedlings, bringing their own sewing machines from their homes. They also made mosquito nets.

In return for the cooperation of the people of Batusangkar we tried to contribute to their welfare as much as possible. Because the atmosphere of the town was very pleasant owing to the harmony between the school and the town, the Japanese surrender struck us as especially bitter. When we announced the surrender and the closure of the school, all the students began to cry: 'Teacher! Why don't you fight to the death. We will join you!' There was nothing we could say to placate them, except: 'Japanese always follow the orders of the Emperor'. However, they repeatedly visited us later, and insisted on continuing the war. It goes without saying that they soon joined the struggle for independence with the **Heiho** and **Giyugun**.

AOKI EIGORO

Law Reform in Aceh, 1943

Aoki Aigoro worked as a lawyer and court official in Osaka, before becoming in 1942 a Civil Administrator (**Shiseikan**) in the service of the military administration of the conquered regions in the South. Based initially in Singapore, he volunteered for the more challenging role as the first **Shihobucho** (Head of the Judiciary Department) for Aceh, with responsibility for implementing the changes in the legal system which the Japanese were hoping to bring about on a uniform basis throughout Sumatra. He spent only one year in Aceh, taking up his new appointment in April 1943, and being forced to return to Singapore by an outraged **Chokan** (Resident) of Aceh the following April. In that short time he had an extraordinary effect on the politics of Aceh, demonstrating once again the importance of individual initiative in the Japanese military system.

Aoki sympathized and fraternized almost exclusively with the reformist Islamic movement PUSA, with whom he came into contact through Tuanku Mahmud. He accepted their argument (which seems not to be supported by the Fujiwara extract above) that the Japanese **F Kikan** had promised PUSA a larger share in running the country in return for its cooperation in 1942. He therefore organized the judicial changes in such a way that control of the courts would pass from the hands of the **uleebalang** territorial aristocracy into those of PUSA sympathizers. The **Chokan**, Iino Shozaburo, who sought minimal disruptions to the Dutch colonial order, found himself confronted with a **fait accompli** after Aoki had first gained support from the 25th Army Headquarters in Bukittinggi, over Iino's head, and then stacked the new courts with PUSA people. The changes therefore stood until the end of the Japanese period, although surrounded by intense controversy and bitterness. Conflict over the role of the courts after the Japanese surrender was one of the factors which precipitated the civil war of 1945-46 in which the **uleebalang** were crushed (see Ushiyama extract below).

PUSA supporters were understandably delighted at the major victory Aoki had given them. When Aoki left Aceh in official disgrace in April 1944 he was given emotive farewells in Kutaraja and Sigli by PUSA leaders. Daud Beureu'eh presented him with a sacred **kris** and thanked him for his services to Aceh. The **Atjeh Sinbun**, edited by PUSA sympathizers, declared that Aoki's name 'is written in gold in the pages of the history of the rise of New Aceh'.* When, shortly after the Japanese surrender, a group of Japanese intelligence agents selected Aceh as the best base for continuing the anti-Allied struggle on a new basis, they took Aoki with them to ensure a warm reception from at least one important element in Aceh. The operation was, however, stopped by Japanese commanders soon after the boatload of potential subversives had reached Sumatra at the end of August 1945.†

Despite his dramatic and controversial intervention in Aceh affairs, or perhaps because of it, Aoki has suppressed his own role as far as possible in the account which follows. In part this was because he wrote it as an official report, intended only for the Department of Overseas Trade, in 1955. It has never been published, and the author was surprised to discover in 1973 that a copy of it had been used for some years by scholars in Cornell University Library. Even though written in the third person in the style of an official report, this is an intensely personal document. It is filled with information only Aoki could have known, and presents his personal and partisan view of the Aceh problem as if it had been the official one. Our extract begins characteristically, as the 'section of the Japanese military administration' he mentions can only refer to himself.

* **Atjeh Sinbun**, 29-iv-2604 and 6-v-2604.

† Interviews with Adachi Takashi, Kondo Tsugio, and Aoki Eigoro, August 1973.

Aoki Eigoro

ACHIE NO MINZOKU UNDŌ

[The Nationalist Movement in Aceh] (Typewritten mimeograph, no
publisher shown, 1955)

Chapter VII: The Change of Policy

About the middle of 1943, a section of the Japanese
military administration [**Gunsei Kikan**] began, with the help of
Tuanku Mahmud,* an administrative advisor to the Gunseibu, an
investigation of Acehnese history, religion and customs, and a
study of the Dutch policy towards Aceh. During the Dutch
period, Mahmud had held the highest position possible for a
native official, but, although belonging to an ex-Sultan
family, he stood on a different political platform from the
uleebalang. He had been a supporter of the F Kikan and PUSA
even before the Dutch retreated. It was he who had striven to
secure the release of Said Abu Bakar, when the latter had
slipped into Sumatra from Malaya and been imprisoned in
Kutaraja by the Dutch police.†

It was through the cooperation of Tuanku Mahmud that the
investigators were able to study the reports of former Dutch
Residents, Assistant Residents and **controleurs**, all of which
had been secretly preserved. Among the reports were 'Nota van

---

* Tuanku Mahmud (1895-1954) was a descendant of a side branch
of the sultan dynasty, all of whom carried the title Tuanku.
The Dutch had declared the Aceh sultanate abolished in 1874.
Several descendants of the dynasty, lacking a power base in
the uleebalang structure, became particularly useful to the
Dutch. Mahmud had a good Dutch education before entering the
colonial administration in the early 1920s. He was appointed
to represent Aceh in the Volksraad (People's Council) in
1931. In the last years of the Dutch regime he came into
sharp conflict with the more political uleebalang, who
opposed first his position in the Volksraad and subsequently
what they saw as his attempt to revive the Aceh sultanate at
their expense. Because of this antagonism he found himself
in alliance with PUSA despite his very different background.

† See Fujiwara, above, pp.14-16, 18.

Caron',* a Dutch manual concerning the control of the uleebalang, and 'Amok Teungku'. We were able to draft the blueprint of our own policy by comparing these reports with petitions submitted from various places in Aceh to the Dutch authorities.

Concomitant with these investigations, another section of the Gunsei Kikan was able, through the mediation of people such as the Tuanku and Teungku Joenoes Djamil, a former member of the F Kikan and teacher of Abu Bakar, to make contact with Daud Beureu'eh and other PUSA leaders.†

PUSA leaders followed on each other's heels to Kutaraja from all over Aceh, even from such remote places as Kutacane and Blangkejeren in the east and Tapaktuan in the west (the area of the Residency of Aceh is said to be about 1.7 times as large as that of Taiwan). They gathered at the residence of a Japanese administrator in the town. Contact with the leaders was made with great secrecy. The Japanese investigating the reports of these leaders came to the same conclusion as that reached by the group investigating the reports and petitions. It was clear that the Japanese would have to change their policy in Aceh as a matter of great urgency. To do otherwise would be to fail to honour their earlier pledges.

The Japanese investigators felt it expedient that the facts of the cooperation of Acehnese members of the F Kikan with the Japanese Army be clarified, in order to make the Gunseikambu in Sumatra recognize the necessity for changing its policy and to bring home to the military authorities the special circumstances surrounding the Acehnese. Accordingly, Teungku Joenoes immediately began collecting reports from responsible F Kikan members of actual events in their respective areas. In this way **Aceh Shū Kōgun Kyōryoku Shi** [A History of Acehnese Cooperation with the Advancing Imperial Army] was produced, and copies of it sent to the military authorities [of the 25th Army] and to the Gunseikambu. Details of this report are contained in the memoirs of former Lt.-Col. Fujiwara.#

* Presumably a report by L.J.J. Caron, a senior colonial official who became Governor of Celebes in 1929, after a period in charge of administration in Aceh in the early 1920s.

† For Joenoes Djamil, Abu Bakar and Daud Beureu'eh, see above, pp. 14, 17, 18, 26. Joenoes Djamil had been appointed in March 1943 to a strategic position as Secrtary of Maibkatra, the Japanese-sponsored Islamic organization for Aceh.

Fujiwara Iwaichi. Portions of his memoir are translated above.

So it was that the powers-that-be in the Gunseikambu came to realize the truth concerning the F Kikan and PUSA, and to appreciate the necessity of a special policy towards Aceh. However, it was hardly possible to strip the uleebalang of all their powers immediately. Such a measure might result in the disruption of the entire military administration. The Japanese promise which the F Kikan (and PUSA too, for that matter) most wanted to see implemented was that concerning religious observation, or in other words the reform of the religious system. This reform had to be implemented whatever the cost. However, such a reform entailed also a reform of the judicial system, since the two systems were inseparably related. This is to say, a prerequisite to reform was to strip the uleebalang of their judicial powers. The Japanese decided to carry out the reform along these lines.

After repeated consultation with Teungku Joenoes, Teungku Daud Beureu'eh and other PUSA leaders, by the end of 1943 the Japanese in charge of the reform* had finished writing a draft ordinance [**gunseirei**] relating to the two systems. Mr Amin,† now Governor of North Sumatra, also joined in these discussions. He was then a judge in Sigli.

The draft was submitted for consideration to the **Aceh Shū Gunsei Kyōryoku Kaigi** [Committee for Cooperation with the Military Administration in Aceh], which consisted mainly of uleebalang. First, the ordinance for the reform of the judicial system was discussed. Notable among the members of the Committee were Teuku Hasan and Teuku Njak Arif.# Njak Arif had joined the F Kikan at one point, but had transferred his

* i.e. Aoki himself.

† Mr is the title borne by Dutch law graduates. Mr S.M. Amin, of Mandailing descent, had been the only private lawyer in pre-war Kutaraja. He joined the judiciary during the Japanese occupation, and the administration thereafter.

For Njak Arif, see Fujiwara, above, p.17. Teuku Mohammad Hasan (1893-1944) was one of the most effective and well-educated uleebalang, succeeding his father in 1935 as ruler of Glumpang Payung, in Pidië, after 16 years as a prominent government official in Kutaraja. As Consul of Muhammadiah for Aceh (1930-35) he had established contacts with the Indonesian national movement. In the last years of the Dutch regime he became the leader of the politicized uleebalang of Pidië in their resistance to the idea of a restored Aceh Sultanate, and in consequence was drawn into conflict with PUSA. This conflict probably contributed to his subsequent arrest and execution by the Kempeitai in 1944, despite the early favour of the Japanese, who had appointed him leader of the 1943 Sumatran delegation to Japan.

allegiance to the anti-PUSA faction since the beginning of the Japanese occupation. He and Teuku Hasan had made a factfinding trip to Japan. After the war he became one of the most important leaders of the anti-PUSA movement, but was arrested and died in prison.

Some members of the Committee, such as Teungku Daud Beureu'eh, of course approved the draft. The problem was the attitude of Teuku Hasan and Teuku Njak Arif. However, as a result of long discussions which lasted for one whole day, these two also finally agreed to the draft. They were actually quietly optimistic that, judging by previous Japanese policy, it would be the uleebalang who were entrusted with the implementation of the ordinance. They felt that their power might even be enhanced without any effort on their part, for if they were to be authorized to select the judges in charge of civil cases, they could appoint their own henchmen. It did in fact seem inconceivable that the Japanese would be able to select all the judges for the whole of Aceh. At the meeting it was decided that the ordinance would be officially announced on 1 January 1944, and would be operative from 1 March.

At another meeting of the Committee held shortly after-wards, the draft ordinance for the religious system was discussed. Prior to this meeting, the Japanese had organized a meeting of 15 authoritative **ulama** in Aceh, in order to obtain their consent and to avoid any criticism by traditional ulama and uleebalang that the heathen Japanese were interfering with Islam.

As had been expected, people such as Teuku Hasan and Njak Arif at first opposed the draft on the grounds of Japanese interference with Islam, but they had to change their stance when presented with a letter of consent to the draft, signed by the 15 authoritative ulama. They stood firm, however, on one point, that the village Islamic judge be appointed on the recommendation of the uleebalang. In the draft these judges were to be appointed by a **Shukyo Hoin** [Religious High Court] based in Kutaraja. Just as with the judicial system, these delegates wanted to secure the power of appointment. An amendment to the draft, the result of a compromise with these delegates, proved the source of much trouble later. The amended ordinance was also promulgated on 1 January 1944.

Chapter VIII: Events Leading up to the Appointment of Judges

The **Atjeh Sinbun** of 1 January 1944 headlined the new ordinance. The people were excited because their aspirations were being taken seriously for the first time. Their support was shown by the many telegrams containing expressions of gratitude and promises of cooperation which poured into the Gunseikambu in Bukittingi and the Gunseibu in Kutaraja from all over Aceh. There were over 300 telegrams. The Gunseikambu reported this to Imperial Headquarters [**Daihon'ei**] as evidence of the success of the Japanese military administration in Sumatra.

Nevertheless, many obstacles and pitfalls lay in the way of implementing the ordinance. These had been anticipated from the moment of drafting. According to the plan for the new judicial system, **Son Hoin** [Village Courts] and **Gun Hoin** [District Courts] were to be set up in all villages and districts of the extensive area which constituted Aceh (remember that it is said to be 1.7 times the size of Taiwan). Moreover, all judges were to be selected from among the people of the respective villages and districts, the total number being about 1,000 if we include reserve staff. These appointments were to be finalized within two months of the day of the public announcement. It was therefore not altogether unreasonable for the uleebalang to have surmised that the Japanese, who were unfamiliar with the population, might be unable to make the appointments. They anticipated that the task of selection would be entrusted to them. Their intention was to emasculate the judicial system. It was evident that, had this happened, the population would have felt totally betrayed, and the Japanese military administration would have lost all its credibility.

At the end of December 1943, when the announcement of the ordinance was imminent, the Japanese had secretly summoned about 20 PUSA leaders from various places to Kutaraja, and asked them to select the judges. They had stipulated three necessary qualifications: each nominee should be (1) trusted by the population, (2) well acquainted with **adat** law, and (3) determined to resist obstruction by uleebalang. The PUSA leaders had accepted the task with enthusiastic cries of 'boleh' [we can].

However, the task was not at all an easy one. The PUSA leaders had only 40 days to compile their lists and return to Kutaraja. Apart from an initial subsidy advanced by the Japanese, they had to meet all costs, including travel expenses. The transportation system in Aceh was indescribably bad. From Kutaraja to the East Coast of Sumatra Residency only a rattletrap tram railway was available - and even this was often out of action. In West Aceh and other regions, old buses were the major means of transportation. No one in Japan could imagine just how dreadful these buses were. Once a bus developed mechanical trouble, it was quite common for it to remain stranded for half a day - and not infrequently for a whole day. Nevertheless, the buses were always packed and consequently one had to book seats often one or two days in advance. If buses or bicycles were available at all one had to consider oneself relatively lucky. In order to visit villages in the valleys between the mountains which traverse Aceh from north to south (and some of the mountains are as high as Mount

Fuji), it was necessary to cross chain upon chain of steep mountains where tigers and leopards lurked.

The PUSA leaders travelled from village to village. Their comrades were to be found hidden in every village without exception. In each village the leaders selected nominees for the position of judge, through secret consultation with their comrades and other local notables. This was the same method which had been adopted earlier by the F Kikan. The PUSA leaders took the opportunity of their selection trip to breathe new life into the bodies set up by the F Kikan.

On the appointed day, the PUSA leaders arrived back in Kutaraja with their lists of nominees. Their faces, smudged with sweat and filth, bore proof of the difficulty of their task. However, they were evidently very satisfied that they had achieved their objectives.

The lists of applicants were first studied by Tuanku Mahmud, Teungku Joenoes, Tengku Daud Beureu'eh and other PUSA leaders, and final selections completed a few days before the announcement of the ordinance. It was decided that the final list should be shown to Teuku Hasan and Teuku Njak Arif for their comments. They were shocked, as they had expected the selection to be done by uleebalang. However, they could not object as they did not know the village candidates. Reluctantly they gave their assent. In this way Acehnese judges were selected who could be expected to respect the will of the people.

Chapter IX: The Kaikyo Hoin [Religious Court]

The uleebalang faction, forestalled in the case of the judicial system, attempted a counterattack on the question of the reform of the religious system. They demanded that their views be reflected in the selection of staff for the **Kaikyo Hoin** (the highest religious court in Aceh) to be established in Kutaraja. They submitted a list of candidates to the Gunseibu. Included were various notorious individuals, of the same ilk as Abdul Djalil of the Bayu affair.* The PUSA faction nominated only the elderly Teungku Haji [Hasballah] Inderapuri. It was

---

* Although Aoki makes no secret of his own prejudices, Teungku Abdul Djalil became a hero for many Acehnese when he began to preach against the barbarous Japanese invaders and the misguided PUSA element which had invited them in. He and over a hundred of his followers and pupils had finally been massacred by the Japanese in November 1942, dying in the heroic tradition of Acehnese Islamic martyrdom. Abdul Djalil, however, belonged to the traditional type of ulama unsympathetic to PUSA, as did the uleebalang nominees to the Kaikyo Hoin.

evident that if we were to accept these nominated candidates, the Kaikyo Hoin would be under the control of the uleebalang and the reform of the religious system would be in name only.

With the consent of the Shu Chokan [Resident], the planning committee replaced half of the nominees with their own selections, including Daud Beureu'eh and Said Abu Bakar, who were especially detested by the uleebalang. As a result, the Kaikyo Hoin staff consisted of two from the conservative faction, two from the neutral faction, and three from the PUSA faction.

A telegram was sent recalling Abu Bakar, who was then in Malaya.* He returned in haste to Kutaraja, having been given permission to travel on a Japanese Army mailboat. Although he was only 26 years old, his knowledge was said to compare with that of other ulama. In view of his contribution to the Japanese Army, it was proper that he should be recalled to Aceh to participate in that reform of the religious system which had been his heart's desire. His return to Aceh gave great hope to former members of the F Kikan, but constituted a serious threat to the uleebalang class.

Chapter X: Conflicts over the Courts

When the names of the judges were published, the people discovered that the judicial system was indeed created for them. As soon as their appointments were official, judges of the Son Hoin began to demand that uleebalang hand over court documents and office buildings. As the buildings in question had always been used for court cases, the Gunseibu had taken it for granted that they would continue to be so used, and had not appropriated any sum in the budget for new ones. The uleebalang reluctantly agreed to hand over the documents, but obstinately refused the use of court buildings. This was the source of a fresh conflict over the new court system.

Buildings for the Son Hoin had to be obtained. In one village the notables contributed money for the purchase of roof materials and bamboo, and the villagers provided voluntary labour service [kinrō hōshi], enabling the construction of a court building in a few days. It was literally a building of 'bamboo pillars and thatch roof'. Nevertheless, the villagers were very pleased with their first court, and hung a placard saying 'Son Hoin' at the entrance. In another village a merchant offered his shop, which until the day before had been the local coffee shop. The facia of the shop was replaced by a

---

* Abu Bakar had withdrawn to Langkawi Island, off northern Malaya, in early 1943, after the attacks from uleebalang rivals and the disappointing reward from the Japanese administration described by Fujiwara above.

sign proclaiming 'SUN HOIN'. Someone who had a typewriter donated it, and those who had desks and chairs brought them along. In this way Son Hoin were quickly established in every village. As paper and pencils were then in very short supply, the Gunseibu was flooded with requests from every village. Gunseibu vehicles loaded with straw paper and pencils bumped over rough roads from village to village.

Despite the poor physical conditions, the villagers were satisfied with the courts. Those appointed as judges worked like cart-horses. In some cases they worked so hard that their main means of livelihood suffered, and they had to be cautioned by the Gunseibu. Through the enthusiastic counsel of these judges, reconciliations were brought about in civil cases which had been languishing for years. Suspects who had been wrongly charged were immediately released, and those who had been accused of minor crimes were given suspended sentences or released on payment of a small fine. The villagers had complete confidence in the judges. Now they were free of the fear of the power formerly wielded by the uleebalang, villagers became bold enough to start asking for the return of land which had been unlawfully taken from them by the uleebalang.

At first the uleebalang could not believe that **orang kampong** (country people), dressed in dirty sarongs and running around barefoot, could manage a court. In due course, however, they were astonished at the unexpected success of the new judicial system. The ever increasing authority of the Son Hoin meant a corresponding decline in their own power. They began a campaign of obstruction.

First the uleebalang began circulating, through their henchmen, disparaging rumours about the Son Hoin along the lines of: 'The judges are all PUSA members'; 'There are even illiterate judges'; and 'They are quite incapable of conducting a trial'. Some members of the Gunseibu who were not familiar with the situation were beguiled by these slanders, but investigation proved them to be completely groundless. It was true that many PUSA members were functioning in the role of judge, but they were trusted by the villagers. Moreover, there were also judges from uleebalang families who were similarly trusted. There certainly existed illiterate judges, but they were indispensable for court trials because they were well acquainted with adat law.

The next step for the uleebalang was to resort to more vicious obstruction. They ordered judges to perform unwarranted military service, so interrupting court work. However, such interruptions were stopped by an order from the Gunseibu exempting judges from such service. The uleebalang then shifted the target of their attack to the villagers, making outrageous demands on them for labour service. They brought charges in court against villagers for violating Japanese orders by failing to perform these services. It was obvious that, were the Son Hoin to punish these villagers, they would lose their authority. The strict letter of the law required that they be punished, but the Son Hoin rejected all such unreasonable accusations.

The uleebalang then propagated the malicious rumour that the Son Hoin did not support the labour service originally ordered by the Japanese Army. Leaders of the F Kikan and PUSA, who had been endeavouring to enlighten and lead the population since the establishment of the courts, took precautions against the danger of being trapped by the provocation of the uleebalang. They urged judges to exercise their discretion and to persuade villagers to perform the labour service for the Japanese army. Thus the slanderous attack of the uleebalang was foiled.

As a final resort the uleebalang had recourse to physical obstruction. They used ruffians to hinder people involved in court cases from entering the court, and to incite riots near the Son Hoin buildings. Village policemen under the control of the uleebalang tacitly condoned such activities. The Son Hoin for its part organized self-defence units with the cooperation of the villagers, to try to prevent this obstruction. The result of all this was, contrary to the expectations of the uleebalang, a strengthening of the organization of the Son Hoin and a sense of unity among the villagers.

Thus, in meeting the opposition challenge, the new judicial system took root among the villagers and firmly established its authority. In addition, the Son Hoin system, backed as it was by F Kikan and PUSA and having an extensive network throughout Aceh, proved an exceedingly useful mechanism when it came to organizing a civil defence corps to meet an Allied attack.

Chapter XI: Until the Final Settlement

The achievements of Abu Bakar in the Kaikyo Hoin were quite remarkable. He immediately hung a large sign proclaiming 'Mahkamah Agama Islam Atjeh' (Islamic Court of Aceh) on the eaves of the building allocated by the Gunseibu. Owing to his youth and physical strength he was able to scour the streets of Kutaraja with such success that a reception centre and treasury could be established. On one occasion the head of a local court,* who was responsible for the Kaikyo Hoin budget, asked Abu Bakar: 'Aren't you in need of money?' He replied smiling: 'Not at all. I will certainly suffer no loss from buying things on credit now, bcause prices will surely rise later'. Abu Bakar was even then displaying a keen business sense. It was therefore not surprising that he played an important role

---

* Presumably Aoki himself.

in the economy of Aceh after Indonesian independence.

The establishment of the Kaikyo Hoin was accomplished by Abu Bakar almost single-handed, since Daud Beureu'eh had complete trust in him, and other **kadi** (Islamic judges) were totally lacking in such talent. Abu Bakar had himself experienced many hardships, and was now more mature than when he had been in conflict with the uleebalang a few years earlier. A cheerful, witty person, he was able to win the hearts of senior ulama quickly. His descent from an Arab family was another factor which aided him in commanding the respect of these elders. Even the exceedingly troublesome Teungku Hasbi* rated Abu Bakar above himself. Hasbi is currently the General Advisor to the Islamic Bureau [of the Ministry of Religion] in the Indonesian central government.

Thanks to the efforts of Daud Beureu'eh and Abu Bakar, popular ulama were selected as judges at the district level. The majority of these were members of PUSA. Among them were Teungku Haji Ujongrimba, famous for his skill at shorthand in the difficult Arabic script, which runs across the page from right to left; and the daring Teungku Hasan, who enjoyed the reputation of being the most skilled sword-fighter in Aceh. Incidentally, the reputation that the Acehnese had for producing good sword-fighters was confirmed by the Japanese corps which put down a peasant attack on a Japanese construction team - an attack caused by excessive demands on the peasants for the construction of an airfield - near Bireuen in May 1945.†

The selection of judges for village Islamic courts was fraught with difficulties, as had been expected. The uleebalang would oppose a nomination, and themselves nominate an unacceptable person. Abu Bakar adhered to the policy of appointing the most suitable and rejecting the unsuitable. The

* Teungku Mohammad Hasbi As-Siddiqy (1904-74) was among the ablest young Acehnese ulama though his modernist education in Surabaya put him outside the mainstream. He was one of the very few Acehnese ulama to join Muhammadiah, which was dominated in Aceh by Minangkabaus and a few prominent uleebalang. Hasbi became Muhammadiah consul for Aceh in 1942, and was often used by the Japanese as a counterweight to PUSA ulama.

† Unlike the followers of Teungku Abdul Djalil above, the '43 martyrs' of Pandraih, in Samalanga, took a heavy toll of the Japanese unit sent against them before the last of the group were gunned down. Skill in the martial arts, frequently combined with a magical invulnerability to bullets and swords, is associated with the Islamic mystical tradition in Aceh as elsewhere in Southeast Asia.

delays in appointing judges created difficulties for peasants anxious to finalize marriage, divorce and inheritance cases. The villagers directed their criticisms against the uleebalang. When the uleebalang refused to change their attitude, judges of the district Islamic court would go to the village and settle the matter. The villagers would laugh at the uleebalang, who lost face through such settlements. The uleebalang, through their obstructionist activities, were ensnared in their own trap.

What the uleebalang feared most was an investigation by the Kaikyo Hoin into **wakaf** [religious endowments] and **baitul-mal** [religious property], both of which they had appropriated for themselves. Abu Bakar instigated such an inquiry with an order to the judges of district Islamic courts. Investigation proved that the uleebalang had appropriated vast areas of land. Abu Bakar demanded that the uleebalang return the land. They, however, had absolutely no intention of complying with such a demand. This was the cause of a fresh confrontation between the Kaikyo Hoin and the uleebalang.

The Acehnese had long looked for the recovery of the wakaf and baitul-mal, which were the symbols of Aceh's prosperity. These funds had the potential to succour the poor and to build schools and hospitals. One of the aims of the Japanese in establishing the Kaikyo Hoin was to gain control of these funds. The Kaikyo Hoin had to pledge itself to carry out that aim. Abu Bakar took the lead in honouring this commitment but, in spite of repeated demands that the uleebalang return the funds, they stubbornly held their ground and continued to refuse. Abu Bakar at last made up his mind.

A mass Islamic meeting was held in the square in front of the great mosque in Kutaraja. Before a large audience, Abu Bakar made a powerful and persuasive speech. He spoke of the glory of Aceh and the destiny of the followers of Islam. At the same time he bitterly attacked the uleebalang who would not return wakaf and baitul-mal and who were not only apostates to the Islamic teaching but great thieves as well. His speech, which was as it were an explosion of the indignation which the masses had long harboured against the uleebalang, won the acclaim of the audience. The uleebalang, seeing their reputation damaged, appealed vehemently to the Japanese. The result was the dismissal of Abu Bakar from his position as judge in the Kaikyo Hoin. This was the sort of man Abu Bakar was.

However, members of the former F Kikan and PUSA did not retreat. They built up a strong sense of unity based on the two judicial systems. Many youths loyal to PUSA joined the **Giyugun** in anticipation of an attack by the Allies.* This also

* For the **Giyugun** (in Java, PETA), the Japanese-trained Indonesian army, see Miyamoto below p.220-34.

constituted a preparation for a confrontation with the uleebalang at some time in the future. Those who did not join the Giyugun strove to establish civil defence corps, with the aid of the Japanese Special Task Team [**Tokumu-han**]. It goes without saying that the prime movers were Abu Bakar and Daud Beureu'eh. The civil defence corps was designed by Lt. Adachi.* He, together with Masubuchi† and Kurai Hajime, a senior administrator (and now prosecuting attorney with the Tokyo District Police Force), was one of the few Japanese in the Gunseibu to defend the F Kikan and PUSA. After Lt. Adachi was transferred to Singapore, Daud Beureu'eh sent more than ten able Acehnese youths to Singapore at the latter's request.

PUSA and the uleebalang were destined to continue to fight each other. The final settlement of the conflict came soon after the Japanese surrender. It was precipitated by the uleebalang faction, which was over-confident of its power. However, it was obvious from the beginning that there was no chance of the uleebalang winning the battle, for they were the enemies of the people. More than 80 leading uleebalang were executed. Aceh was returned to the hands of the people, under the guidance of PUSA leaders. The Acehnese called this final settlement the 'Social Revolution'.

* Lt. (later Capt.) Adachi Takashi was a graduate of the Nakano Intelligence School, trained to prepare for long-term action behind enemy lines. He identified PUSA as the element most likely to wage a long-term struggle against the Allies even in the event of a Japanese retreat, and worked with it for this reason.

† For Masubuchi, see Fujiwara, above, p.11.

Inoue Tetsuro

II) RURAL MOBILIZATION IN EAST SUMATRA
(Bapa Jango: Bapa Djanggut, pp. 80-109)

The Talapeta Period

As soon as I returned from Brastagi to Medan after recovering my health, the Seicho of East Sumatra issued an order appointing me president of a projected institution called **Tokaigan Shu Nomin Renseijo** [Agricultural Training Centre of the East Coast Residency].* The establishment of the Centre was motivated not only by military requirements, but also by the Chokan's friendly concern for me - to reduce the psychological burden which I had so far borne in connection with the **aron** affair and to give me a chance to exert my specialist skills. I accepted the Chokan's recommendation to run the Centre and began the preparations to open it, struggling with the shortages of materials and with transportation difficulties. First, I chose 1,500 hectares of land located 40 kilometres south of Medan, straddling the boundary between the Upper Serdang and Upper Deli districts, and commanding a view of the holy Sibayak mountain on the Karo plateau, with an average altitude 300 metres above sea level. My second concern, based on my principle of using as few Japanese staff as possible, was to search enthusiastically for Indonesian heads to take responsibility for agriculture, cattle breeding, building works, man power and clerical work. I chose as the Indonesian name for the Centre **Taman Latihan Pemuda Tani**, or Talapeta for short.

In the four months following my appointment I largely completed the equipping of such essential facilities as an office, a big Karo-style boarding house, a hall, a big kitchen, roads for vehicles within the farm, seedbed plots, a bulk storage, a storehouse and stock yards. Next, about a hundred capable Indonesians were recruited from the whole of East Sumatra as the first group of trainees. I set the initial goal of the Centre as the attainment of self-sufficiency, and this was to be achieved through cooperation between the trainees and the hundred or so existing agricultural labourers, who were to constitute the core of Talapeta.

The purpose of Talapeta was officially defined as 'the training of able Indonesian youths in rural areas, and education for modern and rational agricultural management in

---

* This authorization was on 5 May 1943.

order to foster agricultural leaders of the peasants or pioneers of intensive farming'. However, it seemed almost impossible in a short period to educate youths who for so long had not been given any moral training, as part of the deliberate policy of the Dutch East Indies government. Nevertheless, my confidence never faltered. I was determined to fulfil my responsibility, moved by a burning passion and that true love and sincerity which a father has for his children.

In order to propagate the aims of Talapeta I established 'Five Vows of Talapeta', which were recited by the trainees every morning. The vows had roughly the following meanings in Japanese:

1. We understand the sacredness and the value of agriculture and maintain our pride as peasants.
2. We work to our utmost.
3. We live with ideals and hope, and study to improve ourselves constantly.
4. We honour heaven, we give thanks to the earth, and we love mankind.
5. We devote ourselves to our fatherland.

At the same time I laid down 'Four Gratitudes of Talapeta', which were recited every night before the trainees went to bed.

1. Let us see the sun shine with gratitude.
2. Let us work with gratitude.
3. Let us eat even plain fare with gratitude.
4. Let us sleep with gratitude.

I still felt one thing missing - we did not have a 'Talapeta Song' yet. After laborious composition, I produced the following:

Born at the dawn of the great age of the Emperor
Let us construct our fatherland.
Ah, flying in the sky, flying in the sky.
The hope of the development of Asia is shining!
This is the time to devote ourselves to agricultural morality.

In the garden full of flowers and moonlight,
Our ideals are blooming.
Let us test our ability.
Ah, we stand on the hill of light
Holding aloft the banner proclaiming for our nation
'Prosperity, prosperity!'

This text was beautifully translated into Indonesian by Murni, who was happy to cooperate. Then, a musician living in Medan composed a melody for it, and so the 'Talapeta Song' was completed.

Again, realizing that our primitive method of rice-husking (stamping by five men in a row) did not have a suitable accompanying song, I tentatively wrote the text of a 'Rice-Husking Song of Talapeta' in the hope of helping to cultivate an aesthetic sense.

Gather around when you hear the **tong tong**,
For this is Talapeta, the land of rice.

The ears of rice are growing well and this year will be a bumper crop.
A hundred girls are working, their necklets beads of sweat.

Let's husk the rice of Talapeta
To the colour of the girls of Karo.

Rather than the colour of the girls of Karo,
Hull it to a colour like the name of our mountain, Sibayak.

War wages outside, but we husk rice,
The hateful ... under the pounder.

Husk as much rice as possible -
Mt Sibayak is watching us from above the clouds.

We must finish hulling by the time
The clouds disappear and the sun shines forth.

This Japanese text was also translated by Murni into beautiful Indonesian, and set to a tune reminiscent of a lullaby. The trainees loved to sing this song while they worked.

In the course of time, **padi**, tapioca, sweet potatoes, onions, beans, vegetables, pasture grass, cotton, bananas, papayas and pineapples were planted. A shed, a stud horse enclosure, henhouses, a goatshed and a big pig-breeding shed were also gradually built. All of these were made possible by the sincere work of the Talapeta family - the staff, students and the **romusha**.

Our bright opening ceremony was held on a day chosen for its auspicious qualities, about the time when the rice, 20 hectares of which had been planted as an initial experimental crop, began to lengthen.*

Present on that day from the Japanese side were the Shu Chokan, high-ranking officials of the Gunseikambu, those involved in the farm, and representatives of the news media; and from the Indonesian side, five sultans and their relatives, advisers to the Japanese administration, educators, those connected with the farm, and journalists. The most remarkable feature of the occasion was not the attendance of the outstand-

* 29 August 1943.

ing journalist, Adinegoro,* the political sphinx Dr Mansur,† or the Japanese female novelist Koyama Itoko,# but rather the fact that even Iwan Siregar accepted the Japanese invitation to the ceremony, in the full knowledge that he would be in the company of his most bitter opponents. (Iwan had been released eight months earlier, through an amnesty to celebrate the 2600th anniversary of the foundation of the Japanese nation,+ and since then had been working as an adviser to the Special Higher Police Division of the Police Department.

As indicated in the words 'the garden full of flowers and moonlight' in the 'Talapeta Song', we were blessed with a good environment. Every morning and evening we could see the beautiful, proud volcano, Sibayak, and we fell into the habit of calling it 'Bapak' [Father], as it symbolized our spirit of reflection and self-correction. Directly opposite 'Bapak' was our **Bukit Cahaya** [Hill of Light], on the peak of which stood an observatory we had made. We could obtain a bird's-eye view of the whole farm, which spread over 1,500 hectares and included various facilities and fields. Furthest away was the big pig-breeding shed and its attached facilities; then the goatshed, the cowshed, a barnyard full of manure, several rows

---

* Adinegoro was the pen name adopted by Djamaluddin, born in Sawahlunto (West Sumatra) in 1903. He was the most professionally qualified Indonesian newspaperman of his day, having studied journalism in Wurzburg and Munich (1926-30). He edited the leading Indonesian-language daily in Sumatra, **Pewarta Deli** (Medan), from 1931, and the Japanese-controlled **Kita-Sumatora-Sinbun** from 1943.

† Dr Tengku Mansur (1897-1955) was a younger son of the former Sultan of Asahan (East Sumatra). He studied medicine in Batavia and Leiden, and practised in Sulawesi and Java before returning to Medan in the mid-1930s. A political conservative, he was the first President of the student movement Jong Sumatra (1917-19), and later led the regionalist political movement Persatuan Sumatra Timur (1938-41) and the Dutch-backed federal State of East Sumatra (NST) (1947-50).

Koyama Itoko (1901-) made her mark when her first novel **Kaimonkyō** (Kaimon Bridge) was awarded a prize by the women's magazine **Fujin Kōron** in 1933. She was active in literary circles from 1935 to 1944 and became known for her works on social problems. In 1950 she was awarded the Naoki Prize for her novel **Shikkō Yūyo** (Probation).

+ This festival, Kigen-setsu, fell on 11 February 1943. It commemorates the supposed founding in 660 BC of the Japanese nation by Emperor Jimmu.

of henhouses; then, a little removed, the big dining hall and the bulk store; while immediately below one was the office building, the storehouse and a drying shed. In front of the office building was a Minangkabau-style bell tower which I named **Lonceng Dadung** [The Bell of Happy Singing]. A little to the right were the staff residences and the big seedbed field. At the immediate foot of the 'Hill of Light' were the big dormitory and lecture hall, with their elegant Karo-style roofs. It was a beautiful landscape which we never wearied of seeing.

Sometimes tigers which had killed pigs were trapped, rock snakes which had swallowed goats and become incapable of moving were easily caught, or big lizards which had been trying to catch the chickens found themselves chased by the dogs instead. Far from disturbing our work, these events added pleasure to it.

It was at the end of December, when we had almost finished harvesting and the Talapeta family was busy practising their dances for the harvest festivals, that I had a strange long-distance telephone call.

'Hallo. Hallo. Sini Mak Murni bicara (This is Murni's mother speaking).' It was indeed the familiar voice of Saniam, Murni's mother.

'Is that **tuan**? I just want to give **tuan** quickly a message from Murni: "I am now staying in Room 5 of the maternity ward of Medan Municipal Hospital, as the mother of **Anak Daitoa** [a son of Greater East Asia] called Abdi. Perhaps you would like to come and see me after getting permission from Iwan according to Indonesian custom". This is all I want to say. Have you understood me? Well then, goodbye.'

I was completely taken aback by the news. Unless it was some kind of lie or joke, it was a real bolt from the blue. I had never been told that Murni was pregnant, nor had I even imagined it myself. Moreover, when I had met her to ask her to translate the 'Talapeta Song', I had not noticed anything. At the opening ceremony of Talapeta a short time before, I had even asked Iwan whether Murni was ill because she had not accompanied him... Recalling how Murni had once murmured to me that the head of the Medan Municipal Hospital had diagnosed Iwan as having a physiological defect, I had a gloomy sense of foreboding as I realized that someone else must be involved. 'But then...', I thought, 'couldn't Iwan's six months' detention in prison have brought about a change in his body chemistry?'

Luckily, I was planning to go to Medan on duty that day, so I immediately ordered the chauffeur to prepare a car in order to set out earlier and visit the hospital. On arriving in Medan I first visited Iwan, who was fortunately at home. As my visit happened to coincide with the Islamic New Year, we exchanged New Year's greetings according to the custom. I had to say, 'Happy New Year. Please forgive all my misunderstandings and mistakes in word and deed over the last year'. After these formalities I asked him, as if I knew nothing, 'How is your wife?'

Iwan replied smiling, 'Ah... My wife? To tell the truth she gave birth to a boy last night, and so is still in the Municipal Hospital'. However, his smiling face looked somewhat vacant to me.

As a matter of formality I expressed surprise and offered my congratulations. In response to my inquiry whether I might visit her at the hospital, he answered lightly, 'As you like, **tuan**'.

Before long I was in Murni's room at the hospital, my hands full of lilies I had bought at a flower shop on the way.

It was Saniam who opened the door to see me. And Murni... she was lying quietly in bed, her face pale but divinely pure. I put the white lilies in a vase beside the bed and approached her softly. All I could manage to say was, 'Congratulations'. Murni was unexpectedly lively. She sat up in bed, turned around and removed a piece of gauze to show me a soundly sleeping baby. The boy was fair-skinned, with clear-cut features, and he did not have frizzled hair like Iwan. I was just beginning to think how much he resembled his mother when Murni opened her mouth for the first time.

She murmured, 'Abdi! A good name? One of my two aspirations - a son of Greater East Asia? Don't you think his eyebrows look like somebody's?'

I was at a loss how to answer, but she persisted, 'I became the mother of this boy in the full knowledge that I was dealing with fire'.

I wondered at the time why she said such a peculiar thing. My thoughts were in turmoil. I felt like a miserable insect struggling in a spider's silken web. Just then a nurse came around the room. Taking advantage of this opportunity, I asked to be excused and left the room.

Meantime, the young men of Talapeta were steadily developing into sturdy, diligent, wise and sensible rural youths, as described in the 'Five Vows'. However, we had only too short a time to give them lectures on academic subjects. One of the reasons for this was that I had been entrusted by the Chokan with supervising the **Tokaigan Shu Kaijo Jikeidan** [East Sumatra Self-Defence Marine Corps] in addition to my job with Talapeta. The development of the war in the latter half of 1944 was placing a serious strain on security in East

Sumatra, which faced the Melaka Straits. The infiltration of Allied spies and special task forces was intensifying all the time. This was also the time when unidentified submarines began to approach very close to the shore and to fire at Indonesian fishing boats. The constant surveillance against these activities was hardly within the capacity of the Kempeitai and police forces alone. The relevant Japanese authorities naturally placed ever greater demands on the Corps, and insisted that it be strengthened. The **Kaijo** (as the Indonesians called the Corps) relied entirely on the voluntary services of young fishermen, who received not a cent of financial support from the Japanese Gunseibu. It was under the leadership of Iwan Siregar, a sworn friend of mine, and it had a surprising coherence and solidarity. Because of its members' total lack of training for intelligence and counter-espionage activities, however, I had to help them in these fields, and this tended to curtail my involvement in Talapeta.

Once again I indulged in song-writing - this time the 'Song of Kaijo'. Again this was translated into Indonesian by Murni - as a present to the members.

Dawn breaks in Sumatra,
Over the sea of hope.
The people are all prosperous,
The sun is rising.
Come to Kaijo Jikeidan!
The Melaka Strait is calling us today!
Let us go to the Melaka Strait. (I omit the remainder.)

The young men to whom I gave this song were kept very busy training hard during their spare time, both morning and evening. The pressure worsened in proportion to the increased reliance of the Japanese Army upon the Kaijo, especially after the Kaijo assumed responsibility for placing a cordon of fences in the water as part of our coastal defences.

Kenkoku Teishintai (KTT)

The beginning of 1945

Although on the one hand the Kaijo was becoming increasingly a useful and effective instrument through its baptism in blood and its incessant training, on the other the counter-espionage activity of the Special Higher Police Division of the East Sumatra Police Department was not producing a remarkable success. This was one of the Chokan's headaches, along with the prevalence of spies and of enemy special task forces. I could not remain indifferent to this and I asked the Chokan's opinion on the feasibility of establishing a secret counter-espionage organization from among the ablest members of the

Kaijo, after first having sounded out Iwan on how much confidence he had in such a proposal.

Since by that time the Chokan had great confidence in Iwan, he immediately agreed with my proposal. I immediately consulted with Iwan, and our discussions bore fruit in the successful establishment of a special counter-espionage organization which was to operate through an elaborate cell system and rigid discipline, recruiting leaders of the former Gerindo party and able members of the Kaijo, and dividing the whole Residency into eight parts. In this way, the organization which we called 'B operation' began its active work. The 'B operation' lived up to expectations, and secretly extended its activities as far north as the northern coast of Sumatra. It rendered distinguished service, such as the elimination of an anti-Japanese group of Malayan Chinese, the annihilation of a 'Secret Club to Support the Allied Landing in Sumatra', and the uncovering of spy activities for the enemy by an estate owner from a neutral country. In comparison, the Special Higher Police Division of East Sumatra had no remarkable achievements to show. The Chokan once summoned the head of the Division to reprimand him. This gave rise to a subtle worsening of relations between Iwan, who had functioned as an adviser to the Special Higher Police Division, and its head. Iwan came to dislike attending the office, grew depressed, and tended to seclude himself at home.

One day while working at Talapeta, I had a telephone call from the Chokan, who asked me to come to Medan immediately. I reached Medan in one hour's hectic drive. When I arrived at the Chokan's residence, he as usual offered me a high seat, while himself taking a lower seat, and in addition, on this occasion he personally poured me a glass of the best quality Bordeaux wine.

He began, 'To be frank, the Chief of Staff complained to me about ten days ago that the Giyugun were becoming increasingly unreliable. By chance I received an emergency order this morning from the Gunseikan [of the 25th Army] which confirms the validity of the Chief of Staff's complaint. You will get a chance to read the complete text tomorrow at the office. Anyway, its essence is that, in order to prepare for a possible landing of the Allies in Sumatra, we should organize and train a secret commando corps [**Yugeki Butai**] in East Sumatra. This would be quite distinct from the existing Indonesian corps such as the Giyugun and Heiho, and would have its own independent status and capacity to pursue operations in cooperation with the Japanese Army'.

'They've left it to the eleventh hour, haven't they?' I replied.

The Chokan went on, 'After thinking over the issue, I have come to the conclusion that the quickest and most practical course is to leave the matter in the hands of Iwan under your supervision, since he has already exhibited his abilities in relation to the Kaijo and the "B operation". I invited you in to hear your opinion of this idea'.

'I think your plan is quite reasonable', I said, 'in view of Iwan's popularity among the people of North Sumatra, the peasants in particular, and his experience in the Kaijo and "B operation". If the plan were realized it would rekindle some inspiration in Iwan, who has been depressed recently about his relations with the Police Department head. So I would urge you to implement the plan in the way you suggest'.

'Well then', said the Chokan, 'could you visit him now and ask how he feels about this. But first I must make clear the conditions for this operation. First, the business should be carried out secretly (it is not even necessary to reveal what is going on to the Division authorities or the Kempeitai at this point). Second, the focus should be on quality not quantity. Third, we should not offend the sensibilities of the sultans. Fourth, the organization should have no political implications. Fifth, it should concentrate on training and education'.

'Yes, I understand. I should be able to report back to you in an hour', I replied.

It goes without saying that this proposal was eagerly accepted by Iwan and his group. Soon the Chokan officially but secretly appointed me Commander-in-Chief of the secret commando corps, and Iwan Deputy Commander-in-Chief. Everything else was left to me and Iwan.

I felt it necessary to give the commando corps a definite name. In view of the fact that what was to become the Committee for the Preparation of Indonesian Independence* had already been recognized, that a name is very important for the morale of members, and so forth, I decided to call it 'Kenkoku Teishintai' [Unit Dedicated to Upbuilding the Country] (KTT). The next step was to establish the principles on which the unit would be based. After due consideration of Indonesian history, religion and ideology, especially the ideologies of leaders and youth groups, I adopted: 1. piety (**ketuhanan**), 2. humanity

---

* Since the Panitia Persiapan Kemerdekaan Indonesia (Committee for the Preparation of Indonesian Independence)(see below p.295) was not decided upon until the end of July nor announced until 7 August 1945, this remark presumably refers to the Badan Penyelidik Kemerdekaan Indonesia (Body for the Investigation of Indonesian Independence), whose formation was announced in Jakarta on 1 March 1945. Its membership was restricted to Java.

(**kemanusiaan**), 3. democracy (**demokrasi**), and 4. social justice
(**keadilan social**).* I demanded that all members be not only
men of absolute integrity and imbued with a spirit of self-
sacrifice, but also devoted to the pursuit of peace and
prosperity for the population as a whole. The four principles
also reflected my expectation that Kenkoku Teishintai, though
obviously an organization aiming at Indonesian independence,
must realize that only Japan could give Indonesia the opportunity for independence, and must face the Allies on the basis
of the mutual interests of Japan and Indonesia.

Then I had to decide on staff, which was easy because I
had only to choose from among members of Iwan's group, as shown
below.

The next step was the registration and organization of
the KTT members, both of which could be done easily and quickly
because there was already in the coastal area a total of about
10,000 men in the Kaijo, a sophisticated corps; while in the
mountain areas I could make use of the former Gerindo party.
After registering them all, I divided the 30,000 KTT members
into two groups; the Mokotai [Wild Tiger Corps] embracing those
members in the mountain areas, and the Hiryutai [Flying Dragon
Corps], embracing those in the coastal areas. In addition I
organized the Junkyotai [Martyr Corps], composed of fanatical
Muslims. The Indonesian names for the Wild Tiger Corps, Flying
Dragon Corps, and Martyr Corps were respectively, Barisan
Harimau Liar, abbreviated as BHL, Barisan Naga Terbang, and
Barisan Sabilullah.

After completing the organization of the KTT, we had to
commence immediately the education and training of members.
Although I intended to establish a tough training programme for
about 400 key officers with ranks between platoon leader and
battalion leader, even the selection of a training place, for
instance, required a lot of care, because of the Chokan's
condition that the whole plan had to be 'top secret'.
Fortunately, as I was supervising Talapeta at the time, I did
not hesitate to use its premises as the training ground of the
KTT, since it was an isolated area and had suitable facilities
for both large scale drilling and training in guerilla warfare.

* These principles closely follow four of the five **sila**
proposed as the basis of Indonesian national identity in
Sukarno's famous speech to the BKPI on 1 June 1934, and later
canonized as Indonesia's national philosophy, the Pancasila.
Nationalism is the one principle omitted by Inoue. Unless
these principles were defined towards the end of KTT's brief
history, they must have preceded Sukarno's speech - perhaps
because both drew on a common pool of ideas within the
nationalist movement, for example, Taman Siswa's Panca-
Dharma.

ORGANIZATION OF THE KENKOKU TEISHINTAI

Position in KTT	Name	Status before and during the Japanese Occupation	Functions during the Period of Independence Struggle
COMMANDER-IN-CHIEF	Myself		
DEPUTY COMMANDER-IN-CHIEF	Iwan Siregar	Gerindo and F-movement leader	Deputy Minister of Defence, head of the Association for Independence in North Sumatra
CHIEF OF STAFF	Suleiman	Deputy Leader of Gerindo, poet and dramatist	Deputy Resident of East Sumatra, a member of PNI North Sumatra, commander of Barisan Harimau Liar or Mokotai, President of the Young Fishermen's Association
VICE-CHIEF OF STAFF	Mohammad* Kasim	Gerindo member	Mayor of Siantar
STAFF OFFICER FOR STRATEGY	Abdullah† Jusuf	Gerindo member	Chief of the Propaganda Section
STAFF OFFICER FOR INTELLIGENCE	Nulung# Sirait	Gerindo member, head of Kimboshi Gekidan [Golden Star Drama Company]	Secretary-General of Young Fishermen's Association
STAFF OFFICER	Mansur	Gerindo member	(in Java?)
ADJUTANT	Anwar Darma	Gerindo member	Secretary-General of labour union in East Sumatra

* Mohammad Kasim was born in 1901, the son of an Islamized Toba Batak who had become a religious teacher in Medan. After attending a two-year course for primary teachers, Kasim went into retailing, eventually having his own small shop first in Pematang Siantar, and from 1935 in Kisaran (Asahan). He took over from Adam Malik the leadership of Partindo in Siantar (1933-34), and later led the Gerindo branch in Kisaran.

† Born in Medan in 1915, Abdullah Jusuf was the younger brother of Mohammad Kasim. He studied at the English-medium Methodist School in Medan and at a nationalist 'Sekolah Republikein' in Bandung before returning to Siantar in 1930 to work as a trader, journalist and legal agent. He led the Siantar Gerindo branch from its inception in late 1937. He became the Simelungun PNI leader after 1950.

Nulung Sirait's power base was among the fishermen of Asahan, where his Serikat Nelayan Merdeka (Free Fishermen's Association) was a powerful force during the early revolution.

201

While I was engaged in this work, the general situation in North Sumatra was constantly fluctuating in response to changes in the war situation in the Pacific:

1. In spite of the frantic counter-measures of the Kempeitai, the police and the Kaijo, the spying activity of the Allies was still continuing.

2. Either through their own conceit or because they took advantage of the ever-worsening Japanese war position, the anti-Japanese words and actions of Giyugun members in various places grew steadily worse.*

3. In North Aceh, attacks by the people on Japanese units took place frequently, arising from religious issues, voluntary labour service, and taxation.†

4. The German Ambassador to Tokyo, Otto, visited Medan by submarine, and had secret talks with Chokan N[akashima].

5. The Allies commenced air raids upon North Sumatran cities such as Medan and Pangkalan Brandan.#

6. The Kempeitai was preparing measures to be taken against pro-Dutch and pro-sultan elements.

7. A start was made on the conscription of Japanese civilians in North Sumatra and the military training of Japanese civilians attached to the military administration. At the same time, a plan to fortify Medan was put into action.

8. The activities of Indonesian political leaders and of the Committee for the Preparation of Indonesian Independence were becoming ever more prominent.

Shortly before noon on 20 March 1945, the big square at Talapeta near the Bukit Barisan mountain range was filled with about 400 key officers of the KTT who had gathered there secretly from all over North Sumatra, each in his own dress,

* These tensions climaxed in two acts of mutiny, by two Acehnese platoons led by T.A. Hamid in November 1944, and by an East Sumatran Company near Siantar led by Hopman Sitompoel in July 1945. The latter episode is described from the Japanese side in Tomon Hiroshi, **Murudeka** (Tokyo, Ōgi Shuppan, 1975).

† The most serious of these attacks was the so-called 'Pandraih rebellion' in Samalanga (North Aceh) in May 1945, in which many Japanese as well as Acehnese died.

Allied aircraft attacked Belawan Deli, the port of Medan, on 20 December 1944, and various other centres, including Pangkalan Brandan, on 4 January 1945.

having traversed mountain and sea to get there. Among them were all sorts of Malays, young and old, Karo Bataks, Toba Bataks, Javanese, Mandailings, and so forth. When they had all fallen into line, about 200 Talapeta members in simple uniforms entered and also lined up behind them to share the delight of initiating the first KTT training session. Soon it was noon. The 'Bell of Joy' reverberated over the forests, the plains, the farm lands, the people and the cattle as if to announce, 'Awake'. Its solemn echoes were wafted gently on the breeze to the holy mountain Sibayak.

The inaugural ceremony ended with a calm closing speech by the poet and Chief of Staff, Suleiman. Here I must refer to two striking events which occurred during the ceremony, as I feel obliged to try to convey the deep emotion of those who were taking part. The first was the raising of the new red and white flag [the **merah putih**], the national flag of Greater Indonesia, after the Japanese Rising Sun Flag; and the other was the singing in unison of the Indonesian national anthem after the Japanese 'Kimi ga yo'. It is beyond my ability to describe the way the dramatic scene affected the Indonesian soldiers and students. As they embraced each other in a touching demonstration of surprised and delighted sentiment, it seemed as though, had the occasion permitted it, they would have broken down in tears.

Whether or not they knew that these generous gifts to Indonesia - neither of which had been seen before in North Sumatra* at least - had been due to the daring resolution of their Commander-in-Chief as well as the Talapeta leader, they looked at me with eyes full of gratitude.

The KTT training began the day after the ceremony. The training, consisting of lectures and military exercises, was allocated as follows:

	Instructors	Subjects
Lectures	Commander-in-Chief (myself)	Strategy for guerilla warfare, peasant spirit, handy fertilizer methods...
	Deputy Commander-in-Chief (Iwan)	Ethics, applied psychology...

* This is puzzling, as the flying of the Indonesian flag had been officially authorized in Sumatra since celebrations of 'gratitude for the promise of independence' in early October 1944.

Chief of Staff (Suleiman)	Indonesian history, history of Indonesian struggle, politics, international affairs.
Exercises Commander-in-Chief (myself) assisted by Sgt. Agura	Basic combat training, guerilla warfare, agricultural routines.
Murni	First aid drill, cooking.

(I forgot to say that one platoon of Karo girls had joined the training, and was led by Murni, who had come there together with Iwan and Abdi Anak Daitoa.)

At about 5 o'clock every morning, when it is still dark in Sumatra, we could hear the lusty singing of the 'Laskar [militia] Song' echoing from a hill across the valley. Iwan, Murni and I stood on the verandah of my residence. The singing gradually sounded closer. It came from 400 KTT officers marching, half naked and with bamboo spears on their shoulders, towards the Talapeta parade ground for the morning gathering. When they reached the top of the valley, they suddenly began trotting down the slope, passing in front of their leaders who applauded them from the verandah. Soon, we heard from the square the cheerful sound of the recitation of the 'Four Deaths of KTT'.

1. We are ready to die for Indonesian independence!
   (Kami bersedia mati untuk kemerdekaan Indonesia!)
2. We are ready to die for holy ideals!
   (Kami bersedia mati untuk cita-cita yang suci!)
3. We are ready to die for the happiness and prosperity of the people!
   (Kami bersedia mati untuk kebahagian serta kemakmuran rakyat!)
4. We are ready to die for responsible leaders!
   (Kami bersedia mati untuk pemimpin yang bertanggung-jawab!)

Normally, after the morning gathering, they practised handling bamboo spears for half an hour as a morning exercise. Then they ran back to the hill, across the valley, where warm bean gruel awaited them, prepared by members of the Karo girls' platoon.

While they were thus engaged, we seated ourselves at the table for a light breakfast. I would ask the cook for fresh milk, soft-boiled eggs and papaya - all of which were produced by Talapeta - as well as specially prepared green-bean gruel. I did not neglect to order a cup of strong coffee, which was indispensable for Iwan. Abdi Anak Daitoa was at a most mischievous stage by this time. He was particularly attached to 'uncle', as he called me. At meals he insisted in sitting on my knee. However, he could not be still even for five minutes during meal times. Sliding down to the floor and picking up a bamboo spear, he would show us a splendid manoeuvre with it. He would usually take on Moppy, our pet dog, and chase it around the table, shouting, 'eigh, yah', copying the adults. Like one of his nicknames, Anak Tidak Nangis [child who does not cry], he was really a tough boy and never did cry even when he tumbled down. As I looked at Abdi I had the same impression as at the hospital in Medan shortly after he was born, that Abdi had no resemblance to Iwan. Apart from his nose and mouth, which resembled Murni's, Abdi looked as if he had Chinese or Japanese blood in him.

Presently we heard the cheerful sound of the 'Laskar Song' once more from the hill across the valley. As this was a sign that the KTT officer training would soon start, we had to get ourselves ready to lead them. Even our Anak Daitoa toddled after us, as a mascot of the illustrious KTT, dressed in a dignified if somewhat comical manner.

In the course of the training, which became ever more intense, the teachers and those who were taught, the trainers and trainees, were as if fused into one by their enthusiasm. Around the 'Hill of Light' the shouting of the trainees echoed forth from morning till evening, and sometimes even till midnight. The labourers and pupils of Talapeta made an effort to provide the KTT officers with sufficient food, and the platoon of Karo Batak girls devoted itself unstintingly to the task of satisfying the officers' stomachs.

In this way the combined fighting spirit of 700 men was simmering at the foot of the Bukit Barisan range, ready to destroy in the name of Indonesian independence whatever enemy might come forth.

The KTT developed far beyond my expectations. Initially its total membership was projected as about 30,000, but it expanded to as many as 50,000.

I had made a secret agreement with the Division that it would provide us with trench mortars, heavy machineguns and so forth, if the need arose. Given these factors, it was impossible to keep the KTT secret from the public. The upper-class Indonesians, the sultans in particular, had an unfounded fear of the KTT. These people eventually pushed the Kyodo Boeidan [Fatherland Defence Corps], which was then under their control, into confrontation with the KTT, resulting in frequent collisions between the two parties. In spite of the attempts Iwan and I made to reconcile the two parties, we did not succeed, and the matter came to the knowledge of the Chokan.

The Chokan warned me to re-check the quality of KTT members and to prevent the occurrence of any further undesirable incidents.

One evening, a meeting of KTT leaders was held at Iwan's place on Mangalaan Street, in connection with the Chokan's warning to the KTT. The Indonesians present, especially Chief of Staff Suleiman, seemed to be distinctly dissatisfied by the Chokan's warning. Late at night, after the meeting, as I was getting into the car to drive myself back to Talapeta, I found a note from Murni fastened to the car door-handle. It read,

> My beloved Tetsu,*
> Iwan and his group have been growing increasingly dissatisfied with the Japanese authorities. Also, the influence of Iwan's group over the people is far greater than you realize. I think you should consider the implications of these two facts, and give Iwan an appropriate position in the administration, in order to prevent a very possible rebellion by the KTT. Murni.
> (From now on I shall drop the title of **tuan** when addressing you.)

The Japanese Surrender and After

On the afternoon of 15 August 1945, I received a telephone call from the Chokan. I set out as usual for Medan, and found the Chokan sitting alone in the huge marble-lined dining room. He looked very weary. As I sat down facing him, he said brusquely, 'We are finally defeated'. I could read in his voice the calm resignation which comes after going through violent emotions, and also the Chokan's tendency to self-deprecation. Even though it was not entirely unexpected, I felt shattered.

The Chokan spoke again, 'I feel I can now say that I have been opposed to the Greater East Asia War ever since I became acquainted with Tojo and the nature of Japanese national power. Moreover, I have been comparing Japanese and American strategy for the past year and have speculated that Japan would be defeated. Anyway, there is no point in complaining now. Everything is finished'.

There seemed to be tears in his eyes. I simply stared at him speechlessly.

'I have put you to great trouble in the past. I can well understand your feelings, as Talapeta and KTT are just about to

---

* 'Tetsu' is an abbreviated form of the author's given name, Tetsuro, and would be used only by someone very intimate. The implication is that Murni was now taking the liberties of a lover.

launch their full activities. But this is our fate. We must
be circumspect and conduct ourselves as true **samurai** to the
last'.

'Yes', I answered clearly for the first time.

'With the Japanese surrender, Talapeta should of course be
closed down, and the KTT dissolved. I will entrust these
matters entirely to you, to resolve as you see fit. However,
please bear in mind that a public announcement to the
Indonesians of the cessation of hostilities will not be made
until the 20th of this month at the earliest, so do not discuss
it with anybody till then'.

'Yes, I understand fully. Please take care of yourself,
too, Your Excellency...'.

After I had withdrawn from the Chokan's official residence
and was about to start my car, a violent squall suddenly broke
as if to mock me. I started the car without knowing where I
was going, feeling as though I was doing battle with the rain
hitting the windshield of my car. I was not in Talapeta or
Medan for the next three or four days. Nobody could have known
what I was doing or thinking during that period. And I,
myself, still do not want to talk about it.*

23 August 1945

The closing ceremony of Talapeta. All those who had been
connected with Talapeta wept with sorrow at parting from each
other. I gave farewell gifts of clothes, agricultural imple-
ments, cattle, seeds and so forth to all the staff, trainees,
and labourers of Talapeta - the only consolation I could offer
them. The trainees were to return home, the staff were to
remain for a while to wind up affairs, and the majority of
labourers were to become part of the Gunung Rintis farm.

25 August 1945

At precisely midnight I ordered the official dissolution
of the KTT in the big hall of its Medan headquarters. All of
the hundred or so present were crying, including company and
battalion commanders. I distributed clothes to all the

---

* Zainu'ddin, 'The Japanese Occupation', in **Indonesian
Nationalism and Revolution: Six First Hand Accounts**,
Melbourne, Monash University Faculty of Education, 1969, p.9,
relates that he was summoned back to Talapeta to be told of
the Japanese surrender on 18 August - perhaps the end of
Inoue's three-day hiatus. Subsequently the failure to obtain
Japanese arms to enable the KTT group to fight the returning
Dutch was the subject of much criticism within the group.
Opinions differ as to whether this resulted from a failure of
will on Inoue's part or Siregar's.

207

members. Vice-Chief of Staff Iwan could not stop his frenzied weeping. As for me, I went off to roam around the city, drinking.

After the dissolution of Talapeta and the KTT, I spent most of my time moping around at Iwan's place or at the houses of other friends in Medan. Iwan himself had not got over the shock even a week after the announcement of the Japanese surrender, and still tended to break down at the slightest provocation, such as visitors trying to console him or the final fly-past by the Japanese airforce. However, Murni's response to the Japanese surrender showed a sharp contrast with Iwan's. Although she looked somewhat shocked when I brought the news of the Japanese surrender to their home, she never wept publicly. She seemed to devote all her energies to looking after Iwan, who had become a silly 'crybaby'.

One day when Iwan looked to be in a good mood, I asked him, 'Iwan, what are you planning to do now? I am afraid that the Allied Forces will land in Sumatra sooner or later, so you can't afford to take things easy.'

He replied, 'At the moment all I know is that I will certainly be arrested by the Allies as soon as they land. I do not know what to do.'

I chided him, 'In contrast to the Japanese who have in effect lost their fatherland, you are a **pemimpin** (leader) who is needed by the Indonesian people. You should therefore respond to the expectations of the people by showing courage yourself. As for the urgent matter of self-preservation, you must find a sensible solution as quickly as possible.'

'Could you take me to Japan now?'

'No, that is impossible because we have no transportation. Such requests have been out of the question ever since the Allies won control of the air and sea. Don't you have any place you want to go, apart from Japan? If I were you, I would go to Jakarta without hesitation, and hide myself among the masses in the capital city. I believe Jakarta is a much safer place to hide yourself than the mountain villages of Sumatra. In addition, you can keep in contact with your Sumatran comrades in Jakarta.'

'You may be right,' Iwan replied. 'I will discuss the matter with my wife.'

In this way, Iwan's family and Suleiman decided to go to Jakarta.

I gave Iwan and Murni all the help I could, but they still had many preparations of their own for the trip. As there were three days left before their departure, I 'borrowed' Abdi Anak Daitoa from them and took him to Talapeta, since I wanted to see how Talapeta had changed. As we drove along, Abdi started to remember the pigs and goats at Talapeta, and mimicked the sounds of these animals, which brought a laugh from me and the driver. When we arrived at Talapeta, I found no vestige of its former prosperity: wild grasses covered the fields and roads; the empty cattle sheds looked really ugly and desolate; and a middle-aged clerk was alone in the dark office, writing something. Abdi and I were welcomed by the cooks and servants who, happily, were still there. I decided to stay at Talapeta that night with Abdi for old time's sake.

At dinner that night Abdi's favourite foods were on the table. Abdi ate to his heart's content on his 'uncle's' knee, along with Moppy who was allowed to join the repast on that special occasion. Then Abdi asked me 'ning ning', which meant to play the piano. He soon tired of that and began to play with a bamboo spear, running around the spacious dining room in pursuit of Moppy. Then, apparently worn out, he came and clung to my knees saying, 'Uncle, boboh. Uncle, boboh', indicating that he was sleepy. I cuddled him in my arms and went out to the moonlit garden. It was late enough for an ordinary boy to start crying because he missed his mother, but Abdi did not seem to be missing his mother. As he lay peacefully in my arms for quite a long time, I looked down at him expecting to find him already asleep, but his eyes were wide open. Suddenly he said, 'Uncle, tong, tong. Uncle, tong tong.' I immediately understood what he meant. He wanted me to sing the 'Rice Husking Song of Talapeta'. This was definite evidence that Abdi was accustomed to going to sleep in Murni's arms listening to this song. I began singing slowly, first in Japanese and then in Indonesian.

Gather around when you hear the **tong tong,**
For this is Talapeta, the land of rice.

Tong, tong, tong ... mari kearah tumbukan padi.
Inilah Talapeta, dusun sumbernya padi.

Before I realized it Abdi was sound asleep. But I went on singing, indulging myself in a sentimentality which only the moon could understand.

Four days later the time had come for Iwan's party to depart. At 3 a.m. they slipped like phantoms from Iwan's house on Mangalaan Street in Medan. I intended seeing them as far as the boundary [between the East Coast and Tapanuli Shu]. I took Iwan's family in my car while Suleiman travelled in another car driven by Iwan's younger brother.* As soon as the car left

* i.e. Thalib Siregar.

Medan, Iwan fell asleep, perhaps because of the sudden slackening of tension. However Murni and I could not sleep at all, in part because Abdi was romping about in the car. Passing through the beautiful scenery of dawn over the Siantar plateau, to a chorus of Toba song, we finally reached Lake Toba at the border of Tapanuli Shu. We had our breakfast on a straw mat on the ground, at a spot where we could see the lake below, though hidden from the eyes of others. It upset me to see Abdi, who could not eat the cold rice ball his mother offered him, because he was used to warm green-pea gruel [**bubur kacang**] every morning.

Meanwhile the traffic on the road was becoming more and more frequent, which meant that it was time for us to part. First, Iwan took my hand firmly and said, as great tears fell from his eyes, 'Please don't do anything rash such as committing **harakiri**'. Next, I shook hands with Murni. Gazing at me she said, 'Let us behave like **pahlawan** [heroes]. Until we meet again.' Then I embraced Abdi. He kissed me vigorously on the cheek as his mother suggested. Finally Suleiman took my hands in his own, which were cold and slim like a woman's, and asked, 'If you can, please give some financial help to my poverty-stricken family, the wife and four children I have left behind.' I watched their car as it travelled around the curve of the lake until it disappeared from view. When I returned to my car to go back to Medan, the driver handed me a paper package saying, 'From **nyonya** [madame]'. Opening the parcel, I found some gifts Murni had secretly left me - the Java batik sarong which Murni loved most, and the velvet **kopiah** [black fez] which Anak Daitoa usually wore.

In September 1945, shortly after Iwan's party had secretly left for Java, a team of Allied officers entered Medan and stationed themselves at the Hotel de Boer. The team consisted chiefly of British and American officers, but I was informed that it included some Dutch officers. In any case Lt. Westerling, an intelligence officer, was certainly in the team.* Under these circumstances I decided to hide in the

* These men were commandos of the Allied Force 136, parachuted near Medan just before the Japanese surrender and installed in the Hotel de Boer by 1 September. Their commander was a South African, Maj. Jacobs, but the senior Dutch officer, Naval Lt. Brondgeest, took most of the early initiatives in the Medan area. Lt. Raymond ('Turk') Westerling, who was to play a notorious counter-insurgency role in South Celebes (1946) and West Java (1950), had his first Indonesian experience with this group in Medan.

house of my friend K on Mangalaan Street and watch the situation, once I had arranged support for Murni's mother, Saniam, and for Suleiman's family.

The Japanese administration in East Sumatra was working for the establishment of a liaison office in order to maintain smooth contact with the Allied Headquarters in Medan, as well as attempting to implement orders from the Allies. In addition, Japanese directors and section heads in charge of the maintenance of estates were meeting every day at Kogen Shrine* in Medan, though they reached no conclusions. In every district Japanese troops began the painful task of handing over power. The Japanese military units in East Sumatra, except for special security units, were ordered to concentrate at various estates in the southern part of the Residency for the hand-over. This was the time when some Japanese began to commit suicide, either with pistol or by harakiri.

Immediately after the Japanese surrender, on 17 August 1945, the two popular leaders in Java, Sukarno and Hatta, proclaimed Indonesian independence in the name of the Indonesian people. I do not know why, but the people of Sumatra still did not know of the existence of the proclamation even in the middle of September. Consequently they continued simply to speculate about their future without initiating any concerted action. But I must confess that I too was one of those who did not know about the proclamation and was just marking time. But had I not established and supervised the KTT for just such an eventuality? Anyway, I felt it was time that I made some positive decision. This I did, with the firm conviction that the people of Sumatra would initiate a struggle for independence...

On 3 October I was still staying at my friend's place on Mangalaan Street. I had finished dinner before my friend, and was reading a newspaper in the living room. Suddenly the phone rang. I picked up the telephone for my friend and found that the man on the other end was evidently Lt. Westerling, the Dutch intelligence officer stationed at the Hotel de Boer.

'Hello, hello. Is that **tuan** K?'

'Yes, yes, I am K,' I answered. 'Do you have something to ask me?'

'I want you to let us know urgently the sorts of popular movements which existed in East Sumatra during the Japanese

---

* One of the very few Shinto shrines built by the Japanese in Southeast Asia, this handsome building became after the war the Medan Club.

occupation, their names and the names of their leaders. And
inform me of the whereabouts of Capt Inoue.'

'Yes, sir,' I replied. 'On the people's movements, I will
report to you soon after I have consulted the Chokan. As for
Capt. Inoue, however, we are still searching for him and
therefore we cannot satisfy your requirement. Is that all
right?'

'Yes, that's all right. But I warn you that it will be
much better for you to find Inoue yourselves, than for us to
capture him. Well then, goodbye.'

'Oh, excuse me, Lt. Westerling,' I interrupted. 'I should
like, as a liaison officer, to ask you the date of the formal
entry of the Allied forces into Medan.'

'Perhaps on the 7th or 8th of this month. Well, goodbye.'
I smiled to myself.

4 October

Completely out of the blue I received a strange piece of
information from my secret messenger. Suleiman, who had left
for Java with Iwan, had suddenly returned to Medan. According
to the messenger's story, when Suleiman was on his way to Java
with Iwan, he had met Doctor A.K. Gani, the top leader of the
National Party in Palembang, and he had learned for the first
time about the independence proclamation on 17 August.
Suleiman accepted Gani's advice that he at least should return
to the East Coast in order to lead an independence movement in
North Sumatra. He had returned immediately to Medan, leaving
Iwan's family to go alone to Java. On his return to Medan,
Suleiman had thrown himself into organizing the movement. The
very night he had returned, an emergency meeting of all-
Indonesian youth groups was held.* I thought, 'He came back
just in time. I will meet him tomorrow.'

5 October

Medan was suddenly flooded with red and white flags. The
bicycles, wheeling around like swallows, each carried a flag;
so did automobiles and horse buggies. People were shouting,
'**Merdeka** (Independence)!' What euphoria! What excitement!
The struggle for independence was at last launched in North
Sumatra.

Day after day unexpected things began to happen. At
about 7 p.m., when it was already getting dark, I was surprised
by a visitor I had not anticipated. It was Salmiah, the

---

* This refers either to an initial meeting of youth activists
  on 23 September, or to a larger rally on 30 September.

sultan's daughter who had been a typist and Murni's companion at the Police Department. When she saw me she said, 'How fortunate to have managed to meet you,' and put her hands on her breast as if giving thanks to God. She seemed worried about being seen, and with a murmured excuse swiftly pulled the curtain to close off the guest room. She sat down in front of me, and though she was still slightly out of breath, she seemed to me to have grown more beautiful than I remembered.

Addressing me as 'Inoue san,'* she said, 'You must get out of this town as quickly as possible. It is said that Lt. Westerling is planning to launch a thorough search of the whole town at 10 p.m. tomorrow, in order to arrest you and Suleiman's group.'

'Is this true?', I asked.

'I got this information by chance from people around Lt. Westerling, so it is pretty reliable.'

'Thank you very much,' I said. 'I too thought that this would happen sooner or later, but I didn't expect them to be so quick off the mark.'

Salmiah said, 'I didn't believe you would let yourself be arrested easily, but I came here to tell you about it just in case.'

'Thank you very much again. I heard that after the surrender you moved from the Police Department of the Japanese administration to Allied Headquarters. Why did you take such a drastic step, which seems to conflict with your own ideas?'

'Is it necessary for you to know now the reason why?' Salmiah assumed a pathetic look and pondered something for a while. 'It was because of the concern Murni and I had for your safety that I went to work at Allied Headquarters. Her concern and mine might seem to be the same, but in reality are quite different. Do you understand what I am saying?'

Salmiah was looking at me mistily. Into my mind flashed the image of her discreet figure following Murni like a shadow on our various meetings.

She went on, 'I never thought I would have a chance to speak my heart to you, or perhaps it was that I persuaded myself not to express my heart. I was convinced I could overcome it... but it's no use, I'm sorry.'

Salmiah put a handkerchief to her eyes as if she could not hold her passion in check. Just then, a **babu** (servant) brought tea, much to my relief. 'Please have some tea,' I said flatly, pretending I was not aware of her emotion.

'I had not dreamed that this was the reason for your present position. I should like to express my deepest gratitude for your special concern over me. At the same time I

---

* In contrast to using his military title as would have been required before the surrender.

213

hope you will continue your present work in Allied Headquarters and contribute to our struggle in a broader sense. Even if what is between us is precious, like a pearl, we should not wear it at the moment. Indeed, I think this is not even the time to argue about whether we can wear it or not.'

Salmiah was silent, so I continued, 'In any case, your friendship has enabled me to avoid the first danger. Now you must trust me to be as smart and cunning as Lt. Westerling. But I want to ask you one more thing. Would you mind waiting for me in the teak forest on the left side of the Medan-Brastagi Road just at the edge of the city, between 9 and 9.30 a.m. tomorrow, dressed as beautifully as possible?'

'Yes, of course. I will be there.'

Covering her face with a blue **selendang** (shawl) and saying 'goodbye' with her eyes, she quietly slipped out the back door and into the darkness. Perhaps it was not only I who felt the insipidness of the incomplete conversation between us. However, I felt inhibited by the tense atmosphere of Medan and unable to talk more deeply.

After seeing Salmiah off, I changed into my usual Chinese black silk clothes and hurried by bicycle to Suleiman's house on Sungei Lungas Street. It took some time to reach it because I had to make many detours to avoid Allied patrols on the way. Although the street was within Medan, it was located towards the outskirts of the city. It transpired that the street lamps were out and the street was dark. However, it was easy to find his house because a few young people with naked swords were on guard around it in the tense atmosphere. As soon as I got off the bicycle, somebody asked in a sharp tone, **'Siapa?** (Who are you?)', but the voice softened when I simply answered quietly **'Soshirei** [Commander-in-Chief]'.

Fortunately Suleiman was at home, but he seemed surprised by my appearing suddenly without warning, and he warned me in English, which was most unusual, 'I think you had better be careful about moving around, as the situation has changed.' Although I could understand his warning, its tone made me feel uneasy. I thought that I had better leave as soon as I finished my business, so I came straight to the point.

'I have decided to leave the Japanese Army because I want to see for myself the result of my training on the Talapeta, Kaijo, and KTT; because I feel guilty and wish to atone for the errors the Japanese committed consciously or unconsciously towards the Indonesian people; because I am opposed to the war tribunal system of the Allies, which is suffused with contradiction; and because I hope that I may find something to live for beyond my patriotic sentiment. I have two ambitions - 'to live and die with you', and to cooperate directly with the Indonesian struggle for independence. On the other hand, I am confident that you have enough strength and fighting spirit for the struggle on your own, while I am well aware that foreigners should intervene as little as possible, so as to preserve the good name of your cause in the international arena. Accordingly, I will content myself with the status of an observer even after I leave the Army, unless you ask for my cooperation. What do you think of this plan?'

'I think everything you have said is reasonable.'

'If you agree, then I have one thing to ask you,' I continued. 'Could you arrange a safe refuge for me to use for a short period? I should like to stay somewhere like the Karo plateau.'

'Well, Bohorok in Langkat district might be ideal in terms of its strategically defensible location; but in view of the relatively pro-Japanese disposition of its inhabitants, its abundant food supplies, and other factors, I think Dahulu on the Karo plateau is the best place. But when will you actually carry out your escape?' asked Suleiman.

'Having considered the way the situation is developing, I am planning to leave Medan at 9 a.m. tomorrow at the latest.'

'Very good. It so happens that Jolin is here at the moment from Dahulu. It might be very convenient for you to leave with him. As I would like to go with you for a while to see you off, I will call at your house at 8.30 a.m. tomorrow. Will that be all right?'

'Thank you very much,' I answered. 'But please wait for me in the forest on the left side of the road, just at the edge of the city, so that we can avoid being seen by anybody. By the way, we will be taking a beautiful lady with us from that point to our destination, in order to distract people's attention. Please bear that in mind.'

Thus the matter was resolved more easily than I had anticipated. Now I had nothing to worry about. I slowly pedalled my way back home, unwilling to bring to an end my last night in Medan.

At 9 a.m. on 6 October, dressed in the formal uniform of an Army captain, I left K's house, telling the family that I had been ordered to change my unit and move to an engineer's regiment which was being concentrated at an estate near Kisaran. My car had been replaced by a decrepit Ford, and Osman, a former batallion leader in the KTT, had taken the place of my former Javanese driver. After driving around the streets for a while to make people think the car was heading towards Kisaran, we left the city and stopped at the spot where we had arranged to meet. While Osman pretended to work on some engine trouble, I dashed in among the teak trees where Suleiman, Jolin and Salmiah were waiting for me. I changed out of my uniform and into a sarong and kopiah. This was effected easily because Salmiah kindly helped me. My transformation complete, we set off. At my request Salmiah sat in the front seat beside the driver, while Suleiman and Jolin took the rear seat on either side of me. As the car passed Arnhemia and

Sembahe and began to tackle the steeper slopes, it began to splutter. As a result we had to get out several times and push the car from behind. It finally boiled over when it reached a hairpin bend after Serbolangit. This happened two or more times after that. Each time we were able to overcome the difficulty, thanks to Osman's remarkable ingenuity and skill. After driving for four hours instead of the normal one, we reached our destination on the Brastagi Road. The place was known to most people as Brastagi Pass and was a desolate place with no houses in sight. Nevertheless, it was located on a busy road so that we had to get ourselves organized as quickly as possible under the guidance of our guide, Jolin. He stepped out of the car first and climbed quickly up a cliff, after making sure that nobody was watching. He looked ahead for a while, then signalled us to come up.

Despite the urgency of the situation I shook hands with each person, beginning with Suleiman. He said, 'Now your job is finished. If you have the chance, please train even one or two youths from this mountain region so that they can live up to their country's expectations.'

Salmiah then came out impatiently and took my hand. 'Please take me with you,' she said. 'I don't care where it is, to the jungle or the mountains. I will do whatever you ask. Please take me as your servant.'

Salmiah was extraordinarily excited, and seemed to be in such a state that she might throw herself on my breast. 'Salmiah,' I said. 'Have you forgotten what I said about the pearl yesterday? That now is not the time to discuss whether we are allowed to wear this pearl or not? If you are really my faithful friend you must not speak in such a selfish way. You must return to Medan now with Suleiman and go on working hard at Allied Headquarters.'

'Suleiman, Osman and Salmiah, goodbye to you all!'

I was aware of Salmiah bursting into tears behind me,* but Jolin was urging me to hurry and I leaped at the cliff telling myself I must cut all my ties and shake off everything. Nothing should exist in front of me but a path leading into a jungle.

---

* Elsewhere Inoue indicates some instability in Salmiah, who appears to have been in rebellion against the closeted environment of the Malay palace. After her father (referred to as 'Ubaishar') was killed in the 'Social Revolution' of 1946, she allegedly drifted into prostitution.

MIYAMOTO SHIZUO

I) Economic and Military Mobilization in Java, 1944-1945

Miyamoto Shizuo was born in Kagoshima in 1908 and graduated from the **Rikugun Shikan Gakkō** (Military Academy). He served as a staff officer in charge of intelligence in Manchuria and North China, before being suddenly assigned to Java in April 1944, with the rank of Major (later Lt.-Col.). His role there was as Staff Officer in charge of supply (including communication and transport), one of four Staff Officers responsible to the Chief-of-Staff of the 16th Army in different areas.

Miyamoto had no knowledge of Indonesia at the time of his transfer, but by the Japanese surrender he had become a key figure in the administration - especially in post-war negotiations with the Allies. Soon after his arrival he made inspection trips to various parts of Java, and was struck by the great poverty and inequality he found there. This led him to adopt a more critical attitude towards the Dutch colonial regime and the wealthy Indonesians who had cooperated with it. Despite the hopeless economic and military position during his time in Java, he appears to have justified the hardship to himself with the hope of eventual victory. Six months after his arrival he concluded, 'At any rate Dutch colonial rule was bad. Our military administration is much better. The harm of colonial rule can be cured by winning the war!' (p.12). His intelligence background had led him to put great emphasis on a strategy of winning 'hearts and minds', a perspective from which he viewed even the PETA/Giyugun army, as is evident below.

After the Japanese surrender Miyamoto's primary concern, in accordance with 16th Army policy, was with the protection of Japan and the Japanese by avoiding Allied accusations of illegal actions. Here he parted company sharply from Maeda and Nishijima of the Navy Office, believing that their support for Indonesian independence jeopardized the safe repatriation of Japanese personnel for which the Army was responsible.

In describing the way Maeda made his house available for drafting the Indonesian independence declaration (not included in our extracts), Miyamoto protests:

> To be honest I felt that Maeda's action was uncalled for. I also felt that it weakened the stance we were taking toward the Allies that the Japanese were not involved in the independence problem at all (p.54).

He also regretted the words 'the transfer of power' in the

declaration, agreed to by Maeda, because it seemed to imply a contractual transfer from the Japanese (p.53). The importance of Japanese participation in the independence manoeuvres was not lost on the Indonesians, Miyamoto believes. He cites a young Indonesian activist who confided to him that the Indonesians felt the need of some sort of 'green light' from the Japanese to convey a degree of legitimacy.

The divergence between the legalistic approach of the Army and the 'romantic' position of the Navy Office caused some bitterness and allegations of disloyalty, both at the time and subsequently. At a Tokyo seminar following the publication of his book, Miyamoto reacted to criticism from Nishijima by insisting, 'We refused to give arms [to the Indonesians] because any such action would have threatened the position of the Emperor' (tape-recording by A. Oki, July 1973). Miyamoto's stance after the surrender was consistently directed to fulfilling Allied requirements wherever possible, forbidding Japanese to fire on Indonesians (often at heavy cost to themselves), and promoting a peaceful settlement between the Allies and the Indonesian Republic. It was an undramatic, even bureaucratic, role compared with that of Nishijima, but a necessary one.

Miyamoto has become in a sense the spokesman for the 16th Army. He decided to write this memoir both as a historical testimony and as an apology to those who suffered economic distress and hard labour in Java, or whose relatives died there as a result of his policies. As the first 16th Army Staff Officer to be repatriated (in March 1947), he made special efforts to collect relevant documents and smuggle them out of Jakarta through Japanese soldiers working on the docks, who in turn passed them to the captain of a Japanese repatriation vessel. These documents form the basis for his narrative and give it its soberly factual style.

Miyamoto Shizuo

JAWA SHŪSEN SHORIKI

[An Account of the Cessation of Hostilities in Java]   (Tokyo:
Jawa Shūsen Shoriki Kankōkai, 1973), Part I, pp. 12-44

CHAPTER III: THE PLAN OF CAMPAIGN AND INDONESIA'S POSITION

1. The General View of the Japanese Army towards Indonesia

The 55,000 soldiers of the Japanese 16th Army, commanded by Lt.-Gen. Imamura Hitoshi forced the Allied Forces in the Netherlands Indies to surrender in the space of only ten days in March 1942, with the loss of 255 Japanese dead and 702 wounded. As a result, the Japanese did not need to use the second and third echelons which had been prepared beforehand in anticipation of heavy fighting. The victory owed much to the voluntary cooperation of the Indonesians. The Japanese themselves felt a spontaneous familiarity and sense of brotherhood towards the Indonesians, with no traces of hostility. This attitude became a tradition of the 16th Army.

2. The Plan of Campaign and the Winning of the Hearts and Minds of the People

It was a maxim of the Japanese army since the Sino-Japanese and Russo-Japanese Wars that an important condition for success in military operations abroad was the winning of the hearts and minds of the people. I myself endorsed this through my experiences in Manchuria and North China. To this end, the **Gunsei Yōkō** [Outline of Military Administration]* directed by Imperial Headquarters to the Japanese army in the field, included (A) the winning of the hearts and minds of the people; (B) the maintenance of order; (C) the acquisition of important resources and their redeployment to Japan.

At the beginning, strategic materials were to be sent from Japan. However, the Japanese eventually had to rely on materials from the occupied regions. The success of (A) and (B) was tied to the security of livelihood of the people, and the best way to achieve this was not to take goods away from the people. On the other hand, such a policy was incompatible

_____
* See Imamura, above, p.52.

219

with (C). In effect, (A) and (B) were essential in order to achieve (C).

Consequently, the Army's most important strategic consideration was how to balance the damage to the people's livelihood against the requirements of military operations. Yet it cannot be denied that the Japanese Army in the field had total confidence in the capacity of such a strategy to win the war, even in the face of the ever-deteriorating Japanese war position, and that there was some degree of arrogance among the Japanese.

3. Japanese Expectations about the Military Strength of Indonesian Forces involved in Direct Defence

Part I: The Volunteer Defence Force [Boei Giyugun]

A: The Process of Establishment

The Java Army [16th Army], which at the time of landing in March 1942 had been composed mainly of two divisions comprising 23 battalions [**daitai**], had been cut back by the Imperial Headquarters to 18 battalions by late spring and early summer of 1942, and to two regiments comprising 8 battalions by early autumn that year. At the same time the recruiting of **Heiho** [auxiliary soldiers] was approved. At the beginning of 1943, the campaign plan in Java was concerned chiefly with the possibility of an Allied attack from Australia; and with such an attack being combined with Allied operations along the north coast of New Guinea. As a result of increasing communication difficulties between Japan and the Southern Army, Java was becoming more and more important as a supply base. Although Imperial Headquarters had planned to enlarge the Japanese force in Java, these plans did not materialize. Consequently, with a total force of two regiments (consisting of 15,000 military men of whom 8,500 were combat forces, and 15,000 Japanese civilians seconded to the army), we were acutely aware of the limitations of our military strength.

We not only developed closer bonds of friendship with the Indonesians, but also, through the Heiho, came to appreciate their military abilities. This came about in part because of the policy of winning the hearts and minds of the people and of promoting Indonesian cooperation with the Japanese, and in part because of the results of tests of military ability undertaken by able Indonesian youths, recruited mainly in Java, at the Tanggerang Special Training Centre, which was under the direct control of Headquarters' General Staff (and the director and deputy-director of which were Lt. Yanagawa and Lt. Tomigashi Takeomi respectively).* These policies were implemented by the

* For Footnote see following page.

Commander, Lt.-Gen. Harada Kumakichi, who succeeeded the first commander, Imamura, and whose administration was influenced by his experience in China - namely, that order among the natives should be maintained by the native military, so that the Japanese army could be held in reserve as a core force.

Moreover, Maj.-Gen. Inada, Vice-Chief of Staff of the General Southern Army, and the Commander, Lt.-Gen. Harada, aware of the scarcity of Japanese forces, in June 1943 made an investigation into the training of Indonesian youths in Java. Both men came to the conclusion that Indonesian youths were capable of meeting Japanese expectations, and reported their findings to Imperial Headquarters in Tokyo, after having first sought the approval of Commander-in-Chief Terauchi. Imperial Headquarters itself - following an imperial conference in May at which it had been decided to permit the participation of indigenous peoples in political matters, and a fact-finding mission by Prime Minister Tojo to the southern regions in July - had come to see the merit of permitting indigenous peoples to contribute to the defence of their fatherland. Accordingly, in August 1943, the General Southern Army issued an order to the armies in Java and Sumatra, approving the establishment of native armies.

As all this took place before I arrived in Java, I do not know whether any thought was given to the harm which might be caused by the creation of a native army - for intance, rebellions when arms were delivered to the people of occupied regions. However, Lt.-Gen. Harada trusted the people implicitly; nor did my own predecessor as Staff Officer seem to have any doubts about the matter.

B. Creation and Expansion

The creation of the **Giyugun†** took the form of accepting applications from those Indonesians who favoured self-defence and cooperation with the Japanese. The Japanese selected

---

* Footnote from previous page:
Although Miyamoto calls this centre **Tokubetsu Kunrenjo**, it must be identical with or a forerunner of the **Seinen Dōjō** (Youth Training Centre), established in Tanggerang in January 1943. The director (of both) Yanagawa Motoshige, an Indonesia-specialist graduate of the famous Japanese Intelligence School (**Nakano-gakkō**), made a great impact on such young students as Kemal Idrus.

† **Giyugun** (volunteer soldier) was the term used by Japanese for this embryo army in Java, Sumatra, and Malaya. The Java Giyugun, however, became generally known to Indonesians as PETA (Pembela Tanah Air = Defenders of the Fatherland).

applicants in September 1943, not from among nationalist political leaders but from nationalists whose convictions sprang from their religious beliefs. In this they were following the advice of Lt. Yanagawa. In contrast to the Heiho, the Giyugun was divided into battalions (called **daidan**) which consisted entirely of Indonesians, though a Japanese officer and non-commissioned officers, about five in all, were attached to each battalion as trainers. These battalions were attached directly to the Japanese garrisons, and their educational and other needs attended to solicitously by a powerful special section established expressly for the training and education of the Giyugun, and under the command of a Colonel or on occasions a Lieutenant-General. The staff of the whole section took part in the education and administration of the Giyugun.

The Giyugun was composed of 33 battalions with 16,500 Indonesians (a battalion [**daidan**] comprised 500 soldiers, divided into three companies [**chudan**], each of which consisted of three platoons [**shodan**], each of which consisted of five squads [**bundan**]), and its members were distributed through each Residency in Java.

At the beginning of October 1943, an order concerning the establishment of the Giyugun was promulgated, and at the end of October a two-month intensive course for commissioned officers ran for the first time at a school in Bogor. From January 1945 the education of ordinary soldiers was entrusted to Indonesian officers in each daidan. The aim of the Giyugun was to defend the fatherland and Islam from the re-occupation of Indonesia by the Dutch, and to train military forces as support troops for the Japanese Army. However, caution was enjoined against any undue haste in meeting the aspirations for independence of the more radical element.

In April and May 1944 American forces seized Hollandia [Jayapura] and Sarmi [in New Guinea]. Moreover, it was strongly anticipated that Allied forces based in Australia would move north and attack Java. Accordingly, the Japanese Army had to prepare for an attack not only from the south, but from the north as well. Thus Java became increasingly important as a supply base for the Japanese Army.

Meanwhile, the results of the training of the Giyugun were most satisfactory, and it was felt that its members would certainly prove their worth. Consequently, between June and August 1944, the Japanese organized a second Giyugun, consisting of 22 daidan, and stationed them in Residencies throughout Java.

I arrived in Java in April 1944 as a Staff Officer for Supply, charged with superintending the maintenance and distribution of arms and munitions along the lines drafted by Obana, Staff Officer for Strategy. As I felt at the outset that the Dutch colonial policy had been good, I entertained some misgivings about giving arms to the Indonesians.* However, I implemented my predecessor's plan, since the Commander and others with long experience in Indonesia regarded it as reasonable.

In June 1944 American forces landed on Saipan Island, and in July the Japanese Army there was annihilated.† Because of the self-maintenance policy of the Southern Army, the role of the Japanese army in Java in making the island a supply base took on a critical importance. At the same time it was expected that the enemy would intensify its manipulation of Indonesians in order to drive a wedge between them and the Japanese. For this reason there were increasing pressures to win the hearts and minds of the people and maintain order on the one hand, and to increase production on the other. It was deemed necessary that the maintenance of order be left in the hands of the Indonesian people, so that the Japanese Army could concentrate on defence and counter-attack. An increase in production was also felt to be of intrinsic benefit to the Indonesians themselves, since it would transform the Indonesian economy from a colonial economy to an independent national economy. The Japanese, having judged that the enemy would not attack Java immediately, mitigated direct defence policies to some extent so as not to prejudice the peoples' livelihood.

In order to carry out the policy of entrusting the maintenance of order to the Indonesians themselves, we concluded, after having studied the location and deployment of the existing two sets of Giyugun forces, that the creation of an additional 12 daidan was necessary. The extra forces were organized and deployed in August. Thus the total strength of the Giyugun became 67 daidan (with an additional three in Bali),# with a manpower strength of 38,000 (35,000 if one relies on paper calculations alone). This was twice as large as the entire 16th Army, and four times the actual combat strength of the Army.

As far as I remember, the quantity of small arms such as ordinary rifles and cavalry rifles held by the Army, including

* The author clarified in an interview that he believed the Dutch had succeeded in winning Indonesian support, so that there was a danger Indonesians would turn their guns against the Japanese.

† **Gyokusai**, i.e. an honourable, but total, destruction.

Miyamoto literally says here 'of which three were in Bali', but the totals following suggest he meant 67 in Java **plus** three in Bali. Bali was the only part of the Navy-administered area to have a Giyugun force, responsibility for which was with the 16th Army in Java.

those captured from the Dutch, was more than 60,000. Since arms could not be supplemented from Japan at the time, everyone - my own seniors, other Armies, as well as the Air Force and Navy - was trying to obtain the arms of the 16th Army. Some units demanded that if the Army had any spare weapons I should give them to them rather than to the Giyugun, on the grounds that their arms had been lost in the sea at the time of the landing and that they had only bamboo spears. Since these claims were reasonable I was prepared to meet them, but something made me want to retain approximately 50,000 small arms under my [16th Army] control. In fact, as I reported to the Allies, the number of small arms held by the 16th Army at the time of the surrender was 53,000 (see table below). Though there may have been some extra arms, the number would not have exceeded a few thousand. I allotted arms to the Giyugun very carefully, for fear of rebellion or of desertion by Giyugun members in response to the worsening Japanese position. In this, I was taking a lesson from history, for the Tokugawa regime [1603-1868] had been able to continue for such a long time in part because of the confiscation of swords and other weapons from the population by Toyotomi Hideyoshi. Then again, the long existence of the Dutch colonial regime had been due to the confiscation of arms from the population. Arms were distributed to the Giyugun as follows:

Table 1: Arms Provided to Giyugun

TYPE OF WEAPONS	NUMBER OF WEAPONS	
	Delivered to the Giyugun*	Total held by the 16th Army
Rifles	17,218	
Cavalry rifles	1,550	
Total	18,768	53,000 †
Light machine guns	197	1,704
Heavy machine guns	697	1,331
Dutch trench mortars	93	201
Cannon	20	
Jeeps	132	
Trucks	330	
Tanks	20	

Note: * The number of arms distributed to the Giyugun was based on a slightly lower scale than that of a Japanese battalion.

† This total is the figure I reported to the Allies at the end of war.

224

In September 1944 the American forces landed on Indonesian territory for the first time, at Morotai. Sukarno agitated for the annihilation of the enemy and an increase in production. The **romusha** labourers brought into requisition also worked well. In police departments, schools and youth associations [**Seinendan**], training for special combat progressed at high speed. The production of munitions necessary for such activity was also increased. However, the building of urgently required wooden ships did not proceed satisfactorily. Investigations into the reasons for this lack of success in ship-building indicated that we could not expect more, as long as we were dependent on the skills of Indonesians who had been under colonial rule.

Part of the enemy force in Morotai might move to the Philippine islands, and another part to the south in order to capture the oil fields [of East Borneo]; or the major force might first attack Java, then turn north after crushing the Southern Army. However, we did not seriously consider the latter possibility. Furthermore, it seemed unlikely that an attack on Java by the enemy based on Australia would eventuate before December, if at all. We therefore decided to watch the situation for a while, and to refrain from immediately implementing defence measures, in order not to prejudice the people's livelihood. Chief of Staff Kokubu approved the above policy reluctantly, saying that it was at variance with the first principle of warfare - being ready for an attack at any time. At that time we were still placing first priority for the defence of Java on East Java and the South Coast, followed by the North Coast.

The Koiso statement of September 1944, admitting the possibility of independence for the East Indies in the future, provided the 16th Army with clear authority to make the Giyugun and Heiho the foundation of a future national army of Indonesia. In October, American forces landed on Leyte, but even in November it seemed unlikely that the major American thrust would be southwards, and an attack northwards from Australia was considered to be only a remote possibility. Thus, the most important role of the 16th Army was still considered to be to increase the capacity of Java as a supply base, and it was estimated that there was still some time left before we need arrange defence measures. I now realize that we made an error in not completely discounting the possibility of an attack from Australia.

In January 1945 the American forces landed on the major islands of the Philippines, but their southward thrust seemed lacking in momentum. Meanwhile, the Japanese position in Burma was under pressure, and the General Southern Army therefore transferred the 46th Division from the Lesser Sundas area to Malaya, in order to step up war preparations on the Singapore front, while the 48th Division in Timor took over responsibility for the Lesser Sundas. The 16th Army helped with the transportation of soldiers involved in this transfer, by providing boats hired from the local population, including even those used in transporting salt from Madura, thus disrupting the salt supply of the population of Java. At that stage an attack from Australia still did not appear imminent, and the priorities of the 16th Army seemed rightly focused on increasing production in Java.

C. Rebellions of the Giyugun

In February 1945 a rebellion occurred in East Java in a Giyugun battalion in Blitar, in the course of which some Japanese trainers and Japanese civilians living nearby were killed. Since the rebellion had taken place at his birthplace, Sukarno seemed worried about possible Japanese suspicions that he was involved in the incident. However, we did not entertain any such suspicions.

Prior to this and to my arrival in Java, some of the population of Tasikmalaya in West Java, led by fanatic Islamic leaders, had risen in protest against their economic conditions.* After my arrival, the peasants of Inderamayu in the Cirebon Residency opposed the excessive rice levy. In this case, Japanese police troops carried out preparatory manoeuvres, while Honda Akira (formerly Kumazawa), of the Ministry of Foreign Affairs, was dispatched to the place with an Indonesian guide, and succeeded in quietening the rebellion, on the condition that the Japanese would reduce the proportion [of the rice crop] levied.

As far as Headquarters was concerned, the Blitar rebellion appeared to have erupted suddenly without any prior warning. The Commander ordered the Chief of Defence in East Java, Maj.-Gen. Iwabe, to pacify the rebellion quickly. Although I felt it necessary, as Staff Officer in charge, to go to the place, I was unable to do so for fear of outbreaks in other battalions. Maj.-Gen. Iwabe dispatched a newly arrived Staff Officer, Tanaka, to Blitar to try to subdue the rebels with the support of the Katagiri battalion from neighbouring Malang. However, the ringleaders had run away, alarmed at the way the situation had developed, and the Japanese were able to put down the rebellion without recourse to military force.

After the rebellion was suppressed, the Commander summoned all battalion leaders and explained that the Japanese sympathized with their plight, and appealed to them as follows, as I remember: 'Because the war is dragging on, the people's

---

* The rebellion in Singaparna district near Tasikmalaya occurred in February 1944. The much less serious Inderamayu affair followed in late June.

livelihood has been disrupted and I sense that some Indonesian people are dissatisfied with the Japanese attitude towards independence. However, I, as Commander, think that the aspirations of the Indonesian people can only be achieved once we have won this war, and in order to win I consider the cooperation of the people indispensable. Furthermore, before independence can be achieved, the content of it must be decided. This is something which you, as senior officers, must understand full well. Hence, mutual distrust between Japanese and Indonesians would have disastrous results.' Of course, the Commander could not say that the Japanese had allotted two-fifths of the arms under Japanese control to the Giyugun. I observed that the majority of battalion leaders present agreed with the content of the speech, and reports reaching Headquarters also indicated the general consent of the battalion leaders. On the following day I left on a fact-finding trip to East Java. By chance I was travelling on the same train as a band of returning battalion leaders, who gave me the same impression that I had received during the Commander's speech.

Two reasons for the rebellion have been suggested: the licentious and luxurious lifestyle of the Japanese, heedless of the hardships of the population; and dissatisfaction among Indonesians over the Japanese attitude towards the issue of independence. Capt. Yamazaki Hajime, who was in charge of the supervision of Giyugun, gave the following report:

> As Blitar is located away from the centre [Jakarta], there was not adequate supervision of the Giyugun there, and the Japanese trainers, civilians seconded to the military and ordinary civilians had been leading a dissolute life. Blitar is the place where the rebel Jayakatwang* originated, and the people of Blitar have a rebellious disposition. One of the leaders of the rebellion, Supriadi, is a strange person, very suggestible but with strong powers of leadership. He has compared himself both with the anti-Dutch independence fighter Diponegoro, and with a mystic who was Diponegoro's spiritual leader. He has managed to manipulate others through the use of such allusions. In such a highly charged atmosphere, antipathy towards the Japanese was the trigger that started a rebellion.

The former head of Giyugun training, Capt. Yanagawa, later reported that a wealthy Japanese had robbed a Giyugun officer

---

* Jayakatwang, ruler of Kediri from 1271, killed his overlord Kertanegara and seized his capital at Singosari in 1292, though he was himself quickly brought down by the combined troops of Majapahit and Mongol China.

of his girlfriend, and that the officer had killed a Japanese trainer in retaliation, and had, moreover, fanned dissatisfaction among the people over the Japanese attitude towards the independence issue, in order to gain wider support for his actions.

I reprimanded Capt. Yanagawa, on the grounds that the training of the Giyugun was at fault. In reality, however, I was not angry at Yanagawa because I regarded the Giyugun as a purely political creation aimed at winning the hearts and minds of the people, rather than as a military force to be used at a time of decisive action. Had I regarded the Giyugun as a military force, I would have had to assume responsibility for the rebellion, Capt. Yanagawa would have been expelled from Java, and the Giyugun would have been completely reorganized.

The 16th Army Headquarters [**Gunshireibu**] put the ringleaders on military trial. According to the forementioned Yamazaki, when he had asked Sukarno about the selection of a jury for the trial, Sukarno had suggested that he himself could perform the role. Though grateful for the offer, Yamazaki had declined it on the grounds that it would do Sukarno no good. Finally, Sukarno had suggested Oto Iskandar [di Nata] for the jury. Yamazaki felt that the unnatural death of Oto Iskandar after the war may in part have been connected with his involvement in the trial.* After the verdicts, Oto Iskandar had suggested to various influential Indonesians that he would try to save the lives of the Indonesians who had been sentenced to death, if some of them were prepared to take responsibility for the condemned men and re-educate them. However, his suggestion had drawn no response. Yamazaki felt that the influential Indonesians were not confident enough to accept the responsibility, or perhaps they felt there was a generation gap between themselves and the ringleaders of the rebellion. I never discovered the sources of his information.

After obtaining permission from the presiding judge (Col. Yoshimoto, head of Giyugun training) to interview the condemned Indonesians for half a day, I gave them five questions to answer in writing, in order to try to find out the character of the Indonesian people and to what extent we could depend on the Giyugun at a time of crisis. A question I still remember is:

---

* Raden Oto Iskandar di Nata (1897-1945) was the leading pre-war Sundanese nationalist, a Volksraad member and editor of an influential Sundanese journal. He was close enough to the 16th Army leadership to be named Adviser to the Security Department in late 1944. His mysterious murder, probably in December 1945, is usually attributed to allegations of complicity in the Japanese takeover of Bandung in October 1945.

Suppose you lost your parents during childhood, but through the help of others you grew up, graduated from middle school, and became a Giyugun officer. Now you have reached the stage of sending your own children to school. Unfortunately, the people who brought you up have died, leaving children with ages similar to your children, and you are to take care of them. However, you cannot send all the children to school on your salary. What would you do under these circumstances?

I had mentally decided that the Giyugun would be allowed to continue in existence if the majority of the officers questioned answered in favour of sending the children of their benefactors to school. I also intended asking the presiding judge to reduce the sentence of those who gave such an answer. The majority of answers were to my satisfaction, and I accordingly asked Judge Onikura Norimasa to take the result into consideration. However, Headquarters Military Administration [**Gunseikambu**] was of the opinion that at least those Indonesians who had killed Japanese should be executed, otherwise any Japanese seconded to the military and any ordinary Japanese civilian working in a remote place would be at risk. In the final analysis, those Indonesians who had killed Japanese in the rebellion were executed, but the rest were exempted. Later we received information that the real ringleader was in hiding at the Bayah coalmine, but we deemed it unnecessary to create another stir.

Apart from the Blitar rebellion, Headquarters received a report of a small incident in a Giyugun unit stationed near Cilacap, but not until it was all over. The incident did not perturb me, but strengthened my conviction that we should not depend on the Indonesians as a military force, but rather leave them to their own devices at a time of decisive action.

D. The Giyugun and the Plan of Campaign in the Event of Decisive Action in Java

In February 1945 the American forces seized Manila, landed on Iwo Jima, and began to advance towards the main islands of Japan. Six months after the Allied forces had captured Morotai, a section of them, consisting chiefly of Australian troops, seized Tarakan in April 1945, with the aim of recapturing the oil resources of Borneo. However, an attack on Java did not seem imminent. It was also speculated that the Allied forces in Australia would not attack the areas which the 48th Division had evacuated. On the Western front the British forces captured Akyab in January. In March the Japanese Army's position in Burma was so unfavourable that it had to face the revolt led by Aung San, while the 7th Area Army decided to seek

229

a decisive action around Singapore on the assumption that the British would surely try to recapture the island.

A decisive war in Java was expected to come last among the regions under the control of the General Southern Army - after Singapore, Banjarmasin and Makasar had fallen into the hands of the enemy. It was felt that there was still time left for the army in Java. During that time the 16th Army was to strengthen the potential of Java as a supply base; that is, to put priority on an increase in production capacity under the Gunseikambu, restrict Army defensive measures to a minimum, and estimate the production capacity of Java accurately so that it could mobilize the population for direct defence in time of war without delay. In pursuance of this, the Gunseikambu singled out Indonesians who could contribute to an increase in production. Had the military authorities anticipated Japan's surrender, they would have nurtured high-ranking Indonesian officials, and technicians who were able to design industrial plants. However, surrender was undreamed of, and the only improvement in skills was at the level of manual work.

The enemy was expected to attack Java with at least ten divisions equipped with tanks and other sophisticated weapons, and under a complete air cover. The Japanese counter-strategy was to fight using only Japanese troops, and to make this their Waterloo (in West Java). This was reasonable in terms of our capacity, and would not involve the Indonesians in battle. Operations over a wider area, as well as being impossible in reality, would only lay waste Indonesian territory and bring suffering to the population. The best way of avoiding this was to let the Indonesians choose their own path of action.

In accordance with the forementioned strategy, I decided to enlist in the Java Army those military cadets directly attached to the General Southern Army and whose corps had just been disbanded in Semarang, and to divide Java into three defence divisions - namely, East, Central and West. In the Central divisions for the time being two undermanned battalions (each battalion had about 150 sick Japanese soldiers and 650 Indonesian Heiho) were to be organized by June 1945, in order to make the soldiers familiar with the particular area. Although there were three strategic roads connecting the East, Central and West divisions - namely, the roads along the north and south coasts, and the one running through the mountainous areas of the hinterland of Java, the first two were likely to be quickly destroyed by the enemy. Therefore it seemed advisable that any decisive action be fought in West Java. In order to do this, the Central division forces would be charged with protecting the central road in the mountains and patrolling both sides of it, while the East division forces were moved safely to West Java. The Central division forces would then also be moved to West Java. I also had a plan for moving the West division forces to East Java to destroy the enemy if he attacked East Java from Tarakan. However, I thought that, judging by our trial manoeuvres, such an attack would not eventuate. Nevertheless, I instructed all officers to learn to drive.

As the central road led only to the west of Purwokerto, I ordered the construction of a new road connecting Ajibarang with Guntung (the construction and selection of the route were carried out by Indonesians under the supervision of Ota, a Japanese engineer), so that the defence forces in East and Central Java could move easily to West Java.

Since it appeared that Java would be the last of the Japanese-occupied regions of the south to be involved in a decisive action, I anticipated being able to construct wooden-hulled motorboats, and so to involve in the action in Java the now idle forces on the Outer Islands, in addition to the Java-based Navy (about 20,000 men?) and Airforce (about 10,000 men?) which had lost ships and planes. As the chances of a northward push from Australia looked very slight, I also planned to bring the 48th Division in Timor (25,000 men) to Java.

The southward movement of the enemy in Tarakan was slow, and did not seem to be on a large scale. In view of this, in June I requested the transfer of the 48th Division to Java, on the condition that the 16th Army be responsible for its transportation. The request was approved, though 5,000 of the 25,000 soldiers were to be sent to Singapore. As a result, the Japanese defence forces in Java consisted of 15,000 men of the 16th Army; 15,000 Japanese civilians attached to the Army; 20,000 men of the 48th Division; 10,000 Airforce men; and 20,000 Navy men - a total of 80,000. If we were to fight a decisive action in West Java with these 80,000 men, there would be no need at all to rely on the Giyugun as a military force. To do so might indeed prove unfortunate.

The total number of small arms of the 16th Army was 53,000 (the figure I reported to the Allies, of which 19,000 had been delivered to the Giyugun, though there were a number of extras held by Indonesian policemen).* In the event of a decisive action involving the 80,000 soldiers in West Java, we would need not only the 53,000 small arms, but also the extra ones allotted to the Indonesian policemen. However, I felt it would be a very demeaning act to confiscate arms already given to the Indonesians. According to an assessment by Lt.-Col. Hayashi Masaki, who was in charge of the munitions factory at Bandung which had originally belonged to the Dutch but was now controlled by the General Southern Army, the production capacity of the munitions factory when supervised by Japanese

* In supplementary information to the translator, Miyamoto estimated that 10,000 weapons may have been in the hands of police.

experts was: 175 tons per month of gunpowder for makeshift weapons; 50,000 hand grenades; and an unspecified number of makeshift trench mortars made of steel tubes. In addition to this, we could utilize a field repair factory for aeroplanes, and the know-how of the Navy. It was out of the question for the Japanese to fight a decisive action in the West, concentrating on mobile forces, against an enemy which could use tanks and artillery corps and had absolute supremacy in the air. In order to render useless the tanks and artillery corps of the enemy, I planned a strategy which took advantage of the complicated terrain around Bandung and the wet-rice fields, and which concentrated on night attacks, using the ammunition as assessed by Lt.-Col. Hayashi. After extensive air reconnaissance (the pilot was Taniguchi Masatsugu of Osaka), I also devised a supplementary plan in which our men, given that they had 40,000 small arms, were expected to fight on equal terms with the enemy.

Accordingly, I left the arms held by Indonesian policemen as they were, and re-allocated the arms of the Giyugun so that it retained 13,000 small arms and returned 6,000. The battalions which had to return their rifles were transformed into units for which the possession of arms was unnecessary, like those in charge of the maintenance and supply of cannon, horse-carriages and automobiles, or else they were combined with other battalions that had small arms.

*   *   *

I planned to establish a school of military arts, in order to foster the Giyugun as the basis of a future Indonesian national army. My idea was that extreme nationalists would be excluded from the actual armed forces, but would be used as teaching staff, to avoid any possible trouble. In developing my plans I took note of the Blitar rebellion of February, selecting Japanese trainers for the Giyugun with great care, and making their training more intensive. I also moved the Giyugun a step closer to becoming an independent national army, by expanding the range of its activities from the maintenance of order at the Residency level to operations crossing these boundaries. Although Staff Officers had so far been unable to become directly involved in the education of the Giyugun because they were too busy, I decided to try to facilitate such involvement wherever possible. I selected members of the Giyugun and Heiho whose continued cooperation we could rely on, and set up a special task force of intelligence activities, headed by Capt. Yanagawa.

In brief, it was not intended to rely on the Giyugun and Heiho as military forces in the event of a decisive action in Java, but they were to be used as political instruments until the time of such action, as a token of thanks [for Indonesian cooperation]. Accordingly, I regarded these troops as a windfall, to be left to follow their own inclinations in the event of a final military showdown. In order, however, to keep the Japanese frontline troops well-disposed towards the Giyugun and Heiho [i.e. despite the secret official attitude that they would not be militarily reliable], I ordered the Japanese instructors to train the Indonesians diligently, and to stress the slogan, 'We fight together and we die together'.

In view of these considerations, I regulated the distribution of arms as listed in the table below. I summoned those Japanese concerned with the training of the Giyugun to the official residence of the Commander in Cipanas to explain my ideas, and while we were discussing the reorganization of the Giyugun, I received the news of the Russian entry into the war. Accordingly, I immediately sent the Japanese back to their units. It should also be mentioned that the Allies landed on Halmahera and Ternate at the end of June, and at Balikpapan on 1 July.

Table 2: Modified Plan for the Distribution of Arms and Weapons to the Giyugun

TYPE OF WEAPONS	NUMBER OF WEAPONS			
	Old Plan	New Plan	To be returned	Extra delivery
Rifles	17,218	12,109	5,109	--
Cavalry rifles	1,550	564	986	--
Light machineguns	197	0	197	--
Heavy machineguns	699	134	563	--
Dutch trench mortars	93	48	45	--
Special trench mortars	20	16	4	--
Jeeps	132	133	--	1
Trucks	330	332	--	2
Tanks	20	0	20	--
Horse carriages	193 *	330 *	--	138

* These figures were reversed in Miyamoto, presumably by mistake (ed.).

E. Training of the Giyugun

As has been mentioned before, the education of the Giyugun officers was carried out through an intensive two month course at Bogor, while the soldiers were trained by Indonesian officers. The education of battalion commanders was focused more on leadership ability than on the command of soldiers, while that of company and platoon leaders focused on effective deploying of troops, and that of the soldiers on increasing

233

their combat efficiency. In addition we trained Indonesian military doctors and accountants. Although we used translated versions of the Japanese **tempan** [military code] and **naimu** [i.e. **naimu kitei**, the discipline of soldiers], the **sentō kōryō** [the military manual for ranks higher than regiment commander] was not used.

The majority of Japanese trainers attached to the battalions were young Japanese officers conscripted while at school. They were thrown into the mass of young Indonesians without being given sufficient orientation beforehand - five youthful Japanese trainers for each 500 Indonesian youths. Thus, immature youths of both nations were thrown into the same melting pot. The young Japanese officers tried to educate the Indonesians by means of physical force, presumably because they saw them as similar to fresh Japanese recruits firmly imbued with patriotism and loyalty to the Emperor, or because they felt a sense of brotherhood with the Indonesian youths. Some Japanese trainers may have looked down on the Indonesians.

Ammunition was collected and stored in ammunition dumps at each barracks, and there was ample opportunity for looting or pilfering. However, the atmosphere was such that when the Japanese trainers requested that ammunition be transferred back to Headquarters, the youths, who had not even had time to have their first lessons in target practice, assisted in bringing in the ammunition and then calmly went back to their drill. While some Japanese trainers ignored the Giyugun officers and concentrated on the soldiers, or insulted the Indonesian officers in front of their men, others helped the Indonesian officers to establish their authority. There seem also to have been some Japanese who resorted to forceful methods during training, either because of a zeal to teach the Indonesians as much as possible in the brief two months of the intensive course, or because that just happened to be the way they were inclined. However, it seemed that the results of the training were better when the Japanese trainers entrusted the Indonesian officers with the training of the soldiers than otherwise. Headquarters provided the young Japanese trainers with sufficient financial resources to act on their own initiative. There were very few Japanese in the army who were given such freedom of opportunity to test their ability.

F. The Selection of Giyugun Officers

The selection of Giyugun officers was based not on favouritism, social status or birth, but on the ability of the individual. We ordered each Residency to recommend able youths, in the hope of initiating social change.

234

Part II: Heiho

The Heiho system was fully integrated into the Japanese army structure. As mentioned before, the Heiho corresponded to the soldiers of lower ranks in the Japanese military system. In order to avoid a situation where the Japanese led too easy a life, the number of Heiho was fixed at less than one fifth of the combat corps. Nevertheless, there were still 3,000 Heiho in combat corps, and 6,000 in non-combat corps. Three times as many Heiho as Japanese served as guards for ammunition magazines; 2,000 served in the air defence corps, constituting 17 companies [**chutai**]; and 1,000, constituting six companies, served in the motorized corps. At the end of the war the total number of Heiho amounted to 25,000.

We were working on the basis that, in the event of the Giyugun becoming a national army, which would be short-staffed in areas such as air defence, transport and supply corps, these men would be able to assume positions of responsibility. In the area of air defence, the Indonesians had reached the stage of being able to shoot down planes themselves, but as for the motorized corps, the Indonesian mechanics were completely incompetent. It was intended that, in the event of a decisive action, the majority of the Heiho would be disbanded and only a small number retained as scouts attached to the Japanese Army. The Army authorities relieved the Japanese troops from matters of military administration, so that they could concentrate solely on military training, but it counted on the Heiho more than the Giyugun to foster sympathy towards Indonesia on the part of the Japanese troops.

Part III: People's Organizations and Movements
(The Unity of the People)

The prime concern of the Army, in gaining acceptance for its military administration, was winning the hearts and minds of the people. The Army mobilized the people - not only the Indonesian leaders, but also the masses - so as to make the Indonesians defy their colonial rulers. Accordingly, the Triple A Movement [**Gerakan Tiga A**], the Concentration of the People's Power Movement [**Pusat Tenaga Rakyat**, or Putera], and the People's/Public Servants' Loyalty Organization [**Hokokai**] were set up with the aim of consolidating cooperation towards Japan. Sukarno and Hatta were encouraged as the most influential leaders in an attempt to generate unity among the people. Furthermore, the Japanese established **Keibodan** [Vigilance Corps], **Seinendan** [Youth Associations],* **Tonarigumi** [Neighbourhood Associations], **Fujinkai** [Women's Associations],

* For Footnote see following page.

235

and **Sangyo Hokokukai** [Associations for Service to the State through Industry] all over Java; as well as fostering a spirit of unity and collective action through education in schools and **Seinen Kunrenjo** [Youth Training Centres]. There were also some Japanese who took it upon themselves to open private schools and training institutions. All of these contributed to giving Indonesians - not only those from feudal, hereditary, aristo-cratic families, but especially those with talent from among the common people - an opportunity to better themselves and a locus for their activities.

Not all these organizations were established by order of Headquarters and the Gunseikambu - some originated independently through the enthusiasm of individual Japanese in various occupations and locations. From the point of view of Headquarters, some of these organizations were not worth the outlay of energy and resources, but their development was not impeded. Despite this, there was criticism from Indonesians that the Japanese policy was coercive and fascist. However, we thought the Indonesians would come to understand the situation sooner or later. As will be mentioned later, a member of the Dutch military police, in answer to a question I put to him, said that the Japanese had tried to Japanize the Indonesians too hastily. By Japanization, he seems to have meant the above movements. We did not intend to pursue Japanization forcefully, but all we knew were the ways and traditions of Japan. We favoured the development of a national consciousness which could provide the natural basis of an eventual state.

* Footnote from previous page:
  The author subsequently provided the figures he had given the Allies at the end of the war on the strengths of these and other semi-military bodies: student corps - 50,000; **Seinendan** - 500,000 to 600,000; **Keibodan** - 1,300,000; **Barisan Pelopor** (Vanguard Corps) - 80,000; **Hizbullah** - 50,000; **Barisan Berani Mati** (Suicide Corps) - 50,000; Special guard corps for police duty - 140,000. He added:

  > Although the establishment and training of these bodies was initiated by the Japanese, their management was gradually entrusted to the Indonesians. The members of the student corps were intended as reserve Giyugun officers, and the others as reserve Giyugun soldiers. To be frank, these bodies only consumed resources of the military administration in money and food without necessarily being welcomed by the Indonesians. In establishing these corps there was even an element of self-satisfaction on the part of the Japanese, never having been colonized themselves.

CHAPTER IV: THE POSITION OF JAVA AS A SUPPLY BASE

Summary

As communications with Japan became increasingly difficult, the General Southern Army was required to procure from occupied territories such necessities as food and clothes, and such facilities as railways, ships, radio transmitters, electricity, machines, timber and skilled labourers, in order to be self-sufficient in supplies and operations. However, Java and Malaya were the only regions in the southern part of the General Southern Army's command which could satisfy such requirements. Moreover, the procurement of such supplies was not an easy matter. For instance, even in Sumatra, which was considered to be fairly advanced, the total industrial potential was estimated to be smaller than that of prewar Shimane Prefecture.

1. The Role of Java in the Total Southern Section of the Area Occupied by the General Southern Army

We will consider the role of Java from data of the 7th Area Army, which was in charge of the southern part of the area occupied by the General Southern Army (with Commander-Gen. Toihara, later succeeded by Gen. Itagaki; Chief of Staff Lt.-Gen. Ayabe; Staff Officer Col. Imaoka Yutaka; and Staff Officer in charge of military administration, Col. Mori Fumio).

2. Implementation of the Policy of Increasing the Supply Capacity

Summary

I really only understood the nature of a colonial economy, and how different it is from an independent national economy, when I saw the situation in Indonesia, where there was not even a single ironworks, chemical factory, or carbide factory, and even the necessary technology and attendant facilities such as electricity, radio communication and medicine production were lacking. What facilities there were had in most cases to be transferred from Java to other parts of Indonesia. We transferred surplus sugar and tea manufacturing equipment and so forth, all of which had formerly been owned by Dutch, British and American citizens; but, with an eye to the establishment of an independent Indonesian economy, no Indonesian properties were removed.

Table 3: Results of Mutual Exchange of Non-Military Commodities (September 1945) [in tons except for cigarettes]

DESTINA-TION	COMMODITY	PLACE OF ORIGIN	1942	1943	1944	1945 (UNTIL JULY)
MALAYA	Rice	Burma	30,000	10,000	--	--
		Thailand	150,000	200,000	100,000	35,000
		Indo-China	100,000	160,000	50,000	5,000
		Java	--	--	--	30,000
		Total	280,000	370,000	150,000	70,000
	Cereals	Java	1,000	70,000	20,000	
	Salt	Java	37,000	37,000	15,000	6,500
		Thailand	2,000	2,000	--	--
		Philippines	--	2,000	1,000	--
		Total	39,000	41,000	16,000	6,500
	Sugar	Java	55,000	30,000	15,000	8,000
	Coal	Sumatra	100,000	120,000	60,000	30,000
	Coking coal	(Indo-China	--	4,000	--	--
		(Sumatra	--	--	--	1,500
		Total	100,000	124,000	60,000	31,500
	Cigarettes (millions)	Java	600	720	500	70
SUMATRA	Rice	Thailand	20,000	--	--	--
	Salt	Java	30,000	24,000	16,000	6,000
	Sugar	Java	26,000	20,000	14,000	5,000
	Tobacco	Java	240	360	300	45
JAVA	Coal	Sumatra	150,000	200,000	120,000	40,000
NORTHERN BORNEO	Rice	Indo-China	20,000	20,000	10,000	--
	Salt	Java	1,000	800	500	300
		Philippines	200	200	200	--
		Total	1,200	1,000	700	300
	Tobacco	Java	48	60	30	--
	Sugar	Philippines	800	600	400	--
		Java	200	100	100	--
		Total	1,000	700	500	--

Table 4: Trade Plan for the Civilian Sector for 1944 (Malaya-Indonesia)

REGION	EXPORTS (tons)		IMPORTS (tons)		
MALAYA	Pig iron	5,500	Zinc ore	8,900	
			Damar	200	
			Cereals	28,000	
			Cigarettes	900	*
	Unprocessed		Manila rope	600	
	Rubber	2,400	Coal	115,000	
			Cement	25,000	
			Quinine	20	
			Buffaloes	14,400	†
			Turpentine	250	
			Plaster	1,000	
			Rice	124,000	
			Rice powder	600	
			Timber	687,000	
			Manganese Dioxide	150	
			Antimony/ iron amalgam	700	
			Sugar	30,000	
SUMATRA	Coal	275,000	Pig iron	400	
	Cement	36,000	Sugar	24,000	
	Resin	750	Quinine	25	
	Palm oil	6,000	Salt	30,000	
	Timber	97,000	Plaster	8,000	
	Zinc ore	1,700	Cigarettes	500	*
	Damar	700			
	Tin	200			
	Quinine	1,440			
	Cigars	3,800			
JAVA	Salt	55,000	Pig iron	5,000	
	Sugar	70,000	Coal	15,000	
	Manganese		Cement	17,000	
	Dioxide	2,200	Tin	200	
	Zinc ore	1,000	Palm oil	6,000	
	Cigarettes	1,800 *	Timber	36,000	
	Cereals	28,000	Damar	1,000	
	Plaster	15,000	Quinine	1,440	
	Quinine	98	Turpentine	500	
	Cigars	7,900	Cotton	700	
NORTHERN BORNEO	Damar	500	Cement	1,000	
	Antimony ore	700	Salt	1,800	
			Cigarettes	100	*
			Rice	4,500	
			Sugar	1,800	
			Quinine	3	

* = millions   † = head

Table 5: Plan for Self-Sufficiency in Industry (23 July 1944)

	COMMODITIES	PRODUCTION CAPACITY IN 1944		ANTICIPATED PRODUCTION PLAN FOR 1944 (ACCORDING TO REGION)				
		EXISTING PLAN	REVISED PLAN	MALAYA	SUMATRA	JAVA	BORNEO	TOTAL
t	Charcoal	103,300	63,300	20,000				20,000
t	steel manufacturing — Open hearth	93,000	73,000					
	Electric-furnace	85,700	19,400	3,000		3,000		6,000
t	Revolving-furnace	9,600	9,600	1,000		2,000		3,000
	Rolling	177,000	109,000					
t	Stretching	25,800	20,000	6,000	1,000	2,000		8,000
t	Coke	37,200	37,200	7,000	4,000	12,000	2,000	25,000
p	Fire-bricks	8,700	8,700	2,000	300	3,000	200	5,500
t	Cement	446,000	455,000	30,000	200,000	8,000		238,000
t	Carbide	10,200	6,500	1,300				1,300
m³	Oxygen	2,860,000	2,860	1,510		1,350		2,860
t	Ammonia	520	530	5		20		25
t	Sulphuric acid	25,000	22,500		11,000	2,000		13,000
t	Nitric acid	500	500					
t	Caustic soda	13,000	9,600	300		5,000		5,300
t	Hydrochloric acid	1,300	500			100		100
t	Chlorate	840	250	20		200		220
t	Glycerine	1,200	1,200	100		400		500
t	Materials for explosives — Gun powder 'Carlit'	1,000	1,000			250		250
t	[perchlorate]	2,000	2,000					
t	Dynamite	250	250					
t	Amatol	700	700			500		500
p	Detonators	21,000	16,000			800		800
km	Fuses	28,000	24,000			8,000		8,000
t	Priming powder	3	3					
t	Electrodes	1,100	1,600	100		100		200
t	Zinc tubes	4,300	4,300	1,500		1,500		3,000
p	Car tires	320	320	15	5	50		70
p	Wooden casks	1,050	1,045	350	100	30	10	490
p	Tire cords	700	700	10	200	210		720
p	Cotton cloth	48,210	48,210	1,000	3,000	24,100	70	28,170
t	Paper	33,240	33,210	1,500	2,500	6,800		10,800

Key to the table: t = tons, p = 1,000 pieces, km = kilometres, m³ = cubic metres.

240

**Table 6: The Construction of Wooden Ships in 1944
(at the end of June 1944)**

CLASSIFICATION		MALAYA	SUMATRA	JAVA	NORTHERN BORNEO	TOTAL
NUMBER OF WORKERS	Japanese	466	45	215	190	914
	Indonesians	15,198	2,463	44,455	3,033	65,149
NUMBER OF SHIPS	Existing	135	55	96	39	325
	To be in-creased by	70	--	73	11	154
PLAN FOR SHIP BUILDING IN 1944	150-ton ships	280	100	700	80	1,100
	150-ton oil tankers	20	20	--	--	40
	250-ton ships	50	10	--	--	60
TOTAL	Ships	350	130	700	80	1,260
	Tonnage	57,500	20,500	105,000	12,500	199,500
1943 TOTAL	Under construction	74	20	51	33	178
	Launched	16	6	127	15	164
	Completed	30	0	56	7	93
1944 TOTAL	Under construction	79	12	68	26	185
	Launched	23	5	163	14	205
	Completed	11	3	18	3	35
PLAN FOR 1944	Hulls	420	100	600	40	1,160
	Motorized lighters	160	700	150	--	410

Table 7: The Production of Engines for Wooden Ships in 1944 (by end July 1944)

	TYPE OF ENGINE	MALAYA	SUMATRA	JAVA	NORTHERN BORNEO	TOTAL
PLAN FOR 1944	New	150 (100)	50	920	0	1,220
	Remodelled	150 (30)	0	0	0	180
ACHIEVEMENT BY THE END OF JULY	New – underway	30	7	14	0	51
	– completed	17	3	37	0	57
	Remodelled					
	– underway	55	0	0	0	55
	– completed	0	0	0	0	0

Note: (a) The plan for 1944 includes for Java 104 diesel engines of Osamu model to be fitted to 150-ton ships.

(b) Figures in ( ) indicate engines for ships to be used by the military.

242

Table 8: Modified Plan for the Production of Wooden Ships and their Fitting with Engines (July 1944)

CLASSIFICATION	MALAYA	SUMATRA	JAVA	NORTHERN BORNEO	TOTAL
WOODEN SHIPS					
150-ton model	130	25	343	30	528
150-ton oil tankers	20	10	10	0	40
150-ton ships for horse transport	0	0	7	0	7
250-ton model	20	5	0	0	25
Total	170	40	360	30	600
TUG BOATS					
200 h.p.	10	0	10	0	20
70 or 75 h.p.	10	5	10	5	30
50 h.p.	10	5	10	5	30
Total	30	10	30	10	80
ENGINES FOR SHIPS (remodelled)	75	17 (81)	322	0	465*
NATIVE BOATS					
Sampans	(18,000)	(500)	--	(500)	(19,000)
Sailing boats	--	(1,000)	(15,000)	(1,000)	(17,000)
Total	110 (18,000)	20 (1,500)	80 (15,000)	20 (1,500)	230 (36,000)

* Apart from this the Army had 70 engines.
( ) = tonnage

A. Industry

We desperately hoped to increase the production of wooden ships, to enable us to send medical supplies to New Guinea, and also to launch an attack on Morotai. To this end, great numbers of beautiful teak trees were felled without compunction. Although General Southern Army Headquarters anticipated being able to produce from 60% to 70% of the required total of ships and engines in Java, it was unable to put this plan into effect (Nakayama Jiro, of the former Ministry of Posts and Communications, and Watabe Iwao, of the former Ministry of Railways, know the details of this).

According to the Gunseikambu, which I believe had comprehensive information on Indonesian engineers and facilities, there were in the whole of Java 235 Indonesian engineers, 1,297 (2,551) skilled (and semi-skilled labourers, and 22 (91)* electricians; while repair factories numbered only 29, with three additional ones for electrical equipment. There had been 23,000 Dutch engineers in Java in the prewar period, and the reason the Indonesians were unskilled is that they had never been placed in positions of authority.

Consequently, the ship-building in 1944 was undertaken by 45,000 Indonesian workers under the supervision of 215 Japanese engineers.

B. Rice

(a) The rice situation in the South and Java

As can be seen from the table below, there was a shortfall of 100,000 tons of rice in Java in 1944, when the army's rice requirements are included. However, the production figures are not altogether reliable.

Table 9: Rice Supply and Demand in Java in 1944

Production	4,630,000 tons
Consumption	
a. civilian sector	4,350,000 tons
b. military sector (incl. stockpile)	380,000 tons
Total	4,730,000 tons
Deficit/shortfall	100,000 tons

* The alternative estimates in parentheses were obtained by the author from other sources.

Table 10: Production and Consumption of Polished Rice in the Southern Areas in the Pre-War Period (quantity in tons, population in thousands)

REGION	YEAR	HARVEST	IMPORT	EXPORT	CONSUMP-TION	TOTAL POPULA-TION	ANNUAL PER CAPITA CONSUMPTION
British Borneo	1940	28,500	16,928	0	45,423	285	0.15
Brunei	1940	3,265	3,235	0	6,500	40	0.15
Sarawak	1940	31,800	38,239	0	70,039	490	0.14
Indo-China	1938	3,757,800	10,336	937,250	2,830,886	23,030	0.12
Burma	1938	8,169,000	1,215	2,786,060	5,384,155	14,647	0.36
Malaya	1938	303,995	831,195	205,967	929,223	4,385	0.21
East Indies	1938	4,168,950	334,290	16,640	4,486,600	60,727	0.07
Philippines	1938	1,437,490	9,360	290	1,448,580	16,000	0.07
Thailand	1938	4,555,699	0	1,398,360	3,157,339	14,465	0.21
Japan	1939	9,697,000	1,460,000	99,000	11,058,000	72,827	0.15

* NB: Eight parts of unhulled rice converts to five parts of polished rice.

245

(b) Rice consumption of the Japanese in Java

The average Japanese rice consumption per capita per diem during the war was estimated at 640 grams. Thus, the 74,000 Japanese in Java at the end of the war would consume 17,000 tons per year. Therefore the rice consumption of the Japanese alone was unlikely to have upset the rice situation.

At the end of the war, the 16th Army had the following stockpiles of rice: 10,000 tons in West Java and 7,000 tons* in East and Central Java (estimated on the basis of these two regions having 70% of the former). The resulting total is the figure of 17,000 given above.

In July 1945, because of the likelihood of a decisive battle in Singapore, the 7th Area Army assigned to the 16th Army in Java the task of acquiring the following amounts of rice for the year 1945 by means of a levy:

Destination	Quantity
South Sumatra	15,000 tons
South Borneo	nil
Celebes and Lesser Sundas	6,000 tons
Navy	15,000 tons
Java	100,000 tons
Singapore	40,000 tons
Total	176,000 tons

Until that time, the bulk of the rice for Singapore had been supplied by Indochina and Thailand (see Table 3). With the severing of naval supply lines, however, and the resultant need to stockpile rice for a decisive action in Singapore, Java's rice requirements increased. It is not clear how much rice was actually sent to Singapore from Java. Whatever the case, transportation was not easy because of the shortage of ships.

(c) Demand for rice for semi-military purposes

Apart from rice for the Japanese, the Army was obliged to acquire rice for the Heiho, Giyugun, and the Indonesian labourers [**romusha**] to whom it was obliged to supply special rations. The number of such recipients is listed in the table below. The rice which the 7th Area Army instructed the 16th Army to procure was intended chiefly for these romusha.

* Miyamoto's Japanese text has 17,000 tons here, an apparent misprint.

Table 11: The Number of Romusha [in Java]

		ARMY	NAVY	GUNSEI-KAMBU	TOTAL
Heiho	male	14,394	877		15,271
Giyugun	male	36,067			36,067
Regular romusha	male	38,370	27,832	239,071	105,273
	female	4,862		446,136	450,998
Occasional romusha	male	112,980	6,990	549,529	669,499
	female	7,675		61,670	69,345
Skilled workers	male	49,909	38,600	184,039	264,548
	female	1,795	1,400	9,410	12,605
Voluntary labourers	male & female	50,000		150,085	200,085
Total		316,052	67,699	2,239,940	2,623,691

* This list should be understood to include all those workers for whom the Japanese were obliged to provide rice, including both full-time ('regular') **romusha** and workers used on a rotation basis. 'Skilled workers' includes all artisans as well as typists, nurses, etc.

(d) Military strategy

The military strength of the 16th Army in 1943 and 1944 was inadequate for any decisive action. Accordingly, we planned to stock food and munitions in advance at scattered places in order to dispense with labour for replenishments. However, this plan was not implemented. When the strategy of transferring the troops in East and Central Java to West Java was decided on, I ordered the troops to set up redoubts,* just in case there was any delay in moving, and also ordered Japanese civilians attached to the Army to set up redoubts so that they would be able to conduct good administration in their respective regions until the end. Apparently both the Army and civilians attached to the Army misinterpreted this order and tried to accumulate excessive quantities of foodstuffs and munitions.

* The word used here, **fukukaku,** is an archaic military term evoking a hilltop defensive position from the samurai past. It was presumably intended to imply a heroic stand to the last man.

To meet the demand for rice, the Gunseikambu placed its first administrative priority on an increase in food production, especially rice, and despatched Japanese agricultural experts into the countryside. This resulted in an increase in the supply of rice in excess of that required by the military.

In order to calculate accurately the demand for rice from the military and civilian sectors (most of the demand came from the civilian sector) and to distribute the rice to the whole of Java, Headquarters prohibited the movement of rice out of any Residency, and fixed the rice levy for each Residency. Army vehicles were provided for the transportation of rice for the civilian sector. However, in implementing the levy the ration was arbitrarily increased at the lower levels of the administration; the prohibition on moving rice out of the Residencies appeared extremely repressive to the population; and furthermore the problems of maintaining a flow of rice, already posed by transportation difficulties, were further aggravated by the Japanese controls on the price of rice as an anti-inflation measure. It is now evident that our policy on rice was completely useless because of our inability to recognize early enough that there would not be a northward attack from Australia. However, I was gratified some time later, after my repatriation to Japan, to hear that Mori Hideo, who had been engaged in the increase of rice production in Indonesia for a time during the war, had been very pleased to find a photograph in **Life** Magazine showing the regular planting of young rice plants in Indonesia, as this seemed to be a result of the Japanese endeavour to increase production.

C. **Textiles**

The demand for textiles in Java before the war was 100 million yards annually. In January 1944 the total stock in Java was 50 million yards, most of which had been confiscated during the initial stages of the war, and carefully stored. After the pacification of Java, the Gunseikambu took over all four textile factories which had operated in the Dutch period, and entrusted the management to Japanese companies. The Gunseikambu further tried to expand these by introducing machines and experts from Japan, and to increase textile production by concentrating on simply manufactured textiles, and by encouraging the cultivation of cotton. Military requirements were to be met first, and the balance used to meet civilian needs. However, as the import of materials from Japan gradually became impossible, we were forced to release stockpiled reserves; and because of the requirements of the military it was necessary to commandeer the civilian textile allowance. Since virtually none of the existing stock remained in the hands of the indigenous people, the textile shortage reached the point where the population had to try and utilize gunny sacks for clothes, and special procedures had to be set up for distributing the white material in which the dead were wrapped. Even the Army had to make economies wherever possible, such as patching clothes. However, according to the reports of Japanese officers in charge of textile procurement, great hordes of relatives would turn up to see the Giyugun and Heiho soldiers at the barracks on visiting days, and all would be neatly and tidily dressed. I felt that the population would look back with nostalgia to these hard times, as long as Japan won the war.

D. Labour

The number of Javanese romusha assigned by the 7th Area Army was as follows:

Destination	Number
Malaya	22,100
Sumatra	92,700
North Borneo	17,000
Lesser Sundas	6,000
Celebes	20,000
Reserves	7,200
Total	165,000
Navy Area	63,000
Grand Total	228,000

With these numbers of labourers, each region was supposed to fulfil the objective of self-sufficiency. However, fortunately or otherwise, the transfer of romusha was not fully implemented because of the shortage of ships. I do not know the details of the situation, and have been unable to check with those in charge.

At first, the Japanese expected the Indonesian romusha to be able to work as efficiently as the Japanese, without appreciating the low nutritional value of their diet. Consequently, we tended to regard the romusha as lazy, because of their inefficiency. After a while we came to realize the extent of romusha undernourishment, and succeeded in preventing casualties which might possibly have eventuated, by reassessing the labour capacity of the romusha at one quarter that of the average Japanese, or by providing them with regular meals. I was told that the times allowed for raising and lowering goods by ships' derricks were regulated in accordance with the reassessed labour capacity of the romusha.

The transfer of romusha from Java to the Outer Islands was

similar to the migration encouraged both by the Dutch before the war and by the Indonesian government after independence. Nobody would deny that many unreasonable policies were followed in the turmoil of war. As few ships were available, however, the actual number sent to the Outer Islands would not appear to have exceeded 150,000, although this number is not verified.

*   *   *

6. *Okada Fumihide, in later retirement.*

7.   General Staff of the 16th Army at a ceremony at the Governor-General's 'palace' in Jakarta on 29 April 1945. Lt.-Gen. Harada is in centre front. To left of him are Maj.-Gen. Yamamoto (Chief of Staff) and Maj.-Gen. Nishimura (Chief of General Affairs). To right of Harada is the Chief Medical Officer, Maj.-Gen. Sugino, and immediately to right of him, in the second row, is Lt.-Col. Miyamoto Shizuo, our author.

8. Group photo in Jakarta, November 1944, to farewell Sato Nobuhide (who is in centre wearing Sukarno's pici). Front row, left to right: Yoshizumi Tomegoro, K.H. Mas Mansur, Sato, Sukarno, R.M.A.A. Kusumo Utoyo, Mr A. Subardjo; Second row: Josef Hasan, Dr Rasyid, Mr Suwandi, Mr A.A. Maramis, Mr Iwa Kusuma Sumantri, Nishijima Shigetada; Back row: Professor Soepomo, Mr Raden Sudjono, Mr Mohd. Yamin, Taguchi Tadao, Arai Toshisuke.

9. *Ceremony to inaugurate PETA battalions, in Governor-General's palace, Jakarta, 1944.*

10. *Makasar Airfield, 28 April 1945. Admiral Shibata, followed by Sukarno, alighting from their military transport.*

NISHIJIMA SHIGETADA

I) The Nationalists in Java, 1943-1945

As its title shows, this book was intended as a historical testimony as much as an autobiography. It was not the first time for Nishijima to give his 'testimony'. In 1951 he wrote an unpublished memoir, **Dai-san no Shinsō** (The Third Truth), now deposited in the Institute of Social Sciences of Waseda University. He had two reasons to write. In 1951 he had applied for a visa to Indonesia which was refused with no reason given. Nishijima was exasperated because he believed he had contributed to Indonesian independence and expected to be treated warmly. Later he learnt that Sukarno avoided receiving any Japanese involved in the independence question for fear of suspicion by the Dutch, who had claimed that independence was a Japanese creation. Secondly, Nishijima was dissatisfied with the accounts of the independence proclamation by Mohammad Hatta and Adam Malik, as each of them omitted to mention that the independence declaration was drafted in Admiral Maeda's residence, that some Japanese participated in drawing it up, and that there was a special relationship between the Navy and Indonesian leaders. Nishijima saw his own account as 'the third truth' in relation to Hatta's and Malik's. The same motive runs through this autobiography, where he quotes 'The Third Truth' frequently. Nishijima was also a joint author of **Indoneshia ni okeru Nihon Gunsei no Kenkyū** (Tokyo, Waseda University Institute of Social Sciences, 1959), translated by the Joint Publications Research Service as **Japanese Military Administration in Indonesia** (Washington, 1963).

Nishijima Shigetada was born in 1911 in Gumma Prefecture, north of Tokyo, the son of a school teacher and principal. His mother's family were among the notables (shizoku) of the district, his grandfather being president of the Maebashi City Education Association. The author was brought up in this intellectual atmosphere. His childhood and youth witnessed a Japan in turmoil, as territorial expansion and rapid industrialization was accompanied by extremely low wages and peasant distress. The communist movement developed during this period, and Nishijima joined it as a student. He was arrested twice, in 1931 and 1933. Like many others he became very disillusioned with the Japan Communist Party while in prison in 1933, rejecting the Comintern slogan of 'converting the war into a civil war'. Nishijima withdrew completely from the communist movement in 1933, apparently convinced by the argument that 'the invasion of China is intended to liberate Asia' (**Shōgen**, p.35).

Nishijima attributes to the English lessons he had from an American woman in his youth the overcoming of his racial prejudice and his first thoughts of going abroad. After release from prison he was drafted into the army for two years and deliberately became a 'model soldier', because he wanted to show that a man who had been involved in the communist movement could be a diligent member of the existing society. Following the suggestion of the 'supervisor' responsible for his good behaviour, Nishijima decided to go to Indonesia because there could be little future for an ex-communist in Japan.

Nishijima left Japan for Indonesia in July 1937, and portrays this romantically as his 'escape to the Southern Cross' (p.52). Until the outbreak of the Pacific War he worked for the Chiyoda Hyakkaten Department Store, in Surabaya, Batavia, and Bandung. He studied German, Indonesian and Dutch, and used as his Dutch textbook Blumberger's **De Nationalistische Beweging in Nederlandsch-Indië**. This aroused his interest in Indonesian nationalism. He was critical, however, of the prevailing nationalist strategy of gradually developing a power base independent of the Dutch (**machtsvorming**), believing independence was only possible through the physical sacrifice of revolution.

In the closing years of Dutch rule, the Japanese in Indonesia were asked to cooperate with the Japanese military to collect information and organize a 'fifth-column movement' (**dai-goretsu katsudō**). Nishijima joined the movement with the motive of 'expelling the Dutch and enabling Indonesia to achieve independence' (p.82). The fifth column secured the cooperation of such Indonesian nationalists as Jusuf Hasan, Subardjo, A.A. Maramis, Tadjoeddin Noor, Samsi Sastrawidagda, Douwes Dekker and Muhammad Yamin. Nishijima's contact with these nationalists was to lead to the formation of the so-called 'Navy group' after the Japanese invasion. He was involved in the establishment of a Committee for Indonesian Independence, surveying possible invasion sites, and most importantly, the investigation through Jusuf Hasan of the likely response of young Indonesian nationalists to Japan.

Immediately after the declaration of war, the Japanese in Indonesia were arrested and transferred to Australia as prisoners of war. Nishijima was detained at Love Day, 180 miles north of Adelaide. His memoir describes his journey from Batavia to Adelaide, life in camp, and the return journey from Adelaide to Singapore as part of an exchange of prisoners of war. One or two days before the detainees arrived in Singapore, a senior Japanese officer boarded the ship and urged them to return to Indonesia as most of them could speak Indonesian and therefore had a contribution to make. Nishijima agreed to go, 'to witness the change in the Indonesian situation' (pp.124-5).

On 1 October 1942 the **Kaigun Bukanfu** [Navy Liaison Office] was established in Jakarta under Admiral Maeda, to facilitate communication between the 16th Army in Java and the Navy authorities in eastern Indonesia. Nishijima was employed by the research section of the Bukanfu on the recommendation of N. Sato, one of the fifth-column organizers connected with the Navy. Nishijima's responsibilities included promoting better Japanese-Indonesian relations, which brought him into frequent contact with the leading Indonesian nationalist politicians. He became increasingly sympathetic with their demand for independence. He and other members of the Bukanfu were able to provide a degree of support and protection to the nationalists by virtue of the almost extraterritorial position of the Navy. At the critical moment of the Japanese surrender, the Bukanfu group was particularly disposed to support Indonesian independence in the interest of long-term Japanese-Indonesian relations, rather than to take a narrow view of international legal obligations.

Nishijima Shigetada

SHŌGEN: INDONESHIA DOKURITSU KAKUMEI -
ARU KAKUMEIKA NO HANSHŌ

[Testimony: Indonesian Independence and Revolution - A Half
Life History of a Revolutionary] (Tokyo, Shin Jimbutsu
Ōrai-sha, 1975), pp.149-72

Blood Comrades

It was natural for me to have frequent contact with
Indonesians, as my task in the Research Section of the **Kaigun
Bukanfu** [Navy Liaison Office] was to investigate political and
economic relations between the Japanese and Indonesians. I
myself also tried to meet Indonesians as much as possible in
order not only to listen to their complaints and grievances but
also to discuss how Indonesia could achieve independence and
what shape an independent Indonesia should have. I functioned
as a mediator between Sukarno and Hatta, since these two
occasionally argued with each other due to the difference in
their ideas, though their conflict was not serious. When I
intervened, they usually accepted my arbitration and listened
seriously to my opinions. The relationship between me and the
two was more than that between Japanese and Indonesians. We
were clearly blood-comrades. I feel I did whatever I could for
them. In any case it is certain that we trusted each other.

As well as Sukarno and Hatta, Achmad Subardjo,* Adam Malik
and Chaerul Saleh† also had a comradely relationship with me,

---

* Mr Raden Achmad Subardjo (1897-1979) was hardly an 'ordinary
young man'. He obtained his law degree at Leiden in 1933,
taking a leading part in anti-colonial politics as President
of the Perhimpunan Indonesia. After returning to Indonesia
he worked as a lawyer and a journalst, and then spent six
months in Japan in 1935-36 writing articles for the **Matahari**
newspaper. Subsequently he accepted a position in the
Economic Affairs Department in Batavia. He became
Indonesia's first Foreign Minister in 1945.

† Adam Malik (1917-84), who eventually became Indonesian Vice-
President (1978-83), was born in Pematang Siantar, East
Sumatra. He was active in both Partindo and Gerindo, before
moving to Batavia in 1934. After a year in prison because of
alleged links with Tan Malaka's PARI party he became one of

though they were still ordinary young men at that time. All
the persons mentioned above played a great role in achieving
independence and in the construction of the nation thereafter.
I believe it was because of our comradely relationship during
the occupation that these people talked frankly with me even
after Indonesian independence.

The time was shortly after I returned to Java after being
released from detention camp in Australia [October 1942].
Sukarno was living on Pegangsaan Timur, next to the house of
one of Ishii Taro's brothers.† This brother hailed my safe
return from Australia and invited me for a welcome dinner party
at his house. Notable Indonesian nationalists were invited to
the party.

*   *   *

I was very pleased to meet eminent Indonesian nationalist
leaders. Both Sukarno and Hatta were still young at that time.
Sukarno appeared to be a frank person while Hatta had the
serious manner of an earnest scholar. I do not remember the
details of what they said at the party, since it happened
thirty years ago. Nevertheless, they certainly criticized the
Japanese administration explicitly. They may have been willing
to criticize the Japanese because they knew my reputation
already. The gist of their criticism was as follows:

> We had great expectations of being liberated from
> Japan by the end of this war. However, this hope has
> been withering. We have, naturally, no intention of
> returning to **white** domination, and we must cut our
> ties to them on the one hand, but we have been forced
> to detach ourselves from Japan on the other. This is
> our serious dilemma.

* Footnote continued from previous page:
  the founders of the Indonesian press agency, Antara, in 1937.
  He worked for the Japanese press agency, Domei, during the
  war.

  Chaerul Saleh (1916-68), a Minangkabau from West Sumatra
  in 1916, and was a student of the Law Faculty in Batavia in
  the late 1930s. Although never completing his degee, he was
  very active in Indonesian student politics, becoming chairman
  of the radical student organization PPPI.

† Ishii Taro, like Nishijima, had been working in a Japanese
  firm in Batavia before the war, and had also played a role in
  fifth-column activities.

Japan used to be our example. 'The Japanese victory
over Russia, a big country, aroused the peoples not
only of Asia but even of the Middle East. We were
unfortunately   disappointed   by   Japanese
'rudeness' when we actually met them.

The   rudeness   of   the   Japanese   seems   to   have   embarrassed
Indonesians considerably. I therefore put a clause 'to improve
the rude behaviour of the Japanese' in the 'direct petition'
[see below]. Subardjo, who played an important role in the
independence question, later commented on this problem.*

It is common for soldiers to be brutal in wartime.
The British and Australian soldiers who landed in
Java shortly after the end of the war behaved more
savagely than Japanese troops in matters such as the
violation of women. With the Japanese it was their
bad manners which struck us more forcefully than in
the case of the British and Australians, since our
expectations of the Japanese had been so high.
Because of their strict military discipline, the
Japanese did not commit offences against women.
However, they roared at Indonesians and hit them,
which hurt people's feelings and dominated their
reactions.

There are positive points in these words of Subardjo. In
those days, he and many of Indonesian leaders were Western-
educated   and   acquainted   with   international   manners.
Consequently they seem to have viewed critically aspects of
Japanese behaviour which were not internationally accepted, and
to have been unable to tolerate Japanese rudeness. The image
of the Japanese among the Indonesian younger generation was
somewhat different from that of their elders. Some of the
Indonesian youths who joined the **Giyugun** [volunteer corps] and
Heiho [auxiliary corps], developed a sense of solidarity with
the Japanese soldiers who like them were rigorously trained and
hit by their Japanese trainers. In any case there is no doubt
that hitting people in itself gave the Indonesians a bad
impression of the Japanese. Even now there are Indonesians who
complain about the Japanese, instancing the name of a
particular Japanese who used physical force on them.
    It must not be forgotten that the Indonesians observed
with real hatred that the Japanese acted as if they were the
leaders, superior to the Indonesians. Japan pursued the
occupation of Indonesia under the slogan of the construction of
the Greater East Asia Co-Prosperity Sphere. Even Sukarno did
not object to this idea. On the contrary he showed an attitude

* We have not been able to trace this quotation.

of cooperation with Japan on the grounds that Asia should be united and mutually supportive. That famous communist, Tan Malaka, had a similar idea. However, the Indonesians disliked the idea that only one of the Asian peoples should become the leader of the whole, like a conductor in an orchestra. The Indonesians could not accept this because of their nationalism.

Once Admiral Maeda invited Dr Matsumoto Noriaki (the present director general of Shiba Gakuen) to Jakarta in order to let him talk with Indonesian leaders. Dr Matsumoto was a specialist in Indian philosophy and an eloquent speaker as well. He explained the idea of the Greater East Asia Co-Prosperity Sphere to Indonesian leaders: 'To use a musical analogy, the Greater East Asia Co-Prosperity Sphere is something like an orchestra. Indonesia plays a violin, Burma plays a flute, and others play their respective instruments. Japan is to conduct the orchestra.'

The Indonesian leaders present listened to this explanation quietly. After a while they asked, 'Why cannot Indonesia or Burma be the conductor?' The question should be understood to contain a strong protest against Japan. That is, why would Japan not allow Indonesian independence despite the fact that it had been proclaiming the similarity of the skin colour between the two, the equality in position of both countries, and the liberation from the Dutch.

At the time the meeting mentioned above was held, Indonesian nationalist leaders of the younger generation such as Adam Malik (the present Minister of Foreign Affairs) had not yet come to the fore. Adam Malik is one of those who played an important role at the declaration of Indonesian independence, and a politician who has exercised considerable influence over Indonesian politics in general since independence. He makes a criticism of the Japanese occupation in the Introduction of his book, **Riwajat dan Perdjuangan sekitar Proklamasi Kemerdekaan Indonesia 17 Augustus 1945** (Widjaya, 1950). From his writing we can glimpse how his generation viewed Japan:

> If we look at the social structure when the Dutch fled to Australia at the end of March 1942, we can clearly see that the Indonesian masses were excited and astonished by the arrival of Japanese imperialism which put an end to Dutch imperialism. However, the heavy-handedness of Japanese oppression throughout the Archipelago during the occupation, both through the controlled wartime economy and other measures such as forced labour and systematic drilling of all social strata, meant that the impact of the four-year occupation upon our national mentality was very great. We could say that during those four years our whole nation underwent a fundamental spiritual revolution. In the course of four years of

257

> oppression the economic and social bases of Indonesia were extinguished and destroyed to the point where there was no social group which did not feel the heavy burden of the Japanese Army.*

The reason why the Japanese invasion evoked tremendous excitement in Indonesia was that the Indonesians expected not only to be liberated from Dutch imperialism but to be able to achieve independence as a result of the invasion; the people had been dreaming of independence for a long time. History clearly teaches us that the dream was pitifully smashed, as Malik says. Malik further points to a spiritual revolution among the people as a result of the Japanese occupation. I agree with this interpretation, which Tan Malaka also shared.

It seems to be necessary to explain this spiritual revolution. The Japanese authorities pursued several policies which unconsciously undermined the existing Indonesian feudal social system. The forced labour, as Malik called it, mobilized peasants who had never seen beyond their own villages to go to the area of other ethnic groups to construct defence facilities. In this way the peasants could see a new world. Furthermore, the Japanese appointed the 'rebels' of the Dutch period, i.e. those involved in the nationalist movement, to be **Guncho (Bupati)** and **Soncho (Camat)** in place of members of feudalistic aristocratic families. This policy had the effect of undermining the feudal structure from inside.

The training drill which Malik mentions introduced a strict military training in Japanese style to the Indonesians, who had had the reputation of being the mildest people in the world and had not been allowed to bear arms and weapons. Because of this training, Indonesians were able to acquire the basic military knowledge necessary for the revolution. There were other important contributions by the Japanese administration to the achievement of the revolution, such as the exaltation of nationalism, which was also encouraged by Sukarno and Hatta deliberately drawing the masses into organizations and giving them political training even though within the framework of the Japanese occupation.

The Japanese implemented the policies above not to promote Indonesian independence but to mobilize the population in pursuit of war. The Indonesians on their part made use of Japanese policies and their results for the revolution, though not without trial and error. In any event, the nationalism of the people was intensified and their rush along the path to independence more rapid as the oppression of Japan became heavier and its war position worse.

When mentioning my relationship with Indonesia, I have to

---

* The quotation is on page 9 of the 1970 edition.

refer to Subardjo, a friend and blood-comrade of mine. As I said before, Subardjo joined the nationalist movement shortly before the war with considerable expectations about Japan. At the time of the declaration of independence and successive struggles for independence, he was an important figure. Whenever we talk about the Indonesian revolution we do not fail to mention Sukarno and Hatta, and it is a historical fact that these two persons were the main figures of the revolution. Nevertheless, we should not forget Subardjo who functioned as a producer of modern Indonesian history behind the scenes of the revolution. I feel an invisible string which connected Subardjo with me, because of the fact that he was attached to the Kaigun Bukanfu and was regarded as a member of 'the Navy group' by Adam Malik during the occupation.

Some Indonesian leaders seemed to be disappointed to find that I was not in the Japanese Army which landed in Java at the beginning of the war, since they had been expecting me to come back to Java again. Subardjo was one such leader. He had been convinced that independence would be achieved once the Japanese landed in Java. He became very depressed when the Japanese rejected a blueprint for the composition of a new Indonesian cabinet - the blueprint he prepared before the Japanese landing.*

While Subardjo was in this state of depression, the Japanese authorities in Java set up the so called 'Hatta Office'† which was intended to listen to the complaints and requests of the population in order to promote a smoother administration. As Hatta was the head of this Office, it was also called **Hatta Kikan** [Hatta Organization]. It was rather natural that Subardjo came to work in this Office, since he had shared the experience of the independence movement with Hatta as a senior member of the Perhimpunan Indonesia while studying in the Netherlands.

One day, perhaps at the beginning of 1943, A.A. Maramis#

* The composition of this proposed cabinet and the manner of its submission to the Japanese, in which Abikoesno rather than Subardjo appears to have taken the main initiative, are discussed in Kanahele, pp.31-2 and 260-1, and Nishijima, Kishi et al, **Japanese Military Administration in Indonesia** (Washington, 1963), pp.342-3.

† On the Hatta Kikan, see Miyoshi, above, p.114-15. It may be related to the **Shijun-in** described by Imamura, above, p.73-4.

Mr A.A. Maramis (1897-1977) was a Menadonese, who graduated from Leiden in law in 1924. Thereafter he practised law in various Indonesian cities. He married a Dutch woman and

came into the office of the Research Section with a threatening look. He brought the news that Subardjo had been arrested by the Kempeitai. Incidentally Maramis had studied in the Netherlands and joined the Perhimpunan Indonesia like Hatta and Subardjo. He was also involved in the independence struggle. After independence he assumed the positions of Minister of Finance and Foreign Affairs. In relation to his arrest, the outward charge made against Subardjo by the Japanese was a minor offence during the Dutch period, when he had been working as a lawyer in Bandung. The Japanese authorities dared to use their power to arrest Subardjo on such a negligible charge because they considered Subardjo a communist.

Subardjo had attended the Conference Against Colonialism and Imperialism in Brussels in 1927 as a representative of the Dutch East Indies, together with Hatta. He had even visited Moscow. In addition, he was close to Hatta whom the Japanese army regarded as a communist, working in the Hatta Kikan. Although the Japanese Army labelled him a communist on these grounds, it had no definite evidence to prove the charge. Hence it brought up the incident from the Dutch period and arrested him. Subardjo was certainly a devoted nationalist, but he was neither a communist nor a member of the Communist Party. Maramis appealed to Sato: 'In spite of my efforts I was unable to obtain permission from the Japanese authorities for his release. Could you please try to rescue him?'

Sato immediately acted to appeal to the director of the judicial department of the Gunseikambu, Adachi, for Subardjo's release. However, he was told that this request could not be granted, as the Gunseikambu had imprisoned Subardjo after a formal trial. Despite this rejection we continued to appeal for his release. One day Sato and I visited Subardjo at Suka Miskin prison near Bandung. Subardjo, in a blue uniform, was in tears when he saw us. We were also in tears as we spoke to console him. He seemed not to be being badly or unreasonably treated, working as a librarian in the jail. After a while he was released after half his term, obviously as a result of our efforts. He told us later, 'I was convinced that the Navy could rescue me. When Mr Nishijima and Mr Sato visited me at the jail I thought you must have made the kind effort I had expected'.

Although Subardjo was released, he was unwilling to return to the Hatta Office which belonged to the Gunseikambu. We wondered how to deal with him. Meanwhile the Hatta Office was dissolved, for in reality it had become a kind of 'complaint

* Footnote continued from previous page:
  spent most of the years after 1950 outside Indonesia –
  initially as an ambassador, and from 1957 in retirement in
  Switzerland.

bureau against the Japanese administration' as Indonesian criticism of the Japanese began to develop, in spite of the positive aim the Japanese had initially entrusted to the Office. Taking advantage of this decision to close the Office, Sato proposed to Miyoshi Shunkichiro,* a liaison officer at the Office, that the Bukanfu take over Subardjo. Needless to say, Miyoshi, who sympathized with Subardjo, gave his immediate consent. Thus Subardjo joined the staff of the Research Section of the Bukanfu, where he could find his old comrades from the Dutch period.

It was not without reason that Sato employed Subardjo in the Bukanfu. Taking advantage of his authority and inside knowledge, Sato had taken pains to obtain the release of Subardjo evidently out of sympathy with Subardjo and consideration for his safety. For the Kempeitai would not have allowed Subardjo, whom it labelled a communist, to return to the Hatta Office even if it had continued. On the other hand, Sato thought Subardjo could not be left on his own because he was likely to be still suspect by the Kempeitai, not to mention the financial difficulties he might suffer. The best solution was to employ Subardjo in one of the Navy organizations which were 'extraterritorial jurisdiction' from the point of view of the Army. In addition, the Research Section was considered a good place for him to find his old comrades.

When we employed Subardjo, there was no work which could justify demanding an additional grant from the authorities. We therefore created a task for Subardjo, making 'military maps of New Guinea', as we thought this task provided a reasonable claim on the budget. This project was approved, and a branch office of the Research Section was established in 1943, with Subardjo as head and myself in charge of communication between the new office and the Research Section. The staff of the branch office consisted purely of Indonesians and was called the Subardjo Kikan. It was really a daring decision of the [Navy] authorities to allow the establishment of such an office in view of the general tendency of the Japanese at that time to intervene in everything. All members of the Research Section agreed to help the work of the new office without interfering, trusting the Indonesian staff entirely. As soon as the project was initiated, however, we discovered that none of the staff had a knowledge of military maps. Consequently we translated Dutch books concerning New Guinea into Japanese instead. I myself joined in this work.

*   *   *

* Miyoshi Shunkichiro was a professional diplomat seconded to the military administration. Sections of his memoirs are translated above, pp.113-25.

Direct Petition to Prime Minister Tojo

What I heard from Indonesian nationalist leaders on my
return to Java from Australia were complaints over the Japanese
refusal to grant Indonesian independence:

> The Japanese stated before the war that they would
> allow independence to Indonesia. We have cooperated
> with the Japanese, taking these words at face value.
> But the Japanese have not listened to our request for
> independence at all. This is a betrayal by the
> Japanese.

I could fully understand their views, as I knew what Japanese
propaganda had said before the war and how cooperative had been
Indonesian response. After seeking refuge in Japan, Jusuf
Hasan appealed to his comrades in Indonesia to cooperate with
the Japanese Army.* Pamphlets with the Indonesian national
flag in red and white and the Japanese rising sun were
circulated in order to publicize the unity and friendship of
the two peoples. There was a radio message saying that
Indonesians would not be killed by Japanese soldiers when they
landed if the Indonesians showed the mark of the sun on their
palms. Committees were set up by Indonesians to achieve
independence through cooperation with the Japanese.

Shortly after the Japanese landed in Java, they began to
follow policies quite contrary to their previous propaganda.
The ban on raising the national red and white flag, which had
initially been permitted, was one of those policies. The sweet
words of the Japanese before the war turned out to be nothing
but devices to facilitate a successful invasion. The most
shocking thing to me and to Indonesians was that Indonesians
were mercilessly shot and bayonetted to death by invading
Japanese soldiers even when the Indonesians showed the mark of
the sun on their palms. In connection with this Japanese
cruelty, Masu Genjiro once asked the High Command, 'Hasn't the
matter of the sun on the palm reached the High Command?' The
reply was, 'If soldiers were given details of operations
beforehand, their morale would be reduced. We have to give
orders simply to follow instructions'.

Hearing this reply, I could see that war was like that.
It is not impossible to understand that there may be special

---

* Jusuf Hasan was a Sumatran who went to Japan in 1930 to study
  economics at Meiji University, where he joined the
  ultra-nationalist Black Dragon Society. He was probably the
  most active Indonesian propagandist in Tokyo, taking part in
  establishing the Kainan Ryo centre for overseas students. In
  the middle of 1941 he returned to Indonesia as a secret
  Japanese agent. Kanahele, pp.8 and 17-18.

circumstances in the battlefield which do not allow the execution of the original plans of the Central Authorities. What would have happened, for instance, if Dutch agents put the mark of the sun on their palms. Although I have no intention to plead in defence of Japanese behaviour, the Japanese might have been precipitated into danger [by adopting a milder approach], as Masu told me. It seems that war is merciless and demands sacrifice.

My conclusion was that independence should be granted to the Indonesians in order to win the war. As a Japanese I did not wish to see Japan defeated and in a miserable condition. To win the war, Japan had to strengthen Indonesia, and for the strength and the cooperation of Indonesia its independence was indispensable. Most of the Bukanfu staff, including Maeda and Sato, were of the same opinion. Accordingly, I argued against those who insisted that Japan had to win the war even at the expense of the Indonesians. Moreover, I was one of the Japanese who tried to persuade the Indonesians to cooperate with the Japanese in order to achieve their independence, and promised them that they could attain independence if they so cooperated.

I will quote from **Daisan no Shinsō** [The Third Truth] to describe how I was feeling at that time:

> It was a great betrayal of the Indonesian people by the Japanese to have subsequently banned the hoisting of the flag. How could Japan excuse itself for this ban, in view of the fact that the overseas service of Radio Tokyo had constantly broadcast the independence song [**Indonesia Raya**] and that Japanese aeroplanes had dropped posters over Indonesia depicting a scene where Japanese soldiers holding the rising sun and Indonesians holding the **merah putih** exchanged good wishes? I was very depressed and annoyed when told about the ban by Indonesians during the occupation. When I returned from Australia to Java in October 1942 without having stepped down on the ground of my fatherland, I had first of all to be confronted by this Japanese deception. When Indonesians attacked the Japanese on this subject, I made up my mind to fight against Japanese policies which were wrong.

Just about the time the national flag issue was sensitive, the problem arose of entrance into higher educational institutions for people from the Outer Islands. After the invasion, the Japanese Army closed the Law School in Jakarta and changed the building into the head office of the Kempeitai, while the Medical College was re-opened. The Japanese closed the Law School, perhaps because they feared it would become a breeding ground for political activities and leftists. During the Dutch period many students from the Outer Islands were

enrolled in the Medical College. With the Japanese occupation,
however, it became difficult for applicants from the Outer
Islands, particularly such Navy-occupied islands as Celebes
(Sulawesi) and Borneo (Kalimantan), to enter the Medical
College in Java, i.e. in the Army-occupied area. In addition,
many who had been enrolled in the Dutch period were unable to
return to the College because of the difficulty of receiving
money from their homes. Apart from the odd situation that the
Navy and Army areas appeared to be 'independent states',
special permission was necessary for moving from one to the
other. As permission was not granted easily, not a few
applicants from the Outer Islands had to give up going to the
College.

One day, the leading figures from the Outer Islands,
Latuharhary* (later a governor of Ambon), Ratulangie (later a
governor of Celebes) and Tadjoeddin Noor† (later a member of
Parliament) visited Sato, the director of the Research Section,
in order to plead for the return of students from the Outer
Islands to the Medical College. It goes without saying that
Sato offered 'to do his best'. While negotiating with the
Gunseikambu, Sato explained the situation to Azuma Ryutaro,
then the Chief of the Health Department of the Southwestern
Area Minseifu (the headquarters of which was located in Makasar
in Celebes). Taking advantage of an opportunity to accompany

---

* Mr Johannes Latuharhary (1900-59) was an Ambonese who gained
his Leiden law degree in 1927. Thereafter he practised law
primarily in Surabaya until the war, when he moved to a
judicial post in Jakarta. He had been active in the Parindra
party.

† Dr G.S.S.J. Ratulangie (1890-1949) was a Christian
Minahassan, born in Tondano, North Celebes. He was in Europe
for 11 years before returning with his doctorate in science
from Zurich in 1919. He became a prominent journalist and
politician, and one of the longest serving nationalist
members of the Volksraad (1927-37). In 1944 the Bukanfu
arranged his transfer from Jakarta to Makasar, where he
headed the nationalist organization Sudara. Named first
Republican Governor of Sulawesi, he was imprisoned by the
Dutch there in 1946.

Mr Tajoeddin Noor was born in eastern Kalimantan of Bugis
descent in 1906, and obtained his law degree from Leiden. In
the 1930s he sat in the Banjarmasin Municipal Council with
support from Parindra. He too was sent to Makasar in 1944.
After 1945 he opted, unlike Ratulangie, to pursue his
nationalist goals within the structures set up by the
returning Dutch. For both these men see also Shibata, below,
p.281.

him to Bandung, I also asked for his help during the drive. Azuma simply said in a businesslike way, 'Yes, I will'.

Soon after Azuma returned to Makasar, money was sent to the Bukanfu for something like 30 students, meaning that the affected students were able to return to the College. Incidentally, Azuma became governor of the Tokyo metropolitan area and played an important role during the Tokyo Olympic Games after the war. While in Indonesia he studied Dutch, reading old Dutch books, as he was originally proficient in German which was similar.

In the meantime I was to go back to Japan on leave. Hearing the news of my return to Japan, some students came to my office and repeatedly questioned whether I was to be deported. I could not hold back my tears of thankfulness for their concern over me. Although I tried to persuade them that I would certainly come back again, they seemed not to believe it. Zus Ratulangie, a daughter of Ratulangie working in the Bukanfu, was one of the [medical] students. She was carrying out a research project on the women's movement and the communist movement. On her identification card which was returned to the Bukanfu was written in Indonesian, 'kepada seorang mau berguna' (to a person who wants to serve). **Daisan no Shinsō** describes the association between the students of the Medical College and myself as follows:

> I had received frequent visits from students of the Medical College since they joined the revolution. I still remember having criticized such students, mainly by using quotations from Lenin's **Leftism: An Infantile Disorder**.

*   *   *

There were many incidents during the occupation which arose from Japanese misunderstanding, or were often even deliberately framed by Japanese. Even when it was clear the Japanese had distorted reality, the Indonesians had to give in to the Japanese Army, the ruler, for, as the Japanese proverb says: 'You may as well reason with a crying baby as try to resist the authorities'. Many critics of the Japanese administration and suspected communists were made to suffer, particularly in cases framed by the Japanese.

G.M.T. Kahin, a famous Indonesianist, in his book **Nationalism and Revolution in Indonesia**, writes as if there were strong underground organizations during the occupation. Little evidence can be found to prove this. I believe that the number of Indonesians arrested and charged as enemy agents in the strict sense was not large, in view of the circumstance mentioned above. Of course, there were numerous criticisms of the Japanese administration and Japan, but most of them proposed points which should be improved in the administration rather than representing a total rejection of the administration or of Japan as such. People were arrested even on charges of minor criticism. Such were the circumstances at that time. Arrest in fact depended on whether a person raised his voice and how loudly he cried out, not on whether he had criticisms, since undoubtedly everybody was critical of the administration in their minds.

Among the so-called anti-Japan plots was 'the Muchtar affair'.* Although the truth of this affair is not clear, I will introduce it by quoting the 'Miyoshi Memoir':†

> The Muchtar affair was an anti-Japan plot in which a professor of microbiology in the Jakarta Medical College, Dr Muchtar, put tetanus bacteria into preventive serum with the purpose of killing Japanese. Although the truth of the whole affair was not clear, many romusha [forced labourers] in the Outer Islands died a mysterious death on several occasions in 1944. As a result of far-reaching investigations, it was proved that the preventive serum was the cause of death. In the course of further investigation of those who were engaged in the production of the serum, the Army eventually discovered evidence of the cultivation of tetanus bacteria in the laboratory of Dr Muchtar. The Japanese accordingly concluded that the murders were an anti-Japan plot by Dr Muchtar.

This 'Memoir' claims that the cultivation of tetanus bacteria in the laboratory of Dr Muchtar was definite evidence of his plotting against Japan. However, it could be quite natural for the microbiology laboratory to cultivate tetanus bacteria for experiment, since a large number of people were killed by tetanus in Southeast Asia until recently. Moreover, if Dr Muchtar really intended the killing of Japanese, why would he leave the evidence in an explicit way? There is a distinct possibility that the Japanese forced him to make a false confession by means of torture.

Although there was a department in charge of political crimes in the Gunseikambu, similar to the Tokkō Keisatsu [Special High Police], it was smaller and less powerful than

---

* On the Muchtar affair see also Sukarno. An Autobiography, pp.193-4, and the much more critical account of Abu Hanifah, Tales of a Revolution (Sydney, 1972) pp.125-7. During the occupation Professor Muchtar had become Director of the Eykman Institute for medical research.

† See note, p.261.

the Kempeitai. As the Kempeitai dealt with serious cases in advance of the department, its reputation was worse than the latter's. The Kempeitai was notorious for its tough interrogation. It arrested suspects on the charge of conspiracy when some people died of tetanus, and on the charge of anti-Japanese murder when several Japanese were seized with typhoid.

Latuharhary, the first governor of Ambon after independence, was one of those arrested by the Kempeitai as alleged culprits in such an affair. He was born in Ambon and was working in the Gunseikambu during the occupation. Ambon, together with Minahassa in Northern Celebes, was called the 'Thirteenth Province of the Netherlands' because of the pro-Dutch attitude of the Ambonese and Minahassans. Most of the population were Christians. With such a background there were many Ambonese who enjoyed privileges during the Dutch period. Many Ambonese and Minahassans were enrolled in the Dutch colonial army. Considering these circumstances during the Dutch period, the Japanese authorities employed non-Christians in preference to Ambonese and Minahassan Christians as administrative staff in Java and Sumatra where most of the population were Muslims.

The fact that many Ambonese were arrested in the tetanus and typhoid affair may not have been unrelated to the sceptical Japanese attitude towards Ambonese. Latuharhary was arrested in the typhoid affair without any firm evidence. I came to know of his arrest when his wife visited me and asked for my help: 'Please rescue my husband. I hear he has been arrested and his friend killed'.

The following day Sato and I negotiated with the Kempeitai in Bogor where Latuharhary was detained. We asked them to release him. They replied, 'He cannot be released because he is an enemy spy'. 'On the contrary,' I protested, 'he has been close to us since prewar times, joining the nationalist movement against the Dutch. If he is really a spy you may behead me. Please reconsider.' 'Very well,' they eventually agreed, 'We will re-examine the case'.

Latuharhary told me that he intuitively felt 'the help of the Navy' in the improvement of food after we had asked the Kempeitai for his release. He was soon released, but was arrested again afterwards by the Kempeitai. Latuharhary had been a political leader in a youth association called Jong Ambon during the Dutch period. Furthermore, he was a member of a nationalist group formed by Subardjo and Hasan before the war. Although I had not met him, I knew his name at that time. He was checked by the Kempeitai simply because he had been an activist of the nationalist movement before the war.

R. Pandji Singgih* was also one of those who were marked

* For Footnote see following page.

267

by the Kempeitai. He had joined the nationalist movement while studying in the Netherlands. At the end of the war he was the **Chokan** [Resident] of Malang (in East Java), but was unfortunately murdered by rioters, perhaps due to a misunderstanding, after the independence declaration. As the Research Section of the Bukanfu was also pursuing intelligence tasks, we were able to obtain information from the Kempeitai. On one occasion the Kempeitai in Bandung let us know of its intention to arrest Singgih, alleging that he was involved in the Pontianak affair. The Japanese claimed that Dr B.J. Haga, the Governor of Borneo (Kalimantan) at the end of Dutch rule, had organized officers of the former colonial army, former colonial officers, and intellectuals in the Banjarmasin district in order to destroy the Japanese Army and the civil administration there. Thus the affair was also called the 'Haga affair'. According to one report a plot to murder Japanese in Pontianak by poison was disclosed through the confessions of those arrested, the plot to be launched on 3 November 1942. Subsequently a total of 12 or 13 hundred Chinese and Indonesians were arrested, many of whom were executed without judicial process. The 'Haga affair' is often quoted as the largest conspiracy against the Japanese during the occupation. On the other hand the affair has also considered a fabrication of the Japanese side.† I strongly insisted to the Kempeitai that Singgih 'could absolutely not be involved' in such a plot. The Kempeitai was eventually unable to ignore my protest and arrest him, presumably because it had not sufficient evidence.

At the end of the war Adam Malik was arrested by the Kempeitai in Jakarta. I tried to rescue him through an

---

* Footnote from previous page:
  Mr Raden Pandji Singgih (1894-1946) was born in Malang and gained his law degree in Leiden in 1922. He practised law in Ambon and various Javanese cities, and was active in Budi Utomo, the PBI and Parindra parties. In November 1944 the Japanese appointed him **San'yo** (Adviser) to the Labour Department.

† Western accounts describe the 'Haga affair', in which about 250 people including seven missionaries were executed, as well as the ensuing Pontianak executions of 1943 which left over 1000 dead, as the most outrageous of Japanese atrocities in Indonesia, seemingly caused by the paranoia of local officers. I.J. Brugmans et al, **Nederlandsch-Indië onder Japanese bezetting: gegevens en documenten over de jaren 1942-1945** (Franeker, T. Wever, 1960), pp.245-51; Kanahele, pp.308-9; C. van Heekeren, **Rode Zon boven Borneo. West Borneo 1942** (The Hague, 1968), and **Helden, Hazen en Honden, Zuid Borneo 1942** (The Hague, 1969).

unofficial channel, but Malik seemed to escape from jail by himself in the end. B.M. Diah* was a journalist with **Asia Raya** during the occupation and was once arrested by the Kempeitai on the charge of criticism of the Japanese. In this case also I demanded his release from the Kempeitai through a backdoor route. Diah was active in the field of journalism, and he assumed the position of Minister of Information after independence. In addition to the cases mentioned above, I tried to release Indonesians who were arrested by the Kempeitai for minor incidents, some of which were evidently Japanese frame-ups. It may sound as though I am blowing my own horn, but I am quite proud of the fact that my humble endeavours through negotiation with the Kempeitai saved the lives of some Indonesians.

The worse the Japanese war position became, the stronger the Indonesian demand for independence appeared. Behind this tendency was the Indonesian dissatisfaction that they were not allowed independence while the population of the Philippine Islands, also in Southeast Asia, had already been granted it. It was only in September 1944 that Japan offered the independence of the Indies at some time in the future, in the statement of Prime Minister Koiso at the Eighty-fifth Imperial Diet.

However, the date of independence was not suggested, nor was the establishment of an official committee for the preparation for independence permitted. This inflamed dissatisfaction and anxiety among the Indonesians. Indonesian leaders expressed their distrust in the Japanese.

In the Army-occupied area the hoisting of the **merah putih** flag was permitted soon after the Koiso statement, pleasing part of the population. Observing Indonesians proudly flying their national flag in the towns, not a few Japanese must have realized how precious independence was for the people. In the Navy-occupied area, however, the hoisting of the national flag was permitted only on 29 April 1945, that is, on the Emperor's birthday. This took place when Shibata, Maeda, Yoshizumi, Sukarno, Subardjo and I visited Makasar (Ujung Pandang). During this visit I had the strong impression that the Navy was far behind the Army as far as the independence issue was concerned. At the beginning of 1945 the Central Authorities conducted an inquiry into the opinions of the Navy and Army on

---

* Burhanuddin Mohammad Diah was born in Aceh in 1917 and trained as a journalist after completing his Dutch secondary education. Before the war he worked for newspapers in Medan and Jakarta, and since 1945 he has managed the prominent Jakarta daily **Merdeka**. He was frequently an ambassador in the period 1959-68, and Minister of Information in 1968. He married Subardjo's niece.

the independence of the East Indies. At that time the 16th Army was of the opinion that independence should be given, preferably to Java and Sumatra, but if that was impossible then to Java and Madura alone. In contrast to this, the 25th Army had the idea that as far as possible Sumatra should not be given independence.

The Second Southern Fleet of the Navy was to hold a meeting of Staff Officers in Surabaya in February 1945, in order to prepare a report on its view of independence for the Central Authorities. We in the Research Section were worrying about the content of the report, since the Navy had a conservative view on independence and it was likely to make a report similar to that of the 16th Army. The Indonesians would certainly be disappointed and we would lose face if such a report was sent to Japan. I immediately visited Hatta and, after explaining the situation, asked his opinion.

'If the Japanese government plans to allow the independence only of Java and Madura, can you accept that?'

'We definitely cannot accept such an independence; we would refuse it. Independence should include the whole of Indonesia.'

'I fully understand your thinking.'

Needless to say I conveyed Hatta's reply to Maeda. Although Maeda just nodded sagely while I talked, he seemed to have already made up his mind to propose a plan for the independence of the whole of the East Indies as the general view of the Second Southern Fleet. Maeda, Yoshizumi and I were to attend the meeting to represent the Bukanfu. That such a low ranking officer as myself was able to attend the meeting of Staff Officers obviously owed much to Maeda's deliberate arrangements. On the other hand, however, I still believe that the invisible force of Indonesian opinion also contributed to letting me attend the meeting.

Among those present at the meeting were such high-ranking officers as the Commander-in-Chief of the Second Southern Fleet, Shibata, and the Chief of Staff, Nagatani, and this made me full of fight. Maeda was not good at speaking, and Yoshizumi was not the type of man who speaks logically and theoretically, though he was able to speak passionately. Accordingly I was asked to make a speech on behalf of the Bukanfu, which turned out to be a long one. I was not necessarily an eloquent speaker, but I was not weak in speaking theoretically. In addition, I had had a long experience of Indonesia. I appealed with all my might that Japan should let the whole of the East Indies attain independence because it was the dream of the population, and the only way to conduct the war was by winning the cooperation of the population. In this way the view of the Bukanfu was adopted as the proposal of the Second Southern Fleet on the independence issue, and it was sent to Tokyo. We jumped for joy over this result and raised our glasses.

*   *   *

One of the highlights of my activity after returning to Indonesia was without doubt 'the incident of the direct petition to Prime Minister Tojo'. This incident occurred in June 1943, that is, immediately after the so-called Tojo statement was issued. In May that year the American army landed on Attu Island,* making it clear even to the population in regions occupied by Japan that the Japanese war position was worsening. Prime Minister Tojo then made a speech about Japanese policy for the Greater East Asia Co-Prosperity Sphere at the Eighty-second Imperial Diet, referring in part to the East Indies. Tojo presented a programme for the political participation of the population, to be implemented gradually during the year according to the level of cultural maturity [**mindo**]† of the inhabitants of different regions, though participation was to be implemented as quickly as possible in Java. This policy was obviously intended to secure the East Indies and strengthen the southern defence lines of Japan. Despite the great divergence between Japanese intentions and the Indonesian aspiration for complete independence, this new guideline opened the way for the political participation of the population.

The Indonesians received the Tojo statement with mixed feelings. About this time the Minister for Greater East Asia, Aoki Kazuo, visited Java. In connection with this visit a memo was sent to me from Doi Akira who happened to be travelling in Central Java, asking 'How about appealing to the Government about the dissatisfaction and the aspirations of Indonesians, through my friend, Capt. Tanaka Minoru of the Ministry of Greater East Asia. When I consulted Sato, I was advised to do so. We did not inform Maeda of this, since we considered he would not be able to sanction such an appeal in view of his position, and feared bringing trouble upon him in case the appeal developed in an undesirable way. Indeed, we anticipated such trouble even if Maeda was not directly involved.

After discussion, Sato and I reached the conclusion that

---

* The American conquest of this tiny Aleutian island was a shock to Japanese opinion, less because of its strategic importance than because every Japanese defender was killed – the first total defeat.

† The term **mindo** [economic and cultural standard] was frequently used during the war to categorize the different levels of civilization of the peoples under Japanese rule.

the petition should be sent to Prime Minister Tojo by way of
Minister Aoki, and that the documents should be signed by
Sukarno, Hatta, Ki Hadjar Dewantara, and Kiyai Haji Mansoer.
Of these, Dewantara* was a man who had participated in the
foundation of the Indische Partij together with Douwes Dekker,
was exiled to the Netherlands, and concentrated on the
educational movement after returning from exile. During the
Japanese occupation he functioned as a senior staff official of
Putera and a member of the Chuo Sangi-in, and he assumed the
position of Minister of Education after the independence
declaration in 1945. Mansoer had joined Sarekat Islam after
graduating from the University of Al-Azhar in Cairo, and became
one of the principal Islamic leaders after he was elected
president of Muhammadiah, an Islamic social organization, in
1937. During the Japanese occupation he took the positions
successively of vice-chairman of Putera, member of the Chuo
Sangi-in, and director of general affairs for the Jawa Hokokai.

These four leaders were called the **empat serangkai**, i.e.
'the united four', and inspired great respect from the
population. In order to ask them for their opinion of the
petition, we hastily visited the head office of Putera on Sunda
Street and eventually obtained their consent. The points of
the petition were as follows:

1. To clarify the status of Indonesia after the war.
    To declare the unification of administration
    policy in the Navy and Army areas of occupation.

2. To allow the hoisting of the national flag and
    the singing of the national anthem.

3. To rectify the rudeness of the Japanese.

When a draft of the petition was completed, the four
leaders expressed their fear of 'a backlash' from Prime
Minister Tojo: 'Is this really all right?' We encouraged them
by saying it was 'absolutely safe'. Sukarno and Hatta did not
show any sign of uneasiness once I assured them of their
safety, but the other two repeatedly questioned their safety
apprehensively. Each time we encouraged them by guaranteeing
their security. We translated the draft into Japanese and had
the translation typed secretly, using the official letter paper
of the Navy on the advice of Sato. We used this paper in the
hope that the official Navy letter-head might give the
impression that the direct petition was backed by the Navy, and

* Ki Hadjar Dewantara (1889-1959) came from the second palace
  of Yogjakarta, the Pakualaman, and first became politically
  prominent under his original name Suwardi Suryaningrat.
  After his period of exile he devoted his life to building his
  Taman Siswa school system.

accordingly that even Prime Minister Tojo would not ignore the appeal because of the significance added by the Navy's name. We also expected that the Prime Minister, who came from the Army, would not dare to punish directly people who belonged to the Navy, which was 'extraterritorial' from the point of view of the Army. When I called on the four leaders for their signature, Dewantara and Mansoer were still scared of the results, asking, 'Are we really safe?'.

The petition was first put in an envelope addressed to 'Prime Minister Tojo Hideki'. Then this envelope was enclosed in another envelope addressed to 'the Minister for Greater East Asia, Aoki Kazuo', and finally it was handed over to Capt. Tanaka. We did not address the outer envelope to the Prime Minister, since if we had it was likely to be read only by his subordinates, its contents ensuring that it was not passed to the Prime Minister. In this way the die was at last cast. Although we had assured the four leaders of their safety, in reality we felt very anxious. Sato pretended to be confident, stroking his bald head as usual, but to judge from his increased drinking he seemed unable to keep his mind from worrying about the matter. He tried to ease his anxiety by drinking and roaming around the town by **becak**.

Although I am not certain how many days elapsed after Minister Aoki went back to Japan, **kempei** [military police] suddenly came to investigate Sato and me. Even before the incident of the petition we were 'marked men' for the Kempeitai, because we talked loudly about Indonesian independence when drinking, quarrelled with kempei, and talked big at restaurants. Thus it was not surprising that the Kempeitai kept their eye on us. However, the way in which the Kempeitai watched us became more forceful and severe, evidently because of the petition. In addition to keeping my house and Sato's under surveillance, the Kempeitai began to follow us when we went out and even to observe us entering a small room near the porch of my house. The surveillance was intensified to the point where kempei pursued Sato by motorcycle when he took a car. Generous person as he was, Sato looked annoyed. Under these circumstances I felt, 'the time has come'.

Previously there had been indications that irritations of this sort might be in store for us. Shimizu Hitoshi of the propaganda section of the Gunseikambu hinted to Sato about the repercussions of the petition letter. Shimizu was on intimate terms with Mrs Tojo Katsuko, and was told of the affair by her when he happened to return to Japan. After coming back to Jakarta, Shimizu told the story to Sato, who in turn described it for me as follows:

> Shortly after Minister Aoki returned to Japan, I had a telephone call from Shimizu enquiring whether he could meet me. We had a meal together in the evening

at a Japanese style restaurant. On seeing me he
blurted out, 'What a nasty thing you have done!' As
I pretended to know nothing, asking what that was, he
referred to the direct petition affair. When Shimizu
had visited Mrs Tojo Katsuko in Tokyo, she had given
an account of the incident and commented, 'There are
reckless people in the Navy'. A few days after I met
Shimizu I came to be followed by kempei.

Judging from Shimizu's story, the letter seemed to have
been read by Prime Minister Tojo. In the testament written
just before he was executed, Tojo says: 'I think that the
reason for the Japanese defeat in this war was that Japan
failed to acquire cooperation from the peoples of East Asia'
(quoted from Yasuda and Fukushima (ed.), **Shōgen: 1945 Nen 8
Gatsu 15 Nichi** [Testimony: 15 August 1945], Shin Jimbutsu
Orai-sha, 1973). Presumably he had in mind the incident of the
direct petition. In view of the fact that Shimizu surmised us
to be the ringleaders of the affair, the Central Authorities
must also have been aware of us. And this must be the reason
why we were watched by the Kempeitai.

At first the kempei responsible for watching me would not
talk to me. In due course, however, he responded to my
chatting and gradually became friendly. This is human nature,
I believe. I said to myself, 'Now I have it', when our
relationship improved, and I offered him a glass of whisky. He
at first rejected my offer, but eventually accepted a drink.
The kempei proved to be a rather hard drinker. It was indeed a
funny scene that a watcher and the watched were exchanging
glasses with each other. As we got drunk, we came around to
discussing the subject in question. Since he was a kempei, I
could not make a careless statement. Thus I tried to perplex
him, deliberately using ambiguous language, and phrases
understood to be those of a leftist and those of a rightist.
As for the kempei, he raised one question after another in
trying to catch my real intention. Although the issue of
independence was a taboo subject at that time, I endeavoured to
convince him in one way or another of the necessity of
independence for the Indonesians.

Sato became unable to stand the impudence of kempei who
appeared not only at his residence but also at his office. At
last he called on the head of the Jakarta Kempeitai, Maj. Naga
Yukinosuke, in order to protest against this impudence: 'I
cannot work properly because of surveillance by kempei from
morning till night. Please put a stop to it'. According to
Sato, Maj. Naga looked embarrassed at the protest and excused
himself on the grounds that he was ordered by Headquarters to
watch Sato, and that he could do nothing about it. After the
end of the war Naga was arrested by the Allied Forces, and
executed at the end of February 1947 on the charge of

274

'organized terrorism and the torture of citizens'. Though a military man, he was small, mild and respectable. When I was working in the Japanese lawyers team for war criminals after the war, a Dutch judge referred to him as 'a rare officer'. Naga may have been forced to send kempei to our houses, the order doubtless having been issued by Prime Minister Tojo. I believe that Naga was unable to ignore the order, but made a show of performing the surveillance as ordered. Otherwise it cannot be explained why kempei were sent so overtly.

I still wonder why the Kempeitai could not uncover my past record - that I had been arrested and imprisoned as a political offender and had been a member of the Japan Communist Party. Anyway, I was very disappointed with the result of the petition. My feeling at the time may be fully described in a section of **Daisan no Shinso**:

> I must confess my naivety at that time, in having believed that once the petition letter reached Tokyo, the Central Authorities would realize the actual circumstances of the occupied regions. I am also very much aware of the dilemma faced by the four Indonesian leaders in having to put such a sacred trust in the hands of one as powerless as myself. Mansoer has passed away, and Tojo, the object of the petition, is now hanged.

Looking back on those days, I am struck by what a daring thing I did. Japanese politics changed drastically after the war. The power of parliament was strengthened and the freedom of speech was recovered. During the war, however, everything was concentrated on the pursuit of war. The Prime Minister, Tojo, had enormous power, backed by the Army. As a result, the voice of the people was thoroughly suppressed and parliament's role became purely nominal. It was, accordingly, quite reckless to have sent a direct petition to the Prime Minister, since the content annoyed him considerably. Had we been in Japan and had we not belonged to the Navy, what would have happened to us? Perhaps the punishment would have been much more severe than just surveillance by kempei. I was young and enthusiastic about the achievement of Indonesian independence in those days, which made it possible for me to do such a bold thing. Recalling those days, I occasionally experience a chill of horror. However, I do not regret the unsuccessful petition, because it must have made the Indonesian leaders feel that there were some Japanese who had a profound love for Indonesia.

I) Nationalist Propaganda in the Navy Area, 1945

Surabaya had been the leading Dutch naval base in Indonesia, and it remained so for the Japanese after falling almost intact into their hands in 1942. This involved the paradox that the headquarters of the Second Southern Expeditionary Fleet, which had administrative authority for Borneo, Celebes, and the eastern islands, was situated in the second city of Army-controlled Java. A further paradox was that the Navy suppressed Indonesian nationalism completely in the areas it administered, for reasons explained by Shibata, whereas the Navy representatives living in Java and having no responsibility for government there developed good and often sympathetic contacts with nationalists. In the last stages of the war this gave these naval officers an important role in mediating between nationalists in Java and Indonesians in the eastern islands whose preparation for independence had been left so far behind.

Admiral Shibata (born 1889 in Toyama Prefecture) was the most senior naval officer in Indonesia, as Commander-in-Chief of the Second Southern Expeditionary Fleet since January 1945. Like many Navy men his background was relatively international. In addition to the usual periods of active service in China (1927-29 and 1938-40), he had spent a year touring Europe and America in 1936-37 to study war preparations. He had visited the Philippines twice before the war, and warmly welcomed the Sakdalista leader Benigno Ramos to Tokyo in 1935. He had been posted from Japan to Indonesia only in March 1943, when he took command of the operations base in Ambon. He is remembered gratefully in Indonesia for his readiness to exploit the naivety of the incoming Allied officers after the surrender to turn most Japanese weapons in Surabaya over to the Indonesians (see extract below).

Shibata Yaichiro

SHIBATA SHIREI CHŌKAN NO SHUKI

[The Memoirs of Commander-in-Chief Shibata] (Tokyo, privately published, 1976), pp.33-40

Chapter VI

1. The Japanese Forces and the Nationalist Movement during the Occupation

In this section I will give my impressions of the actual situation in the East Indies during the Japanese Military Occupation. When the Second World War broke out and the Japanese Forces occupied Indonesia, those people who backed the Nationalist Movement in Indonesia enthusiastically welcomed the Japanese as their liberators. As for the positioning of the Japanese troops, Sumatra was placed under the command of the 25th Army, Java under the 16th Army and Borneo, the Celebes, Lesser Sundas and the Moluccas under the Second Southern Expeditionary Fleet.

The basic policy of the Administration of the Occupied Areas was decided at Headquarters in Japan, and the main point of this policy aimed at permanent possession in order to acquire those resources necessary for economic needs. It therefore laid down that the Nationalist Movement was not to be encouraged.

However, the actual execution of this policy in fact differed remarkably in each region according to the mood of the Indonesians in the area and the personalities of the military leaders.

In Java, where the Nationalist Movement was regarded as being the most fervent and autonomous, the 16th Army organized political movements to promote a sense of national consciousness amongst the Indonesians. These movements were the Triple A Movement (a Pan-Asian enlightenment organization which placed Japan at the centre as the light of Asia and the mother of hope), the Putera Movement (it concentrated and combined the forces in Java), and the Jawa Hokokai (an organization designed to gain cooperation for the war by concentrating the political power of the nationalist leaders and the government officials). On the other hand, the 25th Army in Sumatra and the Second Southern Expeditionary Fleet did not permit political movements in the light of the low living standards of the people in the Outer Areas and the lack of people with ability.*

The announcement by Prime Minister Tojo in spring 1943 made it possible to grant political participation to the Indonesians in the middle of that year. As a result, Representative Councils, State Councils, etc. were established, but in fact they were nothing more than advisory bodies. Therefore, the fact that Burma and the Philippines were granted independence and Indonesia was not, led to great dissatisfaction amongst the nationalist leaders in Java and especially the young radical elements amongst them. This, together with the unfavourable war situation, was responsible for disturbing public order in various areas.

On 7 September 1944 Prime Minister Koiso publicly announced a pledge to recognize Indonesia's independence, but the pace of each of the Military Administrations in Indonesia was not necesarily in keeping with this.

The Navy established a Navy Liaison Office in Jakarta with Capt. Maeda, an expert on the South, as its Chief; it was responsible for such activities as investigations into the situation in Indonesia and political manoeuvres. This Office acted as the Fleet's policy adviser. The staff included two people by the names of Nishijima and Yoshizumi,† both of whom had, since before the war, devoted themselves to the Indonesian Nationalist and Independence Movement.

After completing my first tour of inspection I held a conference of the Chiefs of the Military Administration in Surabaya. Naval Officer Maeda from the Jakarta Navy Liaison Office was accompanied by Yoshizumi and Nishijima, and

---

* Both economic and educational standards were on average slightly higher in the Outer Islands, though the highly educated elite naturally congregated in the big cities of Java. Another relevant factor was that resources of interest to Japan were all in the Outer Islands.

† For Nishijima, see above pp.251-3. Yoshizumi Tomegoro (1911-48) was a journalist and businessman in the pre-war Netherlands Indies, and was recruited as an agent of the Japanese Consulate in Batavia, working primarily among Chinese. He was taken to Australia as a prisoner at the outbreak of war, and like Nishijima repatriated in an exchange of prisoners. His first task during the occupation was with the Navy intelligence unit, **Hana Kikan**, in Makasar, but in 1944 he was transferred to Maeda's Naval Liaison Office in Jakarta. He gradually came to share the views of left-wing Indonesian nationalists, and joined the Republican cause after the Japanese surrender, adopting the name Arif. He died, apparently of tuberculosis, in the mountains near Blitar in August 1948.

Yanagihara, Chief of the General Affairs Bureau of the **Minseifu*** was also present.

Nishijima and Yoshizumi spoke on the trend of public sentiment in Indonesia and emphasized the importance of permitting the use of the national flag and the national anthem, and the acceleration of Indonesian independence. The conclusions we arrived at and which I reported to Imperial Headquarters in Tokyo were as follows:

1. The national flag and national anthem should be permitted in the Navy area immediately.

2. The big names of the Nationalist Movement in Java should be sent to the Navy area to promote the Nationalist Movement there.

3. Independence similar to that in the Philippines and Burma should be granted to Indonesia swiftly.

Concerning (1), I decided that it did not deviate from the basic policy laid down by Headquarters, and so I used my discretion as a Commander away from Tokyo to take arbitrary action without seeking instructions from Headquarters.

Regarding (2), I negotiated the selection of nationalist leaders, made by Naval Officer Maeda and his staff, with the Army. Since in Java too the Army and Navy were at odds with each other, the Army would not cooperate in sending leading nationalists to the Navy area. However, due to the afore-mentioned relationship I had with the then Commanding Officer of the 16th Army, Lt.-Gen. Harada, he readily consented to the dispatch of Sukarno and Hatta, two great nationalist leaders.

2. Journey with Sukarno to Makasar to Promote the Nationalist Movement

As part of the process of carrying out the decisions of the conference of the Chiefs of the Military Administration, I summoned Naval Officer Maeda, Yoshizumi, Nishijima, Sukarno and Subardjo† to Surabaya, and on the night of 25 April [1945] I invited Sukarno, Subardjo and Dr Samsi# as well as 12 or 13

---

* For details of **Minseifu** organization, see Okada, above, pp. 130-1.

† For Achmad Subardjo, see Nishijima, above, p.254.

Dr Samsi Sastrawidagda (1894-1963) obtained his doctorate in the Rotterdam Business School in 1925. He was in government service but also an active nationalist, notably in Sukarno's PNI of 1927-29. In 1941 he appears to have been contacted for fifth-column work by Japanese in Batavia who included

11. *Nishijima
Shigetada
in 1943.*

12. *Admiral
Shibata
in 1945.*

13. Sukarno's visit to Makasar in April 1945. Group photo in front of the residence of the Minseifu Chokan (Governor). Front row, left to right: Dr Ratulangie, Admiral Maeda, Ichiki (Secretary-General), Mitsuhashi Koichiro (Minseifu Chokan), Sukarno, Tadjoeddin Noor, Mr Subardjo; Back row: Hayashi Kenichi, Capt. Yanagihara Masuzo, Nishijima Shigetada, Mr Sumanang, Yoshizumi Tomegoro.

14. *Sukarno and Soetardjo Kartohadikoesoemo, Resident of Jakarta, lead a demonstration of gratitude for the Japanese promise of independence, October 1945. (Miyamoto).*

15. Ceremony of gratitude for the promise of independence, October 1944. From left: Mangkunegara, Pakualam, Susuhunan of Surakarta, Sultan of Yogyakarta. Seated right is the Gunseikan, Miyoshi.

representatives from the various outer regions to a grand
banquet at the Chokan's official residence on the bank of the
Kalimas River. On the eve of Sukarno's campaign tour the
excitement of these people was indescribable. Although this
group were strict Muslims who did not drink alcohol, all,
including Sukarno, drank a toast, and then, when Sukarno stood
up to sing an Indonesian folk song, they joined in singing.
Staff Officer Kinoshita then explained and sang a typical
Japanese folk song called 'Esashi Oiwake', and received hearty
applause from the Indonesians. It was an evening in which we
all became mutual friends.

On the following day, 26 April, I flew to Makasar in the
Chokan's aeroplane - a type 97 flying boat. Sukarno accompanied my group.

Then on 29 April, the auspicious occasion of the Emperor's
Birthday, I held a ceremony at which the national flag was
raised. I sent a telegram to Headquarters just prior to the
ceremony so they would not have time to tell me to 'wait'. The
ceremony was held at the central parade ground near the
Suikosha. The Japanese present were the **Minseifu Sokan**, the
Celebes **Minseibu Chokan**, and the Commanding Officer of the 23rd
Special Base Company.* Among the Indonesians who attended were
Dr Ratulangie, Tadjoeddin Noor,† and many of the Rajas from the
regions. While I was reading my speech at the rostrum, the
enemy air-raid warning siren was rung. For a moment I was
startled and at a loss what to do. The crowd at the back had
begun to panic. However, the occasion was one of great
importance so I continued reading as if nothing had happened.
The aeroplane came into sight but, because of the large trees
unique to the south, the public square was sheltered. The

Footnote continued from previous page:
Maeda and Nishijima. Prominent throughout the Japanese
period, he became adviser to the Finance Department of the
Java administration in December 1944, and in consequence
moved up to fill the finance portfolio in the first
independent cabinet, August-September 1945. See also below,
p.342.

* The **Minseifu Sokan** or Inspector-General of the **Minseifu** was a
civilian and the highest authority within the Naval Civil
Administration Office. There were three **Minseibu** - for
Celebes, Borneo and Ceram (later the Lesser Sundas),
respectively - under the authority of the **Minseifu**. The
Celebes **Minseibu Chokan** was the head of civil administration
for that island. See also Okada, above, pp.130-1.

† For Ratulangie and Tadjoeddin Noor see Nishijima, above,
p.264.

aeroplane appeared not to recognize the crowd and turned back. We were saved by a divine spirit in the sky. When the ceremony finished and I turned back to leave, I passed along a line of Rajas including the famous Raja of Bone,* and I greeted them. They expressed pleasure and bowed to me. The Shiseikan noticed this and afterwards said to me, 'The Rajas were extremely pleased, weren't they.' After the ceremony I was taken on a tour of Makasar. I then retired to my lodgings, and when I walked out to the front garden I met this group again. They bowed to me one by one and walked on. They are indeed wonderful natives.

I think it was when I made a tour of inspection of the internment camp of those women and children regarded as enemies, that I awarded Yamachi, the camp supervisor, with a letter of commendation and other awards for good deeds. His story, entitled 'White Skins and Yellow Captain', was published in the journal **Bunshun**. Later it was released as a separate volume and according to Matsutake, made into a film. What surprised me most during my stay in Makasar was the number of bomb attacks during the day. At times there were even five a day. Whether they were carried out on the basis of the deciphering of radio messages, or on spy intelligence information, I don't know, but either way it was exceedingly dangerous. Although Sukarno and I were lodged in separate quarters, we took refuge in the same air-raid shelter. We would greet each other inside with, 'They're persistent, aren't they?' I missed out on the evening meal once because of the air-raid attack, so I took a **Hi-no-maru bento** along and munched on it. There is no doubt that during my five days' stay I gave Sukarno and his party much to hope for in the way of future independence. If conditions allowed, I had intended to fly on to Borneo, but while I was in Makasar, the Australian troops had begun operations to land at Tarakan in the northern corner of [Dutch] Borneo,† so I returned to Surabaya for the time being.

*   *   *

* Andi Mappanjuki, Raja or **Arumpone** of Bone from 1931 to 1946, was the dominant figure among the many rajas of South Celebes after 1942, partly because he had an anti-Dutch reputation dating from the years of resistance in 1901-4. He fell foul of the Dutch during the revolution and was exiled by them in 1946.

† Australian landings at Tarakan began on 1 May 1945, after heavy aerial bombardment from 12 April.

3. The Trip to Borneo with Hatta

One week after returning from my trip to Makasar (I think it was 12 May), I flew to Banjarmasin with Hatta and the nationalist Pangeran Noor,* who was born in Borneo. This trip too was full of dangers. Fifteen minutes before arriving in Banjarmasin, we received a radio message from the control tower on the landing strip that an enemy plane was approaching. Fortunately there were a great many clouds in the sky, and Katayama, a skilful pilot, was able to weave through the clouds so that we could land safely without detection by the enemy plane. During the evening meal at the hotel, I interviewed influential Indonesian leaders from the countryside.

At 9 p.m. I opened the meeting at which Hatta was to make a speech at the theatre. At the beginning of the meeting I stood on the stage while three representatives from the region delivered moving speeches expressing gratitude to me. Then the Chairman introduced Hatta. He began eloquently, commencing with Hatta's personal history and then went on to describe the long history of the Independence Movement. It went on for ten, then 15 minutes, and he would not stop. My Chief of Staff grew impatient, wrote something on a piece of paper and took it up to the platform. Just when the speech was drawing to a climax, the air-raid warning siren rang. Through the aid of my interpreter I made the following announcement: 'There will be an air-raid so disperse quietly and wait. If the air-raid finishes by 11 p.m. I will re-open the meeting. If it does not, the meeting will be cancelled for tonight and will commence again tomorrow.' There were 1560 people in that audience, but they dispersed without any panic or confusion. I can't help but be ashamed of the Japanese today.

I went to the official residence of the Minseibu Chokan and sat and waited. Three or four enemy planes came and they dropped several bombs. There was very little actual damage done though. The enemy planes finally disappeared a little after 11 p.m., but the meeting was not re-convened. I heard later on that 120-odd enthusiastic young Indonesians besieged Hatta at his lodgings and stayed up all night listening to his views and stating their own. A strong desire for independence was smouldering within them.

That night I stayed with the Head of the Political Affairs Department of the Minseibu, and early in the morning I was

* Ir Pangeran Mohammad Noor was born in South Kalimantan in 1901, and obtained an engineering degree. He succeeded his father, the district chief Pangeran Mohamad Ali, as representative of South Kalimantan in the Volksraad (1931-39). He was named first Republican Governor of Kalimantan in 1945, but never functioned as such.

woken up by another air-raid siren. I reluctantly got dressed and joined the others in the shabby air-raid shelter. The four enemy planes bombed the Chinese section of the town which was situated on the river just beneath us. Six Chinese were killed and several small boats were damaged. Hatta opened the meeting at 11 a.m. and deeply impressed the audience with his speech. I had planned to continue my journey on to Pontianak, but the airport at Pontianak had been bombed to smithereens the day before. For the time being it was impossible to land there, so I had no choice but to cancel the trip and return to Batavia.

4. An unforgettable evening and morning at Kintamani

On 25 July I flew to Bali, accompanied by Naval Officer Maeda, his staff, Sukarno and Subardjo. This was one of a wonderful series of trips in which, together with the big names of the Nationalist Movement, like Sukarno, Hatta and Subardjo, I visited various areas outside of Java to promote the Nationalist Movement. Sukarno spent several years of his childhood in Bali, and he had many friends and relatives in the vicinity of Singaraja.* He later grew up in Java and studied civil engineering at Bandung University. There he devoted himself to the Independence Movement. How he must have been proud to return to his homeland, Bali, as the number one leader of the Independence Movement! I recall that I invited along a film crew to record his home-coming. It was a real spectacle to see the Balinese welcome Sukarno. Late in the afternoon of the day we arrived I opened a rally in the big public square at Singaraja. There were more than 10,000 people in the audience. Sukarno began his speech immediately, and when he said, 'I am half Balinese,' the applause sounded like thunder and went on and on. His persuasive and enthusiastic speech gripped the audience and, at the time, I was convinced he was an even greater orator than Japan's Nagai Ryutaro.† Of course, I didn't understand what he was saying. The interpreter, though, told me the meaning of the sections which the audience applauded. Sukarno was indeed a skilled orator. That evening and the next morning Sukarno was allowed time to himself, and he chatted with old friends and relatives. The film crew

* Although Sukarno's Javanese father and Balinese mother married in Singaraja, they were transferred to Kediri, in Java, before his birth. None of his biographies mentioned any significant childhood period in Bali.

† Nagai Ryutaro (1881-1945) was a Waseda University Professor and prominent politician of the Minseito Party. A Minister for Colonization (1932-34), and for Communications (1938-40), he was best known as an eloquent speaker.

followed him around and recorded live situations. (Unfortunately this film was burnt at the end of the war.)

The next night we stayed at the Kintamani Hotel - Kintamani has been famous since the Dutch era. It is over 2,000 metres above sea level and allows you to forget the heat of the tropics. Below one's eyes can be seen Lake Batur, and nearby, Batur volcano. Far off in the distance the lofty peak of Agung towers up and provides a spectacular sight. After the Japanese Occupation began, the name of Kintamani Hotel was changed to Kegon Inn...a sign board with Kegon Inn written in beautiful Japanese characters was hanging up. I heard that it was the Commander of the parachute troop which landed at Menado, Capt. Horiuchi, who wrote this sign, and that it was he who was responsible for the introduction of physical education amongst the natives in the Navy area. Horiuchi was interrogated as a war criminal and executed by the Dutch Army. In fact, though, he was a wonderful person. We made ourselves at home at the Kintamani Hotel (that is Kegon Inn), and in Japanese fashion sat around the fire eating sukiyaki, drinking and singing. Subardjo took out his violin that he had brought along and began to play it. Sukarno sang along with him, and I can assure you he would get three gongs on the television programme 'Nodo Jiman' [Amateur Singers on the Air]. Sukarno said to me, 'Chokan, if the Nationalist Movement doesn't succeed, Subardjo will be able to survive by playing the violin'.

Subardjo laughed and replied, 'If I aspire to playing the violin, I'll rot in the street'.

We spent the rest of the night watching Kintamani dances.

The next morning there was a particularly thick fog, and unfortunately I could not see the lake or mountains. Sukarno suggested that we visit the gallery of a German artist well-known in the area.* Sukarno was indeed a cultured man for he knew music well and had an interest in art. The Minseibu Chokan, Koshino, and my aide had a busy schedule and were unable to go. I gladly accepted however because it really didn't matter if I ended up being 10 or 20 minutes behind schedule. Sukarno was delighted, and we went along together. The result was that I was 30 minutes late in leaving. However, you can never tell what disguise good fortune comes in. We climbed down the mountain, and on reaching the look-out point,

---

* Probably Walter Spies (1895-1942), a Russian-born German, whose house at Campuan, near Ubud, became a Mecca in the 1930s for Balinese artists as well as international travellers. He did much to publicize and revitalize Balinese art, but died in January 1942 when the ship carrying German internees away from the colony was sunk by a Japanese torpedo.

we could see a superb view of the mountains. It was as if
Allah had granted Sukarno's prayers. As if by a miracle the
mist suddenly cleared. The rising sun appeared in the eastern
sky over the mountains and the lake. I involuntarily shouted
for joy. Sukarno, too, was delighted to see this unexpected
sight.

*   *   *

We continued on down the mountain, and when we approached
one village, both sides of the street were lined with people
waving Japanese and Indonesian nationalist flags. We also
called in at a primary school and inspected the pupils engaged
in drill and sports. I enjoyed myself thoroughly.

5.   Miss Chawan and the Bali Dance

A rally was also held at the public square in Denpasar.
It was equally successful as that of Singaraja. Sukarno gave a
fiery speech, emphasizing, 'The Japanese are unified as one
race. They do not feel they are different from one another
because they come from Kyushu, Tokyo or Osaka. But what is the
situation with Indonesians? We even use different terms like I
am Javanese, I am Balinese. There is no unity; I am half
Balinese'.

There was great applause and much cheering. Sukarno was
certainly a skilful speaker. The fact that Sukarno was deified
after Independence, like Russia's Stalin, China's Mao Tse-tung
and India's Nehru, and that his position as President did not
weaken, was of course due to his achievements as a leader of
the Independence and Nationalist Movement. There is no denying
the enthusiasm which he expressed through his magnificent
speeches emphasizing his love of the Indonesian race.

*   *   *

At night I saw the famous Balinese dancing. Sukarno told
me that Javanese dancing had deteriorated, and he repeatedly
asked me whether I would permit an expert from Bali to be lent
to Java for about one month. The next day he visited the house
of Miss Chawan, one of the top Balinese dancers at the time.
To satisfy Sukarno I invited Miss Chawan to have lunch with me
at the Denpasar Hotel one day. This pleased Sukarno
enormously.

This was an enormously successful trip. From Bali I
returned home. Three times I accompanied three great leaders
and fighters of the Indonesian Independence Movement on trips
to prepare the people for Independence. It was the first time
such a thing had ever been done. I treated the nationalist
leaders as distinguished guests - they rode with me in the

Chokan's plane, and we shared in danger together. There was no wall between us. As a result, the Navy was able to establish an extremely close relationship with the Indonesian Independence Movement.

HIRANO SAKAE

Policy for Sumatra

Hirano was born in Saga Prefecture, Kyushu, in 1901, and graduated from a Japanese College in Shanghai in 1926. This knowledge of China led him into a career in foreign intelligence and research. From 1926 to 1934 he did research on the Japan-China trade for the Osaka Municipality, spending the last five years of this period posted at Tientsin in China. He then moved to the Manchurian Railway Company, which had a much bigger research staff working on China. In 1941 he was sent by the Company to Shanghai, and the following year to Singapore, along with 46 of his colleagues who were all to be attached as research staff to the 25th Army. When the 25th Army Gunseikambu moved to Bukittinggi, in Sumatra, in May 1943, Hirano followed. He became a key figure in the 25th Army's attempts to understand the situation in Sumatra and develop policies designed to gain popular support there.

This account was originally published in 1974 in the journal of the Sekidokai [Equator Association], the Tokyo organization for civilians who had been posted in Sumatra. The following year it was republished as part of a book produced by the same Association.

Hirano Sakae

SUMATORA NO OMOIDE: MINSHIN HAAKU TO DOKURITSU MONDAI

[Memories of Sumatra: Winning the Hearts and Minds of the
People and Problems of Independence], in **Sekidōhyō** (Tokyo,
Sekidōkai, 1975), pp.433-6

I. Introduction

For the following reasons I put great emphasis upon
winning the hearts and minds of the people [**Minshin Haaku**],
both officially while working in the Gunseikambu [of the 25th
Army] and privately.

1. From my experiences as an official of the Manchurian
Railway Company specializing in intelligence and research, I
felt strongly the importance of winning the hearts and minds of
the people when we were working overseas.

2. When I was attached to the Gunseikambu in Singapore as
a member of the **Mantetsu Chōsadan** [Research Team of the
Manchurian Railway Company] (consisting of 47 members),* we
were asked by the Officer in Charge to investigate how to deal
with the aftermath of the Occupation as quickly as possible,
because the Army had been troubled by the unstable conditions.
As a first step, we decided to make a field survey focusing
upon the appropriate measures for winning the hearts and minds
of the people and maintaining order.

3. After following the Army to Sumatra,† we organized a
research section made up of a few teams in the Gunseikambu. We
needed the cooperation of the people in carrying out our
surveys.

---

* The Bureau of Research of the Manchurian Railway was one of
the largest research establishments on Asian affairs in
pre-war Japan. In late 1942 much of its staff was sent to
the South to assist the Army administrations - in addition to
these 47 to Singapore, about 30 were sent to Burma. They
were usually attached to the research and planning section of
the Gunseikambu in each administration, but had a
considerable degree of autonomy from the military hierarchy.

† The 25th Army had initially administered Malaya and Sumatra
from its Headquarters in Singapore. In May 1943, however, it
relinquished responsibility for Malaya and moved its
Headquarters to Bukittinggi, in West Sumatra.

4. As the Japanese war position deteriorated, we were asked to concentrate our research on how to lead and mobilize the people. Accordingly, my reminiscences of Sumatra mainly concern the policy of winning the hearts and minds of the people, and the independence issue.

For the title of this memoir, I first thought that **Dōyō Bōshi** [The Prevention of Public Disquiet] or **Kyōryoku no Kyōka Suishin** [The Promotion and Strengthening of Mass Cooperation] might be preferable to **Minshin Haaku**. However, I adopted the latter because I understood it to be a broader concept than the other two.

II. The Sumatra Administration and Minshin Haaku

It can be said that the substance of administration was better in Sumatra than in other occupied regions. I think the most important reason for this was good administration which succeeded in winning the hearts and minds of the people in the early stages, in the following ways.

1. The population of the island had a favourable perception of Japan from the beginning, and therefore the administration could begin smoothly. In addition, administration in Sumatra was consistently mild to the end, since Sumatra was never directly involved in battle, permitting the Japanese to direct their efforts to improving the social welfare of the population.

2. When the Gunseikambu organization was established, the Residency and Sub-Residency Administrations [**Shu/Bunshu seicho**] were set up at the same time. This made it possible for the central and local administrative apparatus to guide the population harmoniously and to gain in return the goodwill of the population.

3. It must be noted that we moved decisively to establish the **Shu Sangikai** [Residency Advisory Council] in each Residency at an early stage, and next we set up the **Chuo Sangi-in** [Central Advisory Council] allowing the population to participate in the administration as advisers.* The establishment of the Chuo Sangi-in caused a greater response among the people than we had expected, and contributed much to promoting popular cooperation. Furthermore, the establishment of the Council strengthened the aspirations for independence in the

---

* The formation of **Shu Sangikai** in each of the ten **Shu** (Residencies) of Sumatra was announced in November 1943, five months after Tokyo had recommended such a policy, and two months after Java had implemented it. The **Chuo Sangi-in** for Sumatra was not announced until March 1945 and did not meet until the end of June -- almost two years after its Java equivalent.

hearts of the people in general and the intellectuals in particular. I often observed or heard about reactions of this sort.

4. The policy of winning the hearts and minds of the people was also advanced by the good manners of the Japanese there, which were appreciated by the population.

III. My Own Ideas and Efforts

Although the phrase **Minshin Haaku** is often used, there were all kinds of ideas and policies in relation to it according to the circumstances, the degree of cultural development of the people concerned, their sensitivity and so forth. In fact, I changed the strategy for this area of policy four times in response to the deterioration in the Japanese war position. Sometimes I presented advice to higher authorities, and sometimes I tried to win the people round directly through my wide contacts with them.

1. At first, finding that the Minangkabau people possessed a family-centred spirit, I planned to try to assimilate them to the Japanese, who in those days were also inspired by a family spirit. However, I abandoned this plan because my research in due course revealed the difference in the nature of the family spirit in the two peoples.

2. In the second stage, I sought to evoke a patriotic spirit, namely that Sumatra should be protected by the Sumatrans themselves. I encouraged the people to cooperate with the Japanese voluntarily for the defence of their fatherland. This tactic seemed to arouse general sympathy among the population, and to have been quite successful.

3. In the third stage, I thought that the Japanese should allow the people independence. As the Japanese war position deteriorated, the cooperation of the population became an increasingly urgent necessity. In fact, the most important issue among Japanese at the time was how to obtain more active cooperation. As it was obvious to me that the population were strongly attached to the ideal of independence, I personally reached the conclusion that there could be no better course than to promise independence to them in return for their cooperation. Just about the time I was contemplating this, I had a chance to exchange opinions with a young **Shiseikan** [Civil Administrator] from Java, and was encouraged to learn from him that the argument of [promising] independence [in order to obtain the people's cooperation] was also prevalent in Java. I expressed my personal opinion about the value of promoting independence when I reported on the Sumatran situation to the Chief of the Bureau of Military Affairs in the Ministry of the Army, when I visited Tokyo in April 1944 to discuss the question of altering the membership of the research section of the Gunseikambu. The Chief naturally did not give me an

answer, but he kindly listened to me for about three hours without condemning the idea as a lot of silly nonsense. He even invited me for dinner.

I recall this fact with deep emotion in view of the eventual Japanese decision to grant independence to Indonesia as a whole.

4. In the fourth stage, I advised the Gunseikambu of the 25th Army to make use of religion. Because the probability of an enemy landing on Sumatra grew ever greater, we were required to mobilize the population so that they would cooperate with the Japanese and participate in the defence against the enemy invasion. I thought the best way to achieve this was to make use of religion, and I advised my seniors accordingly. Although the Gunseikambu immediately requested Tokyo to dispatch Japanese [Islamic] priests to Sumatra, to our great disappointment the answer came back that no such priest was available in Japan. Then I visited Djamil Djambek* to ask for his cooperation. He was one of the most influential Muslim leaders in Sumatra and was appointed principal adviser to the Commander on matters concerning Islam when the Chuo Sangi-in was opened. I said to him, 'As the Greater East Asia War is a holy war not only for Japan but for the Muslims as well, you Muslims should take an active part in the war alongside the Japanese army. And you should work for a revival of Islam by sending Sumatran Muslims to the holy places of Islam, Mecca and Medina'.

Mr Djambek was deeply impressed with the arguments I put to him, and promised that he would fight to the death. When I visited him at the Japanese surrender for a final greeting, he began to cry audibly. 'How tragic', he exclaimed. 'My life has ended now!' I presented him with an automobile and petrol, both of which had been provided by the Gunseikambu.†

* Sjech Mohammad Djamil Djambek (1860-1947) was one of the great reformist ulama of West Sumatra, and his 'surau' in Bukittinggi was an influential centre for religious instruction to both Dutch-educated and Islamic-educated Muslims. In May 1945 he was appointed supreme adviser on Islamic affairs for Sumatra.

† In Medan, as well as in Bukittinggi, the Japanese provided cars to those leaders who seemed likely to suffer after the surrender for their identification with the Japanese. Hamka, the favoured Islamic leader in East Sumatra, was given the same treatment. The implication was that they would need to flee from their local enemies or the returning Allies.

5. Speeches at Meetings

I made speeches once or twice at big rallies with the aim
of winning the hearts and minds of the people and preventing
any spirit of panic from spreading among the population. The
first speech was made when Germany surrendered, and the second
one when the American forces landed on Okinawa. On the first
occasion I tried to reassure the population by telling them,
'Don't worry about the German surrender. Even though Germany
has been defeated Japan will fight alone until final victory'.
On the second occasion, after frankly admitting the landing of
American forces on Okinawa, I again tried to calm the people by
emphasizing that Japan would win in the end because she was
adopting an old Japanese military tactic: 'Allow the enemy to
cut our skin, but cut his flesh in return; let the enemy cut
our flesh, but cut his bones at the same time'. I also alluded
to an old Minangkabau dance in which a man in trying to kill a
tiger puts his left hand forward so that the tiger eats it, and
then stabs the tiger with the knife in his right hand. While
relating this I acted out the scene on the stage. After I
finished my speech, a storm of applause went on for a few
minutes.

Later a kempei came to my house to say that my speech had
been unexpectedly successful in overcoming the uneasiness.

IV. Independence of Sumatra

1. It was, as far as I remember, a few months before the
surrender that I was summoned by a senior official of the
Gunseikambu and told that Japan had decided to allow Indonesian
independence.* He asked my opinion about the idea of Sumatran
independence. I surmised that 'the Centre'† was thinking of
the independence of Indonesia as a whole, while the Sumatra
military command was looking to the separate independence of
Sumatra. It appeared that the Sumatra military had even begun
to draw up a blueprint for Sumatran independence. I sensed the
difficulty of the position in which the Army was placed in
having to adjust its plans to those of 'the Centre'.

2. As a matter of fact, when I referred to independence
earlier it was to the separate independence of Sumatra. During
the session of the Chuo Sangi-in [27 June to 2 July 1945], I
secretly asked all the members in turn about their preferences,

---

* This appears to be a reference to the meeting of the Supreme
  War Guidance Committee in Tokyo on 17 July 1945, which
  approved independence for the whole former Netherlands Indies
  at 'the earliest possible moment'.

† See Imamura, above, p.53.

and was very surprised to find that all of them hoped for the independence of Indonesia as a whole, and none foresaw the separate independence of Sumatra. As I was still reconsidering my plan for Sumatran independence as a result of this discovery when the official asked my opinion, I explained to him the reasons I was having second thoughts. However, I added that there was only one way we could persuade the population to accept Sumatran independence - if we explained it to them in the following way: 'Because of communication and transport difficulties caused by the deteriorating Japanese war position, independence is impractical for such a broad area as Indonesia as a whole. Accordingly, each region should first become independent as a temporary measure. When the situation allows, all regions should be united centered around Java.'

3. I also advised the senior official that, if independence was to be given at all, negotiations with the Indonesians would not proceed smoothly unless the Japanese entrusted the management of all the relevant organizations to the natives, apart from the minimum involvement of essential Japanese advisers. I should like to refrain from writing about the military's plans for Sumatran independence.

V.   Independence of Indonesia as a Whole

1. After my discussion with the senior official on the independence issue, the Sumatra Army seemed to give up its plan for Sumatran independence and to fit in with the plan for the independence of Indonesia as a whole according to instructions from 'the Centre'. The 25th Army ordered me to bring three Sumatran delegates to Jakarta where a meeting of the Committee for the Preparation of Indonesian Independence was to be held on 16 August.*

2. We left Sumatra on 10 August and arrived in Jakarta on the 13th via Singapore. However, as a result of the Japanese surrender on the 15th, the Japanese withdrew from the independence issue.

3. However, the three delegates from Sumatra insisted on

---

* This committee, known in Indonesian as the Panitia Persiapan Kemerdekaan Indonesia (PPKI), was to put the final touches to a constitution previously drafted by a committee representing Java only. Eight of the 22 PPKI members specifically represented areas outside Java. The three Sumatrans were Dr Mohammad Amir (a Minangkabau) and Mr T.M. Hasan (an Acehnese), both living in Medan, and Mr Abdul Abbas, a Mandailing living in Lampung. Unfortunately, Hirano sheds no light on why the Sumatra leadership being groomed by the 25th Army in Bukittinggi was by-passed in this delegation. Hasan was eventually chosen as Governor of Sumatra.

meeting the delegates of other regions. In this way, the delegates from Sumatra and Bali as well as the Japanese who had accompanied them held a dinner party together. During the dinner the delegates seemed to reach the conclusion that independence should be achieved by the Indonesians themselves. From the following day, communication between delegates from the various regions became very intense, and eventually the meeting of the Committee was held.*

4. The Committee first adopted a Constitution, and then selected the leaders of the new government. Sukarno was elected President, Hatta Vice-President, and one of the delegates from each region was chosen as Governor of that region. The Committee announced the manifesto of the long-awaited independence and gave cheers of 'Indonesia merdeka -- banzai'. This was the first step towards independence.

5. On the recommendation of the Sumatran delegates, I attended this historic meeting and observed the dramatic scene. The meeting ended with two cheers of 'Banzai' three times in Japanese. Watching the whole scene, I was deeply moved and there was joy as well as bitterness in my heart as I thought, 'Even though Japan was defeated, it was through Japan that Indonesia attained its independence'. This event is still deeply imprinted in my memory. It leads me to pray still more for the successs of Indonesian independence.

* The first PPKI meeting was on 18 August 1945, the day after independence was proclaimed. The standard Indonesian sources do not mention the presence of Japanese at this meeting.

JAPANESE SURRENDER

AND INDONESIAN INDEPENDENCE

II) THE INDEPENDENCE PROCLAMATION IN JAKARTA

(**Indoneshia Dokuritsu Kakumei**, pp.186-221)

Unforgettable People

The impression of my first meeting with Tan Malaka, one day immediately after the declaration of independence, is still deeply inscribed on my memory. **Merah putih** flags were flying in the town and the exultation of people was growing day by day. The Japanese, in contrast, were left anxious and uneasy because of the defeat of their fatherland and the uncertainty about their future. I myself was in the same mood, seeking desperately for some psychological security. For this reason, I often visited Subardjo. Among the Japanese in Indonesia I may have been rather fortunate to have had many Indonesian friends. Once I was introduced to an Indonesian by Subardjo. I remember that the Indonesian looked tough, and his gold teeth glittered. Subardjo asked me whether I knew who the man was, but I could not hazard a guess. Anyway, we began to talk. I was immediately surprised by the man's abundant knowledge and consistency of thought. It was apparent from his comments on revolution and the political structure after revolution that he was well acquainted with Marxism. Moreover, he talked about the strategy of mass movement, of propaganda, and of warfare. I was deeply impressed by his arguments because they were firmly based on an analysis of the international situation. I thought, 'How could a man who looks like a peasant analyse things so sharply?' This was no simple man. After we had talked for more than two hours, Subardjo said, 'Mr Nishijima! This is the real Tan Malaka!' Needless to say I was first very astonished and then enormously excited. I shook his hand again warmly.

*   *   *

With the outbreak of the Sino-Japanese war, Tan Malaka had moved to Singapore, taking a job as teacher in a Chinese school. When the Greater East Asia War broke out and Singapore fell into the hands of the Japanese, he smuggled himself to Medan, in North Sumatra, with the help of a Chinese friend. Later, he sneaked into the slums of Jakarta, where he lived for about a year, indulging his taste for reading and writing, without disclosing his name. Suffering from financial difficulties, he found a job at the Bayu coal mine as a clerk.

While working there he travelled around Java, including Jakarta, under the alias of Husein. He visited Jakarta as representative of a group in the Bayu area, in order to attend a youth conference to be held there in August 1945, but the conference was banned by the Japanese.

At the Japanese surrender, Tan Malaka appeared at Subardjo's residence. He also visited Chaerul Saleh (later Vice-Premier), one of the leaders of the youth group at that time, but he did not disclose his name. It is quite understandable in view of his long experience as a refugee that Tan Malaka did not trust people. He also visited Sukarni,* another youth leader, and even stayed at his house at the same time that members of the youth group took Sukarno and Hatta into custody at Rengasdengklok. Tan Malaka neither revealed his name to Sukarni nor participated in the abduction of the two leaders. He revealed himself for the first time when he called on Subardjo. Although Subardjo had met Tan Malaka in the Netherlands in 1922, he did not realize that this was **the** Tan Malaka and for a time took him to be Iskaq Tjokroadisoerjo (who later became a leader of the Indonesian Nationalist Party, and rose to be Minister of the Interior and Minister of the Economy), since the two looked alike. Even when Tan Malaka revealed himself, Subardjo could not at first believe it.

Tan Malaka was evidently sought after by the Japanese Army during the occupation, and it was rumoured several times that he had been arrested. However, there was no substance to such rumours. On each occasion, the Japanese arrested a man as Tan Malaka, only to find that he was not. It was also rumoured that Tan Malaka had been arrested by the **Beppan** [the Special Task Team] of the 16th Army, and that he escaped from jail by breaking the roof.

During the occupation I discussed Marxist ideas with Indonesians acquainted with them, and we exchanged views. Indonesians were generally reluctant to talk of Marxism and socialism for fear of being accused by the Kempeitai, but they

---

* Sukarni (1916-71) was born in Blitar, East Java, and while still a schoolboy became involved in the nationalist party Partindo and in Indonesia Muda, whose national president he became for a time in 1934. After a period of arrest he went underground in the late thirties, and appears to have become a contact for Tan Malaka's PARI party. He was arrested again by the Dutch in 1940, released by the Japanese, and worked during the occupation in Japanese propaganda agencies. He and Chaerul Saleh became the **pemuda** (youth) proteges of the Japanese propaganda chief Shimizu, and were well placed at the end of the occupation as national youth leaders. After independence Sukarni became the leader of the Tan Malaka-inspired Murba party, and later an ambassador to Peking.

300

Proklamasi.

Kami bangsa Indonesia dengan ini menjatakan kemerdekaan Indonesia.

Hal² jang mengenai pemindahan kekoeasaan d.l.l., diselenggarakan dengan tjara saksama dan dalam tempoh jang sesingkat-singkatnja.

Djakarta, 17 – 8 – '05
Wakil² bangsa Indonesia

16. The draft declaration of independence agreed at Admiral Maeda's house (see p.324).

17. Admiral Maeda's house, where the independence proclamation was drafted (see pp.321-4). The house, at Jalan Imam Bondjol 1, was the pre-war British Consul's residence.

18. The 19 September 1945 Rally at Ikada Square in Jakarta (see pages 329-30). Sukarno in foreground waving, partly obscuring Hatta. (Photo Ipphos).

19. *Jakarta slogans in October 1945.*

20. *Street-fighting in Surabaya, November 1945. A British soldier takes shelter behind a knocked-out ex-Japanese tank, which had been mobilized by Indonesian marines (T.K.R.-laut) during the fighting.* (I.W.M.)

treated me as an exception. Some Indonesians close to me broke
the taboo rather boldly. One of these was Iwa Kusuma Sumantri
(later Minister of Defence).* Although Iwa was not a Marxist,
he was well versed in Marxism because he had lived in Moscow as
a student and had a Russian wife. He once told me, 'After
World War I, the terms "workers" and "peasants" were in
constant use. Since then, office workers have come to
constitute a large proportion of the working class. In other
words, the substance of the working class has been changing
considerably. This trend will be accelerated after this war.
Even in Russia, a young generation is emerging which criticizes
capitalism without having experienced it'.

I felt that what Iwa said was quite true. When I had been
involved in the socialist movement in Japan, the unions of
manual labourers were the major force in the movement, and the
unions of office workers were rather ancillary. Now, however,
the unions of office workers are the major force in the movement. Even in Russia, the centre of the socialist movement, a
younger generation had grown up who knew of capitalism only in
theoretical terms, and they were expected to guide the
communist leaders of Japan, a capitalist country, and of Italy,
where the leaders had a long experience of the movement. As a
natural result, rifts appeared between the younger generation
of Russians and the [communist] leaders of Japan and Italy. I
had been vaguely aware of this, but Iwa's logical explanation
helped clarify my thoughts.

When I discussed Iwa's views with Tan Malaka, he listened
to me closely, and kindly answered my questions, giving his own
views. Although I did not usually reveal my weakness, I was
unable to conceal the great shock caused me by the Japanese
surrender. I explained my feelings frankly to Tan Malaka: 'We
are defeated. Nothing can be done now. I do not want to go
back to Japan. In short, I am completely confused'.

Tan Malaka listened to me, then answered slightly
reprovingly, 'I met Sano Manabu through my activities in the
Comintern. I also know Ho Chi Minh and have argued with
Stalin. Thus I believe I understand the position of other
countries and the international situation. As far as the
independence of Indonesia is concerned, I don't think it will
be achieved before I die. Independence cannot be achieved
merely by a declaration, but must be substantiated by an

---

* Iwa Kusuma Sumantri (1899-1972), a Sundanese, was born in
  Tjiamis and obtained a Leiden law degree in 1925. He was
  active in left-wing politics while in Europe and published in
  Moscow a Marxist tract, **The Peasant's Movement in Indonesia**
  (1926) under the pseudonym S. Dingley. Highly suspect by the
  Dutch from the time of his return to a Medan law practice, he
  was imprisoned in 1929 and released only in 1941.

independent state. Judging from my experience in underground movements and as a refugee, it is no easy thing to attain a complete independence.

'You said Japan is defeated. That is certainly true. But have you thought how many people now belong to defeated countries? There are more than 200 million in Japan, Germany and Italy alone. Can you imagine how great a number of oppressed people are living in Asia? The earth is revolving and history never ceases to move on. In ten or twenty years, Japan will be changed. This can be said for sure from my experience.'

I understod well what Tan Malaka meant and felt thankful for his encouragement. After this meeting, he went to Central Java where he broadcast messages similar to what he had told me, through a secret radio station. Apart from the activity of Tan Malaka, I was deeply impressed by his words of encouragement. I felt, 'How splendid to be a revolutionary!' At the same time I realized that goals could be achieved only when one had a long-range perspective that would not be distracted by present circumstances. Tan Malaka gave me an Indonesian name, Hakim, meaning a man of justice or a judge, perhaps regarding me as a righteous man. To Yoshizumi he gave the name Arif, a wise or erudite man.

I frequently visited Tan Malaka while he was staying at Subardjo's house. However, I did not visit him openly, because the Japanese Army, even though defeated, was still there and the Kempeitai was functioning. In addition, there were Indonesian leaders who were arrested by the Japanese Army even after the surrender. Accordingly, we could not be too cautious about the safety of Tan Malaka. We asked him to move to the former residence of a senior Japanese civil administrator of the Navy. In the meantime, Tan Malaka began to talk of a plan to initiate guerilla warfare around Banten in West Java, probably through fear of the danger of remaining in Jakarta. Since he had lived in West Java before, he knew the area well. We decided to do our best for him, and we presented him with a car, arms, radio facilities and food. An Indonesian called Chairuddin, and Yoshizumi joined this venture. This was the last time I saw Tan Malaka face to face.

*   *   *

The Name is Dokuritsu Indoneshia Juku   [School for Independent Indonesia]

Immediately before the Japanese surrender, there were several groups striving for Indonesian independence. Adam Malik, in his **History and Struggle Concerning the Indonesian**

* For Footnote see following page.

Independence Declaration of 17 August 1945, * calls these groups 'revolutionary forces'. Among the groups historically acknowledged were the Sukarni group based on the **Sendembu** [Propaganda Section] of the 16th Army, the Sutan Sjahrir group, the student group represented by Chaerul Saleh, and the Navy group. The 'Navy' in the last case means the Japanese Navy, and in particular the Bukanfu where we were working. The Navy group therefore consisted of Indonesians who were working in the Bukanfu. Its core members were graduates of the Dokuritsu Juku. In other words, the Dokuritsu Juku was the origin of the Navy group. Its members played an important role in the promulgation of independence and in the subsequent struggle for independence.

The Dokuritsu Juku was instituted at a time of crisis. As the Japanese war position deteriorated, the Japanese increasingly needed Indonesian cooperation. At the same time they were no longer able to ignore the issue of independence. Japan had up to then maintained a grand design that such sparsely populated regions as Sulawesi and Sumatra be permanently occupied and the population converted into **komin** [lit., Emperor's subjects], while the densely populated regions of Java and Madura were given a high degree of autonomy. In short, independence was not officially considered. Indonesians might talk about independence among themselves but they could not do so openly. The ever-deteriorating war position forced Japan to change its attitude towards independence, as reflected in the Koiso statement [of 7 September 1944].

The Koiso statement gave rise to a wide range of reactions. Generally speaking, however, Indonesians appreciated it as representing some advance, since the Japanese at least officially promised Indonesian independence at some future time. After the statement not only such outstanding figures as Sukarno and Hatta, but even young people began to discuss the issue of independence openly. Naturally this heightened their enthusiasm for independence. The Koiso statement had established the following five guidelines:

1. The timing of independence is not to be discussed.
2. Although the Japanese government permits informal preparation for the study of independence among the population, it does not allow formal activities for independence.
3. Political participation should be promoted in the Indies.

* Footnote from previous page:
  Adam Malik, **Riwajat dan Perdjuangan sekitar Proklamasi Kemerdekaan 17 Agustus 1945,** 1950 (5th edition, Jakarta, Widjaya, 1970), p.24.

4. Enthusiasm for independence should be encouraged among the population, and propaganda conducted for independence.
5. The use of the national flag and anthem of the Indies should be recognized.

Despite these guidelines from the Central Authorities, actual implementation differed according to the characteristics and ideas of the military authorities in each area - the 25th Army in Sumatra, the 16th Army in Java and Madura, and the Navy in the rest of Indonesia. In addition the Army and Navy were in conflict in Tokyo, which further influenced the way the guidelines were implemented in Indonesia. There was, moreover, the general tendency among Japanese, both in Indonesia and Tokyo, to look down upon Indonesians, particularly the people of Borneo (Kalimantan), the Celebes (Sulawesi) and the Lesser Sunda Islands (Nusa Tenggara). Some military authorities in Indonesia wanted to concentrate on the war without being drawn into political complications, so they tended to keep out of the independence issue as far as possible.

Nevertheless, the Japanese in Indonesia felt obliged to do something for independence, in view of the Koiso statement and the ever-increasing enthusiasm of the population for independence. In Java, the expansion of political participation was implemented. It was to be expected that Indonesians viewed this as a deliberate Japanese substitute for the recognition of independence. The promotion of political participation was easy for the Japanese, because it had already been the policy since the Tojo statement and therefore the new policy merely meant increasing the number of Indonesians participating in the administration - for instance, by increasing the number of Indonesian Residents and Advisory Councils and by appointing Indonesians to assist the director of every department of the Gunseikambu. The policy of expanding the **Chuo Sangi-in** [Central Advisory Council] and the **Chiho Sangi-in** [Local Advisory Council]* was in conformity with the new policy. It was also not difficult to stimulate aspirations for independence, and to propagate such aspirations through the radio and publications. The enlargement of the **Giyugun** [Volunteer Corps] was expected to be effective not only for Japanese propaganda purposes but also to be useful as war potential, directly or indirectly, if the Allied forces should land. The Islamic Volunteer Corps called Hizbullah resulted from these Japanese guidelines, and actually fought courageously against the Dutch during the struggle for independence.

In addition, the Japanese devised such measures as the establishment of supporters' associations for the Giyugun and **Heiho** [Auxiliary Corps], and the aid system for **romusha**

* Normally **Shu Sangikai** [Residency Advisory Council].

[requisitioned labour], among other measures. In truth, however, this was all that the Japanese could do. Naturally, dissatisfaction was expressed by Indonesians in various ways, for instance in such complaints as: 'Japan has been claiming that it is going to recognize Indonesian independence. When will it do so?' As mentioned above, Japan had no intention of clarifying the time [for independence]. Dissatisfaction of this sort came to be openly expressed by Indonesians. We thought: 'Something must be done'.

At the time the Indonesian suspicion about Japan's ambiguous attitude towards independence was becoming critical, Maeda told us, 'Japan promised to recognize Indonesian independence in the future. This will take place in the not too distant future. Consequently we must make haste to groom Indonesian leaders who can become the core of the nation after independence'. Maeda was of the opinion that we should establish a school to educate young people in preparation for Indonesian independence. Maeda had expressed similar views to Sato, Yoshizumi and myself before. The time had at last come to implement the plan. Maeda as usual did not mention details of the way this was to be carried out. We immediately started making preparations. First we consulted Subardjo, the person closest to us, who agreed with the plan, saying, 'It is a very good idea. We will look for able young men'. Soon Subardjo found some youths through his connections and brought them to us. The Kaigun Bukanfu, unlike the Gunseikambu of the Army, did not have administrative authority in Java, and accordingly was unable to recruit people through its administrative apparatus. Since Subardjo asked the Indonesian leaders on whom he could rely for recruits, relatives and friends of these leaders were among the youths selected. I remember that the total number of youths was slightly more than thirty.

Maeda named the school **Yōsei Juku**. When asked the origin of the name, he explained that 'yōsei' was the first word of the instructions of Emperor Jimmu. According to the **Kōjien** [dictionary], published by Iwanami Shoten, 'yōsei' means 'to cultivate justice'. It is also possible that Maeda chose the name because the pronunciation of the word is the same as 'yosei' meaning 'to train'. Whatever the case, it was unreasonable to demand that Indonesians use such a Japanese word. At that time the Japanese were forcing on the Indonesians the use of Japanese language and the practice of saluting in the direction of the royal palace in Tokyo, thereby causing much resentment. Indonesians wanted to absorb what was good in the Japanese way of life and were willing to ask for Japanese help, but they showed a strong antipathy towards Japanization. The same can be said of the school. Even though the Japanese had built it as a favour to the Indonesians, it would never appeal to the population if it carried a Japanese name.

Yoshizumi, an active and courageous person, proposed, 'If

Maeda likes the name Yosei Juku then let it be. But as far as we are concerned let us use an Indonesian name'. I agree with his idea. Again we consulted Subardjo, who eventually suggested 'School for Independent Indonesia' or Asrama Indonesia Merdeka. This could be abbreviated as Dokuritsu Juku in Japanese. Before the Koiso statement was issued, the Japanese did not use the term **dokuritsu** [independence] or the Indonesian **merdeka** and there was an official taboo on the use of the word 'Indonesia'. It might appear unimportant to foreigners whether the word 'Indonesia' was used or not, but it was important to the Indonesians. Although the Japanese used the [official] title, 'the East Indies', Indonesian leaders often asked to have it replaced by 'Indonesia'. When Putera and Jawa Hokokai were instituted, the leaders demanded that 'Indonesia' be added to the names of these organizations. The Japanese rigidly refused. As expected, the name Asrama Indonesia Merdeka appealed to the population, and the institution was able to recruit many able youths.

The next problem was how to manage the Asrama. As the matter was entrusted to Yoshizumi and myself, we discussed it together and agreed to leave the management to Indonesians, with Subardjo in charge. When we put this to Subardjo, he suggested we choose somebody who was younger and less close to the Japanese than himself, and who could contact students directly. He excused himself on the grounds that he worked in a branch office of the Bukanfu Research Department, and was rather too old for the position. Eventually we appointed Wikana, who had once worked in the branch office, as president of the school. Wikana, under the assumed name of Sunoto, had once been arrested by the Dutch before the war on the charge of leading a youth movement.

George S. Kanahele claims in his doctoral thesis, 'The Japanese Occupation of Indonesia: Prelude to Independence',* that Subardjo did not know Wikana's background. This is not true. Subardjo told me about Wikana's background, and while Subardjo was working in the branch office of the Research Department of the Bukanfu, I asked him to write an article on youth movements [making reference to Wikana]. I might have felt sympathetic towards Wikana because his experience had been similar to mine in being arrested by the police. Anyway, Wikana played a role in organizing youth groups, taking over public facilities and founding the basis of the Republic immediately after the independence declaration. In later times he became a senior member of the Communist Party. It is not

---

* Kanahele's thesis (Cornell University, 1967), p.312 n 38 in fact states only that in interviews Wikana claimed (and Subardjo denied) that Subardjo had been unaware of Wikana's true identity.

yet known whether he is still alive, has been murdered, or has gone underground following the 'September 30 affair'. With hindsight I suppose it was rash to have used Wikana, in view of his previous career. At the time, however, I only thought: 'Our seniors will not know of Wikana's career unless we deliberately inform them of it. We shall just have to see how things go if we are discovered'. It was proved later that Maeda knew nothing of Wikana's background.

There were problems to be settled concerning the school, namely lecturers and curriculum. We started by selecting lecturers. We planned to invite Sukarno, Hatta, Maramis, Subardjo and Iwa. Subardjo asked us to add Sutan Sjahrir.* Sjahrir was a college of Hatta. The 16th Army had once considered utilizing him, but the idea had been rejected. There was no objection to Subardjo's request on our part, since we had already included Hatta among the lecturers of the school. Then I had to persuade Sjahrir. Sjahrir describes the situation as follows in his bok, **Out of Exile** (New York, John Day, 1949) [p.251]:

> The political policy now altered slightly. Nationalism was no longer so vigorously opposed... It was just about this time that I first came into direct contact with the Japanese. The Japanese information service sent a Japanese to find out my views on the general situation... Thereafter I had at least one visitor a week from the information service: first a Japanese and then an Indonesian. I realized that my movements were being watched. They had evidently found out that I travelled considerably and had many visitors. In fact, toward the end they tried to restrict my movements. They requested me to give courses dealing with nationalism and the Indonesian popular movement in a so-called nationalist institution that had been set up, called the **Ashrama Indonesia Merdeka** (Association for a Free Indonesia). As the situation then stood, I could not refuse. I realized that it was an indirect means of making my travel difficult, and at the same time of keeping an eye on my movements and my ideas.

---

* Sutan Sjahrir (1909-66), a Minangkabau from Padang Panjang, studied law in Leiden (1929-31), where he became a socialist and a close supporter of Hatta. He helped Hatta establish the party Pendidikan Nasional Indonesia, and was exiled with him in 1934. Apart from Amir Sjarifuddin who was in a Japanese prison, Sjahrir was the most prominent politician to refuse cooperation with the Japanese, and thus was in a good position to rise to the premiership after their surrender, in November 1945.

Sjahrir's reference to 'a Japanese' obviously meant me. However, I had no thought of restricting his activities. This seems to be pure speculation arising from his own bias. On the other hand he admits the usefulness of the Dokuritsu Juku in another part of the book, which I will mention later. At any rate, Sjahrir eventually agreed to give lectures.

The content of the lectures and the way of organizing them we entrusted to the Indonesian staff. I believe I stressed this point in trying to obtain Subardjo's agreement. Thus Sukarno came to give lectures on the history of the nationalist movement, Hatta on the cooperative movement, Subardjo on international law, Sjahrir on the principles of nationalism and democracy, Iwa on labour problems, and Wikana on the youth movement. In addition, Yoshizumi and I were in charge of lectures on guerilla warfare and on agricultural problems respectively. The school was initiated in October that year [1944] at 50 Defencielinie van den Bosch street, i.e., the present Jalan Bungur Besar near Kemayoran airport. The students all stayed at a dormitory nearby, the management of which was left in their own hands. The Head of the Juku, Wikana, lived close by the school. All costs were met by the Bukanfu.

At the time we initiated the school we had abundant financial resources. Furthermore, Yoshizumi was good at collecting money. Thus we were able at least to ensure the students did not suffer from hunger, even if life there was not necessarily luxurious. In fact we gave no thought at all to financial problems, for we had in mind obtaining money by smuggling in opium from Singapore in the event of serious financial difficulties.

Once the school was open, Yoshizumi and I devoted ourselves enthusiastically to lecturing. The preparation of lectures took quite a lot of time because of the Indonesian language. Although Yoshizumi and I were in charge of the school, we could not be there all the time since we were obliged to work for the Research Department as well. Nevertheless the lectures went on smoothly, thanks to the ability of the Indonesians to manage their own affairs. As I have said, we made a point of avoiding coercion as far as possible, and consequently we were cautious not to introduce things Japanese in lectures. On the other hand the curriculum was required to cover as wide a range of subjects as possible, since the major aim of the Juku was to groom leaders for a future republic. In view of this we invited an instructor from the Fifth Guard Troop of the Navy to teach **bujutsu** [one of the Japanese martial arts]. I myself occasionally led the students in a training run. I could run as I was still just a little over 30 at the time and had done my military training in the army.

The Dokuritsu Juku automatically ceased to function on the Japanese surrender. The only students were those who had entered in October 1944. Some articles on the Dokuritsu Juku use such expressions as 'graduates of the first year' or 'graduates of the second year', but this is inaccurate. Most students joined the independence struggle without completing the course, and some played a role in founding the Republic.

* * *

In a section omitted, Nishijima describes the role of Major A.K. Jusuf in kidnapping Prime Minister Sjahrir on 3 July 1946, although Jusuf had been regarded as 'one of my best students' at the Dokuritsu Juku by Sjahrir (Out of Exile, p.252). These events are more fully described in Benedict Anderson, Java, pp.370-403.

* * *

Among the students of the Dokuritsu Juku were the subsequent Secretary-General of the Indonesian Communist Party, Aidit; the 'number two' of the Party, Mohammad Lukman; and Sidik Kertapati, who wrote a book on independence and was a member of the Party.* Lukman became acquainted with Aidit only after he entered the Dokuritsu Juku, but was later to support Aidit in his bid for leadership of the Party. Lukman lost his life, together with comrades such as Aidit, in the 'September 30 affair'. Had he not entered the Dokuritsu Juku, the course of his life might have differed.

* * *

Several articles on Indonesia published after the war refer to the Dokuritsu Juku, and many claim that the substance of the curriculum was communist. I grant that it was socialist, but not communist. During the war some people thought that Indonesia should develop in the direction of national socialism. We had the same idea. In the event Indonesia did appear to move in that direction, which was only natural since the management of the school was in the hands of the Indonesians concerned. Many Indonesian leaders were more or less influenced by Marxism while studying in Europe after World War I. Since nationalist movements in colonies like the East Indies aimed to cast off the yoke of the colonial power,

* Sidik Kertapati, **Sekitar Proklamasi 17 Agustus 1945**, first published 1957; (3rd, revised editon, Jakarta, Pembaruan, 1964). D.N. Aidit and M.H. Lukman led the PKI from 1951 until they were killed following the affair of 30 September 1965.

in this case the Netherlands, nationalism had common ground with anti-imperialism.

The keynote of anti-imperialism is socialism - whether in terms of the First, Second or Third International. As a result there is no denying that the substance of the curriculum tended to be socialist. Accusations that the curriculum was communist came particularly from the Dutch, not without reason. After Indonesia achieved independence, the Dutch wanted to annihilate it under one pretext or another. For this reason, I believe, they labelled independence 'made in Japan' or 'a communist fake'. If we look at Indonesian history it is obvious that such criticisms of independence were beside the point.

Looking back on those days, one thing I am proud of is that we did not force anything upon the population. The Army set up its **Kenkoku Gakuin** [Institute for the Founding of the Nation] in March 1945 with the same goals as the Dokuritsu Juku. Despite the mushrooming enthusiasm for independence at that time, the Army gave its training centre a Japanese name and insisted that the Japanese language be used there. The head was also a Japanese. We used the Japanese name of Dokuritsu Juku because we understood the thoughts and sentiments of the Indonesians through associating with them. I wondered why [the Army] did not choose a more effective course, since it had set up the institute at no small effort.

There was certainly criticism in some Japanese quarters, particularly the Army, that the policy we adopted was too close and sympathetic to the Indonesians. I believe that the 16th Army in Java had a more progressive administration than the Army in any other occupied region, and yet it gave the new institution a Japanese name. This seems to reflect an incurable defect in the Japanese. Japanese leaders publicized that the Greater East Asia War was the war for the liberation of colonized peoples. Why then did Japan not allow the independence of occupied countries? The Japanese interpreted the liberation of Asia as liberation from the West - liberation of the Indonesians from the Dutch. Liberation should have been of the Indonesians, the Asian peoples, themselves.

After the Russo-Japanese War, Japan intensified the nature of its imperialism. However, Asian peoples did not view Japan as a purely imperialist country. On the contrary they believed that Japan, having defeated Russia, could liberate them from the yoke of Western domination. Without appreciating these expectations Japan insisted upon 'under Japanese supervision' and 'Japanization'. As a result Japanese policies towards Indonesia inevitably tended to be based on expediency. We, on the other hand, were convinced that Japan would be able to maintain close ties with Indonesia only if she achieved independence in the true sense. Although we were certainly idealistic, I still firmly believe we were not wrong.

The Longest Day: The Eve of the Independence Declaration

Indonesians were increasingly suspicious about their future after Germany surrendered to the Allied Forces in May 1945. Moreover, in August various reports reached Indonesia, including the Russian invasion of Manchuria and the dropping of atomic bombs on Hiroshima and Nagasaki. With each report unfavourable to Japan, Japanese in Indonesia felt more acutely their isolation. They wondered how Japan would be able to carry on the war against the whole world, given that its allies had already surrendered.

It was on 8 August that we received the news of the Russian invasion of Manchuria, and four Indonesians visited me at my home at Kebon Sirih 80 without any prior warning. They were Subardjo, Buntaran, Iwa Kusuma Sumantri and Soerachman.* My residence was open to anybody and visitors often came unexpectedly. The four leaders caught me as I came into the reception room, and asked gravely: 'What course will the war take?' I fully understood what they were trying to say. Japan had been taking the position of recognizing Indonesian independence and the population had been preparing for it. What would become of independence if the Japanese surrendered? When Germany invaded the Netherlands, the Dutch Queen Wilhelmina II had broadcast a message that 'the government of the Indies will be modified after the war', but she had said nothing about granting independence. The Dutch had no intention of allowing the Indies to be independent. On the contrary, they would begin to suppress the Indonesian demand for independence even though it was ever more intense. What sort of fate awaited these Indonesian leaders, who had been cooperating with the Japanese solely in the hope of achieving independence? General Pétain of France, a hero of World War I, was arrested by the Allied Forces because of his cooperation with Germany. There was no guarantee that these Indonesian leaders would not share the same fate as Petain. I realized

---

* For Subardjo and Iwa see above. Dr Buntaran Martoatmodjo (b. 1896) was a prominent member of the 'Navy group' around Subardjo, Deputy Vice-Chairman of the Chuo Sangi-in, a member of both the 1945 committees to prepare Indonesian independence (BPKI and PPPKI), and Indonesian Adviser to the Health Bureau of the Internal Affairs Department. The last position led naturally to the post of Health Minister in the first independent Indonesian Cabinet (September–November 1945).

Ir. Raden Mas Pandji Soerachman Tjokroadisoerjo (b. 1894) was not politically active until he was appointed Chief of the Economic Affairs Department by the Japanese in July 1945. He was also Minister of Finance in two of Sjahrir's 1946 Cabinets.

that the four leaders were worrying not only about the future of Indonesia but also about their own fate.

I recalled my own feelings on my return to Java from a camp in Australia. Guadalcanal had already fallen to the Americans. At that stage I held strong doubts about the Japanese war position, and these grew when Karasawa* gave me his very pessimistic perspective on the war when I stopped over in Japan for a while. Under these circumstances it would not have been unreasonable for me to weigh up whether it would be safer to be in Japan or Indonesia if Japan was defeated. In reality I returned to Java without the slightest hesitation, even though I might never return to Japan alive. My desire to see the development of the Indonesian independence movement with my own eyes was very strong, and I renewed my resolution to cooperate as much as possible with the Indonesians to achieve independence.

There were quite a number of Japanese who were deeply involved in Indonesia and shared its hopes for independence. However, we were outsiders after all. True independence could not be achieved unless the Indonesians, the people concerned, were to acquire it by themselves. To this end the people had to arm themselves and be prepared for real sacrifices. This was my theory, and I reiterated it many times to the four Indonesians that night: 'Whatever may befall you, such as a Japanese surrender, you must achieve independence by yourselves. Never react passively to external circumstances'. I had for a long time taken the view of the war that those who had died in it would be justified as long as Indonesia attained independence. For that reason I wanted all the more to see Indonesia independent. However, it seemed undeniable to me that there was a degree of passivity among the Indonesians.

I often heard complaints from Indonesians such as: 'Even though we asked for help, the Japanese did not provide it'. Of course there were things which could be done only by Japanese, but there must also have been things that Indonesians could do. Every time I heard such complaints I condemned the passive attitude which lay behind them. I had occasion to talk with Trimurti,† a nationalist activist and the wife of Sayuti Melik, who is now a member of parliament and was a minister after the

---

* Karasawa was the 'supervisor' responsible for Nishijima's good behaviour after he had been released from political detention in 1933.

† S.K. Trimurti (b. 1914) and her husband Sayuti Melik (b. 1909) were both on the left wing of nationalist politics, and were imprisoned by the Japanese until rescued by Sukarno in 1945. Before the war Trimurti had been associated with Gerindo, while Sayuti had spent a period of exile in Boven Digul.

war. On that occasion I told her, 'A door will never be opened
if you stop knocking at it simply for fear of hurting your
hand. As long as you are involved in the nationalist
liberation movement, you must possess a will strong enough to
open the door even though you injure your hand, your bones are
bared, and the knocking gives you pain. In other words you
must be prepared to sacrifice yourself for liberation and
independence'.

I had associated with Indonesians who shared the view
described above. The four Indonesian leaders listened
earnestly to me and returned home nodding agreement.

I felt the three days from 15 to 17 August 1945 to be
enormously long. These three days constitute an unforgettable
period of my life. It was on the 15th that the rumour of a
Japanese surrender spread, causing great upheaval for both
Japanese and Indonesian leaders. The Japanese were on
tenterhooks for different psychological reasons - some were
reluctant to acknowledge the Japanese surrender, while others
believed it and feared the grim situation which might develop
as a result. How did the Indonesian leaders react to the
rumour of a Japanese surrender? I quote from Subardjo's book,
Indonesian Independence and Revolution:

> On that unforgettable day, 15 August, a rumour spread
> in Jakarta that Japan had surrendered to the Allied
> Forces. But we were unable to obtain any official
> information from reliable Japanese authorities.
> Sukarno and Hatta tried to get solid information from
> the military administration authorities but they
> could not because the **Gunseikan** [Chief of Military
> Administration] was not in his office.

Sukarno and Hatta tried to enquire about the Japanese
surrender directly from the Gunseikan, Maj.-Gen. Yamamoto
Moichiro, but they were refused permission to meet Yamamoto on
the pretext that he was attending a meeting. I do not know
whether Yamamoto was really in his office or was attending a
meeting elsewhere. Since they were refused by the Army
authorities, they next tried to obtain information from the
Navy. Thus they visited Subardjo at the branch office of the
Research Department, which eventually led to a meeting of
Sukarno, Hatta, Subardjo and Maeda. This meeting was a factor
which connected the Indonesian declaration of independence with
the [Japanese] Navy. Hence this meeting should be given a
prominent place in the history of Japanese-Indonesian
relations.

In the afternoon (perhaps 4 or 5 p.m.) of that 15 August,
Sukarno, Hatta and Subardjo called on Maeda at the office of
the Bukanfu in front of Gambir Square. I was at the office of
the Research Department on Postweg, and was summoned by Maeda
to act as interpreter. First Sukarno explained the purpose of

313

the visit. He asked Maeda, 'Hearing that Japan had surrendered, I visited an Army office to confirm the news, but I could not meet anybody. So we came here to find out whether the report was true or not'. Maeda replied, 'I cannot answer with certainty, since no official report has reached here. In any case I cannot believe that the Japanese would surrender. Please be cautious about believing messages, because many of them seem to be subversive. When we obtain official information we will certainly let you know'.

Maeda did not waste words, and his reply was very short. Probably that was all he could say. However, his attitude and the prevailing atmosphere clearly implied a Japanese surrender. The tone of my translation may also have given a hint of confirmation of the Japanese surrender. As they were leaving the office one of them, perhaps Subardjo, said, 'It is not important whether Japan has surrendered or not. We must continue to fight for independence'. Sukarno and Hatta must have had the same determination. The Japanese surrender was certainly a sad event, but independence had to be achieved since it was the earnest wish of the people. Even if it was to come as 'independence as a gift', independence was near at hand, and in their own hands.

The Allied Forces had not expressed their position on Indonesian independence, and the Dutch had promised only a high degree of autonomy. Consequently, independence seemed likely to be shelved as a result of the Japanese surrender. Nevertheless we must fight for independence. This may have been the resolve shared by the three Indonesians as they left the Bukanfu. Hatta claimed after the war in **Suara Partai** (July-August 1951), 'It was confirmed on 15 August that Japan had surrendered'. However, the Army authorities had not met Sukarno and Hatta, nor had the Navy subsequently given them official information of the Japanese surrender. Hatta may have sensed it instinctively.

After their meeting with Maeda, Sukarno, Hatta and Subardjo discussed the policy to be followed, and agreed to carry out the objectives of the Committee for the Preparation of Indonesian Independence. They decided to convene the Committee at 10 a.m. on the 16th. This Committee had been preliminarily instituted on 11 August as an organization to take over political power from Japan, and it was to commence its activities officially from the 18th of that month. However, Japan surrendered before the Committee officially started. The predecessor of this Committee, the Body for the Investigation of Independence, had been established on 28 May 1945 to implement the Koiso statement. The Body had as its aim the investigation and study of all subjects related to independence and the preparation of reports and materials necessary for independence. Naturally such a project required a lot of time. Thus we can assume that the real purpose of the

Japanese in the establishment of the Body was to gain time on the one hand and to acquire the cooperation of the Indonesians on the other. Contrary to Japanese expectations, however, the Body pursued its tasks at full speed and even began to discuss a draft Constitution after only two sessions. Hence it is obvious that Sukarno and Hatta thought independence just around the corner when they were confronted with the news of the Japanese surrender.

Late in the afternoon of 15 August, Subardjo visited us at Kebon Sirih 80 in order to confirm the news of the Japanese surrender. As Subardjo often said, our residence functioned as a meeting place for Indonesians associated with the Navy. On that day, too, several Indonesians had already gathered at the house before Subardjo arrived. Being unable to accomplish his aim, he went off to Sukarno's residence at Pegangsaan Timur 56, together with Hatta, intending to decide the subjects to be discussed at the meeting of the Committee for the Preparation of Indonesian Independence the following day. They arrived at Sukarno's place at about 11 pm, and found Sukarno arguing with some youths, including the president of the Dokuritsu Juku, Wikana, and Darwis.

*   *   *

In the passage omitted, Nishijima uses published Indonesian and Dutch accounts to describe the confrontation between the youth leaders on the one hand and Sukarno and Hatta on the other. Wikana and Darwis pressed hard for an immediate independence declaration in defiance of the Japanese, while the older leaders wanted to await official confirmation of the surrender.

*   *   *

Subardjo heard at 8 a.m. on the 16th that Sukarno and Hatta had disappeared. Sudiro, Subardjo's secretary, brought him the news. Sudiro had visited Sukarno's residence along with Subardjo the night before, and witnessed the heated argument between Sukarno and the youths. Although Sudiro immediately guessed that the youth group had abducted Sukarno and Hatta, he could not find out from them where Sukarno and Hatta were located. Subardjo also suspected the youth group, but sought to obtain the Navy's support in rescuing them, since if it had been the Army which had seized the two leaders there was no other way than to ask for the intervention of the Navy. Subardjo telephoned me at the Bukanfu to notify me that Sukarno and Hatta had disappeared, adding , 'They may fall into the hands of the Army'. Then he hurried to Maeda's place by car to report the incident directly. I, too, immediately reported to

315

Maeda. To tell the truth, neither Maeda nor I thought the youth group had the courage to carry out such an abduction, and we therefore suspected that the Army had masterminded it.

Maeda went to the Gunseikambu by himself to enquire after the two men. I do not remember precisely which of the two, the Gunseikan Yamamoto or the Chief of General Affairs Nishimura, met Maeda on that occasion. Whichever of them it was, he was taken aback by Maeda's enquiry and replied, 'Although we have been looking for them both, unfortunately we do not yet know where they are'. He added quite unnecessarily, 'As a matter of fact, if they have disappeared it is rather convenient for us, because it will mean less trouble in the future'. I thought the Army was underestimating the seriousness of the matter. Nevertheless, the Army also had to ascertain the whereabouts of the two leaders. Apparently the Army had been looking for them through the Kempeitai and the Beppan, which was in charge of intelligence. Maeda gave me an order: 'It would create a serious situation if communications between the highest Indonesian leaders and the Japanese Army were to be broken at this critical stage. We absolutely must maintain communications. Find the two immediately!'

Maeda's instruction made me realize what a thoughtful man he was. As I was about to leave, his voice behind me said, 'I have nurtured you till now so that I could use you on just such an occasion as this'. I was not angry at his words for he often used such expressions. However, I felt somewhat lost without Yoshizumi, who was in the middle of a meeting with members of an underground organization set up by the Third Section of the Research Department. I calculated that the youth group must have carried out the abduction if the Army was not involved.

We had a close relationship with the youth group, which occasionally asked us to rescue its members when they were arrested by the Kempeitai. We also talked together, held meetings, and argued over the issue of independence – whether it should be 'independence on a platter', or something achieved through struggle. Wikana was the leader of the group. I intuitively thought Wikana would be the only member of the group related to the Navy who could also be connected with the kidnapping. I therefore approached Wikana at the Dokuritsu Juku at Bungur Besar. I remember that I tried very hard to persuade him to talk, but he would not open his mouth. I wondered if an Indonesian might simply close up in such a situation. Wikana sat on the floor as silent as a clam. Despite this attitude I had to find out about the abduction, so I continued to urge him: 'You know very well how much I have worked for the good of Indonesia. I have tried, as you know, to be a bridge between Japan and Indonesia. It is not possible that you cast me aside at this stage and do things on your own, considering what I have done for Indonesia. How could we

316

betray you? I suggest that you hand Sukarno and Hatta over to us.'

I do not remember how long I cajoled Wikana, but undoubtedly I repeated these arguments. Finally Wikana opened his mouth. His face was rather pale, and he was obviously taking the matter hard, 'No, we cannot, because we comrades have made a promise. We want to declare our independence to the world. Even if it is crushed in a moment we will not care, so long as the declaration remains as an historical event. We are ready to be killed'.

Hearing this reply I knew something serious was about to happen. Subardjo also tried to persuade Wikana. Guessing from Wikana's words that they had decided at a meeting the previous night to take Sukarno and Hatta safely out of Jakarta, I concluded that Sukarno and Hatta were detained not far from the city.

After our discussion Wikana seemed to bend a little. He began to move between the youth group and us, perhaps to consult his colleagues. Two messengers from the youth group were apparently dispatched to the secret place where Sukarno and Hatta were held. It must have been conveyed to the members of the group there that we had no intention of stopping their plan to declare independence and indeed were willing to support it. Since a member of the **Kyodo Boeigun** [Home Guard], Jusuf Kunto,* was among the messengers, the [former] Giyugun was evidently involved in the case. In the end Kunto took Subardjo to Sukarno and Hatta at the hiding place. Prior to this, Maeda was asked to promise not to arrest any youths connected with the plot, and to guarantee the safety of Sukarno and Hatta. On the spot Maeda answered, 'Yes'. When Subardjo was about to leave for the hiding place I offered to go with him, but he refused.

*   *   *

The passage omitted discusses the attitude to the kidnapping of Sukarno and Hatta, the 'Rengasdengklok affair', in other published sources, notably Adam Malik, pp.39-43.

*   *   *

---

* Jusuf Kunto is identified by Sidik Kertapati, **Sekitar Proklamasi 17 Agustus 1945** (Jakarta, 1964), p.97, as a pemuda member of Sukarni's group.

I would like to quote from **Daisan no Shinsō**:

> Because of this (kidnapping of Sukarno and Hatta),
> independence was proclaimed outside the orbit of the
> Japanese Army. Historians will judge it in the
> future, but as far as I am concerned it was right.

There was certainly a degree of excess and menace in the
activity of the youth group. However, without their action the
enthusiasm for independence could not have blazed so fiercely
and independence itself would not have been accomplished. In
that event the population would have suffered in anguish for a
long time. If independence had been pursued mainly through
consulting Japanese authorities, as planned by Sukarno and
Hatta, it might have been attained in a purely formal sense,
but on the other hand Indonesia might not have been able to
combat the movement of the Dutch and Allied Forces to return
there.

It was about 4 p.m. when Subardjo left for Rengasdengklok,
but he did not arrive till 6 p.m., due to various accidents
including a puncture along the way. He was not readily
accepted by the youths, partly because they were in an
extraordinary state of excitement, and partly because Subardjo
was suspect to them because of his closeness to the Navy. Adam
Malik claims, in the book quoted above, that since Subardjo was
said to have come as the representative of the Japanese Navy,
he and his secretary Sudiro were almost detained. On the other
hand Subardjo tells a different story in his book, **Indonesian
Independence and Revolution**. He says that when he was asked
whether he was sent by the Navy he replied: 'No! Bung Sudiro
and I came here after discussing with Wikana and other members
of the Navy group'. Thus any suspicion towards Subardjo was
removed. Then Subardjo and his secretary began to negotiate
with Supeno, a **Shodan-cho** [platoon leader] of the Giyugun and a
son of R.P. Singgih. While negotiating, the Shodan-cho asked
whether an independence declaration could be issued by
midnight. Subardjo replied that this was impossible because it
would take time, first to call a meeting of the Committee and
next to prepare the declaration, all of which was expected to
require at least the whole night. After arguing for a while,
Subardjo promised to complete the preparations by 6 o'clock the
following morning, to make it possible to declare independence
by the following noon. In response to this, Supeno asked what
would happen in the event of the failure of this programme.
Subardjo answered, 'If everything fails to materialize, I will
take full responsibility for that failure. You may even shoot
me if that happens'. Only after Subardjo had said this, was he
allowed to meet Sukarno and Hatta. Subardjo hurried Sukarno
and Hatta to the car and they drove off to Jakarta.

I had been waiting eagerly at Maeda's residence for
Subardjo's arrival. It was already 11 p.m. and very dark. A

Japanese officer was slashing at sesame plants with his sword, in despair because of the surrender. As the Japanese had encouraged the cultivation of sesame for its oil, the plant was found everywhere in Java. A kempei was standing under a tree keeping watch on the residence, perhaps in anticipation of some incident. I heard later that Nakatani Yoshio, an Army interpreter, was also watching the residence from next door. It was into this atmosphere that Subardjo and his party arrived. Sukarni had already changed from his Giyugun uniform into ordinary clothes on the way.

First I let Sukarno and Hatta come in and sit down. Subardjo took me out of the room saying, 'Just a moment, Mr Nishijima'. He gave me a brief account of what had happened. Only after I heard his account did I realize that Subardjo had risked his life for the independence declaration. Given the increasingly tense situation, there was a real possibility that Subardjo might be killed if his programme failed to materialize. I sensed that the situation had at last come to a crisis point. In the meantime Yoshizumi, as well as members of the Committee for the Preparation of Indonesian Independence, had arrived. Members of the youth group were gathering in a waiting room. Maeda came down from upstairs and gave a lengthy warning that independence should not be won through bloodshed. Naturally, however, the excited Indonesians would not listen to such pious advice. Then we all began to argue strenuously.

While we were arguing, Sukarno suddenly asked Sukarni, 'Will it really be all right?' Sukarni stood up in surprise and replied, 'It will be dangerous!' He knew of a planned uprising by the youth group, and explained that its timing was imminent. The plan had been adopted on the morning of the 16th, for an uprising to be launched mainly by former members of the Giyugun and Heiho and by students at 1 a.m. on the 17th. Sayuti Melik and I stood up and followed Sukarni out. The three of us stopped at Hatta's house first, whence Sukarni emerged dressed once more in military uniform, and bearing a pistol and sword. The car finally stopped in front of a dormitory for students of the Medical School in Parapatan, after passing along Jalan Menteng. The dormitory was the headquarters of the youth group. Sukarni and Melik went in alone while I stayed in the car.

I could see soldiers of the former Giyugun on trucks, all armed and looking tense. Sukarni and Melik soon came back. They must have announced, 'The uprising is called off for tonight!' Our car then moved in the direction of Koningsplein and eventually arrived at the broadcasting station, which was strongly guarded by military police. Since the youths had been expressing their desire to proclaim the independence of Indonesia to the world, I could well imagine that their plan of rebellion included the seizure of the broadcasting station. Even Maeda had once asked the Army to guard the station, so it

319

was not surprising that the Kempeitai knew some, if not all, of the plan.   There seems to have been a mutual understanding between the Indonesians inside the station and Sukarni that the former would commence activities in response to a sign from Sukarni outside.   Sukarni suddenly shouted, 'The plan is called off for tonight!' Hearing his voice, kempei rushed towards us. They seemed surprised to find the two of us - Sukarni, who had been arrested by the Kempeitai several times, and myself, who had once been under its surveillance.   We were immediately placed in custody by the kempei.   I demanded that one of them contact Maeda, explaining that we were on an urgent mission. The kempei immediately telephoned Maeda, who ordered, 'Release them at once.   This is an emergency'.   In this way we were released.

Indoneshia ni Okeru Nihon Gunsei no Kenkyū* makes it clear that Maeda asked Gunseikan Yamamoto of the Army to come to his house while we were out, but that the request was refused. Maeda asked Yamamoto because he wanted to have somebody representing the Army, as he did not want to give the impression that the Navy had handled the independence issue unilaterally, and he therefore wanted to invite an Army authority to join him in investigating the subject.   Moreover he thought it might facilitate finding a solution to the problem if both Army and Navy authorities talked directly with the Indonesian leaders.

Since Maeda'a request had been turned down by Yamamoto, Maeda visited the Chief of General Affairs of the Gunseikambu, Maj.-Gen. Nishimura.   Sukarno, Hatta, Maeda, Yoshizumi and I went together to Nishimura's house.   It was past 1 a.m. in the morning of the 17th.   Nakatani had been called to the house as an interpreter.   Although Nishimura did not refuse us an interview, his attitude was cool.   Sukarno and Hatta demanded that Nishimura allow immediate independence, and call a meeting of the Committee for the Preparation of Indonesian Independence one day earlier than had been scheduled.   Maeda supported these demands, but Nishimura would not give his consent, and tried to pursue a policy of maintaining the **status quo**.

Yoshizumi, Saito Shizuo (the present Ambassador to the United Nations) and I were in a waiting room.   I was becoming irritated by the stalemate.   Saito said accusingly to me, 'What you are doing is clearly disloyal to the Emperor.   The Emperor

---

* This study was conducted by a group headed by Nishijima and Kishi Koicho, and published for the Waseda University Social Sciences Research Institute by Kinokuniya Shoten in 1959.   An English translation was prepared by the Joint Publications Research Service of the U.S. Department of Commerce in 1963. The incident referred to may be found on pp.473-8 of the Japanese version and p.502 of the English version.

has said that everything is over. If you take any action [like supporting Indonesian independence] the result may affect the status of the Emperor'.

Although my memory is rather vague, I think Saito even used the word **kokuzoku** [traitor] of Maeda. Anyway I was infuriated by what he said. I said to myself, 'What an absurd thing to say. Did not the Greater East Asia War aim at the liberation of Asia? Was not the initial aim of the war to bring Japan closer to Asia? We have striven towards that very end! We must bring the issue to its conclusion in a responsible way. Why else have we propagated the slogan, "To live with [Asia] and to die with [Asia]"?'

I unconsciously put my hand in the pocket where I kept my pistol. As everything was in chaos at that time we carried arms with us. I glared at him, my hand on the pistol. **Daisan no Shinsō** shows how I felt about Nishimura's stubbornness:

> We took our decision. There was no way left but to pursue our policy at our own discretion. The only things we had to be cautious about were that the measures taken should not appear to be associated with Japan in any way, that they would not affect Japan (in this case innocent Japanese living in Java), and that they would not incur reprisals from the Army.

It was past 2 a.m. when the meeting was re-opened at Maeda's residence. Sukarno, Hatta, Subardjo, Maeda, Yoshizumi and I sat down around a round table in the dining room. Members of the youth group and the Committee for the Preparation of Indonesian Independence occupied a reception room and a waiting room. Just before the meeting began, Maeda said, 'We must request the presence of somebody from the Army'. He called Saito by telephone, but Saito refused to come on the pretext of being busy with his work. Next he called Miyoshi and said, 'Please come over, since we have some people gathered here'. Miyoshi was a sociable person and a **Shiseikan** [Civil Administrator] with a good reputation among the Indonesians. He willingly agreed to come there, perhaps encouraged by being a little tipsy. He arrived at the residence shortly afterwards, but seemed to find himself out of place in the highly charged atmosphere of the room. 'Please take a seat', I said. Since the Army was in charge of Java and the Navy had only a secondary position, we needed somebody from the Army to avoid the criticism that the Navy had dealt with the matter unilaterally. Miyoshi was to serve as an Army witness.

The youths in Maeda's house were exerting pressure upon the meeting from the adjacent room. They were unwilling to make the draft declaration at the same table that the Japanese were using. Moreover they opposed every point. For instance, when Sukarno and Hatta proposed to sign a document and read it to the members of the Committee for the Preparation of Indonesian Independence at noon on the 17th, Sukarni and Saleh strongly opposed the proposal. They insisted that there was no need to use the Committee, which was closely identified with Japan, and that the participation in the declaration of the members of the Committee was anathema since they had done nothing for independence. On another occasion, when Sukarno suggested consulting the highest Japanese authorities before making the declaration, the youths bitterly criticized this on the grounds that independence was purely the concern of the Indonesians, and had nothing to do with the Japanese. It was finally decided that independence was to be declared regardless of Japanese approval. The draft declaration was put in order by Sukarno after a heated argument between the leaders' group [centring on Sukarno], which included Hatta, and the youth group.

The first draft read: 'The Indonesian people hereby declare their independence. The existing administrative organs must be seized by the people from the foreigners who now hold them'. In this text the greatest problem was the use of the term 'seized'. If the Indonesians were to 'seize' power from the Japanese Army by force this might exasperate the Japanese and lead to a tragic collision between the two. The surrender notwithstanding, the Japanese Army still remained intact. Here again I will quote from **Daisan no Shinsō**:

> We were not necessarily unable to understand what the youth were thinking, nor the leaders. However, as the latter group admits, the present Japanese Army now, or at least immediately before the surrender, promoted Indonesian independence and approved it. Sukarno's group wanted to avoid a situation where the Indonesians, by issuing a declaration which would immediately cause a Japanese reaction, would compel the Japanese Army to play a role as effective agent to the Allied Forces. As Hatta correctly says, revolution can only be achieved by force, but Indonesian power is still inadequate. Moreover, the enemy – the real enemy the Indonesians have to face – is not the Japanese Army, which is deprived of its authority to exercise power, but the Dutch, who are preparing to suppress the Indonesian people again. It is brave but not wise for the Indonesians to fight the Japanese Army with such inadequate power.

The discussion continued for a long time. Finally the term 'seize' in the text was replaced by 'transfer'. In the expression, 'the transfer of power and so forth should be attempted in a careful manner and as quickly as possible',*

* For Footnote see following page.

the word 'attempted' was changed to simply 'carried out'. This text was written by Sukarno himself on paper brought from upstairs in Maeda's residence, and still exists. One can clearly observe the corrections on the document. Thus the draft of the famous independence declaration was completed. It read: 'We, the Indonesian people, hereby declare the independence of Indonesia. Matters concerning the transfer of power and so forth should be carried out in a careful manner and as quickly as possible'.

Miyoshi was requested to convey to the Army that the term 'power' (**pemerintahan**)† in the declaration meant 'administrative authority'. The transfer of administrative authority had already been pursued as a basic policy and should therefore not provoke any opposition from the Army. Although it took only two or three hours to complete the draft, I felt that never in my life had I concentrated my mental powers more intensely. Everybody there seemed to feel the same and to be exhausted by the great strain of the moment, whether they were conscious of it at the time or not. This exhaustion might have been responsible for compromises on both sides. All of the participants did what they could, which the youths also must have appreciated. The final draft was typed out by Sayuti Melik.

At last the time had come for Sukarno to read the text to the members of the Committee who had been waiting in the next room. I heard Radjiman# asking, 'Is this approved by the Gunseikan?'

I was irritated: 'How stupid to say such a thing at this stage!' I could also hear voices asking, 'Who is going to sign?' and 'Who is to read it?'

According to Subardjo, Sukarni again opposed the contents

* Footnote from previous page:
  Nishijima has compressed things here. This phrase had been substituted, at Hatta's suggestion, for the second sentence in the draft proposed by the youth group.

† The word used in the proclamation was in fact **kekuasaan** (power) not **pemerintahan** (government).

Dr Radjiman Wediodiningrat (1879-1952) had been a stalwart of Budi Utomo since its foundation in 1908. He was one of the first Indonesians to obtain a Dutch medical degree (Amsterdam, 1910), and thereafter became official doctor of the Surakarta **kraton** (palace). As an elder statesman he was named chairman of the Committee to Investigate Indonesian Independence (BPKI) in June 1945, and had travelled to Saigon with Sukarno and Hatta in August to receive the promise of early independence.

of the draft on the grounds that it lacked revolutionary spirit and was too weak in the way it was expressed. As Sukarni's criticisms were supported by the youths, arguments over the draft broke out again. However, the members of the Committee overrode the opposition and decided in favour of the draft.

It was really an extraordinary declaration. It is often said that 'Sukarno and Hatta represented the people', but there are no signs of the two on the document.* Such an independence document is probably rare anywhere in the world. Also we noticed only afterwards that the document was dated '17-8-'05', i.e. 17 August 2605. The year 2605 was based on the Japanese calendar system. The fact that nobody, myself included, realized this may reflect the atmosphere of the meeting. Finally, I should like to raise the question of whether there were any Japanese present. It is true that there were Japanese, including myself, at the place where the draft was written, and that we even expressed our opinions. However, we did not attend the actual reading of the declaration, which was to the members of the Committee. Hatta has recorded his denial of our involvement.† However, Hatta and the others who support his claim confuse the place where the draft was written with the place where independence was declared.

Thus one act in the drama of independence had ended. It had indeed been a critical task. I myself was unable to indulge in the relaxed mood which would be normal after accomplishing such a difficult task, but I did notice that the youth group, the leaders' group, and the Japanese looked relieved of tension, having reached a mutual agreement through compromise. I could not think of the future, perhaps because I was too exhausted by the prolonged strain. All those who had attended went their way with their own thoughts.

* The scribbled original draft, reproduced in Osman Raliby, **Documenta Historica** (Jakarta, 1953), p.4, ends simply 'Djakarta 17-8-'05, Wakil2 bangsa Indonesia' [representatives of the Indonesian nation]. However, the text typed by Sayuti Melik was signed by Sukarno and Hatta, as had been agreed after a stormy debate. The date was also changed to 1945. It was this typed text which was read by Sukarno. See Nugroho Notosusanto, **Naskah Proklamasi jang Otentik dan Rumusan Pantjasila jang Otentik** (Jakarta, Pusat Sedjaran ABRI, 1971).

† We have not been able to trace an explicit statement to this effect. In his **Sekitar Proklamasi** (Jakarta, 1970), p.58, Hatta states that Maeda withdrew upstairs while a five-man Indonesian committee drafted the proclamation, and that Miyoshi remained within earshot but said nothing.

Miyamoto Shizuo

II) ARMY PROBLEMS IN JAVA AFTER THE SURRENDER

Army-Navy Conflict after the Surrender
(from an Appendix by Miyamoto)

All officers of the Headquarters and the Gunseikambu listened to the radio message at noon on 15 August 1945, as we had been told it would be very important. Although we could not hear the broadcast clearly because of interference and static, we could guess that the message was an Imperial statement of surrender, judging from many pieces of information since the Russian participation in the war. But we were not certain of it. Accordingly, confirming the Japanese surrender was the prerequisite for any future action. Of course, I thought we should officially notify the Indonesians and the Japanese in general about the surrender only after such confirmation. However, we did not receive any certain information through official channels.

The Indonesians came to know that the Japanese had accepted the peace on the 14th by intercepting foreign new broadcasts. The population immediately demanded that their leaders take action. Indonesian leaders visited the office of the Gunseikambu on the following day to verify this information. Since all the staff of the Gunseikambu were absent in response to a summons by the Commander to his office, they decided to visit the **Kaigun Bukanfu** [Navy Liaison Office], at the suggestion of Subardjo who worked there. They verified the information from Admiral Maeda. On the 16th the Kaigun Bukanfu evidently received an official telegram which conveyed the Japanese surrender. However, the Headquarters of the 16th Army had not received any such telegram at that stage. Taking Maeda's words and intercepted foreign radio reports as firm evidence of the Japanese surrender, the Indonesians immediately began to act. The Kaigun Bukanfu, accepting the truth of a Japanese surrender, began to act in harmony with the Indonesians, and helped the Indonesians to proclaim their independence on the morning of the 17th.

Army Headquarters expected the cessation of hostilities to take effect very slowly, since orders from the Allies would not take precedence over those of senior Japanese authorities, and Headquarters was planning simply to consult authorities in Tokyo when it received such orders. In any case Headquarters considered Allied orders to have no binding force at this stage. In view of this, Headquarters was investigating how to be helpful to the Indonesians within a framework which was legal with respect to the Allies, as well as protecting the status of the Japanese Army. Thus there was no point in giving unverified information to the Indonesians. Headquarters was planning to publicize the Japanese surrender only after it was confirmed and after having prepared plans to create the optimum conditions for Indonesians. Headquarters estimated that it would take time to implement these plans.

The judgement of the Kaigun Bukanfu on implementing the cessation of hostilities was quite different. The Bukanfu viewed the situation as very imminent. The way in which the Chief of Staff of the Navy at Imperial Headquarters issued the order to suspend hostilities well demonstrates this. The dates on which the Chiefs of Staff of the Navy and Army issued the order to suspend hostilities were:

	Preparatory order	Actual order	Implementation
Navy	17th	19th	midnight 22nd
Army	18th	22nd	midnight 25th

*   *   *

The dates on which the peace agreements were implemented were as follows:

20 August	The opening of communication between the Japanese government and the command office of MacArthur; the order of MacArthur in Manila to Japan to send liaison officers.
27 August	The Rangoon provisional agreement of the General Southern Army.
2 September	The official agreement of cessation of hostilities between the Japanese government and the Allies in Tokyo harbour.
12 September	The signing of the official surrender in Singapore.
29 September	The landing of Allied Forces on Java.

These dates show the correctness of our judgement that there was no problem about delaying notifying the Indonesians about the Japanese surrender until the evening of the 18th when we received the official telegram.

There was no need to announce the Japanese surrender before confirming it, nor to help the proclamation of independence. It can be said that the Kaigun Bukanfu did not study the process by which the peace was implemented, or that its judgement was not sound. I think it would have been best to proclaim independence on the 19th, the date the Committee for the Preparation of Indonesian Independence had originally planned. Had this happened we would have been able to consider the ways to provide the Indonesians with the best conditions for independence, maintaining our trust to Indonesians as during the war. What were the advantages of declaring independence at the expense of satisfying its prerequisites!

Once we announced the Japanese surrender, even when based on ambiguous information, we were obliged to observe international laws as the defeated party, namely to maintain the **status quo** of the time we recognized the surrender. In other words, this hasty announcement made it impossible for us to take steps to satisfy the preconditions of independence. Thus, it was absurd to take an action by which we would be prevented from helping the Indonesians at all.

I think the Kaigun Bukanfu, when consulted by Sukarno and Hatta, should have said that they would give a definite answer after consulting the Army, and should have actually visited Headquarters. Had the Kaigun Bukanfu acted like this, the Japanese authorities of the Army and Navy would have been able jointly to discuss **legal** methods to support the independence of the Navy and Army occupied regions on a unified basis, i.e., Java, Celebes, Borneo, East Indonesia. However, this did not materialize. Moreover, the situation became confused at the very beginning of the cessation of hostilities in Java, the consequences of which were long drawn out.

The Japanese Response to Allied Orders to Dissolve the Giyugun and not to Deliver Japanese Arms to the Indonesians
(from an Appendix by Miyamoto)

It was considered natural that the Allies would order the above in trying to recover their colonies, but we had no legal power to refuse once the orders were issued.

Nothing could be done for the Indonesians by the Japanese Army once the orders were issued. Expecting to receive the orders immediately after the Emperor's radio message of surrender, I had to finish planning the Japanese response to the anticipated orders before we received them (if possible before we confirmed the surrender). From my point of view, therefore, the activities of the Kaigun Bukanfu since 15 August were quite annoying.

A clash between the Japanese Army and Giyugun seemed unavoidable if both were armed and if the Japanese were obliged to maintain order. If such a clash occurred, both the Japanese and Indonesians might suffer fatal losses, since the Giyugun had been trained to fight to the end. Although disarming the Japanese Army was considered to be one way of avoiding the clash, such a measure was likely to be prohibited by the Allies. I planned to take the following steps before we received any order prohibiting the disarmament of the Japanese Army: (1) to dissolve the Giyugun; (2) to disarm the Japanese

327

Army, because there was no further necessity for it to maintain order, and to prevent any spontaneous clash with the Allies which would have been a mortal blow to the Japanese Army; then to make the Japanese wait for repatriation in strategically unimportant places; (3) to entrust the maintenance of order to the Indonesian police forces, though some strengthening of the police forces seemed necessary. With the independence proclamation on 17 August, however, I feared that the implementation of these steps might be held to be illegal and that it might affect the position of the Emperor. Unexpectedly, the Headquarters of the 7th Area Army, based on an order of the General Southern Army, instructed the implementation of the three steps above-mentioned to the Japanese in Malaya and Singapore. The measures appeared to apply only to Malaya and Singapore, not to Java. Nevertheless, I decided to implement the measures in the end under the pretext of having just followed the policy of higher authorities at the sole discretion of the 16th Army, thus hoping to cause no harm to the Emperor. On the other hand I tried to persuade the Indonesians to adopt non-violent methods for independence and to take a peaceful attitude towards the Allies. But my efforts were in vain.

The Indonesian senior leaders aimed at independence through peaceful means, but the youths pursued armed struggle. In response to this circumstance, we decided not to use arms against Indonesians who would try to capture arms from us. The Allies had naturally ordered us to use arms in order to prevent Indonesians from capturing Japanese arms. This order was conveyed by the Commander of the Allies who summoned the Japanese Commander twelve times to the Headquarters of the Allied Forces in Indonesia. We promised to observe the order not to give arms to the Indonesians, but we also refused to use arms against the Indonesians on the ground that this would disturb administration and good order, and therefore the Japanese would be unable to secure the safety of detainees from Allied countries. In addition, I commented that it should be the Allied Forces, not the Japanese, who used arms in an emergency.

*   *   *

Chapter IV: The Prohibition on Hoisting the National Flag and the Gambir Square Incident
(Part III, pp. 69-74)

On 18 Sepember [1945] the Gunseikambu received orders from the Allies to prohibit any gatherings of Indonesians, anyone carrying arms, or the hoisting of the national flag of Indonesia; while the General Staff Heaquarters was ordered to restore complete order.

328

A few days before this, Lt.-Col. Mellsop, whom we later discovered was Chief of Staff of the British Army of Occupation, had been put in charge of transmitting orders from the Allies to the Headquarters of the 16th Army. His office had formerly belonged to the adviser to the military administration, Hayashi (the building is now the office of the supreme commander of the Indonesian National Army) and was located two or three houses from the Headquarters of the 16th Army (now the head office of Pertamina).

As the Gunseikambu had never before received an order from the Allies, it was not clear from where these orders came, but, as an Army Staff Officer, I felt that they could have serious repercussions. However, we could not defy something which had been issued as a military order, especially as we had to maintain a united front. On the following morning, the 19th, Nishimura, the Director of General Affairs of the Gunseikambu, had a serious talk with the Chief of Staff at the latter's place. I was told that the Indonesians, in violation of the previous day's orders, were planning a big rally at Gambir Square* in front of the former official residence of the Governor of the Netherlands Indies.

When I looked in horror at the square from the window of the Staff Office building, a huge crowd of Indonesians was already converging on it and raising flags. Without awaiting the arrival of an interpreter, I jumped out of the building. On every approach thoroughfare large numbers of Indonesians, bearing flags, bamboo spears, guns and **keris** were being stopped by Japanese guards. Machine guns were trained on the crowds. Even so, numerous people had already reached the square. From every direction could be heard the sound of drum bands playing the national anthem.

The Indonesian eyes turned on me were not necessarily hostile. However, I was strongly aware of the delicacy of my position. I felt that it would take only one shot from a weak character, an authoritarian, or someone intent on driving a wedge between the Japanese and the Indonesians, to alienate our two peoples. The national anthem to the rhythm of the drums seemed to be accusing me: 'Can't you understand the feelings of the Indonesian people?' But the very holding of the meeting was a violation of the order of the Allies issued the day before. It occurred to me that the Allied authorities who had issued the order were probably watching me from their office directly in front of me.

As there was no time to obtain permission from the Army Commander [**Gunshireikan**], I ordered the troops nearby to lead

* Known as Koningsplein under the Dutch, Ikada under the Japanese, and subsequently Gambir and Lapangan Merdeka, this is the largest open space in the city, with the principal national buildings around it.

the demonstrators to the square. They pushed forward like an avalanche. The chief of the guard corps of the Kempeitai raced over to me, furious with anger, and said, 'How can a Staff Officer take this upon himself? The head of the Kempeitai would not countenance it'.

I answered, 'Well, the head of the Kempeitai need not take responsibility for this. Let all the demonstrators in'.

Soon Senior Staff Officer Obana appeared anxiously on the scene. He agreed with my decision, and rushed off to obtain official sanction.

In the meantime Sukarno and Hatta, in an overcrowded car guarded by youths, were moving at a snail's pace towards the square. I was unable to speak Indonesian, nor was I accompanied by an interpreter. The car drew up in front of me, and we saluted each other. Fortunately, an Indonesian youth who could speak Japanese (I later discovered it was Yono,* who was to become a major general), kindly interpreted for me. Platoon commander [Zulkifli] Lubis,† who later became Vice-Chief of General Staff, was apparently there also. I told Sukarno that I would be in trouble if he incited resistance towards the Allies. He said that he would not do so. As the Allied Forces would soon be arriving, he would be appealing to the people to unite in order to achieve independence. I therefore told him that he could carry on, and asked if I could listen to his speech, which he was quite happy for me to do. I listened to his speech from a tiered stand. The interpreter, Nakagawa Masakazu, caught up with me, fearing the worst, and listened to the speech beside me. He told me that Sukarno was telling the crowd to work together and to do their utmost.

Since the audience kept shouting in response to Sukarno's words, the speech, though simple in itself, took quite a long time. When it was over, the huge crowd dispersed with light steps. Surveying the scene, I felt that the question of the

---

* Although clearly 'Yono' in the Japanese, this may be a reference to Achmad Yani (1922-65), who was trained in the PETA and eventually rose to be a Lt.-General, Minister of the Army and Chief of Staff, before being murdered in the September 1965 coup attempt.

† Zulkifli Lubis, born in North Sumatra in 1923, appears to have been one of the Indonesian Giyugun/PETA officers selected for the special training in intelligence activities referred to by Miyamoto above (I, p.18). He was the first intelligence chief of the Indonesian Army after 1945, and became Deputy Chief of Staff and a key figure in Army politics in 1952-56. He resigned his post in opposition to the Army leadership in 1956, and became a leader of the subsequent PRRI revolt.

sovereignty of Indonesia was an Indonesian matter affecting the Indonesian people, and therefore it should be dealt with by the Indonesians themselves. Their leader should be an Indonesian, not a Japanese Commander, nor a Britisher or Dutchman. I decided that if I were arrested by the Allies over the incident I would tell them my feelings on the matter, but I was not summoned.

Chapter V: The British Instruction to Maintain Order

In view of the Gambir Square incident of the previous day, it was with much trepidation that I presented myself at the liaison office of the British Army on the morning of the 20th, as ordered. There I received the following instructions:

Following consultations with the Army and Navy, the British Army orders the following to the Japanese Army:
The Japanese Army is responsible for the maintenance of law and order until the Allied Forces land on the island and take over the task. There will be no sympathy for anyone who disturbs order.
The Japanese Army is to maintain order at all costs. It is advised to use tear gas shells if necessary.

Meanwhile, I was receiving complaints from the Japanese troops that they were unable to prevent Indonesians, by persuasion alone, from seizing Japanese arms. In Surabaya we increased the number of checkpoints in order to strengthen our guard.

Chapter VI: The Feelings of the Indonesian Side

The Staff Office of the 16th Army had taken the view that matters concerning Indonesia were the province of the Gunseikambu, and that we should not by-pass the Gunseikambu in our approach to such matters. Moreover, in taking the lead in collecting information on Indonesians we did not seek to preempt the Gunseikambu, as we felt that to do so would somehow be a breach of propriety. Then again, we were afraid that if we approached influential leaders, people might get the impression that they were puppets of Japan. After the Gambir Square incident, however, I concluded that all problems concerning Indonesia came within the orbit of military operations, and therefore I resolved that the Staff Office should take the initiative on such matters.
Having been charged with the maintenance of order in the Jakarta district, I informed Major Naga, head of the Jakarta Kempeitai, that I should like to hear the feelings of the Indonesians, and requested that he arrange a meeting with some

appropriate people. He brought Kasman,* Chairman of the
Provisional Peoples' Council and former battalion leader;
Minister of Justice Soepomo;† Dr Ratulangie;# and so forth.
All with one accord demanded arms. They would not listen to my
advice that it was folly to try to attain independence by
force, and that they should rally together and pursue
independence through peaceful methods with the support of
international public opinion. The gist of their argument was
as follows:

> We have endured three and a half centuries of
> colonial rule. We have tried peaceful methods, which
> were the only ones possible at the time, but all such
> efforts have ended in failure. Generations before us
> have reached the conclusion that independence must
> ultimately be attained by force of arms. Our fore-
> fathers tried violent methods several times, but
> failed through lack of arms. We once hoped to attain
> independence with the help of Japan, but Japan is
> defeated. We feel we have lost our mainstay.
> However, the Japanese surrender has spurred us to
> seek independence immediately by ourselves without
> relying on others. If we miss this chance, we cannot
> count on another chance of gaining independence.
> This is why we need arms now, above all else.
>
> Hearing your words, we envy the [optimism of you]
> Japanese. The colonial ruler would never give up any
> vested interest in his possession unless deprived of
> it by force. From our three and a half centuries of
> experience, we know the Europeans better than the
> Japanese do. The Indonesian people are determined to
> die. Even the entire student population has entered

* Kasman Singodimedjo (b. 1908) received a law degree from
  Batavia in 1939 and was an active youth and Islamic
  leader before the war. He was chairman of the first
  Republican assembly, the Komite Nasional Indonesia
  Pusat, from August to October 1945.

† Dr R. Soepomo (1903-58) was Indonesia's leading jurist,
  a lecturer at the pre-war Law School and principal
  architect of the Republican Constitution. As Adviser to
  the Justice Department under the Japanese, he naturally
  became Justice Minister in Sukarno's first
  (transitional) cabinet.

For Dr Ratulangie, see above, p.264. Miyamoto appears
  mistaken here, as Ratulangie had returned to Sulawesi as
  Republican Governor on 19 August.

the army. The only arms are those held by the
Japanese Army. Although we are reluctant to break
with the Japanese Army, it may prove necessary. The
Japanese arms will sooner or later be handed over to
the Allies, and then will be used against us. We
cannot take a wait-and-see attitude. People are
already accusing us of being too compromising with
the Japanese. The will of the people is very strong.
We are amazed that we are still alive now.

I could not promise to give arms, but repeated my advice
that they adopt peaceful methods in the face of the overwhelming power of the Allies. However, they refused to
compromise, saying they would fight even though the land be
laid waste.

I thought it unavoidable that incidents similar to that at
Gambir Square would spread all over Java, and that Indonesians
would try to seize Japanese arms. In anticipation of such
incidents the military authorities despatched Col. Obata, of
the commander's office, on the 22nd [September] to East and
Central Java to check the situation. On the 23rd, Col.
Nakagawa was murdered at Cirebon, and was immediately replaced
by Col. Nagai. However, details of the murder were not clear.
On the 24th, I summoned the intelligence officers and explained
the basic problems concerning the Indonesians, and the use of
arms in particular. I had actually been worried about the
safety of these intelligence officers as they made their way to
Jakarta.

As the landing of the Allied Forces was expected soon,
Army authorities called out the liaison officers in Jakarta in
order to hear their views on what attitude the Japanese should
take towards the Allies and the Indonesians. The meeting was
attended by the Chief of Staff, the Director of General Affairs
of the Gunseikambu, and all Staff Officers. The majority
considered that the power of the Allies was overwhelming, and
the Japanese must obey their instructions. Only Lt. Matsuura
Kojiro, of the Department of Munitions, argued on the basis of
his experience in Australia and Surabaya before the war that
Indonesia merited becoming an independent nation, and that the
Japanese approach should take account of this.

Chapter XIV: The Situation in Central Java
(Part III, pp.146-53)

I. General Situation

From the point of view of command, the Japanese Army in
Central Java (headed by Maj-.Gen. Nakamura Junjiro) was placed
in a most pitiful position. The Headquarters of this Army had
its origins in a training school for non-commissioned officers,
under the direct control of the Southern Area Army. During the

process of preparing for war, the top candidates of this establishment were transferred to the 16th Army, which used them to make up a regiment. As the aim had been continuously to expand troop strength, this had grown by the end of the war to two battalions (each battalion having 150 sick soldiers). Then, after the surrender, the 16th Army incorporated into its ranks troops which had been on their way to Singapore, and placed them under the command of the Army in Central Java, in order on the one hand to reduce the necessary food provisions to West Java, and on the other to strengthen the ability to maintain order in Central Java.

Naturally the newly absorbed troops had little sympathy with the Giyugun and Indonesian society in general, nor even with the Japanese administrative apparatus or personnel in Java. As a result, Japanese civilians seconded to the Army tended to choose separate concentration camps from those of the military, making effective communications and control very difficult for Headquarters in Java. In addition, Central Java had special problems, such as the largest rice shortfall in Java and consequently a large number of radicals, including communists, as well as the largest number of female internees from Allied countries (30,000-40,000 persons?). In anticipation of an early attack by the Allies on East Java, Headquarters had transferred the prisoners of war and male detainees in East Java, who might have been enlisted in the opposing forces immediately on their release, to the highlands of West Java, where it seemed there would be no problems with supervision. Since it was unlikely that the female internees would be enlisted by the enemy, the majority had been moved to Central Java, while a small number remained in East Java. One can see the situation in Central Java from a memoir of the head of the Japanese Army there, Maj.-Gen. Nakamura.*

II. From the Memoir of Maj.-Gen. Nakamura

1. Special Circumstances in Central Java

(a) Although tens of thousands of the sick, the old and women (the exact number is not clear because of the lack of sources) were initially released from detention camps in Central Java such as Magelang, Semarang, Ambarawa, etc, most returned to the camps as a result of Indonesian hostility. The

---

* The remainder of Miyamoto's memoir appears to be taken verbatim from Maj.-Gen. Nakamura Junjiro, Commander of Central Java with his Headquarters in Magelang. Nakamura was arrested when the Allies occupied Semarang, on the charge of having furnished arms to the Indonesians, but was eventually released.

Japanese in Central Java, therefore, found themselves unexpectedly having to protect the returned detainees and find food for them. Under orders of a lieutenant-colonel of the British Army and a Dutch medical team, who had been sent to investigate, the Japanese had to collect medical supplies, beds and clothing, as well as large amounts of foodstuffs (meat, eggs, vegetables etc.) for the daily consumption of the detainees, and were exceedingly hard pressed to do so. At first the procurement of these goods was carried out relatively smoothly. In the course of time, however, it became increasingly difficult as the Japanese Army's stockpiles in the Central area were depleted and the Japanese were called upon more and more to provide the Dutch with food and supplies. Japanese attempts to collect the goods were increasingly blocked or obstructed by the Indonesians. Eventually the Japanese organized foraging parties with armed escorts, which went out all over the countryside desperately trying to buy up goods. These activities only further irritated the people, and the rumour spread that the Japanese Army was supporting only the Dutch. This in turn required the Japanese to strengthen their guard, and caused minor clashes with Indonesians everywhere. Nevertheless, we adhered to the policy of not using arms against the Indonesians.

(b) Many of the Japanese defence corps had been formed immediately after the surrender, and had little or no sympathy towards the organs of military administration in their respective areas, and still less towards the Giyugun and the population in general. The Japanese officers in charge of these corps had originally come from the education section of Headquarters, and their imperfect understanding of, and lack of contact with, the Giyugun was probably one of the reasons for the unsuccessful negotiations with the Giyugun after the war.

(c) The closure of Japanese firms and businesses, and the assembling of the Japanese in concentration camps, did not proceed smoothly because people were forced to move to areas far removed from the location of their businesses, and where they had no contacts.

2. The Major Incidents in which Indonesians Seized Arms from the Japanese by Force

(a) In addition to cases where Japanese guards of foraging parties and members of the transport corps were robbed of their arms, individual Japanese, both military and civilian, holding arms, came to be attacked by Indonesians.

(b) The Kempeitai in Pekalongan, surrounded by rioting Indonesians, fired warning shots, but this only further provoked the rioters. Eventually the Kempeitai settled the problem by lending part of the arms in its possession to the

Indonesian Resident, under the pretext that he needed them for extra guard duties.

(c) A Japanese company, attached to the army in Central Java only after the surrender, while travelling by train to join the Otsuka Battalion in Yogyakarta was tricked by an ex-Giyugun officer from Yogyakarta into handing over arms in exchange for a deposit receipt.

(d) As a result of the handover of arms to Indonesians in East Java, the Kempeitai in Solo (Surakarta) were also pressed into giving arms to Indonesians. Ex-Giyugun soldiers armed with these weapons entered Yogyakarta and Magelang, creating serious disturbances there.

Shortly before and after this incident, I met several times with the Sultan of Yogyakarta and the Residents of Magelang and Semarang on the subject of law and order, explained to them the position of the Japanese Army, and requested them to maintain order. However, no improvement was apparent and the region was, on the contrary, totally under the control of young radicals and armed student corps. Since these groups controlled even transportation and communication, the Japanese troops were left isolated. Indonesian officials of the Residency government, sensing that their lives were in danger, allowed themselves to be manipulated by the young patriots. The Resident of Magelang was taken into custody somewhere by volunteer partisans on 30 September (?).

(e) The special defence corps of Yogyakarta: In Yogyakarta, enthusiasm for independence and revolution was particularly strong. The Otsuka Battalion, which had just arrived there from Timor, took stock of the rapid rate at which young Giyugun soldiers were becoming armed, and tried to maintain order and to negotiate with the Indonesians. However, not only were their attempts at persuasion unsuccessful, but the battalion was surrounded at night by armed Giyugun soldiers. Since Japanese policy was not to fight the Indonesians, their response was limited to firing warning shots, and so the Giyugun soldiers broke into and robbed several arms stores.

(f) An Indonesian attack on Magelang: According to the Indonesians, Solo (or Surakarta) belonged to Central Java. However, to the Japanese it was included in East Java. Many of the arms of the Mase Battalion and those formerly allotted to the various Giyugun battalions were stored there, and all fell into the hands of the Indonesians. With the seizure of arms in Solo and Yogyakarta, the arming of ex-Giyutai soldiers proceeded quickly. They then moved to threaten Magelang from both sides.

There were a few thousand Dutch people under Japanese protection at each of several scattered spots in Magelang and Ambarawa. We feared that if it came to a clash between Japanese and armed Indonesians the security of the Dutch would

certainly be in jeopardy, and moreover such a clash might bring
unexpected results. We obtained the consent of the British
Colonel-in-Charge that, in order to assure the safety of the
Dutch, the Japanese would not use arms against the Indonesians
under any circumstances. This policy was reinforced by an
instruction from the Japanese Commander on 11 October 1945, as
well as by the urgency of the situation. In keeping with this
policy of not using arms, we decided to dismantle all arms so
that they could not be used, and to conceal the parts. In
addition, munitions were to be gradually disposed of.

The Indonesian head of the Magelang Residency government
was taken away into custody, resulting in a breakdown of law
and order there. The region was now under the control of armed
youths. The Japanese Army strictly prohibited its troops from
using arms, while seeking to win over by methods of persuasion
the Indonesian youth leaders, who were former company and
platoon leaders in the Giyugun. However, on 13 October (I am
uncertain of the date) armed Indonesian troops broke into many
places, occupying command offices and detention camps as soon
as they realized that the Japanese Army would not use arms.

The Area Commander, who had responsibility for the whole
of Central Java, unable to carry out his task of maintaining
law and order, took a wait-and-see attitude and resigned
himself to bearing the responsibility, as if the situation were
due to his personal mistakes.* Having once decided to bear all
responsibility, his course of action was dictated by his one
desire to avoid any needless injury or death, not only among
the Japanese but also among the Dutch detainees, such as might
result from a clash with the Indonesians. Japanese were
dispersed throughout Central Java and held in custody.

I myself was put under house arrest in Yogyakarta. It was
therefore three days after the event that I heard of the
Semarang incident.

(g)   The Semarang incident: While I feel very bitter
about the Semarang incident, I should like to refrain from
writing about it here.†

*   *   *

III.   **Supplementary Information from the Viewpoint of
       Headquarters   [Gunshireibu]**

*   *   *

* Nakamura's confusing shift to the third person in describing
  his attitude here is presumably out of feelings of delicacy.

† For a description of the murder of hundreds of Japanese in
  and around Semarang, see Shibata, below, p.368.

2. The Yuda Battalion in the Banyumas Residency

The Yuda Battalion, which had absorbed those Japanese who had been robbed of their arms on the North Coast of Central Java, distributed arms to the Indonesians through negotiation, while communications were broken. Its members just stood by and watched the Indonesians carrying away their arms.* The Japanese Resident at Banyumas was Iwashige Takaharu, an open-hearted person who had built up close contacts with the Indonesians through a long time spent in the area. In addition, the two Japanese interpreters, Maeda Naomi from the battalion and Tamura Saburo from the civil administration, performed the functions of ball bearings and lubricating oil. I presume that the battalion commander, Yuda, in handing arms over to the Indonesians, resigned himself to certain death when brought to trial by the Allies. Although the British Army ordered Headquarters to get the Yuda Battalion to Bandung, Headquarters did not pass on the order, on the pretext that it was impossible to get through.

3. The Otsuka Battalion in Yogyakarta

After the pacification campaigns in Java at the beginning of the war, this battalion was transferred to Timor, where it stayed for over two years. At the end of the war, only part of the battalion returned to Java. Thus, it was a field army with absolutely no familiarity with Java. Faced with Indonesian demands for arms, the battalion fired shots in the air to demonstrate their capacity to resist, although they had absolutely no intention of starting a real fight. Once the arms were given to the Indonesians, however, the power of life or death over the Japanese was in the hands of the Indonesians. The members of the battalion were forced to walk to prison barefoot, as a warning to others, and by the time of their release most of them were affected by deficiency diseases. I have great respect for their fortitude.

---

* This wholesale transfer of arms made the Banyumas Battalion the best equipped in the whole Indonesian Army, and helped launch its young commander, Soedirman, on his rapid climb to Supreme Army Commander.

	WEST JAVA	CENTRAL JAVA	EAST JAVA	TOTAL OF CENTRAL AND EAST JAVA	GRAND TOTAL	CENTRAL AND EAST JAVA AS %AGE OF TOTAL
Rifles	25,379	6,671	19,648 (19,000)	26,318	51,698	50
Automatic rifles	1,070			242	1,312	20
- ammunition	35,040,000			18,880,000	53,920,000	30
Pistols	10,628			3,646	14,274	25
Automatic pistols	796	445	846 (700)	1,145	1,941	59
- ammunition	4,950,000			4,710,000	9,660,000	50
Light machine guns	827	157	422 (720)	877	1,704	51
- ammunition	36,150,000			26,980,000	63,130,000	40
Machine guns	662	212	504 (480)	669	1,331	50
- ammunition	31,030,000			12,370,000	43,400,000	30
Grenade barrels	239	77	148	225	464	50
- ammunition	61,000			36,000	97,000	40
Artillery cannon	24	7	17	24	48	50
- ammunition	32,156			6,043	38,199	20
Trench mortars	93	45	63 (makeshift 408)	108	201	53
- ammunition	44,690			18,488	63,178	30
Anti-tank guns	27	4	14 (25)	29	56	50
Field guns	31	6	19 (27)	33	64	50
- ammunition	114,449			68,347	182,796	40
10 & 12cm cannon	16			11	27	40
- ammunition				9,433	48,143	20
Cannon	24	3	3 (4)	7	31	23
- ammunition	17,573			4,239	21,812	20
Anti-aircraft guns	284	8	142 (145)	153	437	33
- ammunition	650,000			410,000	1,060,000	40

Table continued

	WEST JAVA	CENTRAL JAVA	EAST JAVA	TOTAL OF CENTRAL AND EAST JAVA	GRAND TOTAL	CENTRAL AND EAST JAVA AS %AGE OF TOTAL
Tanks	34	0	16	16	50	32
Armoured cars	124	3	62	65	189	32
Automobiles	910	118	591 (550)	709	1,619	44
Trucks	2,307	243	1,309 (1,250)	2,169	5,431	40
Repair cars	45	0	8			15
				(in kilos)	(in kilos)	
Dynamite	0			7,625	7,625	100
Carlit				6,825	15,161	40
Gun powder	**48,263**			7,228	55,491	10
Ammonium nitrate	not known			44,017	not known	---
TNT				13,694	not known	---
Grey powder				1,057	not known	---
Ammonium sulphate	**261,381**			2,627	264,008	1
Hand grenades	**223,116**			95,388	318,454	30

Notes:

1. These figures are based on those reported to the Allies after the war, and do not include the thousands of arms which were manufactured by the Army nor the arms held by the Navy and Airforce. While the number of arms held by both forces is unclear, the Navy is thought to have had between 1,000 and 3,000 rifles. This can be offset by the fact that the above figures for Central Java include the arms of the Semarang division, which fell into Allied hands.

2. Apart from the above, there were many pistols belonging to Japanese officers (3,300 in total) and to civilians seconded to the military (about 5,000).

3. Arms belonging to the police of the Gunseikambu (24,000 policemen in all) are not included. These arms would have included heavy and light machine guns (80), rifles (10,000) and pistols (16,000).

4. Explosives used in industry are not included.

5. There are no figures to demonstrate strategic power at sea.

6. The figures in brackets were obtained from a Staff Officer in East Java after repatriation.

7. The figures in **bold** have been calculated by the editors by extrapolation from other columns.

II) SURABAYA AFTER THE SURRENDER
(Shibata Shirei Chōkan no Shuki, pp.51-77)

Chapter VII: The Surabaya Coup d'etat -
            The Story of the End of the Japanese Navy

1. The Fateful Day - 15 August

When I received the Imperial Proclamation accepting the
Potsdam Declaration, at midday on 15 August, I quietly shed a
few tears. It was the first crushing defeat of the Japanese
Empire since its foundation, and it caused me to be overcome by
a flood of inexplicable emotions.   After the Potsdam
Declaration I was ordered to cease hostilities and was given
various instructions relating to the termination of the war,
from both the Imperial Headquarters and the Commander-in-Chief
of the Allied Fleet. My mission in the South had come to an
abrupt end. I never thought I would survive defeat in war.
The problems I encountered immediately after the war, however,
were more immense than those associated with defeat. After the
surrender there were tens of thousands of soldiers under my
control, scattered over the whole of Indonesia except Sumatra.
I had to organize and assemble that defeated army, and carry
out the armistice arrangements smoothly. I needed strength and
determination to do this.

My first responsibility was to announce the surrender.   I
had to think of when and how I would do this. I wondered
whether there was any way I could get out of it. I had,
though, absolute confidence in the military discipline of my
subordinates. I therefore issued orders to the unit commanders
to make a straightforward and honest announcement of the
surrender to their men, to guard against rash behaviour and to
wait quietly for further instructions.

At the time of the surrender, the 22nd Special Base Force
was still engaged in a life-and-death battle with the
Australian Army in the jungle on the outskirts of Balikpapan.
I ordered them to stop fighting immediately. These men were in
desperate need of food and medical supplies, so I sent my Chief
of Staff, Kinoshita, there to issue relief supplies. The
tragic news of the defeat did not cause any serious wave of
reaction, but there was a little bit of backlash. For
instance, my Chief of Staff, with tears in his eyes, pleaded
with me to request the higher authorities to make some sort of
condition with the Allied Forces regarding the future of Japan
after the unconditional surrender and the existence of the

Emperor. I respected the sincere nature of this person, and considering the request to be very important, I made arrangements to forward it by telegram to Navy Headquarters in Tokyo and to the superior authorities.

Another incident involved a group of young officers who believed Japan should cooperate with the Indonesians in gaining Independence. Some crew members aboard a Navy mine-sweeper seized a number of guns, deserted the ship and took refuge in the mountains. Similar disruptive action was taken by a unit led by a warrant officer in the vicinity of Yogyakarta. The men involved in both these incidents were brought under control and returned to their units within a few days. Thereafter the situation quietened down.

In Batavia, on 17 August, a Proclamation of Independence was issued signed by President Sukarno and Vice-President Hatta. The Indonesian people felt sympathy for Japan due to her defeat. For instance, one morning which I shall never forget, a former close friend of mine, Dr Samsi,* on hearing of Japan's surrender, fell head-over-heels as he rushed into my office and expressed his grief for Japan's misfortune. I tried to console and comfort him by saying, 'Japan has finally been defeated. However, there is no doubt that Indonesia will succeed in becoming independent. Stand firm so you can have the strength to fight for that independence'. He was appointed Minister of Finance in the first cabinet, without having to run for election. Dr Samsi died a year before I visited Java [in August 1964]. He was the man I most wanted to meet there.

2. The Surrender Ceremony in Singapore

I was ordered by telegram to participate in the surrender ceremony to be conducted by Lord Mountbatten, Supreme [Allied] Commander in Southeast Asia, in Singapore on 12 September. On 11 September I flew to Singapore accompanied by my senior staff officer and deputy Commander-in-Chief.

Singapore at that time was in absolute chaos. The Allied Forces had entered the city and most of the Japanese Army and Navy personnel had been ordered to move elsewhere.

I stayed at the Headquarters of the 7th Area Army (Raffles College). Gen. Terauchi, Commander-in-Chief of the Combined Southern Forces, was absent due to illness. Those present were General Chief of Staff Numada and his staff of two or three; Gen. Kimura, Commander-in-Chief of the Burma Area Army; Lt.-Gen. Nakamura, Commander-in-Chief of the Thailand Area Army; Lt.-Gen. Kinoshita, Commander-in-Chief of the Air Force, and three of his staff; Vice-Adm. Fukudome, Commander-in-Chief of both the 10th Area Fleet and the 1st Southern Expeditionary

* For Dr Samsi Sastrawidagda, see Shibata, above, pp.280-1.

Fleet; and myself and my two staff. All together there were six Commanders-in-Chief.

In Singapore at that time, an Operations Unit was sent out every day to clean up the city. A major or a captain was made commander of this unit. They would leave their quarters at about four in the morning, run for one or two hours to the work site, and then work like slaves for a day. It was indeed unbearable work. These men experienced more than enough of the hardship of defeat. The Chinese antagonism towards the poor Japanese exploded into violence, and eventually the situation became so critical that it was too dangerous for Japanese to leave their homes during the day or night. The handling of Army units ordered to move out of Singapore was completely chaotic, and because they were limited to taking only what they could carry themselves, the looting of their valuable possessions became an everyday occurrence. They had no protection whatsoever from the heavy rain, and although they were drenched, they were made to sleep out in the fields. The Japanese Navy personnel, on the other hand, were well looked after by the British Navy. The handling of men was efficiently organized, there was no ill-treatment, and the British even used their own ships to transfer us. They were indeed very polite. Similarly, while I was met at the airport by a captain from the British Navy, and was taken by car to my quarters, Gen. Kimura and Lt.-Gen. Nakamura were taken home by truck. Nevertheless, when on the way home my car drew near to the Japanese Fleet Headquarters and I asked for permission to discuss some matters there, my request was refused.

The six Commanding Generals and Admirals of the defeated army did not talk with each other at great length. Gen. Kimura did, however, relate the story of how, when the Allies first entered Burma, the Army was forced to set up Headquarters in a temple and to live together with the Buddhist monks. Unfortunately, this was just at the time of the rainy season which meant they became extremely vulnerable to Allied attack. On the Thai Front, as in Java, it seems that they were bracing themselves ready for the attack.

That night I slept in the downstairs room with Vice-Adm. Fukudome and I fell asleep with the sound of Lt.-Gen. Nakamura's snoring coming from upstairs.

3. The Loud Jeers of 'Baka Darō' ('You fool')

We ate breakfast together on the morning of the 12th. I remember the nostalgic smell of dried sea-weed that was served for breakfast that morning.

The surrender ceremony was to take place in the City Hall, but I was not sure at what time it was to begin. At about 8 a.m. a Medical Officer from the British Army gave us a medical examination. He made me open my mouth wide, and with a miniature light bulb, he carefully inspected the inside of my mouth. After the war I was subjected to innumerable medical examinations, but this was the only time I had such a strange inspection of the inside of my mouth. Vice-Adm. Fukudome and myself were driven to the ceremony in a jeep sent round by the British Army. On the way, the jeep suddenly stopped outside the Governor's residence (formerly the residence of the Commander-in-Chief of the Japanese Army) and we were kept waiting outside for about one hour. A large number of Chinese, seeing the pathetic figures of Army and Navy Generals who just a few days before had been tyrants, began to move towards us. The MPs desperately pushed them back.

Eventually we arrived at the Hall. Both sides of the road leading up to the Hall were lined with British soldiers, and sailors in white uniforms. Behind them were rows of Chinese who had come to watch. As we approached the Hall, the crowd swelled in numbers and the Chinese began to jeer incessantly, 'Baka darō, baka darō...' At the entrance we got out of the car and climbed 20 or 30 stairs up to the doorway. Cameramen and other interested people took photo after photo of us. We were told to rest for a while in a room to the left of the hall entrance. Here English people, most of whom were women, stared in at us from the doorway and window. Their eyes were full of hatred and curiosity. Once they had finished looking they would change places with others so they could have a turn at staring at us. These women made me feel uneasy. The Lt.-Col. who was our guide first explained the lay-out of the ceremony hall and then led us to it. It was a fairly big hall with a large picture of the British monarch hanging on one wall, and a stage. We sat facing the stage, with Gen. Itagaki sitting in front and the rest of us behind him. Facing us was a line of Generals representing the Allied countries, with Gen. Percival sitting out in front. Directly opposite me was a Lt.-Gen. from China. The expression on Gen. Percival's face was particularly memorable. For the first time I discovered how it felt to be the General of a defeated army. I was overcome by a myriad of emotions. The hall was packed full with Allied civil and military officials.

Shortly Lord Mountbatten appeared at the rostrum. He struck a noble figure and possessed the dignity and grace characteristic of the British aristocracy. He spoke eloquently. I was only able to understand about half of his speech, but the gist of it was something like this: '...if you had not surrendered, the Allied Forces would have physically seized Japan with the soldiers already positioned for invasion'. Lord Mountbatten finished speaking and signed the Document of Surrender. Under the intent gaze of the representatives from the other countries, Gen. Itagaki remained calm and unruffled as he picked up the pen to sign his name. Looking at him from behind, I thought he was a truly great man.

344

I did not feel at all humiliated in having to face defeat in war and a surrender ceremony. The General slowly signed his name seven times, and then the ceremony ended.

I left the ceremony hall, and after having a rest in the room we had waited in before, left the building. In the square in front of the hall a large number of soldiers were assembled as if there was going to be a troop review. The crowd had greatly increased in number and the cry of 'Baka daro' had become more intense than before. Many of them had broken through the barricade of soldiers and, trying to throw stones at our car, they pushed towards us. A Second Lieutenant from the British Army, who acted as our body-guard, and one other man, got out of the car, stood at both doors and protected us from the mob. It grieved me greatly to think that the Chinese felt such intense hatred towards the Japanese Army.

At a few minutes past midday I returned to my Headquarters, and after finishing lunch I went with my two staff members to the airport. We were escorted by officers from the British Army. The plane left Singapore just after 3 p.m. While in Singapore, I was only able to spend one evening chatting with Commander-in-Chief Fukudome, his Deputy, and the Navy staff stationed in Singapore. In addition, I was not permitted to visit the Headquarters of the 1st Southern Expeditionary Fleet.

I stayed the night of the 12th in Batavia, and discussed the surrender ceremony with Army Commander-in-Chief Nagano, Rear-Adm. Maeda, and his subordinate commanding officers. In particular, I talked about the Chinese hatred towards the Japanese in Singapore, and the measures we should adopt in the future. I left Batavia on the 13th, but due to engine trouble we were forced to land at Semarang. I used the opportunity here to tell the **Chokan** [Resident] and the Commander of the Kempeitai about the situation in Singapore. At that time the atmosphere in Semarang was peaceful, but because it had become a place where the Japanese had gathered and where they had to look for their own food, all sorts of problems were beginning to develop. Since it was necessary to make repairs to the plane, I left by car and arrived in Surabaya at 3 a.m. the next morning. (The crew of this plane were all massacred in the Semarang Incident which occurred later on. I will never forget the pilot and crew of that plane, because throughout the war we had been together many times in dangerous situations.)

4. Arrangements Relating to the Termination of the War

When I returned to Surabaya, I called a meeting of my commanding officers and told them of the surrender ceremony and the arrangements I had made with the Army in Batavia. I concluded by saying, 'In Singapore, the Chinese hate the Japanese intensely. In Java, however, the Indonesians feel sympathy towards the defeated Japanese. This is because we treated them well during the war. I sincerely hope that until the time we leave this country these warm feelings will continue, and that a binding and lasting friendship between us will remain. However, we must pay full attention to the direction of their actions'. At that time, no one could have predicted the crisis of the days that followed.

The strict attitude adopted by the Allied Forces towards the officers and men of the Japanese Army was revealed in the following daily broadcast. Lord Mountbatten issued an order forbidding officers and men of the Allied Forces in the South East Asian Region to fraternize on an intimate level with officers and men of the Japanese Army. He ordered that:

1. Officers of the Allied Forces must not shake hands with officers of the Japanese Army.
2. Officers and men of the Allied Forces are not permitted to eat in the same room as officers and men of the Japanese Army, and are not permitted to sit beside each other at the same table.
3. Officers and men of the Japanese Army must hand over their swords to the Allied Forces at the time of disarmament.
4. Officers of the Japanese Army must salute officers of the Allied Forces regardless of their rank. The Japanese officer must salute first and the officer of the Allied Forces must return the salute.
5. The Japanese flag must not be raised in areas occupied by the Allied Forces.
6. Those officers and men of the Japanese Army who, regardless of their rank, do not obey these orders, and display a lax attitude will immediately be reduced to the status of prisoners of war.

On 15 September Rear-Adm. Patterson, a representative of the Allied Forces in Southeast Asia, arrived in Batavia.* I despatched Rear-Adm. Maeda, Commander of the 5th Garrison, together with one of my own staff officers, to receive instructions from him.

The main points laid down by Patterson were as follows:

(a) Contact with and medical treatment for the Allied prisoners of war and internees.

* Rear-Adm. W.R. Patterson of the Royal Navy was the first high-level Allied representative in Indonesia, reaching Batavia/Jakarta aboard HMS **Cumberland** on 15 September. He remained the senior Allied officer in the Netherlands Indies until the arrival of Lt.-Gen. Sir Philip Christison at the head of a substantial British military force on 30 September.

346

(b) With the exception of troops needed to maintain public law and order, auxiliary units and armed squads must be disarmed and their weapons guarded. Those who have been disarmed must be evacuated to fixed areas and military discipline must be maintained.

(c) Orders were also given relating to the handling of Japanese ships and warships.

I instructed my subordinate units to carry out the orders from Imperial Headquarters and from the Allied Fleet. In order to execute meticulously the orders and instructions received from the Allied Forces I organized a Navy Security Force to assemble personnel, arms and military supplies, to protect ships, warships, aeroplanes, heavy vehicles and other equipment, and to maintain public law and order. With the aim of taking every possible precaution regarding the handing over of military equipment to the Allied Forces, I established a Transfer Committee and appointed Rear-Adm. Tanaka, Commander-in-Chief of the 21st Special Base Force, as Committee Chairman. The other Committee members were selected from each unit.

I also set up a Liaison Committee, with a Rear-Admiral who was Chief Accountant in the South as the Committee Chairman.

Firstly, in order to maintain public peace in the city of Surabaya, the following steps were taken:

(a) Recreation facilities like cinemas, theatres, dance halls, clubs, restaurants, hotels, cafes and bars were opened.

(b) The wartime camouflage was removed from the buildings, roads cleaned and repaired, neon signs in shop windows restored, and constructions and decorations reminiscent of the war, like welcoming arches, were destroyed.

Next, the following measures were taken to promote law and order:

(a) Assistance was given to the International Red Cross which helped those released from internment camps, and to those who were unemployed as a result of the cessation of hostilities.

(b) Assistance was given to religious and medical institutions.

(c) Newspapers (English and Dutch language), posters and leaflets were made use of for propaganda purposes.

Another important point concerns the measures I took on the advice of Mr Ayukawa of the **Mainichi** newspaper regarding the problem of half-blood children born in Indonesia during the war. During the occupation of Java a considerable number of

347

children were born through relationships between Japanese, including soldiers, and Indonesian women. The fathers of these children had either already returned to Japan, were about to return, or had died through war injuries. I felt that we were obliged to give money to the mothers for the upbringing of these children, and so I issued orders to my subordinates both to make an appeal to the Government and to advertise in the newspaper for this purpose. Ayukawa and Miss Yabe, who herself was born in Java, took responsibility for the issuing of money. It was an extremely humanitarian action.

5. The Committee for the Re-Occupation of Surabaya Enters the City

In the middle of September Allied Forces officers belonging to RAPWI* arrived in Surabaya, and my subordinates cooperated with the Japanese Army unit responsible for assisting them in their duties. Our main task was to hand over medical facilities, supplies and heavy vehicles to the Red Cross Committee in Surabaya. However, in carrying out this job, we took great care not to arouse the nationalist sentiment of the Indonesians.

On 21 September Allied Forces Navy Capt. Huijer landed in Surabaya† and showed his letter of authority addressed to the

---

* RAPWI (Recovery of Allied Prisoners of War and Internees) teams were quickly organized throughout Java and Sumatra following the Japanese surrender, largely from among Allied personnel who had been clandestinely parachuted into Japanese territory either before or shortly after the surrender. Their task was to provide emergency relief for Allied prisoners, but as the first Allied representatives in many areas they also assumed various other functions.

† Capt. Petrus J.G. Huijer (b.1899) was the first Allied representative in Surabaya, largely because of the insistence of the commander of Dutch forces in the area, Adm. Helfrich, on whose personal staff Huijer had served in 1943-44. Anxious that at least in the city of the great pre-war Dutch naval base the Allies should be represented by a Dutch naval man, Helfrich had sent Huijer to Batavia in a Dutch Catalina with instructions to be the first to reach Surabaya by whatever means. Adm. Patterson allowed him to reconnoitre Surabaya on his own on 21 September, and to return there on 23 September with authority to serve as Patterson's representative. Huijer's small staff was entirely Dutch, which made it virtually impossible for them to play a useful mediating role in the tense situation which quickly developed.

British Commander-in-Chief. He gave instructions to me relating to the preparations to be made for the stationing of Allied troops in Surabaya. This involved the mine-sweeping of Surabaya's canals, the preparation of camps for the soldiers, and the arrangement of heavy transport vehicles, naval vessels and planes for use by the troops. Capt. Huijer was a Dutch Reserve Captain who had worked in a sugar company before the war and thus knew Surabaya well. When he arrived he immediately took me to his former villa and instructed me to repair it. He was now the Navy Commander-in-Chief in Surabaya and was excited about where to have his office and so forth.

On the one hand I was responsible for carrying out orders, but I also made requests when necessary. For instance, I sent a petition to Adm. Patterson via Capt. Huijer explaining that I wished to assemble the Japanese Naval Units located in East Java at a camp in Pujong village, Malang **Shu** [Residency]. I received permission in principle from Capt. Huijer. My plan was to avoid chaos and confusion when the Allied Forces landed in Surabaya, by evacuating Navy personnel in Surabaya, with the exception of the Navy Security Force and members of the Transfer Committee, to Pujong.

However, at that time the anti-Dutch sentiment in Western Java had gradually begun to spread to East Java and there were clear signs that the Indonesian people in the city of Surabaya and the surrounding areas would try to oppose the occupation of Surabaya by Dutch troops. The situation had become very insecure. Having been advised in a note from the Commander of the Army Units, I set up a close liaison link with the Army Units and the Military Administration, and kept a very close watch on the situation in Surabaya. At that time, I received the following instructions from Capt. Huijer, Officer-in-Charge of the Allied Forces Navy in Surabaya:

1. Increase the number of soldiers involved in the mine-sweeping of Surabaya port. Speed up the operations at the port.
2. Increase the number of soldiers in the Navy Security Force to 3,000 men, and arm all the men.
3. Stop the evacuation of the Japanese Navy from the Surabaya area. This does not include the evacuation of civilians working for the Navy.
4. If the Indonesians riot, the Japanese Navy must make a counter attack. This does not constitute a violation of the Rangoon Agreement.
5. From 2 October one Douglas DC3 transport plane must be made available for use by Capt. Huijer as a communication link between Surabaya and Batavia.
6. Preparations must be made for sea-planes to be sent out immediately on order.

On receiving these instructions I ordered the return of the necessary number of Navy soldiers who were on their way to the assembly centre at Pujong. In order to fully equip these men with weapons I arranged for the return of the weapons and ammunition which had already been collected.

On 1 October the Navy military strength located in Surabaya was as follows:

Military Force on the Land	-	3,110 soldiers 1,455 civilians attached to the Navy
Military Force on the Sea	-	a fleet consisting of fewer than 11 torpedo boats 6 ships some small motor boats
Military Force in the Air	-	planes for sea battle) reconnaissance planes) Total 30 water patrol planes)
	-	4 transport planes (including 1 flying boat)

6. From the Time of the Japanese Surrender to the Surabaya Riots

Even today I still greatly appreciate the fact that immediately after the Japanese surrender on 15 August, the Indonesian people felt sympathy for us and lamented our defeat. With the passage of time this sympathy cooled somewhat. However, because they never showed any feeling of antagonism toward us, the situation remained relatively peaceful.

When in Batavia on 17 August the Indonesian nationalist leader, Sukarno, was elected President and the Proclamation of Independence was announced, the Indonesians' sense of nationalism was immediately aroused. The people of Surabaya at once raised the national flag and became excited with the glorious feeling of Independence. When this excitement subsided, the Indonesians tried to oust the Japanese military administration and requisition buildings and installations. They even demanded that the national flag be raised at the Fleet Headquarters building. Just at this time, Dutch planes scattered leaflets over Surabaya. When the Dutch internees began to pour back into the centre of the city and demand that we return to them their homes, industries and cars, fights broke out between them and the Indonesians all over the city.

On 19 September a fight began when the Indonesians tried to pull down the Dutch flag raised over the Hotel Oranje.*

* For Footnote see following page.

After that, anti-Dutch incidents increased daily in Surabaya, and demonstrations by groups of Indonesians occurred frequently.

The Army Unit stationed in Surabaya then issued a proclamation prohibiting meetings, group processions and the carrying of arms. The strength of the Kempeitai and the Auxiliary Kempeitai was increased and all efforts were made to suppress the Indonesians. However, when a large number of Dutchmen associated with RAPWI marched into Surabaya, the anti-Dutch feelings of the Indonesians exploded, and frequent attacks were made on the Dutch throughout the city. At this point, the Army Unit cooperated with the Navy Security Force to protect and guard the area which the Navy was responsible for defending. Together they operated to suppress the Indonesians.

I felt that the situation had now become extremely dangerous, so I made a request, through the 10th Area Fleet, to the Supreme Allied Command, Southeast Asia: 'With regard to the maintenance of law and order amongst the Indonesian people in Java, and particularly Surabaya, I consider the landing of Dutch troops to be inappropriate and a great hindrance to the execution of the end of war arrangements. I would therefore like Surabaya to be occupied by no one other than the British'.

The Japanese Army bore the responsibility for maintaining law and order, and so was obliged to suppress the anti-Dutch movement. We were in an awkward position because we had to cooperate as much as posible with RAPWI which was organized to aid the Dutch. The Indonesians began to despise the Japanese, because we were helping the Dutch who were deliberately obstructing Indonesian Independence. As a result, it seemed that the anti-Dutch movement would rapidly develop into an anti-Japanese movement.

On 30 September Lt.-Gen. Christison, Supreme Commander of Allied Forces on Java, arrived in Batavia. I despatched my Chief-of-Staff and one other staff officer to Batavia and appointed them liaison officers representing Fleet Headquarters.

7. Surabaya Becomes the Scene of Mass Rioting

As I have just mentioned, the anti-Dutch movement soon developed an anti-Japanese side to it as well. The main reason for this antagonism lay in the fact that, according to the

* Footnote from previous page:
  This famous incident led quickly to the first major outbreak in Indonesia of fighting between Indonesian youths and newly released Dutch internees. One Dutch captain died in the 19 September violence, which was soon replicated in many other centres.

the Japanese Army was completely prohibited from distributing news or propaganda to the natives. As a result, the Indonesian people were not able to interpret correctly the real feelings of the Japanese Army.

At 3 p.m. on 1 October I called a meeting of my commanding officers, laid down instructions concerning the maintenance of law and order in Indonesia, and explained the Fleet policy on this matter.* I told them that the law and order situation amongst the natives had deteriorated to an alarming degree, and in various places incidents of anonymous violence and shooting had become commonplace. Moreover, part of their antagonism was directed toward the Japanese. I warned them that we had now come to an important stage in the execution of the end of war arrangements and it was necessary to handle the current situation with the utmost care. Although the responsibility for public security in the greater part of Surabaya lay with the Army, the Navy had the responsibility of protecting the naval port and other Navy facilities. It was therefore necessary to take appropriate precautions, like increasing the guard in insecure areas. Concerning this problem the basic policy of the Fleet was as follows:

1. To strengthen the soldiers on patrol, to act in an authoritative manner, and to remove all opportunities the natives could take advantage of to cause disruption.

2. If a dangerous situation arises, try to persuade the natives not to take action and to make them see they are mistaken.

3. In the event that, despite your attempts at persuasion, they try to resort to mass violence, use a variety of threats to try to discourage them. (For instance, by calling out troops, arranging weapons and preparing for action.)

4. If it becomes necessary to use arms for self-defence, endeavour to limit the number of casualties.

* This meeting may well have been an important turning point, for Capt. Huijer later believed that the Japanese Army commander in Surabaya, Gen. Iwabe, changed his attitude fundamentally between 30 September and 1 October, and thereafter ceased to cooperate with Huijer's attempts to control the Indonesians. 'I cannot help thinking that Iwabu's attitude changed that Sunday night...on secret orders he received from Japanese High Command.' Tweede Kamer der Statengeneraal, **Enquêtecommissie Regeringsbeleid 1940–1945. Verslag houdende de uitkomsten van het onderzoek**, Deel 8 A & B ('s-Gravenhage, Staatsdrukkerij, 1956), p.596.

In short, the policy aims at avoiding the use of weapons, attempting to pacify the Indonesians, and taking the edge off their aggression. It is imperative that the commander of each unit do his utmost to prevent the outbreak of dangerous incidents. In addition to using persuasion as a tactic, you must also change your own opinion of the natives, consider what their feelings are, and take pains not to upset them by your language and attitude. You should restrain yourselves from behaving arrogantly, speaking in a loud voice and acting in a high-handed manner.

Furthermore, in situations which are potentially dangerous, do not talk directly to the mobs, but try to persuade one of their representatives, and if you succeed in persuading him, use the opportunity to sway the mob. If they do not accept your advice you must take the utmost care so as not to provoke a dangerous incident.

In addition, I made the following points:

1. In regard to policing and surveillance there should be close liaison between all the units, and plans should be made in cooperation between them.
2. The use of weapons will be decided upon by the commander according to the situation. In such a case he will inform Fleet Headquarters of his decision, and Fleet Headquarters will seek permission from the Allied Forces.
3. Units located in isolated areas will establish close contact with the Army and will exchange information with them. Furthermore, where possible, an extremely effective policy is to attempt to win over the influential natives.
4. When soldiers are to be transported, a careful analysis of the situation must be made to determine whether or not it is necessary to arm the men. When supplies are to be transported, as far as possible always attach a police guard.
5. Each unit must at all times make an effort to gather information and maintain contact with neighbouring units.
6. Thieves and looters must be dealt with strictly. However, care must be taken to explain the punishment of criminals to the people, so that rumours will not be spread that we ill-treat the natives.
7. Lessons can be learnt from recent incidents involving the Army in which there was bloodshed.

These incidents occurred due to -

(a) forcefully trying to break through a mob of natives with vehicles;

(b) commencing to drive into a mob obstructing the pasage of a vehicle without trying to find a satisfactory solution;

(c) displaying bad attitudes towards the natives, and thereby upsetting them.

This meeting continued on into the evening until we were interrupted by a report from the 21st Special Base Force Headquarters. The report went as follows:

At about 6 in the evening a crowd of Indonesians, worked up by a fight with some Dutchmen and planning to loot weapons and vehicles, had finally become riotous. In cooperation with the Indonesian police whose responsibility it was to guard the city, they had assembled groups of rioters throughout the city, and there were obvious signs of imminent upheaval.

The Commander-in-Chief of the Base Force immediately issued orders that all Navy personnel located in Surabaya were to increase their surveillance and guard against looting by the rioters. In particular, all patrolmen and sentries were to be armed, as well as the emergency units who were to stand by in readiness for action. A strict watch was to be kept over weapons and explosives, and emergency arms were to be supplied quickly to each Navy unit. With this the meeting adjourned and each commanding officer returned to his post. However, by this time the riotous masses had already begun kidnapping Japanese and plundering weapons and vehicles. Some of the commanding officers returning from the meeting were kidnapped on the way.

That night each Navy unit maintained a strict guard. However, throughout the city, rioters had been gathering in groups and had become violent. We could not make contact with the Army unit, and therefore had no idea how the situation was progressing.

We later found out that this was because our telephone wire had been cut. That night about half the rioters occupied the airport, including the Navy sea-plane base. In addition, most of the Army units which had hastened to Surabaya on hearing of the crisis were disarmed by the Indonesian units. Although we had predicted that this type of incident would occur and had taken the necessary precautions, we were thoroughly defeated. I fell asleep that night thinking about the situation outside and the Indonesian rioters.

8. Don't Point Guns at the Natives!

2 October was a bright sunny day. In the morning the

centre of the city appeared as if everything had quietened down, but Japanese passing through the city still feared being kidnapped, we were still cut off from communication with the outside world, and a strict watch over the city continued. As on every other day, I had breakfast and went to the staff officers' room. But just as I started speaking to the communications officer, about 30 or 40 Indonesians carrying rifles, pistols and bamboo spears, and led by an Indonesian police officer, barged in. For a second I was speechless, but then I ordered, 'Don't resist them! Stay as you are! You must not shoot!' There were in all about a thousand rioters – or should I call them revolutionaries? – equipped with tanks, heavy machineguns, spears, swords and other weapons. They had raided the 21st Communications Unit which was located adjacent to Fleet Headquarters, had locked the personnel in a room, and had then disarmed them. They then surrounded our Headquarters, demanded we surrender our arms, and searched the building for weapons. Apart from each individual's personal long sword, there were only a few pistols in the building. My aide-de-camp was alarmed when they came into my room and carried away my long sword. He argued with the police officer that the Commander-in-Chief's sword was extremely important, and could he please return it. The police officer, who seemed to be the most senior member of the group, consented. He raised the sword up high in his hands before me, politely bowed in respect and returned it to me. They then began to withdraw peacefully. In the meantime, one platoon of the Security Unit of the 21st Special Base Force had suddenly arrived at the front gate to rescue me. The platoon consisted of a commander, 28 men, two light machineguns and a few rifles. The rioters demanded that they hand over their weapons. They again surrounded the Fleet Headquarters, and the situation became extremely dangerous. The Security Unit attempted to use threats to make the mob retreat, but the crowd was increasing in numbers all the time and it seemed that at any moment they would start shooting at each other. Originally the rioters had been mainly young men, but this time there was a great number of boys of about 12 or 13, with bare feet, spears in hand and shouting out 'Merdeka'. It was really an incredible sight.

There were about 40 swords for use by officers and 20 revolvers in the Fleet Headquarters building. For a moment I thought we would have to fight for our own self-defence with these weapons and the aid of the Security Unit. Navy Capt. Huijer of the Allied Forces had instructed that if the Indonesians rioted we were to use armed force to suppress them. In my opinion, though, once we opened fire here, the rioters would become irritated, enraged, and eventually violent. The Allied Forces soldiers and civilians, and particularly the large number of Dutch and Japanese interned in the southern part of the city, would all be massacred and the entire city would be thrown into complete disorder and chaos. I was also aware that while on the one hand they were a mob of rioters, on the other hand they were a group of men determined to win independence for Indonesia. If the Japanese Army shot and massacred them now, their animosity toward Japan would remain forever. I realized that I would be charged with disobeying orders, but, after all I was now no more than a commander of a defeated army. I was prepared to discard my honour as a soldier for the sake of preserving the peace. If we had fought against the Indonesians then, our friends and allies would have been killed or wounded. I was determined not to drag into war again the officers and soldiers who had ceased hostilities for the sake of their Emperor and their country. There was only one way the situation could be brought under control without blood being shed.

I reluctantly accepted the demand of the mob, disarmed the 28 members of the Security Unit, and placed the weapons under the joint supervision of the Indonesian police and the Japanese Army. I entrusted the handing over of the weapons to Sudirman, the Vice-Resident of Surabaya Shu.* The rioters agreed to disperse and the problem was tentatively solved. During the confusion all the personnel, including the commander, of the 21st Communications Unit in the adjacent building, had been kidnapped by the mob. Fortunately the communications equipment escaped serious damage. For the time being, though, we had no communication. When the rioters invaded Fleet Headquarters, I had immediately arranged for the escape of one of my staff officers. He proceeded to the Main Office and Branch Office of

---

* Raden Sudirman was born in Semarang in 1890, and after a Dutch-medium education jointed the Customs Department in 1912. He was a member of the Surabaya Gemeenteraad (1921-24) and a leading supporter of Dr Soetomo in his Indonesisch Studieclub from 1925 and Parindra from 1935. In 1943 he became chairman of the Surabaya Shu Sangikai. The Japanese named him **Fuku-chokan** (Vice-Resident) of Surabaya Shu at the end of 1944, as part of a general move to prepare Indonesians to take over as Residents. In 1945 he was also appointed to the final session of the Java **Chuo Sangi-in** (Central Advisory Council) and the Committee to Investigate Measures to Prepare Independence. As the highest Indonesian official in Surabaya, Sudirman was pressed into proclaiming a Republican apparatus independent of the Japanese on 3 September, and he was subsequently recognized as Resident by the Republican Central Government. Shibata, however, refers to him throughout by his former Japanese title as **Fuku-chokan**. He was never more than an ineffective mediator between the youth activists on the one hand and Japanese and Allies on the other.

the Indonesian Peace-Keeping Organization [BKR - the nascent Republican army], and to the Residency Government Office. There he demanded that the Vice-Resident bring the mob under control. However, the Vice-Resident displayed no inclination to act, and on the contrary replied that it was a revolution, and he would not agree to negotiate to bring the situation at Fleet Headquarters under control.

9. Surabaya City under Coup D'etat

At about 11.30 a.m. I could hear the sound of gun shots in the vicinity of the Surabaya Residency Office. The rioters had attacked the Kempeitai Unit and both sides were shooting at each other. Eventually the rioters managed to occupy the Headquarters of the Kempeitai. The situation was becoming increasingly serious. We now had absolutely no contact with the Army units, and judging that the Military Administration no longer had any power to control the situation, I sent a letter to Vice-Resident Sudirman, via an Indonesian police officer, stating that I wished to have an interview with him. However, I received no answer. At 2.40 p.m. a crowd of rioters driving tanks surrounded the 21st Special Base Force Headquarters and the barracks of the Land Garrison, and began firing. The Land Garrison followed the policy I had laid down earlier, and did not resort to armed conflict. They endeavoured to pacify the rioters by means of persuasion, but when after repeated attacks eleven Japanese were injured and three killed, they lost their patience and began to return the fire. A full-scale fight broke out as the Land Garrison tried to stop the mob from entering their barracks. On hearing the sound of these shots at Fleet Headquarters, I orderd by telephone that shooting stop. Soon after the Japanese had begun to shoot back, a Chief Medical Officer and three of his subordinates were killed by the rioters at the military installation barracks. I feared that if the Land Garrison continued to fire in self-defence, the life of every Japanese living in Surabaya would be endangered, and that the whole of Surabaya would turn into a massive blood bath. So I repeated my order to the Commander-in-Chief of the Base Force to stop the shooting. As a result of this order to cease fire the weapons were seized by the rioters. However, I knew that I would be the only person held responsible by the Allied Forces for the disappearance of these weapons, so I did not hesitate to forbid armed resistance.

My Chief-of-Staff, Commander Kinoshita, related this incident in his book **Merdeka** in the following way:

> In Surabaya at that time there was a total of about 5,000 to 6,000 soldiers belonging to both the Army and the Navy, including the men of the Army Eastern Self-Defence Force. This alone was probably

sufficient to suppress and subdue the Indonesians. However, there was a large number of Japanese military personnel and civilians attached to the Army, all of whom had no weapons and were scattered throughout the city of Surabaya. Also there were many Eurasians and Dutch who had returned to the city after being released from internment camps. Therefore, if a head-on collision had occurred between the Japanese and Indonesians, the situation would have deteriorated into revolutionary chaos, and there would have been no way of securing the life and property of a great many of these people.

Commander-in-Chief Shibata's decision was based primarily on his concern for humanity. In addition he deeply sympathised with and understood the Indonesian independence cause. His decision was derived from his broad-minded outlook on the situation. He issued the following important and urgent order by radio to his subordinate units: 'I have tried every possible way to answer the Indonesian demand that we hand over our weapons, and I have explained the reason why it is not possible. On no condition whatsoever are you permitted to use armed force. When no peaceful solution can be found, there is no alternative other than to let them seize the weapons. The responsibility for this lies with me'. Shibata was determined to avoid armed conflict.

I dispatched one of my men under police escort to the Indonesian police headquarters, and he arranged for a mutual ceasefire and the handing over of part of the weapons, belonging to the Special Base Force, to the Indonesian police officials. This was on the condition they would be held in custody and would not be handed over to the rioters. With this they finally agreed to stop shooting and the situation was brought under control. It was then just past 5 p.m. [2 October].

Taking into account what had happened in the last two days, at 4.20 p.m. I had ordered, 'All naval vessels and ships which can be navigated must set sail immediately and take shelter elsewhere'. This was intended to secure the safety of the ships anchored in Surabaya port. At 4.45 p.m. I had also issued the following order by Navy telephone:

Due to the development of a thoroughly revolutionary situation in Surabaya, it is now extremely dangerous to provoke the Indonesian masses. It is therefore absolutely prohibited to fire at them. It is essential that each administrative office does its utmost to persuade and pacify the Indonesians and to protect

358

facilities and equipment without worsening the situation.

1. In the situation where the Indonesians demand that the Indonesian flag be raised, you are permitted to agree to it.
2. In the situation where the crowd demands your weapons, etc, and there is no alternative but to give in, you are permitted to hand over the barest minimum of arms. However, when handing over the weapons to the person responsible for them, make out a document stating clearly the particulars of the weapons.
3. In the situation where they demand the handing over of installations, offices, etc, do your utmost to try and negotiate with the person in charge of the crowd, and, depending upon the situation, consult with the Allied Forces regarding the joint custody of the installation. Try as best you can to satisfy for the time being the demands of the Indonesians and to preserve the peace.
4. Each department will assemble together, and take strict precautions to prevent unnecessary disaster.
5. In the situation where it is advisable to use an [Indonesian] policeman as guard, get him to cooperate positively with you by occasionally consulting with him.

At 2.16 p.m. on that same day I informed the Southern Combined Army and the 10th Area Fleet by telegram of the situation in Surabaya. I expressed my opinion that, because it was absolutely impossible for the Japanese Army to maintain law and order in Surabaya and it was extremely difficult to protect weapons and installations, the British Army should now move in and occupy the town. That night the commander of the Army unit in Surabaya dispatched a liaison officer to inform me of the situation on their side, and it was obvious that it was impossible for the Army unit to control the situation.

From 1 October the Navy had planned to strengthen its military power by increasing the supply of light machineguns and rifles, as well as the small arms used by the Security Force. However, because we were in the middle of carrying out the end of war arrangements at that time, there was not a sufficient amount of small arms and weapons available to distribute. Therefore, since the Army unit had already lost its power of authority, it was impossible for the units scattered throughout the area even to defend themselves with their inadequate supply of weapons.

In my judgement it served no purpose to use weapons, for

it would only aggravate and complicate the already dangerous situation. It would both endanger the lives of the large number of Allied nationals in Surabaya, especially the Dutch internees returning from places in Java, and also result in the destruction of buildings and installations. I referred this opinion to the Commander-in-Chief of the East Java Defence Unit. He was the man responsible for the maintenance of law and order in East Java. Recognizing that the situation could only be brought under control if weapons were not used, he agreed with my decision and thus brought Army policy in line with that of the Navy.

As yet the vicinity of the Surabaya Naval port had remained peaceful, but at about 7 a.m. on 3 October a group of rioters attacked the area and demanded they be given the weapons located there. The Commander at the port refused to comply with their demand, saying, 'Since the property of the Japanese Navy must be handed over to the Allied Forces, I cannot give it to Indonesia'. However, they would not accept this as an answer, and the situation became very dangerous indeed. Since it looked as if there was going to be bloodshed, an agreement was made whereby the Indonesian flag was temporarily raised, and the custody and guarding of the arsenal was placed in the hands of the Indonesian Peacekeeping Organization [BKR] and the Indonesian Police. The rioters then gradually retreated.

At about 11.30 a.m., I sent two Staff Officers from Fleet Headquarters to the residence of Vice-Resident Sudirman to request a meeting. His representative, Dwidjo,* Chief Justice of the Surabaya High Court, met them and they requested a reply to these proposals from me:

1. A meeting with the Indonesian authorities responsible for controlling the situation, with regard to the recent riots.
2. It had become impossible to carry out the mine-sweeping operation of Surabaya port as ordered by the Allied Forces, because since 1 October the captain of every mine-sweeping vessel had been kidnapped. Recognizing that the responsibility for these kidnappings lay with the Indonesians, I demanded the immediate release of the ship captains.
3. I demanded that the ship-building yard in the merchant shipping area of Surabaya be protected from attack by rioters.

* Presumably Mr Dwidjosewoyo, a lawyer and second vice-chairman of the Surabaya National Committee (KNI).

4. Since the transport vessel, **Kitakai Maru**, moored to the commercial wharf, was now being looted, I demanded it be guarded and protected.

At 3 p.m. the same day [3 October], I visited the Headquarters of Mr Dwidjo and received the following reply to the above proposals:

1. Vice-Resident Sudirman expressed his regret over the incident which occurred yesterday. The members of the National Committee [KNI] were powerless to do anything in the present situation. Until the people's feelings subsided, there was nothing that could be done but to sit and wait.
2. It was the Vice-Resident's intention to release all the ship captains, but because there was a danger that the rioters might harm the captains, nothing could be done to save them immediately. Furthermore, when they were released, they were to be placed in an internment camp.
3. The Indonesian police would guard the shipbuilding yard and the **Kitakai Maru**.

After conveying this official message, he chatted with me on an informal level. He said that the youth in Surabaya were wild with a desire for Independence, and even his own child, a 14-year-old middle school student, rushed around with spear in hand, after the mob. He said there was nothing he could do to stop him.

That day the Indonesians again demanded the weapons belonging to the 21st Special Base Force Land Garrison, and began to plunder them. All that day, mobs of rioters roamed Surabaya's streets causing disorder and unrest. From about 7.30 p.m. members of the Indonesian Special Police Force* formed an armed guard outside the Fleet Headquarters. Since the rioting had first broken out, we often heard the dull sound of two pieces of wood being banged together. On hearing this sound thousands of Indonesians would appear from nowhere, and quietly gather together ready for action. That night the same dreaded sound of wood banging together could be heard. Where

---

* The **Tokubetsu Keisatsutai** (Special Police Force) had been first formed in Aceh (Sumatra) in early 1943, and then extended to each residency in Java in 1944. It was a well-armed, mobile, paramilitary force designed to counteract anti-Japanese underground and guerrilla groups. When PETA/Giyugun and Heiho forces were disbanded after the Japanese surrender it remained as the best armed and disciplined Indonesian force, usually responsive to instructions from the official Republican government hierarchy.

were they going to this time? Every now and then I heard the
sound of gunshots. Whizz! A stray bullet shot down the road
outside Fleet Headquarters. It was dangerous, really
dangerous.

10. I Provisionally Surrendered to Captain Huijer

At 7.30 p.m. on 3 October, Dutch Navy Capt. Huijer, a
member of the Allied Forces Committee for the Re-occupation of
Surabaya, visited me. He was escorted by members of the
Indonesian Special Police Force. He issued the following
instructions to me:

> The rioters are preparing an attack at 12 midnight on
> Fleet Headquarters and the Base Force Land Garrison.
> You, as Commander-in-Chief, can make a choice between
> the following two options. On the one hand, you can
> risk your life at the hands of the mob, and thereby
> be discredited. On the other hand, you can acknow-
> ledge me as the representative of the Allied Forces,
> and surrender to me. In the latter case, all
> soldiers and property belonging to the Japanese Navy
> will become the possessions of the Allied Forces, and
> theoretically cannot be touched by the Indonesians.
> I have received a firm promise from the Indonesian
> National Committee in Surabaya that they will agree
> to this measure.

I thought about what he had just said. I had already been
carried off to Singapore and, together with the other
subordinates of Commander-in-Chief Terauchi of the Combined
Southern Army, had surrendered to the Allied Forces. There was
no way the Japanese Army and Navy could bring the situation in
Surabaya under control. The second option made sense. I
decided I had to agree to it. It was true that Capt. Huijer
had come as a member of the Committee for the Re-occupation of
Surabaya. It was not clear, though, that the rioters were in
fact going to attack that night, but if he could bring the
situation under control with the measures he proposed, it would
be a marvellous thing. Therefore, on hearing of his
recommendation I decided to complete the surrender procedure,
and as evidence of my surrender, I handed him my sword.*

* Huijer's report (**Enquêtecommissie**, pp.596-8) makes clear that
  Huijer believed the Indonesian violence was essentially anti-
  Japanese, and that the only chance of saving the remaining
  three Japanese installations, of which the most important was
  the Naval Aviation Yards, was to place these under explicit
  Allied control. Sudirman and his KNI colleagues had
  encouraged this course. Benedict Anderson's judgement (**Java,**

According to a report I heard from the Army Communications Officer the next day, the Army Unit carried out a similar procedure based on exactly the same recommendation from Capt. Huijer. At 10 a.m. on 4 October, I telephoned my Chief of Staff who had been dispatched to Batavia, and through him informed Lt.-Gen. Christison, Supreme Commander of the British Forces in Batavia, and Rear-Adm. Patterson of the British Navy, of the surrender details.

11. Captain Huijer is Missing

At 8 a.m. on the 4th, the Surabaya workshop of the 20th Naval Air Force Squadron sent a message explaining that a critical situation had developed there. Up until then the area of the airport where it was located had remained peaceful. Capt. Huijer immediately went to the workshop, accompanied by two staff officers from Fleet Headquarters, and escorted by Indonesian police officials and members of the Peacekeeping Organization [BKR]. Because this workshop had been taken over by the Allied Forces, they were able to reach an agreement whereby the outside protection of the workshop was to be left to the Indonesians, and the workshop was to continue operation as normal. Since the first test of the new situation had succeeded, at 5 p.m. I reported to each Navy section: 'As a means of bringing the situation in Surabaya under control, I have completed the formal procedure of surrender to Capt. Huijer'. I then issued subsequent orders to each of the sections.

At that time we were still able to communicate by military telephone with Batavia. I received a reply by telephone from my Chief of Staff to the message I had sent to Batavia regarding the following matters which I had already proposed to the Allied Forces Headquarters and to the head of the Indonesian government, Sukarno, as a means of restoring law and order:

1. The restoration of Fleet Headquarters' communication links.
2. The ordering of the release of Japanese Navy personnel who are imprisoned.

* Footnote continued from previous page:
p.153) that this action by Huijer was 'the mistake that precipitated the Surabaya crisis', is difficult to reconcile with the accounts of Shibata and Huijer, who agree that Japanese resistance had ended and the overwhelming majority of weapons had been surrendered before the 'surrender' to Huijer took place.

3. The protection of the lives of Japanese residents in the Republic of Indonesia. Permission to use the Pujong area for this purpose.

On the basis of the third point, I ordered the commander at Pujong to secure the protection of the area. The rioting throughout the city did not cease. The rioters followed the same pattern of calling their friends together and then attacking various places. Communication and traffic with the outside world was cut off, so we had no idea of the situation in the rest of Java. It had also become very dangerous for my liaison officer to travel back and forth to the Allied Forces located in the Hotel Oranje.

At just after 3 p.m. on 5 October, rioters again surrounded the Air Force workshop at the airport, where a temporary agreement had been reached the day before. They eventually kidnapped all the Japanese employees. In the evening a major incident occurred. The munitions warehouse on the island of Madura, which had been seized some time earlier by the Indonesians, suddenly exploded. In Surabaya we could see enormous flames reaching up to the sky, and could hear the incredibly loud bang of explosives. The next day I was told that these explosions continued for four hours.

At 7.30 p.m. the 1st Detachment of the 21st Communications Unit was surrounded by rioters at the Sidoarjo Transmitting Station, and all the staff kidnapped. Probably because of the deafening roar throughout Surabaya caused by the Madura explosions, the rioters gathered together at various places that evening, and eventually occupied the office of the 102nd Operations Unit. All Japanese in the vicinity of the office were imprisoned inside the building. Navy telephone communication with the area was cut off.

One thing that gave me some sense of relief during the rioting period was the success Fleet Headquarters and the Special Base Force had in bringing pressure on the Residency Government Office to release imprisoned Japanese Navy personnel. The Indonesians permitted the release of most of the Navy personnel who had been imprisoned in the city jail since 1 October. They were accommodated at the barracks of the Base Force Land Garrison.

As the night drew on, it began to appear as if the city had quietened down. However, telephone communication between each of the Navy units had been cut off one after the other, and it was now only possible to make a direct call between Headquarters and the Land Garrison. I therefore had no idea of the situation at each of the Navy sections. The Indonesians had strengthened their watch over Fleet Headquarters, and so it was extremely difficult to make communication with the outside world.

On the morning of 6 October two of Capt. Huijer's

subordinates - Maj. de Timmerman, an army doctor, and Maj. Siegers, an accountant - came to Fleet Headquarters to investigate the cash and account books of the 102nd Navy Management Division. They then siezed the cash, worth 2,800,000 guilders, sealed the safe and took it and the key away with them.

In the afternoon of the 7th, the Indonesian rioters occupied the naval base. So that the minesweeping of Surabaya port could continue, I called for negotiations with the Vice-Resident, Sudirman, and he agreed to do his best to cooperate with my proposals. The minesweeping operation had been impossible to carry out since the supplies to these ships had been cut off by the riots.

On 8 October, the Fleet Headquarters liaison officer whom I had dispatched to Capt. Huijer was kidnapped by the Indonesians. The Indonesian authorities in Surabaya had now lost control over the people, and under a situation of near anarchy the rioters were looting and behaving violently at various places throughout the city. The sound of gunshots could be heard continuously all day.

On the 9th and 10th the city deteriorated into a further state of anarchy. At 5 p.m. on the 11th, the British warship **Recruit** and two other ships anchored at the outer end of the northern channel. A torpedo boat guided them into the channel. Wing-Cdr Groom, an Australian Air Force RAPWI officer stationed in Surabaya, called on us at Headquarters to inform us that on that same day every Dutch soldier stationed in Surabaya had been placed under detention by the Indonesian police. He also told us that on the night of the 10th, Capt. Huijer's party had departed by train for Batavia, but they had been kidnapped by a mob in the vicinity of Jombang and had not been seen since.*

12. I Planned to Escape from Surabaya, but Failed

At 1 p.m. on 13 October, the rioters occupied the 102nd Navy Management Division and kidnapped most of the personnel.

On the 14th, I made the following demand to President Sukarno, head of the Indonesian government, through my Chief of Staff in Batavia:

* Capt. Huijer and his party had been taken off the train at Kertosono, past Jombang, and brought back to Surabaya on 11 October to protective detention in the former British Consul's house. On 16 October Huijer and other Allied and RAPWI personnel were transferred to the city jail, from where they were rescued by British troops ten days later.

The ringleaders of the rioters in Surabaya are taking advantage of Japanese paternal concern for the Indonesians. The Japanese are endeavouring to honour international obligations by faithfully carrying out the end of war arrangements, and in so doing are attempting to avoid bloodshed and destruction in the towns and cities. These ringleaders skilfully agitate the masses and use them to indulge in acts of violence and insult. They have seized our weapons and installations and have detained our men. Although they have been pacified to some degree, the fact still remains that the Indonesian authorities and the Indonesian masses have committed a serious violation of international faith. Their actions are regrettable and intolerable. I request you to exercise strict control over these people, and quickly devise some sort of counter measure.

On the 16th, I heard that the Japanese living in Surabaya had been arrested. The city remained in a state of chaos. I had no idea of the exact situation because nearly all communication with the Navy Units and the Army had been cut off. Previously I had decided that I would stay on at Fleet Headquarters right until the end, so that I could maintain communication and liaison with the Allied Forces. But now I realized that there was absolutely no point in staying on any longer here, because it was impossible to communicate with them. Having decided that I should try and move to the warship **Wakataka**, anchored outside Surabaya, I endeavoured to outmanoeuvre the Indonesians, but I did not succeed.

At midday on the 18th the direct telephone line between Headquarters and the Base Force Land Garrison was finally intercepted. At 3.40 that afternoon, Mustopo,* Commander of the People's Peacekeeping Army (TKR), visited me and stated that he had information that a mob was coming to attack Fleet Headquarters to search for any concealed weapons. Since the TKR could regrettably do nothing to prevent this, he requested

* Dr Raden Mustopo (b.1913) graduated in dentistry in 1939. He was among the second intake of officer trainees for the PETA army in 1943, and by the end of the war had risen to **Daidan-cho** (battalion commander), a rank achieved by few Indonesians. The TKR or Tentara Keamanan Rakyat (People's Peacekeeping Army) had been created on 5 October as the army of the Republic, replacing the more informal BKR (Badan Keamanan Rakyat). Both BKR and TKR were primarily recruited from among Japanese- trained soldiers - the PETA/Giyugun and the Heiho. It was frequently the highest-ranking PETA officer who became head of the local TKR.

that this evening we temporarily move out of Fleet Headquarters. Part of my staff and myself went by armoured car and bus to the Hotel Ngemplak (the Navy had used this hotel during the war for the Suikosha), and the others were accommodated at the barracks of the Base Force Land Garrison. We had absolutely no communication with the outside world. Immediately I made the warship **Wakataka** the flagship for communication.

I was lodged at the former residence of the Commander-in-Chief of the Special Base Force. Army Commander-in-Chief Iwabe and his staff officers were billeted at the same place. The first night there were no beds and no mosquito nets. The waiters who worked in the dining room of the former Suikosha where we ate were the same people who had worked there for us during the war. It was lucky that we knew their faces. A man called Atmadji, who had become Navy Commander-in-Chief,* came to visit me there. I had not met the man before, but I was told that he was a former journalist. I said to him, 'Congratulations! Let's celebrate with a beer', so he went out himself to get some beer. He returned and filled my glass up. During the war this hotel had been used as the commissariat of the Army. A group of young officers of the Indonesian revolutionary army, wearing Japanese army uniforms which they had no doubt looted, and looking very important with their Japanese swords, were coming and going from the hotel. They behaved in exactly the same way as the Japanese Army had done ever since the Manchurian Incident. They were crazed with the desire for 'Merdeka'.

We were guarded in this hotel by the TKR, the police and three sentries. I came to dread the changing of these guards, for just as in Japan, they would crash their boots together in unison, and yell out the commands in an extremely loud voice. I sleep heavily in the mornings and loud noises usually do not wake me. However, this noise was deafening and it would invariably wake me. At 10 a.m. on the 22nd, Mustopo, Commander of the TKR, came and announced that Fleet Headquarters had been rescued from the mobs. AT 11 a.m., my staff and myself returned to our old headquarters. A small TKR platoon stood guard, but as usual there was no communication with the rest of Surabaya or Java.

13. Two Sad Events

At 2 p.m. on 22 October I received some tragic news from one of my staff officers in Batavia. There had been a serious

---

* The TKR-**laut**, or naval arm of the TKR, had formed a strong section in the Surabaya dockyard area under Atmadji, a pre-war activist of the left-wing Gerindo party.

clash between the Indonesians and Japanese in Semarang when a mob of Indonesians had tried to seize some weapons from the Japanese Army. One hundred and fifty Japanese had been murdered.* The Japanese killed had been imprisoned in Semarang jail at the time. What was particularly poignant was that just after they had been machine-gunned down, one of them, before he died, had written in blood on the side of the prison wall, a prayer for the success of the Indonesian independence movement. Among those murdered was a man called Saito Fumiya who had been my interpreter when I was Commander at Ambon. His father was an expert on Indonesian affairs, and was known by all the Indonesian nationalists. Saito Fumiya had worked at the Navy Liaison Office in Batavia.

Another of those killed was First Lt. Katayama. He originally piloted carrier-based attack planes, but after the Manchurian Incident he worked for the Greater Japan Aeroplane Company, as a pilot of passenger planes flying between Tokyo and Seoul. After the China Incident he was conscripted, and during the war he was involved in the dangerous task of air transportation in the Solomons and Rabaul theatres. These were areas in which decisive air battles were fought. In 1943 he became chief pilot of the transport planes of the 2nd Southern Expeditionary Fleet. He displayed real skill, both as leader of the Fleet Headquarters' transport plane unit and coordinator of the crews of the '97' flying boats. Most importantly, though, he worked as the exclusive pilot of the Commander-in-Chief's plane, and in that position flew through dangerous areas around Ambon, Timor, Menado and Tarakan. I was often in a plane piloted by him which was involved in near fatal situations. Three such incidents were when I flew with President Sukarno to Celebes and to Bali, and with former Vice-President Hatta to South Borneo. In the last instance our plane was pursued by the enemy, and First Lt. Katayama saved us by escaping through a rift in the clouds. He was an extremely sensible pilot and never took risks. I had enormous confidence in his flying ability. On the way back to Surabaya from the surrender ceremony in Singapore, we were forced to make an emergency landing in Semarang due to damage caused by poor-quality engine parts. Because Katayama had to remain behind until the plane was repaired, he became a victim of this tragic incident. I was deeply grieved to hear the news of his death.

The other piece of tragic news was reported to me by the Commander of the 5th Guard Force stationed in West Java. On 25 October he informed me:

* This terrible slaughter of 15 October, and the even more extensive Japanese reprisals of the following four days, are described in Anderson, **Java**, pp. 146-9.

On the 19th, Capt. Takeshita, Commander Otani and 84 others boarded a train at Batavia bound for a Japanese assembly camp (near Bandung). However, nothing was seen or heard of them past Cikampek. Every effort was made to search for them until the 25th, when the Provisional Indonesian Government reported that the entire group had been murdered by Indonesian rioters. The full details of the incident are still not known.*

I was heartbroken.

14. Farewell Surabaya

On the basis of reports that British troops would soon be landing in Surabaya, the Indonesian Independence Army began hastily to move the Japanese Army in Surabaya to the assembly camp. At 4 p.m. on the 22nd, the Commander of the Special Base Force received instructions from the Indonesians to the effect that the evacuation of Japanese should be completed by 25 October. He reported to me the following orders he had received from the Indonesians:

1. Rear-Adm. Sumiki and 501 others who have been accommodated at the barracks of the Base Force Land Garrison will be transferred to Pujong in Malang Shu.
2. All those remaining will also be gradually evacuated to the same place.

For several days it seemed that the number of rioters in the city had dwindled, and that the situation had calmed down. What had happened though was that the Indonesians had rapidly organized their own army, named it the TKR, and placed it in charge of guarding the city. At 5 p.m. on the 24th a report came in that Sumiki's unit had arrived in Pujong. Another report I received from Sumiki by way of a messenger from Malang indicated that he had received quite different instructions from the Indonesians at Pujong [concerning the evacuation of Navy personnel from Surabaya] from those the Indonesians had given the Commander of the Special Base Force [on the 22nd]. I was puzzled and at a loss what to do [in view of the uncertainty about where we were to be evacuated]. I telegraphed the following two points to the Commander of the British troops:

* This attack must have been a reaction to the Japanese takeover of Bandung on 10 October, at British urging, which had been a bitter humiliation for the **pemuda** Republican movement there. See John Smail, **Bandung in the Early Revolution, 1945-1946** (Ithaca, Cornell Modern Indonesia Project, 1964), pp.58-70.

1. The Headquarters personnel of the 2nd Southern Expeditionary Fleet are accommodated at the Embong Wungu Navy Headquarters; and about 1,600 other Navy personnel, including those of the 21st Special Base Force, are at the Gubeng Land Garrison Barracks. No one is permitted to leave these camps.
2. The Indonesians have made it clear that they will steadfastly resist the Dutch troops.

At 8 pm. on the 25th an Indonesian police officer arrived with a written order from Mustopo, Commander of the TKR. He requested that Fleet Headquarters personnel leave for Pujong at 10 p.m. I was a little doubtful about the authenticity of the written order. This was because Mustopo had promised me, 'Whenever I move you to another place, I will always accompany you'. Indeed he had sat in the same car with me when I was temporarily moved to the Suikosha, and again when I returned to Fleet Headquarters. When I saw him personally order and command even the smallest of operations, I said to him, 'An Army commander in this area surely can't afford to take care of minor operations personally, can he?' He replied, 'The Indonesians don't know how to do anything properly, so I have no alternative but to do it myself'. Since I had no way of verifying the order, I had to obey it. I then telegrammed to the Commander-in-Chief of the 10th Area Fleet, the Minister for the Navy, the Commander of the 16th Army, and my own Fleet subordinates that Fleet Headquarters would move to Pujong. After tidying up and arranging matters at Headquarters, we made some **Hi-no-maru bento** for when we got hungry. We waited and waited but no one came for us. We had nothing to do so we sat down and played solitaire. Still no one had come for us by midnight, so I lay down on the sofa to try and sleep. But I could not sleep at all. It got later and later, until finally, at 4 a.m. on the 26th, they came for us. Mustopo did not arrive, but it was too late by this time to disobey. There was only one bus, so my top-ranking staff and myself boarded this, and the others left by truck.

In January I had raised the admiral's flag at Fleet Headquarters and since then it had been my castle. Ever since the end of the war, though, I had had to face indescribable difficulties in this castle and now I was forced to evacuate it. Samurai in the past probably felt similar emotions when they too were defeated in battle and forced to flee from their castles.

The bus departed and was led through the streets by an armoured car. We soon came out on to the main road. The road to Malang was on the right, but the bus turned left instead. My Deputy Commander-in-Chief, Namaguchi, yelled out, 'Hey, you've gone the wrong way!' but the driver pretended he didn't understand and accelerated. In front of the broadcasting building, he turned in the direction of Gubeng Station. I was alarmed. The bus arrived at the station, and we were told to get out. I tried to argue with them, but they explained that they had brought us here on orders and we were to get on board the train. I was furious to think that I had been deceived. I thought I would try and make a dash for the Land Garrison barracks, but just at that time I heard the sound of gunshots in the direction of the naval port. The British troops had landed. The sound of shooting was close by. Although the Land Garrison barracks were not far away, it was now doubtful whether we could make it there alive. There was no point in dying in vain so I abandoned the idea of escape. The train was going to leave any moment. If we were left behind here we would be completely stranded. The train was packed with the Navy Unit. It was heading towards Malang. I boarded the train and after a short while it departed.

15. My Handling of the End of War Arrangements

When judging whether or not I succeeded in carrying out the end of war arrangements, I feel that one must take into consideration the old proverb that it is easy to throw the first spear but difficult to bring up the rear-guard. Looking back now, I personally don't think I 'performed the job successfully'. Even now I am still grateful for the cooperation I received from my staff officers, my commanding officers and their subordinates. They were all willing to risk their lives in order to help me resolve critical situations.

Since Java was an Army Administration area, it was the Army which was responsible for the maintenance of law and order there. Ever since February 1945 the war operations of the Navy and the entire Army had come under the control of the Southern Combined Army. In the case of Surabaya, then, there was an Army Corps with a Commander. The Commander of the Navy Special Base Force and myself were more senior than the Commander of the Army Corps, but ultimately it was this Army Commander who was in charge of defence and law and order. The Navy was only responsible for the naval port area and the Navy's own buildings and equipment. The political situation in Indonesia became very uncertain and it was obvious that eventually there would be an explosion. Prominent Indonesian citizens began saying that in the event of such a situation I should arise and take the lead. With the consent of the Army, I took over the situation. I assembled these prominent Indonesians at the Suikosha, listened to their views and opinions, and worked out a plan to forestall the crisis. However, the 1 October incident broke out before we concluded our discussions.

When I was a Lt.-Commander I captained a gunboat on the Yangtze River for two years. It was the time immediately after

371

the Nanking Incident. The Japanese Government had decided upon the course it was to take, and so it was relatively easy captaining a patrol ship. Nevertheless, the job of looking after the Japanese residents who lived upstream of the Yangtze River did cause me a great deal of worry. I then went to work in Manchuria and North China, where I learnt how important it was to be not only skilful but also courageous. Still, at the time of the biggest event of this century - Japan's unconditional surrender - I was saddened to think that I had not sufficient mental training. My job of protecting Japanese citizens in Surabaya after the war was much more difficult than the police work on the Yangtze River.

Because of the large number of Japanese in Java, it was impossible to assemble them all in one place and defend them from attack. Therefore, if on 2 October the Land Garrison had not remained calm when they were attacked by 10,000-20,000 rioters, but had resisted, the Japanese living in undefended places throughout the city would have been instantly murdered. Furthermore, even if I had been able to assemble the Japanese in one spot and to protect them for a while, there would have been no reinforcements or relief. We would therefore have been starved into surrender. The Indonesians were wild with the sense of nationalism, and young and old, male and female alike were screaming out 'Merdeka'. Throughout the war the Japanese encouraged the Independence movement, and my staff and I were responsible for this encouragement. Even though the Indonesian people had become riotous, disregarding their international obligations, I could not make them the target for our machine-guns and shoot them down. I believed that such an action would remain as a source of deep regret for Japan for hundreds of years to come, and would thereby serve as an obstacle to Japanese/Indonesian friendship and trade. In addition, my soldiers had fought for their country, and had ceased hostilities in accordance with an Imperial order. If only to retain my dignity as a soldier, I could not order them to go back into war. I was an Admiral of a defeated Navy.

If my decision not to shoot at the Indonesians incurred the displeasure of the Allied Forces, and if it was regarded by them as being a criminal act, I am resolved to accept it as that. I stood by a policy of non-resistance which aimed to bring the situation under control without causing bloodshed. Both my staff and my commanding officers agreed to this policy, and while it was extremely difficult to carry out, in the end we were able to achieve our task. My staff was always willing to go in and out of dangerous areas, even though it meant risking their lives. All of us had thought that the Indonesians were a docile race and were not capable of such radical and violent behaviour. We were wrong. Even now I believe that once the Indonesians started to riot, there was nothing we could have done to stop them. The policy I took in

372

Surabaya (of not shooting at the Indonesians) was the exact
opposite of that taken by the Commander of the 16th Army in
Batavia. I ordered my Chief of Staff, Kinoshita, to attend the
Supreme Conference of the Army and Navy in Batavia, and this is
how he described the opinions expressed at the Conference in
his book **Merdeka**:

> Firstly, the opinion of the Navy as stated by
> Commander-in-Chief Shibata was that in the present
> circumstances, no matter what the situation, the
> Japanese must not resort to armed conflict. There is
> no alternative, in a situation where all other non-
> violent methods of pacification have been exhausted,
> other than to hand the weapons over to the
> Indonesians. In the event of a confrontation between
> Japanese and Indonesians, we have no alternative but
> to bear with their demands. If we are not patient
> with them, the lives of hundreds of thousands of
> Japanese in East and Central Java will be placed in
> jeopardy. Already we have laid down our weapons due
> to an Imperial order, and regardless of what the
> Allied Forces say, it would be absolute stupidity to
> take up our weapons and lose officers and soldiers at
> this late hour...
>
> The atmosphere was tense, and the expression on
> the face of the Army Commander was one of
> disagreement.
>
> The next day, the 9th, the following Army order
> was telegraphed to every region. It opposed outright
> the opinion of Commander-in-Chief Shibata: 'According
> to the orders of the Allied Forces, not one gun must
> be handed to the Indonesians. It is therefore neces-
> sary to use armed force to obey these orders'. This
> was of course an Allied Forces' order which the Army
> had no choice but to issue. Because this predicament
> which the Army Headquarters faced was not communic-
> ated to the units in the field, relations between the
> Indonesians and the Japanese deteriorated seriously.
> In the end, armed confrontation and the massacre of
> Japanese became frequent occurrences. At that time,
> we could not devise a policy upon which both the Army
> and Navy agreed, and which did not take a wrong view
> of things. And so, even today we cannot resist
> feeling repentance...

Even now there remain many points which cropped up during
the rioting which I still do not fully comprehend. For
instance, although Capt. Huijer told the Japanese Army and Navy
that he had 'reached an agreement with the Indonesians' and
therefore we should surrender to him, he was not at all able to
restore law and order at Surabaya. In fact, he himself was

kidnapped by the Indonesians and was not heard of afterwards. Moreover, while the Indonesians on the one hand made firm promises to us, on the other hand they failed to adhere to any of them. Whether this was because they intended to deceive and trick us, or whether it was simply because in the utterly confused state of affairs they were not able to control their men, I don't know. I would especially like to find out, though, why they promised in the first place to send the Fleet Headquarters Staff to Pujong, yet in the end they imprisoned us at Ngawi jail. However, now there is no one left who can explain this to me.

In conclusion, I believe it is appropriate when assessing my handling of the end of war arrangements to apply the old proverb that it is easy to throw the first spear but difficult to bring up the rear-guard. Moreover, I learnt from the Surabaya experience that even though you can resolve to take a certain action beforehand, when it 'comes to the crunch' you begin to doubt your decision. Even though I have experienced more than enough of the heavy responsibilities of the highest in authority, and of hardship which surpasses that of death itself, I still have not had sufficient moral training.

USHIYAMA MITSUO

Conflict in Aceh after Independence

As indicated at the end of Aoki Eigoro's account, the polarization between **uleebalang** aristocrats and their Islamic opponents reached a violent conclusion after the Japanese surrender. The centre of this conflict was the Pidië area of Aceh, with its capital at Sigli, and a few Japanese were on hand to watch the drama unfold.

Capt. Ushiyama Mitsuo was in charge of the small unit which remained in Sigli on Allied instructions after the main Japanese forces withdrew to safer areas in October 1945. Born in Saitama Prefecture in 1919, he had become a postman after leaving school in 1938, but was consripted into the army three years later. After a few months' service in South China and Vietnam (1941) he had returned to Japan to complete a brief officer training course (January 1942). His first assignment as a Second-Lieutenant had been at Tarutung in North Sumatra (1942-43), though he had been in Aceh since the end of 1943.

Ushiyama remained at his post in Sigli until 20 December 1945, feeling increasingly helpless and isolated as the civil war gathered strength around him -- ending in the destruction of uleebalang authority shortly after his departure. Eight months later, immediately after his repatriation to Japan, he wrote down his recollections of this dramatic period while they were still fresh. Much later, in retirement in Tokyo, he had a slightly amplified account mimeographed for circulation among his comrades of the war years.

Ushiyama Mitsuo

HOKUBU SUMATORA SHŪSEN NO KI

[Record of Ending the War in the Northern Part of Sumatra]

The Conflict between PUSA and the Uleebalang

Among the Acehnese of Aceh Shu, which occupies most of northern Sumatra, there was a long-standing conflict between two parties -- the group of sultans and chiefs called the **uleebalang** party, and the progressive Muslim association called PUSA (the initials of Persatuan Ulama Seluruh Atjeh, which can possibly be translated as All Aceh Muslim Association). Sumatra was still lagging far behind the advance of world civilization, with its people locked into the so-called feudal system. The conflict between the two parties seems to have persisted through the period of Dutch colonial rule. This feudalism may in fact have been generated by Dutch rule, which sought to control the population through the landowning uleebalang class, by appointing them as village and district heads* and by transferring to them some degree of administrative and judicial authority. Educational and cultural benefits were enjoyed almost exclusively by this group at the expense of ordinary people, who were left illiterate and forced to work like cattle. The village and district heads employed private policemen,† and it seems that there was always a policeman on guard at their residences.

Class distinctions were very strict here, and the natives had taken it for granted, because of time-honoured custom, that they should be submissive to the uleebalang. This could be seen by the manner of salutation used by male and female servants at the residence of village and district heads. When

---

* In Aceh the village is a small unit of a few hundred families, headed by a **keucik**. The Japanese administrative village is much larger, however, and the uleebalang were designated **Soncho**, usually translated as village head, during the Japanese occupation. It is to be understood, therefore, that the references to village head or Soncho which follow apply to the uleebalang, who ruled on average over about 8,000 people.

† The strength of the uleebalang was traditionally based on his **rakan** (immediate armed followers), while Dutch practice also placed authority for local police in uleebalang hands.

greeting their master they knelt on the ground, stretched out their hands and bowed reverently as if they were receiving something. Women used a handkerchief reverently to take hold of the hands of village and district heads, as if to enfold their hands. The only recognition of this was a slight nod of the head.

The differences in class structure were even reflected in the terms used to address different people -- for instance **tuan besar** (lord), **tuan** (master), **engkau** (you) and **ku** (brother).* Since the Acehnese addressed Japanese soldiers as **tuan**, the Japanese used this word in addressing all Acehnese regardless of class. An uleebalang once complained to us, 'Please don't say **tuan** to such fellows. Call them **engkau** or some such term instead'. People in the Gunseibu were probably careful about these distinctions, but the average soldier could not have cared less. As a matter of fact I seldom used **engkau** myself since it was difficult to pronounce. I always called people **tuan** even if they were peasants or manual labourers. The Dutch had probably been quite strict on this point.

A village head would have a large area of land and live in a fine house. About four kilometres away would be various other villas where beautiful women lived (although the Koran allows a man to have up to four wives, some village heads had as many as six). The village heads wielded a considerable degree of power, since there would always be some villagers of their persuasion who were loyal to their chiefs. PUSA was thus a sort of underground organization with members pursuing their activities clandestinely.

It was PUSA members who, when the Japanese were fighting the Dutch colonial forces after landing in Sumatra, as a result of the expansion of the Greater East Asia War, cooperated with Japan in the initial stages by assisting the landing of the Konoe Division in Aceh and guiding the Japanese soldiers. After the Japanese pacification of Sumatra, the PUSA members seemed to feel that their hour had come and to expect that the Japanese military administration would operate through them. However, things did not proceed as they had expected. I do not know whether this should be blamed on the failings of the Japanese administration or the difficulties in replacing uleebalang in administrative posts by qualified PUSA members. Whatever the case, the Japanese continued the Dutch practice of appointing the privileged uleebalang to most of the important posts, such as village and district headships [**Soncho** and **Guncho**]. The main difference from the Dutch period was that functions of the village and district heads as tax collectors and judicial authorities were removed or limited. These

* Acehnese **ku** in fact means father, and would only be used of an older relative.

functions reverted to the Japanese administration, and the local heads were empowered only to function under Japanese orders and supervision.

From the point of view of the uleebalang, their position was much weaker than in the past, both politically and financially. Their dissatisfaction did not surface, only because of pressure from the Japanese Army. Moreover, the uleebalang must have been seriously inconvenienced by the increased workload and burden resulting from the Japanese defensive preparations against a possible enemy landing, and from the new administrative policies. They may also have been irritated by the Japanese tendency to complain about insufficient uleebalang cooperation with the Japanese. It is understandable that they looked back nostalgically to the Dutch period. The PUSA members were not satisfied either, as their expectations had not been realized, and they were compelled to endure silently because the control of the military made open resistance impossible.

The Merdeka (Independence) Movement

The Japanese Army pushed ahead with the construction of defence facilities through the forced cooperation of the population, and organizing and training the Giyugun. Meanwhile the Gunseibu concerned itself with the policies of social reform and construction which were in the interest of Japan. At primary schools in villages and towns, Indonesian teachers threw themselves into teaching the Japanese language and the singing of Japanese songs under the supervision of Japanese attached to the Gunseibu. From classrooms near the road could be heard the sweet voices of children singing such songs as 'Drawing the Rising Sun in Red on a White Canvas', and 'The Nobility of Pure-White Mount Fuji'. In the streets, too, children would sing Japanese military songs such as 'Aikoku Koshin-kyoku' and 'We Shall Win'.

Thus time passed. The Japanese war position grew ever worse, and at last Japan was defeated... And so the war came to an end. With the news of the Japanese surrender, the Japanese soldiers and the natives alike were for a time in a position rather akin to unemployment. However, a nationalist movement soon sprang up among the natives. At least, the top leaders of the movement in Java seem to have started their activities around the time of the Japanese surrender. The leaders, who had believed Japanese slogans about the establishment of a 'Greater East Asia Co-Prosperity Sphere' and the promises of independence, decided at the Japanese surrender that they would realize the goal of independence on their own. The enthusiasm of these leaders for **merdeka** (independence) was very great, and their spirit spread like a forest fire all over Indonesia. The Republic of Indonesia was proclaimed, with

Sukarno as President and the Minangkabau Mohammad Hatta, born in Bukittinggi in Sumatra, as Vice-President. The leaders set about establishing various organs of government, an Indonesian Army was formed, and the functions of the Japanese administrators in the Gunseibu were taken over by Indonesian officials. Each day change followed change with bewildering speed.

The British forces (from the British and Indian Armies) had been occupying Medan, the capital of Sumatra,* and apart from their measures concerning the Japanese Army on the island they gave indications that it would not be long before the island was once more under white men's rule. The most urgent task the new Republic faced in achieving complete independence, if it were not to be stillborn, was to give substance to its military forces. As everything had to start from scratch, some degree of confusion was inevitable. In particular, the creation of an army produced a situation reminiscent of a pre-battle scene from the Sengoku period [the century of civil war in Japan after 1467]. As the Indonesians were now anticipating fighting not the Japanese but the white man, the strengthening of the Army had to be something more than the mere expansion of existing forces. The leaders moved quickly around the whole of Indonesia, while the natives paraded gravely with rifles and swords. Some were sharpening their parangs (long slender knives), while others kept watch with only bamboo spears in their hands. They demonstrated their fighting spirit at gruesome meetings in various places. However, their serious headache was the lack of arms. The arms of the Japanese therefore tended to become the objects most desired by the Indonesians. Though they had no enmity for the Japanese, their hunger for arms frequently led them to plunder and eventually to perpetrate outrages in which Japanese were killed or injured.

The Military Units Remaining

Prior to the situation described above, the major Japanese forces in North Sumatra were ordered by the Allied Forces to concentrate in the Medan area. The Fourth Regiment of the Konoe Division, under the Divisional Commander, moved to a plantation at Tinjuwan, southeast of Limapuluh in the East Coast Shu, leaving some units of the Regiment behind at their respective posts. The plantation was located about 90 kilometres southeast of Medan. Before the Regiment arrived

---

* Medan was designated capital of Sumatra by the Indonesian Republic in August 1945, though the Japanese (and therefore the incoming Allied Forces) had their headquarters at Bukittinggi, in West Sumatra. The main British force began disembarkation on 9 October 1945.

379

there, it burnt its military flags at Sungei Bisangkar to the southwest of Medan. This, I am told, took place at 10 a.m. on 22 August 1945. The Third Battalion concentrated at a plantation at Tanah Hitam near Tinjuwan.

Among the units which remained were the Second Battalion, led by Maj. Takahara, which was stationed near Kutaraja, the town at the northern tip of Sumatra; and our company, the Eleventh Company of the Third Battalion, which was stationed in Sigli, a small town 100 kilometres east of Kutaraja. Our company eventually comprised 200 men in total, having absorbed one signals squad and several trucks despatched from another company, two rifle platoons under Lts Tsumida, Igarashi, Takaoka and others, and a medical team comprising a few medical orderlies under the military surgeon, Capt. Azuma. In addition, there were various civilians such as **Shiseikan** [Senior Civil Administrator] Muramoto (now Mr Nakata), who had been ordered by the head of the Gunseibu in Kutaraja to come to Sigli as **Fuku-bunshucho** [Sub-district Head]*, Nakamoto, Ogawa and Iwazaki from the Gunseibu staff, and Iseya and others from a Japanese trading company. One battalion of the Konoe Third Regiment was stationed at Langsa, 330 kilometres southeast of Sigli, while another battalion remained at Pangkalan Brandan, a further 90 kilometres southeast of Langsa. These remaining units were ordered by the British Indian Army representing the Allied Forces in Sumatra to maintain order in their respective regions and to look after the buildings (barracks, government offices and public halls), oil-drilling equipment, and so forth which had once belonged to the Dutch Army and to the Dutch colonial government.

Our Eleventh Company had the smallest complement of any of the remaining units dotted over such a broad area. After the major Japanese forces in North Sumatra had hastily withdrawn to Medan, I felt indescribably lost and helpless. Wild fears spread among us -- that we might be abandoned to fall victim to native riots, or sentenced to severe punishment or hard labour, or possibly exiled to some isolated small island by the Allies. However, we managed to overcome these initial fears that we had been marooned, and prepared to meet whatever fate was in store for us. As a first step we cultivated some vacant land around the barracks and planted cassava and sweet potatoes. Moreover, we made countless trips by car to the evacuated battalion headquarters at Lammeulo to collect supplies such as rice, **miso**

---

* Muramoto changed his name after the war to Nakata Eishu. He was a political science graduate of Tokyo University and had been a member of the strategic 'think-tank' of Gen. Iwakura in Tokyo. Posted to Aceh in May 1943, he acquired excellent Indonesian and was used as a political trouble-shooter, particularly in the increasingly polarized Pidie region.

[bean paste], sugar and salt. More important, we also brought back quantities of rifle ammunition, handgrenades and dynamite from Lammeulo, as well as such weapons as rifles and machine-guns made in Czechoslovakia, which we had confiscated from the Dutch during the war. We did this to preserve law and order and to control the number of military weapons. All the arms and ammunition were stored in an armoury and powder magazine made of clay, in the courtyard of the barracks. Since the ammunition at Seulimeum airport and the heavy artillery shells at Lammeulo were too heavy to carry, we were forced to leave them after making an inventory. As for the care of buildings once belonging to the Dutch, maps of them were made by teams of officers and men working for several days, and were then held by the units remaining behind. With the aid of these maps we occasionally patrolled the buildings by car. We had to carry out such tasks in the face of mounting riots, attacks and explosions.

The Violent Demand for Arms

Although such incidents were causing a steady deterioration in the law and order situation, there was nothing we could do about it. Many Indonesians from various organizations came to us for arms - requesting, negotiating, and even threatening. Of course representatives came from the uleebalang as well as from PUSA, each of which was watching the other like a hawk to make sure its opponents did not obtain arms. At the same time they obstructed us on our way to buy vegetables, fish and meat; put a watch on our barracks even at night; and plundered rice, sugar and so forth from our food stores. The tension created by their constantly watching us drove us all slowly neurotic. According to information from Teuku Cut Hasan, a member of the uleebalang party and Guncho of Sigli,* the activities of PUSA were taking on a threatening air and it was planning to destroy the uleebalang. The Guncho and other members of the uleebalang party lived in constant fear. Accordingly, the uleebalang, through the military surgeon Azuma, who had his surgery in the town, and Shiseikan Muramoto, demanded that we hand over about 50 rifles for their defence. The military surgeon and Muramoto tried to persuade us in the following terms:

* Teuku Cut Hasan, younger brother of the uleebalang of Meuraksa, in Aceh Proper, had a good Dutch education and headed the Muhammadiah organization in Aceh from 1935-42. He was appointed Guncho of Pidie and the North Coast of Aceh by the Japanese, and continued in office as Republican **controleur** in Sigli until December 1945.

A clash between the uleebalang and PUSA seems inevitable. In terms of the number of supporters, PUSA is in a far superior position. But if we look at the loyalties of the members of the Sigli unit of the independence army known as TKR, the uleebalang area is in a far stronger position. Under these circumstances the Japanese should secretly cooperate with the uleebalang, the weaker party in the conflict, in order to keep the balance between the two sides and thereby secure the safety of the Japanese unit.

After much deliberation it was decided to hand over a token number of the confiscated rifles, but a means of doing so had to be devised.

As the weapons were coveted by both PUSA and the TKR, they would no doubt be furious if they came to know that such weapons were being secretly supplied to the uleebalang faction, and would prevent us from carrying out our plan or possibly launch an attack on us. It was an undertaking which called for extreme caution.

One night we bundled the confiscated rifles up in mats, loaded them onto a truck, and drove to the surgery which was fortunately next to the Guncho's house. We had put Sgt.-Maj. Yamazaki into the truck on a stretcher, so that we could pretend we were taking a critically ill soldier to the surgery. We travelled several hundred metres, crossed a bridge over the Sigli River, reached the surgery in the centre of the town, and backed the truck into the front garden. A large group of soldiers lifted the stretcher out of the truck, calling encouragingly, 'Are you all right? Take heart', while the patient for his part groaned convincingly. In the meantime, the rifles wrapped in mats were being pushed under the fence of the Guncho's residence, where they were gathered up by the Guncho's subordinates. Such was our little play, and it was a successful presentation. At times during this charade we were almost overcome by the ludicrousness of it all, but there was also the feeling that something bad was happening, in that this was the first step towards handing over weapons. There was also the fear that we might be discovered by PUSA, which would have provoked an incident. The 'invalid', Sgt.-Maj. Yamazaki, must also have been in emotional turmoil.

The Clash of the Two Parties

A few days after the secret delivery of arms to the uleebalang party, a thousand supporters of this party, drawn from rural areas, made a demonstration march towards Gigieng, the principal PUSA stronghold, passing in front of our barracks. Soon one of the PUSA leaders called Husein Sab,* his

* For Footnote see following page.

clothes all worn out, dropped in at the rear entrance of the
barracks. Although he usually wore an insolent grin, he now
looked tragic and even cruel. Breathing heavily, he said,
'Thousands of we PUSA people want to march now into the centre
of Sigli. Please permit us to pass in front of the barracks'.

I asked him, 'What is the purpose of the demonstration? I
suspect you are planning to have a fight with the uleebalang'.

Husein replied, 'No! We simply want to march through the
town. If we PUSA people do not make a show now it will look as
if the Sigli PUSA members had succumbed to pressure from the
uleebalang. PUSA members elsewhere would ridicule the Sigli
PUSA for being spiritless, and we would be condemned by the
PUSA executive. We must therefore show our presence in the
town. We cannot ignore the challenge of the moment.'

Husein also promised not to interfere with the Japanese
Army. But it was quite clear to us that in reality PUSA was
planning to obtain arms from the Japanese by eliminating the
opposing faction.

The factors leading up to this conflict between the two
parties were complex and varied. One of the factors may have
been the manoeuvring of Muramoto. When Muramoto left Kutaraja
for Sigli he was, so I heard, instructed to provoke conflict
among the natives in order to secure the safety of the Japanese
units in Kutaraja, which were under threat of attack by the
natives. Thus, while the plot to maintain the status quo in
Sigli was according to plan, an excessive dose of the medicine
seems to have been administered. In the past Muramoto had
successfully dealt with many incidents caused by the natives.
He was well acquainted with native affairs as a result of his
experience as a civil administrator. As for the independence
movement, he had a deep knowledge of its progress since its
very beginning, unlike us soldiers. He seemed to have great
confidence in the movement and in his own ability to handle it.
He once said to us, 'Please leave to me anything that concerns
movements among the natives in Sigli. As there is a real
danger of the military provoking an unfortunate incident
through some ill-conceived action, I want you to refrain from
any activity in this area'.

Our company did abide by this request, and had it not been
for his efforts in Sigli and our cooperation with them, our
company might have suffered a similar fate to other units, or
even have generated more serious incidents causing still more
casualties than in other units. Only later did I come to know

* Footnote from previous page:
  Husein Sab and his two brothers were small traders from
  Gigieng, near Sigli, and political activists in the PUSA
  cause. Husein had good Japanese contacts and formed one of
  the strongest revolutionary armed units in Pidië.

383

that Muramoto became a marked man for native leaders on account
of his activity (especially his promise to deliver arms at the
time of our evacuation from Sigli), and that even after he
moved to Kuala Simpang he was shadowed by assassins.

*   *   *

*Ushiyama here digresses to praise the role of
Muramoto in the Japanese attack on Langsa (East Aceh)
on 24 December and the maintenance of a defence
perimeter against the Acehnese in that area.*

*   *   *

To return to Husein's request to hold a mass demonstration, I myself became tense, sensing from his mood that developments were taking a serious turn.

'We believe what you have told us, but if even one of your
people were to fire an arrow in this direction we would
retaliate immediately', I emphasized.   Then, to back up my
words, I insisted, 'With your plan of passing along the road in
front of the barracks, there would be no way of being sure you
did not really intend to attack us until you had all passed by.
This would be very confusing and leave the way open for either
side to make a mistake.   Therefore you must turn north at a
point 500 metres east of the barracks and then proceed towards
Sigli along the edge of the coconut plantation which skirts the
coast'.

As this route would involve a wide detour of our barracks,
I anticipated that we would have time to counter in the event
that they did decide to launch an unexpected attack on our
barracks.   I kept my eyes on Husein to see how he would respond
to my conditions.   He replied, 'I understand.   We will
certainly do as you say'.   As he was preparing to leave, I
added as a parting shot, 'If you break your promise we will not
hesitate to fire on you'.   The meeting ended on a very tense
note, and Husein departed.

We stepped up our preparations in case a battle occurred,
decided our strategy and positions, increased the number of
guards, and positioned them at key points around the barracks.
No unusual signs were reported by a lookout on a watchtower
made of bamboos and areca palms.   However, according to
information from a Chinese merchant who regularly delivered
meat and vegetables to our cookhouse, natives and TKR soldiers
of the uleebalang party were deploying along Sigli River in the
town.

Then* an urgent report came from our lookout that a large

* The date was 4 December 1945.

number of PUSA members were gathering in Sukon village, two kilometres east of the barracks. Soon the rest of us could see a long column of people, six or seven abreast, crossing the Sukon bridge and marching towards us. They seemed not to have many rifles, and were jogging along with parangs held aloft. This forest of parangs glittered in the sunshine. We manned our respective positions, prepared for any eventuality. They were drawing closer to the point at which they were supposed to turn northward. We watched tensely. The head of the column suddenly turned to the left [northward], and they proceeded along the promised course. They were all chanting something in unison. It was quite uncanny, sounding like the humming of an enormous swarm of bees. As they drew closer we could see they had palm leaves tied around their necks.

Later I learned that their chant was known as **Perang Sabil,*** a quotation from the Kuran appropriate for a critical battle. I was told, although I cannot vouch for the truth of my information, that according to the **Perang Sabil** a Muslim will go to heaven if he kills non-Muslims, since a battle with non-Muslims is a holy war, and no arrow or bullet would hit a Muslim as a child of God. Such a Muslim would live an idyllic existence in a heaven filled with smiling flowers, singing birds, clear flowing streams, tantalizing sweet smells, beguiling music, and beautiful, seductive women. Apparently one has only to read these words and one falls under their magic spell and wants to kill. It was weird and unnerving that these people should be chanting famous passages from the book, and rousing their emotions to a state of rapture. The palm-leaves decorating their necks were also symbols of combat.

There was an Islamic school about 50 metres from our barracks. On arriving at the school compound, the column demonstrated its fervour by marching around in a circle. With a shout they then split into two groups. I realized that their tactics were for one group to take the road along the coast leading to the concrete bridge over the Sigli River, while the other marched straight on to cross the wooden bridge upriver from the concrete one, and the two groups would attempt to rejoin in the town. Suddenly the column on the upper road, six or seven deep, surged forward to cross the river without making any attempt to utilize the lie of the land, and dashed recklessly in front of the guns of the uleebalang without

* The author may have confused here the brief Kuranic texts presenting righteous warfare (primarily of Madina against Mecca) as a religious obligation, with the lengthy Acehnese poem, **Hikayat Perang Sabil** (Epic of the Holy War), written in the 1880s to exhort Acehnese to fight the Dutch by describing the lavish heavenly rewards awaiting those who died fighting in the way of God.

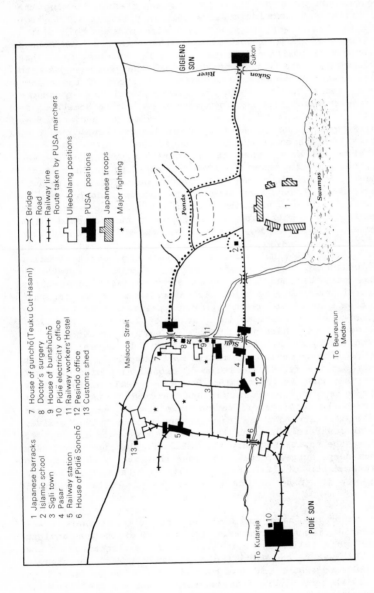

1 Japanese barracks
2 Islamic school
3 Sigli town
4 Pasar
5 Railway station
6 House of Pidië Sonchō

7 House of gunchō (Teuku Cut Hasan)
8 Doctor's surgery
9 House of bunshuchō
10 Pidië electricity office
11 Railway workers' Hostel
12 Pesindo office
13 Customs shed

Bridge
Road
Railway line
Route taken by PUSA marchers
Uleebalang positions
PUSA positions
Japanese troops
Major fighting
★

Sigli, Aceh: 'The first day of the PUSA-Uleebalang Conflict'.

bothering to make a detour. Although the move was made quite fairly and openly, I was in an agony of suspense about the danger involved.

Suddenly I heard a gunshot from the direction of the town **pasar** (market). I had only time to think, 'It's started at last', when the crackle of light machinegun and rifle fire was heard, mixed with the explosion of handgrenades. We did not move outside the barracks, but our men stayed at their posts with their guns trained on the town. Stray bullets occasionally whined over our heads and hit the bamboo walls of the barracks. At last the battle between the two parties had been joined.

It was really a long day. Finally the sun set and the dark fell quickly. In tropical countries evening turns quickly into night. Since there was no point at all continuing the watch through the dinner hour, most of us withdrew into the barracks leaving only a section of the unit on guard. The sound of the light machineguns made me worry that the [Japanese] patrol corps in the town might have joined in the shooting, as the firing of the guns sounded very skilled (tatata-tatata, three point firing, and tatatatata-tatatatata, five point firing). However, when we met up again I was relieved to hear that the patrol corps had not been involved in the battle. I thought it the ultimate in senselessness for the Japanese to become involved in a native uprising. The firing continued intermittently, just as I had foreseen.

Intervention in the Combat

At about 2 a.m. Shiseikan Muramoto came to our camp in a car driven by Nakamoto. He said, 'It would be wrong to let the natives go on fighting indefinitely, as well as being disadvantageous for us. If the two parties were to form a united front directed against the Japanese we could find ourselves in a serious situation. So I am going to visit Pidië (a village about two kilometres away)* to try to persuade the PUSA leaders to stop the fight. In fact the Soncho Pakih Sulaiman, who is an uleebalang leader, and others have come to beg me to intercede and stop the fighting at all costs. Could you come with me to Pidië?'

I decided to go with him. I woke up Sgt. Kobayashi (squad leader of the first platoon), put a pistol in my pocket, and we

---

* Pidië was the name of an ancient kingdom which had given its name to the whole region of Sigli, Meureudu and Lammeulo, but as a result of subdivisions under Acehnese and Dutch rule, the uleebalang of Pidië, Teuku Pakih, was only one of many uleebalang in Pidië region, although his uleebalang-ship (Japanese **son**) embraced the local capital, Sigli.

climbed into the car with Muramoto. Kobayashi is a man of iron nerves. Far from showing any sign of trepidation in joining us, he was smiling. Muramoto's background was that he had met the leaders of both parties, was well acquainted with native affairs, and had a reasonable command of the native language. He was a political science graduate of Tokyo University and had once been a newsman with the **Asahi Shimbun.** He had the inborn samurai disposition of being on the side of justice. He was wearing a white, open-necked shortsleeved shirt and white shorts, with his favourite stick in his left hand and a cigar in his right. His casual appearance seemed at odds with the danger of the mission he was embarking upon, yet I felt it might well be the most appropriate. However, his face looked strained and his eyes were burning.

Since we were driving in the dark there was a real danger of being fired on by both the parties, unless we let them know from a distance that we were Japanese. Muramoto's white clothing showed up well against the night. Kobayashi and I removed our steel helmets and put them on the floor of the car, put on white headbands, and fluttered from the car window a white flag made out of a sheet, as if we were military envoys. I recall the worried look of the soldier on guard as we set off. To tell the truth it was not at all a pleasant experience. My eyes were heavy from days of strain and inadequate sleep, and the cold night air chilled me to the bone. The rain which had begun at about 10 o'clock that night had made the barracks and roads muddy, and it was still raining intermittently as though the pitch-black sky had not fully unburdened itself.

Just as our car was about to cross the wooden bridge leading to the **pasar** we were astounded to see a wall of guns aimed at our headlights, but fortunately we were able to cross the bridge without incident. Along the embankment of the road beside the **pasar**, people, possibly PUSA members, were lying as if transfixed. Twenty or thirty of these rain-soaked natives watched us grimly. From the window we could see what appeared to be dead bodies.

Finally our car stopped in front of the electricity office of Pidië (where there was a small thermal power generator controlled by Teuku Husein). Under the only street lamp in the neighbourhood were assembled several hundred PUSA supporters, armed with bamboo spears and a few rifles with bayonets. Among them we could see Hasan Aly, and the deputy commander of the Indonesian Army, who was said to have come from Kutaraja.*

* Hasan Aly (born 1916) was a Dutch-educated journalist and businessman of Sigli, who had become an assistant secretary of PUSA before the war. From October 1945 he led the PRI (later Pesindo) youth movement in the Sigli area, which

Muramoto spoke eloquently of the need to stop the fighting, suggesting ways of doing so and referring to the Meiji Restoration. He had the air of a tactician from the time of the Sino-Japanese War, even though he lacked the warrior-moustache. He pointed out the futility of the Indonesian people killing each other, explained who the true enemy of Indonesian independence was, and emphasized that independence should be sought through cooperation among all the natives.

We suddenly became aware that we were surrounded on all sides by a rabble of unpleasant-looking soldiers, their eyes hollow with fatigue yet glittering strangely, who were awaiting the outcome of our visit. I felt uneasy because some of the men kept brandishing their parangs about. In any case, the talk led to an agreement and for the second time we drove towards the marketplace in order to meet one of the PUSA leaders, Husein Sab, at the Pesindo Office. However, though we knocked on the shutters and called out there was no answer. A few PUSA soldiers appeared from somewhere around and also called Husein Sab, but still there was no answer. It seemed that he had fled because of the battle the previous night. When we returned to our car we found somebody lying on a cart by the roadside. When we looked more closely we found it was the corpse of a PUSA supporter, his face white through exposure to the rain. At this point we returned to the barracks.

The harrowing night ended, and the second day under constant alert began. During the day the military surgeon, Azuma, treated various wounded natives who were found groaning with pain, while Muramoto continued his parleying. Although only an occasional gunshot could be heard and the battle seemed to have ceased, the strange confrontation continued. Many PUSA people could be seen around the Sukon area and even on the road near the barracks, milling around with parangs and bamboo spears in their hands. There was much aggressive posturing from the two sides.

The shooting started again at night. Muramoto came to us and asked, 'Although I have already persuaded the leaders of both parties to cease hostilities, it seems to be difficult to establish a truce because the orders to do so have not reached the soldiers at some outlying places. I want you to use your forces to take control of Sigli and put an end to the fighting'.

Since we were responsible for guarding the town and

---

* Footnote continued from previous page:
  coordinated the anti-uleebalang struggle. The Army officer mentioned was probably Teuku Hamid Azwar, Chief of Staff of the TKR in Aceh, who was sent with an army detachment after the TKR commander, Sjammaun Gaharu, had been captured by the PUSA group on 4 December.

protecting our units in isolated positions, we decided to intervene in the affair.

Our detachment consisted of about ten men under my command. The barracks had suffered considerably from the long rainy spell, rather like the rainy season in Japan, and my big rubber boots, soaked with muddy water, made an unpleasant squelching noise as I walked. The soldiers looked sleepy and languid as they put on their rubber-soled socks and military boots, covered with red soil and feathers. I went out to the toolshed in the rain and collected three hoe-handles. To these I attached pieces of white sheeting to make white flags, and we set off for the town in two trucks. The time must have been 9 or 10 p.m. On the way we heard heavy gunfire. By the time we reached the railway workers' hostel the shooting had reached a climax, after which it faded away until there was silence once more. Under these circumstances it was out of the question that we should set foot in the town, let alone try to stop the fighting, as any move on our part would inevitably have been interpreted by one of the parties as a move to support the other, thereby resulting in disaster. Even if we were to split into several groups in the darkness and position ourselves at strategic points, this too was likely to provoke a misunderstanding.

I ordered my men to get into the railway workers' hostel, by now quite empty, as quickly as possible. There we huddled together behind the thickest wall of the building. We could hear a violent gunfight outside. From time to time came the strange explosive sound of shells hitting trees in the garden, and the crackling sound of branches falling to the ground. This sound of 'hyun shuru-shuru' was mixed with the explosive 'zu-dan' of the grenades. We passed the time smoking, eating the dried bread somebody had given us, and chatting for a while. Eventually I decided we had better spend the night in the building, and the men settled themselves against the wall of the small room in whatever way they found most comfortable, and fell asleep. I too lay down but, unable to sleep, I got up again and started to read a thin book which happened to be nearby. Just across from me someone else was reading a magazine. The gunfire did not stop. We had had about one hour's rest when a soldier in front of me moved a chair, making a grating noise. Tanaka, who was just in front of me, leapt groggily to his feet shouting, 'Enemy raid! Enemy raid!' and brandishing his gun. Several other soldiers immediately followed suit and tried to rush out the door. I frantically restrained them, saying, 'Wait, wait! It was nothing! Go back to sleep. It was just the scraping of a chair'. The half-wakened soldiers went back to sleep again. They looked like a crowd of sleep-walkers. Looking at the faces of the sleeping soldiers I felt that everybody was exhausted and overwrought, with their nerves completely on edge. I too lay down on the floor, but I slept very badly till morning.

When we awoke, the early morning sun was glaring painfully into my tired eyes. We returned to the barracks, and about noon Muramoto arrived in the style described before, accompanied by Nakamoto and Iwazaki. He asked me for the support of my military forces in helping persuade the PUSA supporters at the Sukon bridge to stop fighting. It was apparent that we had to cooperate with Muramoto's efforts if we wanted to see the matter resolved without getting caught up ourselves in the conflict between the two parties. I and about ten armed soldiers with steel helmets left by truck for the Sukon bridge. As it was daytime we took only one white flag on the truck and did not wear white headbands. Visibility was good, which helped lessen the feeling of uncertainty we had experienced in the darkness the two previous days. However, I felt just as tense as before, since we had to thrust our way in amongst a huge, primitively armed force by following a narrow path surrounded by salt pans and swamps, and since I was not sure what difficult situation might arise should the negotiations be unsuccessful.

On reaching our destination, and while still wondering whether or not to get out of the truck, we were surrounded by hundreds of PUSA supporters. Behind them was a sea of thousands of faces, and from behind these, as far back as the coconut plantation, came the swelling murmur of yet more throngs. Muramoto in particular was jostled by them. Somebody was shouting, 'What have you come here for? Kill them!' There was a seething mass of dissatisfied-looking people. Muramoto for his part was trying to make contact with the leader, calling out his name. A defiant-looking man emerged from the rear, and his followers immediately formed a protective ring around him. We responded by guarding Muramoto in the same way. The tone of their verbal exchanges was very harsh, making me feel that the situation was taking an unexpected turn for the worse.

Muramoto seemed to be being engulfed by the natives, but managed to say to me, 'I am certain that I will be able to win these people over and make my own way back, so don't worry about me, but withdraw your troops immediately'.

I replied, 'It would be dangerous to do such a foolhardy thing. Please try to settle the matter now while we are still with you'.

Muramoto retorted, 'I am convinced I shall be safe, so please withdraw. If you stay here it will only make things more dangerous'.

Muramoto also asked Nakamoto and Iwazaki, who had both accompanied us, to go back. Finally, since Muramoto refused to listen to my repeated pleas that we remain, with a heavy heart I ordered the Japanese soldiers back into the truck. The truck had difficulty turning. As soon as it was under way I looked back, but Muramoto had been swallowed up in a dark mass of natives.

[Back at the barracks] I had guards keep watch on the situation from a distance while I waited, pacing anxiously around the courtyard wondering whether Muramoto would be torn limb from limb. Quite a long time later Muramoto appeared. He came up to me with a daredevil smile and reported the success of his talks with the natives. What follows is his own description to me of what had happened to him in Sukon village.

Muramoto had decided to ask us to withdraw when we were surrounded by over 2,000 natives because he had heard many shouts from the natives like, 'Tuan Muramoto is a traitor! **Potong** (Kill)!* **Potong! Potong!**', and 'You told us not to shoot because you would persuade the uleebalang party to stop fighting, but the enemy has been shooting at us. You are a troublemaker who has betrayed us'. The atmosphere was heavy with the desire to kill. Muramoto felt the situation was extremely dangerous, but that there might be a way out if he were the only Japanese, as the natives would be more excited and not listen to him if he were accompanied by his colleagues (Nakamoto and the others) and the troops. Having thus taken stock of the situation he made up his mind to stay – making this decision in the midst of a mob seething with anger and excitement.

Suddenly he lay on the ground saying, 'Oh, I'm tired', and pretended to fall asleep. This was partly due to the genuine exhaustion brought on by days of insufficient sleep, but it was also a deliberate feint. Although this had the effect of taking the natives by surprise, the voices reviling him did not subside. With his eyes closed he considered his tactics. Exhausted, and overheated by the strong sun, he became extremely thirsty.

After twenty minutes or so he gently raised himself to a half-sitting position, focused his tired eyes on the natives around him, and said, 'Oh, I'm tired. Give me some tea'.

Immediately the natives replied in hostile tone, 'There is no tea here!'

He promptly said, 'If there is no tea, water will do. Bring me some water even if it is muddy. I have not slept a wink since yesterday because of rushing around trying to solve this question. I am completely exhausted'. He lay passively, making no effort to get up, as if he were resigned to his fate and afraid of nothing – not even **'potong'**.

As he lay there a native brought water to him. He drank four or five cupfuls which moistened his dehydrated throat and stomach. In addition to the relief this brought, came the conviction that the crisis was over. 'Since the natives

* Literally 'cut (the throat)'.

brought me water as I asked, I can now take the initiative', he thought, realizing that his intuition had been right.

The angry natives, who had been standing around watching his actions up to now, gradually grew calm. He stood up and began a speech, 'Come now, don't be so angry. I am here not as Muramoto the Japanese, but as Muramoto an Asian like you. As a Japanese I have lost the war and been put under the command of the Allied Forces. So I want to talk to you as a brother Asian. It is very painful for me to see you now. Here you are fighting against the uleebalang, but are not the uleebalang also Indonesians like everybody else? I think this is not the time for the two of you to be fighting each other. Isn't your real enemy somebody else? Look at the situation from a broader perspective. You are talking a lot about **merdeka** (independence), but independence can never be achieved as long as you go on fighting. I have been looking at you from the viewpoint of your **guru** (teacher). If my pupils started fighting for innocent reasons I would not intervene, but when they start fighting at the risk of their lives, how can I, their teacher, stand aloof? Can't you see your real enemy, who is so pleased to witness the spectacle of Indonesians fighting and killing each other, and exhausting their strength?

'I love you too much to be a mere onlooker, and I have been rushing around looking after your interests even at the cost of my sleep. There are some fools among the uleebalang, however, and I was very disappointed to find that some louts have been disrupting my efforts by shooting arbitrarily at you, and betraying you. What benefit would there be for me in cheating and manipulating you? As an Asian I, Muramoto, have struggled to achieve Indonesian independence, even at the risk of my own life, as at the moment. However, if you still insist on calling me a traitor and wanting to **potong** me, then there is no hope for any of us'.

Muramoto went on to talk about the international situation, and then concluded, 'If you do not see the sense of what I am saying, and continue to kill your own countrymen, then do so only after first chopping off my head here and now'.

So saying, he threw his head forward. The throng of natives listened silently to his speech. The younger ones seemed to understand him, and said, '**Tuan** (Muramoto) has studied things a hundred times more than we'.

At this Muramoto heaved a sigh of relief, and immediately went on to talk about how a revolution should be conducted: 'It is the way of Western society to conduct their revolutions in a sharp zig-zag like the teeth of a saw. But revolution in Eastern society is not like that. Eastern society, Japan in particular, prefers a milder undulating curve, avoiding aggressive measures as much as possible and trying to settle matters through discussion. The Meiji Restoration [in 1868]

393

and the Taika Reform [in 645] are good examples. Killing one another is quite inappropriate'.

The anger of the natives seemed to subside slowly, and many of them began to express their agreement with his arguments. I recall that Muramoto had something just visible in his belt that could be a useful tool in bargaining with the native leaders or protecting himself in case of danger. I do not know whether he had recourse to it on this occasion.

So Muramoto returned to our barracks. Shortly afterwards, PUSA leaders began gathering in the yard of the **meunasah** (Islamic school) in front of the barracks. Muramoto went there, stepped up on the elevated platform, and tried to persuade them of the stupidity of fighting and killing among themselves, and urged them to stop the hostilities. Tears streamed down his face as he spoke, and his obvious sincerity succeeded in talking the natives around.

On the morning of the fourth day of the incident [7 December], as I was rubbing the sleep from my eyes and looking about, I saw coming along the road in the mist a procession of old men, women and children, carrying munitions. It seemed that they had come all the way from the village of Gigiëng to the east of Sukon.* The procession was headed by an old man carrying a flag, made from a worn piece of white cloth about the size of a handkerchief, attached to a bamboo stick. Whether or not they were deliberately imitating the idea of our white flag, it was obviously intended to show that the people marching were not combatants.

Both sides seemed to be totally exhausted by the fighting, and stupefied by hunger and by the chill night air. They looked as if all they wanted to do was to go home straight away. I heard that some of the good natives were beginning to criticize their leaders, whom they may have suspected of deceiving them. I could not help feeling sorry for them, with their sad faces and emaciated forms.

In the afternoon Lt. Hino's unit occupied various strategic points around the town, a train was arranged to enable the people of the uleebalang party to withdraw to Beureunun, and the PUSA supporters were made to withdraw to Gigiëng village.† From the barracks I watched the lengthy withdrawal of the PUSA people, as in groups of three and five they headed back to Gigiëng, looking like fugitive soldiers. In this way the war between the two sides came to a temporary halt.

* Gigiëng, about 10 km east of Sigli, was the headquarters of the anti-uleebalang force led by Husein Sab.

† Beureunun was the seat of the rich and powerful uleebalang of Keumangan, and became one of several strongholds where the uleebalang attempted to hold out.

For a few days after the clash the Indonesians could be seen burying their dead comrades. One of the burial places was in the coconut plantation in front of the barracks, and so I named it **Heian Rin** [Peace Forest]. Army Surgeon Azuma told me that when he had visited houses where the dead had been taken and had attempted to clean and dress their bloody wounds, he had been stopped by members of the family, who had shaken their heads firmly and said, 'Please don't do anything to it. This is the pure body of a martyr who died in battle. His spirit is now in Heaven. This brings joy to us as well'.

I thus became aware of the intensity of the people's belief in the relationship between Islam and fighting, and their conviction that anyone who dies fighting the heathens in what they call a holy war will go to a paradise like that described in [the **Hikayat**] **Perang Sabil**, and live there in great happiness.

I heard that in the four-day clash the head of the TKR (the Indonesian Army was later called the TKR), First Lt. Abdoerrahman, lost over 100 men dead or fled, and that at the final count the force had only four men left including Abdoerrahman himself.* Abdoerrahman was the son of the Soncho [uleebalang] of Beureunun, and formerly platoon leader of the Jangkabuya Giyugun unit (the Matsushima unit). In the clash described above he, of course, joined the uleebalang party. At first he had maintained a neutral stance, but he was probably forced to join the uleebalang party for some reason.

---

* Although about 500 people appear to have died in this Sigli incident, the great majority of them were the poorly armed PUSA supporters. Most of the losses to the TKR unit must have been by defections to one of the two warring sides. Teuku Abdoerrahman was the son of Teuku Oemar, the wealthy uleebalang of Keumangan dismissed for malpractice in 1938.

SELECT BIBLIOGRAPHY
of Relevant Books in English

Abu Hanifah, **Tales of a Revolution**, Sydney, Angus & Robertson, 1972.

Anderson, Benedict, R.O'G., **Java in a Time of Revolution, Occupation and Resistance, 1944-1946,** Ithaca, Cornell University Press, 1972.

___, **Some Aspects of Indonesian Politics under the Japanese Occupation, 1944-1945,** Ithaca, Cornell Modern Indonesia Project, 1961.

Aziz, Muhammad Abdul, **Japan's Colonialism and Indonesia,** The Hague, Martinus Nijhoff, 1955.

Benda, Harry J., **The Crescent and the Rising Sun. Indonesian Islam under the Japanese Occupation, 1942-1945,** The Hague/Bandung, Van Hoeve, 1958.

Benda, H.J., J.K. Irikura and K. Kishi (eds), **Japanese Military Administration in Indonesia, Selected Documents,** New Haven, Yale University Southeast Asia Studies, 1965.

Dahm, Bernhard, **History of Indonesia in the Twentieth Century,** London, Pall Mall, 1971.

Donnison, F.S.V., **British Military Administration in the Far East, 1943-1946,** History of the Second World War, London, HMSO, 1956.

Fujiwara Iwaichi, **F. Kikan. Japanese Army Intelligence Operations in Southeast Asia during World War II,** trans. Akashi Yoji, Hong Kong, Heinemann, 1983.

Hatta, Mohammad, **Memoirs,** ed. C.L.M. Penders, Singapore, Gunung Agung, 1981.

___, **The Putera Reports: Problems in Indonesian- Japanese Wartime Cooperation,** trans. W.H. Frederick, Ithaca, Cornell Modern Indonesia Project, 1971.

Kanahele, George S., **The Japanese Occupation of Indonesia: Prelude to Independence,** Cornell University PhD, Ann Arbor, University Microfilms, 1967.

Kirby, S. Woodburn, **The War Against Japan I: The Loss of Singapore,** History of the Second World War, London, HMSO, 1957.

Lebra, Joyce C., **Japanese-Trained Armies in Southeast Asia: Independence and Volunteer Forces in World War II,** New York, Columbia University Press, 1977.

___, **Jungle Alliance: Japan and the Indian National Army,** Singapore, Donald Moore, 1971.

Legge, John D., **Sukarno,** London, Allen Lane: The Penguin Press, 1972.

Long, Gavin, **The Six Years War: A Concise History of Australia in the 1939-45 War,** Canberra, Australian War Memorial, 1973.

McCoy, Alfred W. (ed.), **Southeast Asia under Japanese Occupation**, New Haven, Yale University Southeast Asia Studies, 1980.

Malik, Adam, **In the Service of the Republic**, Singapore, Gunung Agung, 1980.

Newell, William H. (ed), **Japan in Asia 1942–1945**, Singapore, Singapore University Press, 1981.

Nishijima Shigetada, Kishi Koichi et al., **Japanese Military Administration in Indonesia** (translation of **Indoneshia ni Okeru Nihon Gunsei no Kenkyū**, 1959), Washington, U.S. Department of Commerce, Joint Publications Research Service, 1963.

Reid, Anthony, **The Indonesian National Revolution**, Hawthorn, Vic., Longman Australia, 1974.

____, **The Blood of the People: Revolution and the End of Traditional Rule in Northern Sumatra**, Kuala Lumpur, Oxford University Press, 1979.

Sastroamidjojo, Ali, **Milestones on my Journey: The Memoirs of Ali Sastroamidjojo, Indonesian Patriot and Political Leader**, St Lucia, University of Queensland Press, 1979.

Silverstein, Josef (ed.), **Southeast Asia in World War Two: Four Essays**, New Haven, Yale University Southeast Asia Studies, 1966.

Sjahrir, Soetan, **Out of Exile**, New York, John Day, 1949.

Sukarno, **Sukarno: An Autobiography, as told to Cindy Adams**, Hong Kong, Gunung Agung, 1966.

Wigmore, Lionel, **The Japanese Thrust**, Australia in the War of 1939–1945, Canberra, Australian War Memorial, 1957.

INDEX

Abdoerrahman, Teuku, 395.
Abdul Abbas, Mr, 295.
Abdul Djalil, Teungku, 184.
Abdul Hamid, Teungku, 17.
Abdullah, Basuki, 74-5.
Abdul Rahman, Tengku, 18.
Abdul Wahab, Teungku, 19, 21.
Abe, Toshio, 133.
Abikoesno Tjokrosoejoso, 259.
Abu Bakar, Said, 11, 12, 13,
    14-16, 18, 19, 21, 22, 24,
    25, 26, 27, 28, 179, 180,
    185, 187-90.
Abu Hanifah, 1.
Aceh: anti-Dutch revolt of March
    1942, 9-30, 177, 179-80;
    post-independence conflict
    in, 190, 375-95; reform of
    judicial and religious
    systems in, 179-90;
    sultanate, 179, 181. See
    also Aoki Eigorō; Fujiwara
    Iwaichi; Ushiyama Mitsuo.
Aceh Shū Kōgun Kyōryoku Shi,
    180.
Adachi (of Java Gunseikambu),
    260.
Adachi Takashi, Lt., 178, 190.
Agricultural methods, Japanese,
    175, 248.
Agricultural training institu-
    tion. See Talapeta.
Agura, Sgt., 204.
Ahmad Abdullah, 19.
Aidit, D.N., 309.
Air-raids, Allied: on Makasar,
    145-6, 150, 282; on North
    Sumatra, 202.
Almujahid, Teungku Amir
    [Hoesain], 17.
Aly, Hasan, 388-9.
Ambarawa, 334, 336.
Ambon, 159, 267, 277, 368.
Amin, Mr S.M., 181.
Amir, Dr Mohammad, 295.
Anami (Vice-Minister, Army),
    131.
Antara, 255.
Aoki, Lt.-Gen., 63.
Aoki Eigorō, 3, 10, **177-90**.
Aoki Kazuo, 271, 272, 273.

Arif, Teuku Njak, 17, 23, 26,
    181-2, 184.
Arifin Tobo, Tengku, 88,90-1.
Ariga (President, Tokyo Uni-
    versity), 133.
Arms: Japanese procurement of
    Dutch, 13, 26, 33, 47;
    supply of to Indonesians,
    218, 223-4, 231-3, 258, 277,
    328-38, 355-9, 373, 379,
    381-4.
Arnhemia, 82, 83, 84, 86, 87,
    94-5, 99, 101, 102, 215.
Aron: problem of in East
    Sumatra, 83-9; suppression
    of, 89-104, 109.
Asahan, 201.
Asari Seiichi, 162-3.
Asia Raya, 269.
Asrama Indonesia Merdeka
    (Dokuritsu Indoneshia Juku),
    302-10, 315, 316.
As-Siddiqy. See Hasbi
    As-Siddiqy.
Atjeh Sinbun, 177-8, 182.
Atmadji, Navy Commander-in-
    Chief, 367.
Australia: fear of attack from,
    220, 222, 225-6, 229, 231,
    248; Japanese invasion plans
    for, 55, 56; Japanese POWs
    in, 252, 279.
Australian troops: in Borneo,
    229, 282, 341; in Java,
    36-8, 47, 48.
Ayabe, Lt.-Gen., 237.
Ayukawa (of **Mainichi** newspaper),
    347-8.
Azuma Ryūtarō, Prof., 133,
    264-5, 380-2, 389.
Azwar, Teuku Hamid, 388-9.

Bagan Siapiapi, 18.
Baitul-mal, 189.
Bali, 2, 143, 144, 223, 296;
    nationalists visit, 284-7.
Balikpapan, 143, 144, 233, 341.
Banda Aceh. See Kutaraja.
Bandung, 231, 232, 260, 265,
    268, 338; Japanese capture
    of, 36-52 passim; Japanese

takeover of Oct. 1945, 228, 369.
Bangkok, 9.
Banjarmasin, 283-4.
Banten, 33, 302.
Banyumas, 338.
Bapak Janggut. **See** Inoue Tetsurō.
Barisan Berani Mati, 236.
Barisan Harimau Liar (BHL), 200, 201.
Barisan Naga Terbang, 200.
Barisan Pelopor, 236.
Barisan Sabilullah, 200.
Bataks. **See** Karo; Toba.
Batavia (Jakarta), 345, 351, 363, 373; as 16th Army HQ, 39, 49, 53, 55, 67, 71. **See also** Jakarta.
Batusangkar, 173-5.
Beureu'eh, Teungku Mohammad Daud, 14, 17, 26, 177, 180, 181, 182, 184, 185, 188, 190.
Beureunun, 394, 395.
Bireuen, 188.
BKR. **See** Indonesian Peace-Keeping Organization.
Black Dragon Society, 262.
Blangkejeren, 180.
Blang Pidiĕ, 24.
Blitar, 4; rebellion in, 226-9, 232.
Body for the Investigation of Indonesian Independence (BPKI), 199, 311, 314-15.
Bogor (Buitenzorg), 36, 39, 49, 222, 233, 267.
Bone, Raja of (Andi Mappanjuki), 282.
Borneo (Kalimantan), 2, 71, 144, 264, 278, 283, 304; Minseibu office in, 131, 134, 144, 147.
Borneo, North, 60.
Brastagi, 109, 191, 216.
British Army: instructions to Japanese, 329, 331, 337, 346-7; in Medan, 379, 380; in Sura- baya, 359, 369-70.
Budi Utomo, 268, 323.
Bukittinggi, 174, 177, 182, 289, 290, 293, 295, 379.
Burma: independence in, 279, 280; Japanese operations in, 55, 225, 229, 290, 343.
Burma National Army, 29.

Bushidō, 10, 77.

Calang, 24.
Caron, L.J.J., 180.
Celebes (Sulawesi), 144, 264, 278, 304; Minseibu office in, 131, 134, 140, 146, 281.
'Centre' (chūō), 53, 55, 59, 65, 294, 295; views of on Java administration, 56-8.
Ceram, 144; Minseibu office in, 131, 134, 143, 144, 159.
Chadidjah (wife of Jacub Siregar) ('Murni'), 4, 80, 81, 82, 90-3, 104-9, 192, 193, 197, 206, 209-10, 213; birth of Abdi, 195-6.
Chairuddin, 302.
Chian Iji Kai, 26.
China: Japanese experience in, 31, 38-9, 47, 50, 57, 59, 219, 221, 277, 289, 371-2, 375, 389. **See also** Manchuria.
Chinese: antagonism to Japanese, 343-5; merchants, 43, 54, 158.
Christison, Lt.-Gen. Sir Philip, 348, 351, 363.
Chūō Sangi-in (Central Advisory Council), 120-1, 272, 291-2, 293, 294, 304, 311, 356.
Cikampek, 369.
Cilacap, 33, 37, 48, 229.
Cipinang prison, 75-7.
Cirebon, 226, 333.
Committee for the Preparation of Indonesian Independence (PPKI), 199, 202, 252, 295-6, 311, 314-15, 356; and independence proclamation, 318-24, 326-7.
Communications: in Aceh, 13, 16, 20-6; in eastern Indonesia, 156; in Java, 34, 36, 70.
Communism, 265, 306. **See also** PKI.
Cotton, production of, 153.
Courts. **See** Judicial system.
Cultural programmes, Japanese, 155-6, 159-60.

Darwis, 315.
Deli, 79; aron problem in, 82-104.

Denpasar, 168, 170, 286;
    Teacher Training Institute,
    162.
Dewantara, Ki Hadjar, 122, 272,
    273.
Diah, Burhanuddin Mohammad, 269.
Djamaluddin ('Adinegoro'), 194.
Djamil Djambek, Sjech Mohammad,
    293.
Djamin, Dt., 115.
Djojohadikusumo, Margono, 1.
Doi Akira, 271.
Dōmei Tsūshin, 105, 255.
Douwes Dekker, E.F.E., 252, 272.
Duabelas Kota, 95, 101.
Dutch, 179-80; antagonism
    towards, 12, 14, 17, 21;
    Japanese employment of, 54,
    58, 70; reoccupation of
    Surabaya, 348-9; violence
    against, 21-5, 350-1.
Dutch East Indies Army (KNIL);
    surrender of, 25, 40-9, 219.
Dwidjo[sewoyo], Mr, 360-1.

Education: in Bali, 159-71,
    286; in eastern Indonesia,
    154-5; in Java, 63, 68-9;
    in Sumatra, 173-5, 378.
Eguchi Mitoru, 134.
Eguchi Toshio, 135.
Endō Naoto, 144.
Endō Saburō, Maj.-Gen., 37, 46.
Engineers, Indonesian, 225, 244.

Fifth-column movements, 9-28,
    252, 253, 255, 262, 280-1.
    See also F Kikan; Maeda;
    Nishijima.
Fishermen's Association, 201.
F Kikan, 9-30, 86, 87, 107, 177,
    179, 180, 181, 184, 185, 187,
    189, 190, 201.
Foreign Affairs, Ministry of
    (Gaimushō), 40-1.
48th Division, General Southern
    Army, 225-6, 229, 231.
Fujiwara Ginjirō, 130.
Fujiwara Iwaichi, 9-30, 180.
    See also F Kikan.
Fujiyama Aiichirō, 130, 139.
Fujiyama Ichirō, 140.
Fukudome, Vice-Adm., 342-5.
Furui Yoshimi, 132.

GAFI (Gabungan Fucheyama
    Indonesia), 24.
Gaharu Sjammaun, 389.
Gambir Square, 313, 329-31. See
    also Koningsplein.
Gani, Doctor A.K., 212.
General Southern Army, 20, 28,
    33, 37, 55, 59, 60, 63, 71,
    117-18, 221.
Gerindo, 115, 198, 200, 254,
    312, 367; association of
    Siregar with, 80, 81, 88, 89,
    91, 107, 201.
German: artist, 285; contact
    with Sumatra, 202; invasion
    of Netherlands, 17.
Gigiëng (Aceh), 25, 382, 383,
    394.
Giyūgun, 175, 189, 198, 217,
    236, 246, 256, 304, 330, 334,
    335-7, 366, 378, 398; arms
    to, 223-4, 227, 231-3;
    dissolution of, 327-8, 361;
    establishment of, 3, 220-4;
    and independence proclama-
    tion, 317-19; plans for,
    222, 232-3; rebellions of,
    202, 226-9; training of,
    232-4. See also PETA.
Gotō Masao, 144.
Gotō Takanosuke, 132.
Greater East Asia Co-Prosperity
    Sphere, 29, 159, 256-7, 271,
    378.
Greater East Asia War, 145, 154,
    161, 206, 293, 299, 310, 321,
    377.
Groom, Wing-Cdr., 365.
Guadalcanal, 149-50.
Gubeng, 370, 371.
Gunsei Kikan, 179, 180.

Hadikusumo Ki Bagus, 121.
Haga, Dr B.J., 268.
Hakkō ichiu, 53.
Halim, K.H. Abdul, 121.
Hamid, Teuku Azwar, 202.
Hamka, 1, 293.
Hana Kikan, 279.
Harada Kumakichi, Lt.-Gen., 221,
    280.
Harada Kumao, 129.
Harada Yoshikazu, Maj.-Gen.,
    33-4, 37, 49, 52, 54, 60.
Hasan, Jusuf, 252, 262, 267.
Hasan, Mr T.M., 295.

Hasan, Teuku Cut, 381.
Hasan, Teuku Mohammad, 181-2, 184.
Hasan, Teungku, 188.
Hasballah, Teungku Haji Ahmad, 19, 184.
Hasbi As-Siddiqy, Teungku Mohammad, 11, 12, 14, 188.
Hashimoto, 21.
Hashimoto Kingorō, 140.
Hasjim, K.H. Wachid, 121.
Hasjmy, Ali, 18, 19.
Hatta, Mohammad, 1, 74, 75, 120, 121, 235, 258, 259, 260, 270, 284, 303, 307, 308, 330; assassination plan for, 122-4; kidnapped by youth, 300, 315-18; and independence proclamation, 313, 319-24, 327; and Miyoshi, 113, 115, 122-4; and Nishijima, 251, 254-5, 272; tour of Navy areas, 3, 280, 283-4, 368; in Tokyo, 125; and Vice-Chairmanship of Chūo Sangi-in, 121-2; as Vice-President, 296, 379.
Hatta Kikan (Kantor Penasehat Umum), 114-15, 122, 123, 259, 260-1.
Hattori, Col., 55.
Hayasaki (Mayor of Medan), 90, 91.
Hayashi Kyūjirō, 53, 75, 329.
Hayashi Masaki, Lt.-Col., 231, 232.
Health care, 133.
'Hearts and minds' policy: in Java, 217, 218, 219, 223, 228, 235; in Sumatra, 290-2.
Heiho, 175, 198, 220, 222, 225, 230, 232, 233, 235, 246, 256, 304, 319, 361, 366.
Helfrich, Admiral C.E.L., 348.
Hikayat Perang Sabil, 385, 395.
Hino, Lt., 394.
Hi-no-maru (Rising Sun): flag, 96, 97, 262; symbol, 262-3.
Hirano Sakae, 3, 289-96.
Hirose Toyosaku, 140.
Hiryūtai (Flying Dragon Corps), 200.
Hizbullah, 236, 304.
Hōkōkai, Jawa, 235, 272, 278, 306.
Honda Akira (Kumazawa), 226.

Honjō, Gen., 131.
Horiuchi, Capt., 285.
Hotel de Boer (Medan), 210, 211.
Hotel des Indes (Batavia), 61.
Hotel Oranje (Surabaya), 350, 364.
Houston, USS, 33.
Huijer, Petrus J.G. (Capt.), 348-9, 352, 355, 362-5, 373-4.
Husein, Teuku, 388.

Igarashi, Lt., 380.
Iino Shōzaburō, 177.
Iizuka Choichi (Takahisa), 137-8, 146.
Ikeda Seihin, 133.
Imai Hidebumi, 135.
Imamura Hitoshi, Gen., 2-3, 31-77, 221; and Dutch surrender, 40-9, 219; imprisonment of, 75-7; and Javanese Princes, 118-19; lands in Java, 33-9; military administration of, 52-66; and Sukarno, 70-5, 114; trial of, 65-6.
Imaoka Yutaka, Col., 248.
Ina Hirofusa, 161.
Inada, Maj.-Gen., 221.
Inderamayu, 226.
Inderapuri (Aceh), 19, 22, 184.
India: Japanese operations in, 55, 56.
Indian Independence League (IIL), 13; conferences of, 16, 20.
Indian National Army (INA), 13, 20.
Indonesia Muda, 300.
Indonesia: national anthem of, 203, 272, 280, 304, 329; national flag of, 203, 212, 262-3, 269, 272, 280, 281, 286, 299, 304, 328-9, 350, 359, 360; plans for first cabinet in, 259.
Indonesian Army (TKR), 76, 357, 360, 363, 366-7, 369, 370, 382, 384, 389, 395.
Indonesian independence: aspirations for, 115, 200, 205, 217-18, 222, 283, 301-2, 304, 361, 367, 372, 278, 393; Japanese attitude to, 3, 29-30, 71, 80, 142, 162, 227,

228, 257, 262-3, 269-71, 274-5, 278, 280, 287, 292-6, 303-6, 356, 368, 372, 383, 393; proclamation of, 211-12, 296, 323-8, 342; or Sumatran independence, 294-5.
Indonesianization, 73-4, 154, 191, 221, 223.
Industry, development of, 143, 145, 149, 156.
Inoue, Sen. Adj., 41.
Inoue Kōjiro, 134, 144, 147.
Inoue Tetsurō, 3, **79-109, 191-216**; in hiding, 208-16; and Kaijo, 196-7; and KTT, 197-207; relationship with 'Murni', 4, 104-9, 195-6; and suppression of aron, 82-104; and Talapeta, 191-6.
Ipoh (Malaya), 14.
Irie Seiichirō, 152.
Iseya, 380.
Ishii Akiho, 60-1.
Ishii Tarō, 255.
Ishikawa Shingo, Capt., 129, 130, 135, 136, 146, 147, 148, 149.
Iskandar di Nata, Raden Oto, 228.
Islam: Japanese attitudes towards, 3, 15, 158, 177, 182, 293; law, 182, 184-5, 188-9; movements, 12, 14, 17, 184, 188, 272. **See also** Muhammadiah; PUSA.
Islamic oath, in Aceh, 22-3.
Isoya Hirosuke, Lt.-Gen., 131.
Itagaki, Gen., 237, 344-5.
Itō Kenzō, Rear-Adm., 135-6, 141, 146, 149.
Iwabe, Maj.-Gen., 226, 352, 367.
Iwakuro, Gen., 380.
Iwan. **See** Siregar, Mohammed Jacub.
Iwasaki Takehiko, Capt., 136.
Iwashige Takaharu, 338.
Iwazaki, 380, 391.
Izuwa, 132, 134.

Jakarta (Batavia), 120, 144, 295, 300, 302; Law School, 263; Medical College, 263-4, 266, 319; Navy Liaison Office, 279. **See also** Batavia; Gambir Square.
Jalil (agriculturalist), 102.

Japanese: bad behaviour of, 61-3, 140, 227, 256, 272; enthusiasm of teachers, 161-5; language, spread of, 67-9, 145, 155, 165-8, 305, 378; reactions of to Indonesia, 1-3, 34-6, 49, 54, 137, 154-5.
Japanese administration: calibre of personnel, 2, 127, 132-5; division of responsibility, 2, 58-9, 73, 117, 127, 130, 253, 261, 264, 272, 277, 321; mistakes of, 29-30, 214, 234, 236, 247-8, 262-3, 265-9; records of, 1, 159, 218.
Japanese Army-Navy conflict, 117, 135-6, 140-2, 146-52; over independence issue, 218, 277, 280, 320-1, 325-7, 373.
Japanese Imperial Headquarters (Daihon'ei), 20, 183, 220-1.
Japanese surrender, 30, 175, 190, 206-8, 211, 293, 295, 299, 300, 301, 302, 308, 311-15, 319, 325-7, 341-2, 350, 378, 380.
Japanization policy, 2, 3, 79, 158, 160, 236, 305, 310.
Java: as Army supply base, 222, 223, 225, 230, 237-50; Japanese plans for defence of, 55-7, 229-32, 247; 'soft' policy towards, 2-3, 31-2, 52-6, 65-6.
Joenoes Djamil, Teungku Mohammad, 18, 26, 180, 181, 184.
Jombang, 365.
Judicial system: in eastern Indonesia, 154; reform of, in Aceh, 181-9.
Junkyōtai (Martyr Corps), 200.
Jusuf, Abdullah, 201.
Jusuf, Maj. A.K., 309.

Kahin, G.M.T., 265.
Kaigun. **See** Navy.
Kaiho Yoshio, 134, 137.
Kaijō Jikeidan, Tōkaigan Shū, 196-7, 200, 214.
Kaikyō Hōin (Religious Court), 184-5, 187-9.
Kalijati airport, 37, 40, 41, 43, 50.

Kalimantan. See Borneo.
Kamakura Maru, 135, 136, 140, 159.
Kanahele, George S., 306.
Karasawa, 312.
Karo Bataks: aron activities among, 85-104; and KTT, 203-4.
Karo-Karo, Gumba, 89.
Karo-Karo, Kitei, 89.
Kasim, Mohammad, 201.
Kasman Singodimedjo, 332.
Katayama, Lt., 283, 368.
Katsumata Minoru, 133.
Kaya Okinori, 133.
Keibōdan, 235-6.
Kempeitai (Military Police), 4, 27, 58, 61, 76, 107, 181, 197, 198, 202, 294, 300, 302, 330, 331-2, 335-6, 345, 351, 357; and aron problem, 83-94; and Hatta, 122-5; and nationalist leaders, 267-9, 316, 319, 320; and Nishijima, 273-5; and Subardjo, 260-1.
Kenkoku Teishintai (KTT): in East Sumatra, 80, 81, 214; establishment of, 197-206; dissolution of, 207-8.
Kertapati, Sidik, 309.
Kesatuan Melayu Muda (Malaya), 9, 13.
Keumangan (Aceh), 394, 395.
Keumiroe bridge, 22, 26.
Kimura, Gen., 342, 343.
Kinoshita, Lt.-Gen., 342.
Kinoshita (staff officer), 281, 341, 357-8, 373.
Kintamani (Bali), 285-6.
Kisaran (Sumatra), 201.
Kitajima Kenjirō, 53.
Kita-Sumatora-Sinbun, 194.
Kobayashi, Sgt., 387-8.
Kobayashi trade mission of 1940, 113.
Kobayashi Yukio, 134.
Kodama Hideo, Count, 53, 54, 65, 73, 142.
Koesoemo Oetoyo, R.M.T., 122.
Kōgen Shrine (Medan), 211.
Koiso Kuniaki (Prime Minister): statement of 7 Sept. 1944, 225, 269, 279, 303-4, 306, 314.
Kokubu (Chief of Staff), 225.

Koningsplein (Batavia), 67, 319, 329. See also Gambir Square.
Konoe Division, 20, 21, 25, 28, 59, 377, 379-80.
Kōno Yoshitada, 50, 69.
Koshino Kikuo, 144, 285.
Koyama Itoko, 194.
Krueng Raya (Aceh), 25.
KTT. See Kenkoku Teishintai.
Kuala Selangor (Malaya), 16, 18, 19.
Kuala Simpang (Aceh), 384.
Kubota Yoshimaro, 134-5.
Kunto, Jusuf, 317.
Kurai Hajime, 190.
Kuroda, Lt.-Gen., 63-4.
Kutacane (Aceh), 180.
Kutaraja (Banda Aceh), 18, 19, 20, 22, 23, 26, 29, 177, 179, 180, 182, 183, 184, 185, 187, 189, 380, 383, 388.
Kyōdo Bōeidan (Fatherland Defence Corps), 205-6.
Kyōdo Bōeigun (Home Guard), 317.

Labohan Aji, 19, 25.
Lammeulo (Aceh), 380-1.
Lamno (Aceh), 24.
Langkawi Island, 185.
Langsa, 380, 384.
Latuharhary, Mr Johannes, 264, 267.
Lau Cih, 87, 89.
Law: students, 115; courts, see Judicial system.
Leyte, 225.
Lhoknga air base, 22, 23.
Lhokseumawe, 29.
Lhoksukon, 11, 17.
Lubis, Zulkifli, 330.
Lukman, Mohammad, 309.

MacArthur, Gen. Douglas, 48, 127, 326.
Machida Keiji, Lt.-Col., 37, 68, 75.
Madura, 226, 364.
Maeda Naomi, 338.
Maeda Ryūichi, 134.
Maeda Tadashi, Adm., 144, 253, 257, 263, 269, 270, 271, 279, 280-1, 305-7, 313-14, 345-6; and independence proclamation, 217-18, 251, 315-24, 325.
Magelang, 334, 336, 337.

Mahmud, Tuanku, 177, 179, 180, 184.
Maibkatra, 180.
Makasar (Ujung Pandang), 128, 131, 134, 146, 152, 264, 265, 279; air-raids on, 145-6, 150, 281-2; internment camp at, 282; life-style in, 136-40; nationalists' visit to, 269, 281-2; Research Institute, 156.
Malang, 49, 144, 268, 369, 370, 371.
Malaya: Japanese in 9, 13-14, 16, 18, 29.
Malik, Adam, 251, 254-5, 257-8, 259, 268-9, 302-3, 317, 318.
Manaki, Maj.-Gen., 27, 28.
Manchuria, 31, 53, 131, 217, 219, 367, 368.
Manchurian Railway Company, 289, 290.
Mangku Negara, 118, 120.
Mansoer, Kiyai Haji Mas, 121, 272, 273, 275.
Mansur (KTT Officer), 201.
Mansur, Dr Tengku, 194.
Maoe Shigesaburō, 134.
Maramis, A.A., 252, 259-60.
Martoatmodjo, Dr R. Buntaran, 122, 311.
Maruyama Masao, Lt.-Gen., 36, 39, 47, 76.
Marxism, 299-301, 309-10.
Masaki, Hanri, 17.
Mase Battalion, 336.
Masu Genjirō, 262, 263.
Masubuchi Sahei, 11, 13, 14, 16, 20-1, 26, 27, 28, 29, 190.
Matahari newspaper, 254.
Matsue Haruji, 130.
Matsumoto Noriaki, Dr, 257.
Matsuura Kōjirō, Lt., 333.
Medan, 18, 20, 202, 299, 301, 379, 380; and F Kikan, 10, 18, 26, 28-9, 107; as Inoue's base, 79-109, 191-216 passim.
Melaka Straits, 12, 13-14, 16, 28, 197.
Melik, Sayuti, 312, 319, 323, 324.
Mellsop, Lt.-Col. J.A., 329.
Menado, 143, 144, 285, 368.
Mengwi, 163.
Merak, 33.

Midway Battle, 136-7.
Mikawa Gunichi, Vice-Adm., 148.
Military Academy, Yogyakarta, 76-7.
Minahassa, 267.
Minami Kikan, 30.
Minangkabau, 13, 16, 18, 20, 174, 188, 292.
Mineral exploration, 156.
Minseifu. **See** Naval Civil Administration.
Miyamoto Shizuo, 3, **4**, **217-50**, **325-34**.
Miyoshi Shunkichirō, 3, **113-25**, 261, 266; at Dutch surrender talks, 40-1, 43-6, 47; and Hatta Kikan, 114-15; and independence proclamation, 321, 324; intervenes for Hatta, 4, 122-4; and Princely Territories, 116-20.
Mizuike Ryō, 132, 134, 136, 141, 146-7, 148, 149, 151-2.
Mōkotai (Wild Tiger Corps), 200, 201.
Moluccas, 278.
Mori (Commander, Base Force, Makasar), 137.
Mori Fumio, Col., 237.
Mori Hideo, 248.
Mori Katsuei, 144.
Mori Naoki, 135.
Morita (authoress), 140.
Morita Shōji, 66.
Morotai, 225, 229, 244.
Mountbatten, Lord Louis, 342, 344, 346.
'Muchtar affair', 266-7.
Muda, Teuku, 17.
Muhammadiah, 121, 181, 188, 272, 381.
Mukai, 62.
Muramoto (Nakata Eishū), 380, 381-4, 387-94.
Murase, Lt.-Col., 123-4.
Mustopo, Dr Raden, 366, 367, 370.
Mutō Akira, Lt.-Gen., 56, 60; in Java, 56-8; in Sumatra, 58-60.

Naga Yukinosuke, Maj., 274-5, 331-2.
Nagai, Col., 333.
Nagai Ryūtarō, 284.
Nagano, Gen., 345.

405

Nagano Shirō, 135.
Nagata Hidejirō,60, 65.
Nagatani, Gen., 270.
Nakagawa, Col., 333.
Nakagawa Masakazu, 330.
Nakamiya Gorō, Lt., 11, 12, 14,
    16, 17, 27.
Nakamoto, 380, 387, 391, 392.
Nakamura, Lt.-Gen., 342, 343.
Nakamura Junjirō, Maj.-Gen.,
    333-8.
Nakamura Kenjō, 133, 134.
Nakamura Toshihisa, 141.
Nakashima Tetsurō, Lt.-Gen., 79,
    80, 83-6, 89, 90, 91, 92,
    93-4, 101-2, 103, 104-5,
    108-9, 191, 197-9, 202,
    205-6.
Nakata Eishū. See Muramoto.
Nakatani Yoshio, 319, 320.
Nakayama Jirō, 244.
Nakayama Yasuto, Col., 49, 52,
    54, 61-2, 71-3, 74, 118.
Namaguchi, 370.
Namo Rambei (East Sumatra),
    95-7.
Nanyō Kyōkai, 53.
Nasu, Maj.-Gen., 39.
Natal (Sumatra), 16, 18.
Naval Civil Administration
    Office (Minseifu), 280;
    conflict with military,
    140-2, 146-9, 150-1;
    establishes local administra-
    tions, 142-4, 153-4;
    structure of, 130-1, 281.
Navy, Japanese: and
    independence movement, 251,
    252, 270-3, 277, 279-87, 304,
    313-24, 325-7.
'Navy group', 252, 259, 303,
    311, 318.
Navy Liaison Office (Kaigun
    Bukanfu), 144, 252-3, 254,
    259, 279, 305, 313, 315,
    325-6, 327, 368.
Neighbourhood Associations
    (Tonarigumi), 235.
New Guinea, 144, 150, 220, 222,
    244, 261.
Ngawi jail, 374.
Nishijima Shigetada, 217,
    251-75, 279-81, 299-324; in
    Australia, 252, 255, 262,
    263, 312; and Dokuritsu

Juku, 302-10; and indepen-
    dence declaration, 311-24;
    and Kempeitai, 4, 260-1,
    267-9, 273-5; petition to
    Tojo, 262-75; and Tan
    Malaka, 299-302; and Waseda
    University project, 1, 251,
    320.
Nishimura, Lt.-Gen., 21.
Nishimura, Maj.-Gen., 316,
    320-1, 329.
Nishimura Naoki, 134, 137, 144.
Noji Munesuke, 137.
Nōmin Renseijo. See Talapeta.
Noor, Ir Pangeran Mohammad, 283.
Noor Tadjoeddin, 252, 264, 281.
Numada, Gen., 342.
Nur, Teungku, Mohammad, 18.

Obana, 222, 330.
Obata, Col., 21, 28, 333.
Oda, Lt., 40, 43.
Oemar, Mohammed Saleh (Surapati;
    'Suleiman'), 81, 89, 201,
    203, 204, 206, 209-10, 211,
    212-16.
Oemar, Teuku, 395.
Ogawa, 380.
Ogawa, Gōtarō, 140.
Ohara Bunshichi, 135.
Oil: in Borneo, 225, 229;
    Japanese concern for
    facilities, 13, 16, 20, 23,
    25, 49, 54, 70; pricing
    policy, 63-4.
Oka Keijun, 130, 135, 151.
Okada Fumihide, 2, 3, 127-58;
    appointed Minseifu Sokan,
    129-32; conflict with
    military, 136, 140-2, 146-52;
    selects officials, 132-6;
    views of on colonial policy,
    157-8.
Okada Keisuke, Adm., 129, 132-3.
Okamoto Naoto, 134.
Okamura Masayoshi, 43.
Okazaki Seizaburō, Maj.-Gen.,
    33-4, 35, 39, 40, 43, 49, 52,
    60, 65, 66, 144.
Ōki Atsuo, 68.
Okuda Kiminobu, 161, 162.
Ōmori Hiroshi, 134.
Onikura Norimasa, 229.
Ōsawa Toru, 135.
Ōta Takeo, Rear-Adm., 146.

Ōtsuka Battalion, 336, 338.
Ōtsuka Isei, 64-5.
Ōtsuka Tadashi, **173-5.**

Padang Panjang, 19, 307.
Paku Alam, 118, 120.
Palembang, 49.
Pancasila, 200.
Pancur Batu. See Arnhemia.
Pandraih rebellion, 188, 202.
Pangkalan Brandan, 202, 380.
PARI, 254, 300.
Parindra, 264, 268, 356.
Participation, political (**seiji
    sanyo**), 120-2, 125.
Partindo, 88, 115, 254, 300.
Patterson, Rear-Adm. W.R., 346,
    349, 363.
Pekalongan, 335.
Pemuda. See Youth.
Penang, 9, 11, 12, 13, 16-7;
    Radio, 12, 14, 18, 21.
Pendidikan Nasional Indonesia,
    307.
Peramiindo, 19.
Percival, Gen., 344.
Perhimpunan Indonesia, 259, 260.
Pesindo, 388, 389.
PETA (Pembela Tanah Air), 3,
    189, 217, 221,330, 366. **See
    also** Giyugun.
Pétain, Marshall, 51, 311.
Peureulak (Aceh), 25.
Pewarta Deli, 194.
Philippines: American landings
    in, 225, 229; Japanese
    operations in, 55, 60;
    independence in, 279, 280.
Physical education, 160, 168,
    175, 285, 286.
Pidië (Aceh), 181, 375, 380,
    381, 383, 387, 388.
PKI, 309.
PNI (Partai Nasional Indonesia),
    114, 115.
Pontianak, 144, 284; affair,
    268.
Poorten, Lt.-Gen. H. ter, 40,
    42-8.
PPPI, 255.
Prisoners of war, 334-5, 336-7,
    346, 347, 348, 350-1, 355-6,
    358, 360.
Propaganda Unit, 12, 14, 37,
    68-9, 71, 75, 303.
Prostitutes, 141, 150.

Pujong (East Java): relocation
    of Japanese to, 349-50, 364,
    369, 370, 374.
Pulo, Teuku, 24.
PUSA, 10, 11, 14, 19, 25, 177,
    376, 378; conflict with
    uleebalang, 381-95; and F
    Kikan, 14-15, 17, 21, 26, 27,
    179, 180, 377; and reform of
    judicial and religious
    system, 180-90; Scouts, 18;
    Youth, 17, 18, 26.
Putera, 235, 272, 278, 306.

Rabaul, 32, 56, 66, 77.
Radjiman Wediodiningrat, Dr,
    323.
RAPWI teams, 348, 351, 365.
Rasjid, Teuku, 24.
Ratulangie, Dr G.S.S.J., 264,
    281, 332.
Ratulangie, Zus, 265.
Rebellions: anti-Japanese, 30,
    188, 202, 226-9.
Red Cross: in Surabaya, 347,
    348.
Religious system: reform of in
    Aceh, 181, 182, 184-90.
Rengasdengklok, 300, 317, 318.
Rice: in Java, 244-8, 334.
Rōmusha (labourers), 193, 225,
    246-7, 249-50, 257-8, 266,
    304.
Roti, 102, 104.

Sab Cut, 25.
Sab, Husein, 382-3, 384, 389,
    394.
Sabang, 25.
Sabi, Teuku, 24.
Saigon, 28, 50, 54, 71, 149,
    323.
Sailors Training Institute
    (Makasar), 153, 154.
Saionji, Prince, 129.
Saipan, 223.
Saito Fumiya, 368.
Saitō Shizuo, 320-1.
Sakaguchi Brigade, 33, 37, 48.
Sakomizu Hisatsune, 132-3.
Saleh, Chaerul, 254-5, 300, 303,
    322.
Salleh, Mohammad, 11, 13.
Salmiah, 105, 109, 212-16.
Salt, 226.
Samalanga (Aceh), 29.

Samejima Shigeru, 134.
Sangyō Hōkokukai, 236.
Saniam, 105-6, 195, 196.
Sano Division, 49.
Sarekat Islam, 272.
Sasagi Takanobu, Capt., 135-6, 141, 146-9.
Sastrawidagda, Dr Samsi, 252, 280-1, 342.
Satō Nobuhide, 253, 260-1, 263, 264, 267, 271-2, 273, 305.
Sawamoto Yorio, 130, 152.
Second Southern Expeditionary Fleet, 270, 277, 368, 370.
Second (Tōhoku) Division, 16th Army, 33, 36, 37, 39, 40-2, 46, 47, 48.
Seinendan, 163, 225, 235-6.
Sekidōkai (Equator Association), 173, 289.
Self-sufficiency policy, 145, 223, 237-50.
Semarang, 230, 334, 336, 337, 345, 368.
Senjinkun, 54.
Serang (West Java), 33, 34, 36, 38, 39.
Seri Takeji, 132.
Seulimeum (Aceh), 18, 19, 21, 22, 26, 381.
7th Area Army, 237, 246, 249, 328, 342.
Shibata Yaichirō, 3, 144, 269, 270, **277-87, 341-74**; on arms to Indonesians, 355-60, 372-3; at Singapore surrender ceremony, 341-5; and unrest in Surabaya, 345-74.
Shigemasa Masayuki, 133.
Shijun-in (Advisory Council), 73-4, 259.
Shimada Shigetarō, 130, 142.
Shimizu Hitoshi, 1, 71, 75, 273-4, 300.
Shimizu Shigeo, 134, 144, 159.
Ships, construction of, 156, 225, 231, 241-4.
Shōgenji family, 71-2.
Shōgenji Teiji (Tei-chan), 62, 67-8, 71-2, 74.
Shōji, Col., 38-9, 42, 76.
Shōji Regiment, 33, 37, 38, 39, 40, 41, 47, 48.
Shū Sangikai (Residency Advisory Council), 120-1, 291, 304, 356.
Siantar, 201, 202.
Sibayak, Mt., 109, 191, 193, 194, 203.
Siegers, Maj., 365.
Sigli, 22, 26, 177; Japanese occupation of, 25-6; and PUSA-uleebalang conflict, 375-95.
Singapore, 33, 37, 50, 65, 107, 177, 190, 230, 231, 246, 252, 289, 290, 299, 308; administration of compared with Java, 54, 57-8, 64-5; as centre of F Kikan activities, 20, 21, 27-9; meeting of commanders in (July 1942), 63-4; surrender ceremony in, 326, 342-5, 362, 368.
Singaraja, 159, 284; Normal School, 165-6, 171.
Singgih, Mr Raden Pandji, 267-8, 318.
Sirait, Nulung, 201.
Siregar, Mohammed Jacub ('Iwan'), 80, 81, 88, 89, 97, 106-7, 194, 195-6, 197; arrest of, 89-93, 104-5, 108; flees to Jakarta, 208-10, 212; and KTT, 198-208.
Sitompoel, Hopman, 202.
16th Army: administration of Java, 2, 31-72 passim, 217-50 passim, 278; and independence issue, 270, 304, 310; named 'Osamu Troop', 55; and Navy, 253; problems of in Central Java, 333-8.
Sjahrir, Sutan, 1, 303, 307-8, 311.
Sjarifuddin, Amir, 32, 307.
'Social Revolution' in Sumatra (1946), 80, 190, 216.
Soedirman, Gen., 338.
Soedjono, 74.
Soepomo, Dr R., 332.
Soetardjo Kartohadikoesoemo, 74.
Solo. **See** Surakarta.
Son Hōin (Village Courts), 183, 185-7.
Spies, Walter, 285.
Subardjo, Mr Raden Achmad, 1, 114, 252, 254-5, 256, 259-61, 267, 269, 280-1, 305-8, 311-15; and Dokuritsu Juku,

305-8; and independence
proclamation, 311-24, 325;
and Tan Malaka, 299-302;
tour of Bali, 284-7.
Sudara, 264.
Sudirman, Raden, 356, 357,
360-1, 362, 365.
Sudiro, 315, 318.
Sudō, Tetsuomi, 134, 146.
Suetsugu, Adm., 129.
Sugawara Airforce Unit, 37, 43,
46.
Sugita, Lt.-Col., 13, 14.
Sugiyama Hajime, Gen., 55-6.
Suikōsha (Navy Club), 130, 137,
150, 281, 367, 370, 371.
Sukapiring, 95, 101.
Sukarni, 300, 303, 317; and
independence proclamation,
319-24.
Sukarno, 1, 3, 120, 121, 123,
124, 225, 226, 228, 235,
256-7, 258, 259, 303, 307,
308, 312; and Imamura, 32,
61-3, 70-5; and independence
proclamation, 313, 319-24,
327, 350; kidnapped by youth
group, 300, 315-19; and
Nishijima, 251, 254-5, 272;
as orator, 75, 284, 286, 330;
as President, 296, 363, 365,
379; in Tokyo, 125; tour of
Navy areas, 3, 269, 280-2,
284-7, 368.
Sulaiman, Teuku Pakih, 387.
Sulawesi. See Celebes.
Suleiman. See Oemar, Mohammed
Saleh.
Sultans and rulers: in Java,
116-20, 121; in Sumatra, 80,
85, 193, 194, 216.
Sumantri, Iwa Kusuma, 3, 301,
307, 308, 311.
Sumatra: administration of by
Japanese, 2-4, 58-9, 290-4,
see also 25th Army; counter-
espionage in, 197-8; fifth-
column operations in, 9-30;
independence for, 294-6. See
also Aceh.
Sumida Tomo, 135.
Sumiki (Rear-Adm.), 369.
Sundas, Lesser, 144, 225, 278,
304; Minseibu in, 143, 159.
Supeno, 318.
Supriadi, 227.

Surabaya, 37, 48, 49, 141, 145,
148-9, 152, 277, 282, 345;
anti-Dutch violence in,
350-1; anti-Japanese
violence in, 352-74; meeting
of February 1945 in, 270,
279-80; occupation of by
Dutch troops, 348-9; peace
preservation in, 347, 352-4.
Surakarta, 336; Susuhunan of,
116, 118-20.
Suwirjo, Raden, 114-15.
Suzuki, Maj.-Gen., 13.
Suzuki Kantarō, 132.
Suzuki Seihei, **159-71.**

Taiping (Malaya), 9, 12, 26.
Takabe Rokuzō, 132.
Takagi Sōkichi, Capt., 129, 132,
135, 136, 149.
Takahashi, Maj.-Gen., 63.
Takahashi Akira, 133.
Takahashi Ibo, Vice-Adm., 137,
141, 146.
Takashima Tatsuhiko, Col., 43,
49, 52, 57, 66.
Takasu Shirō, 146, 147, 148.
Takeda, Col., 55.
Takei Toshiyada, 161, 162.
Takeuchi Kakichi, 130, 139.
Talapeta, 79-80, 191-5, 196,
197, 198, 214; closure of,
206-7, 208-9; as KTT
training ground, 200-5.
Taman Siswa, 115, 272.
Tamiya Takeo, Prof., 133.
Tamura Saburō, 338.
Tanah Datar, 174.
Tanaka, Rear-Adm., 347.
Tanaka Minoru, Capt.: as
adjutant to Imamura, 42, 43,
72, 74; in Ministry, 271,
273.
Tanggerang Special Training
Centre, 220-1.
Tan Malaka, Ibrahim gelar Sutan,
254, 257, 299-302.
Tapaktuan (Aceh), 19, 24, 25,
180.
Tarakan, 229, 231, 282, 368.
Tarigan, Keras, 89.
Tashiro: in Penang, 11, 12;
as official in Sumatra, 38,
86, 99.
Tasikmalaya, 226.
Teacher training, 162-7, 170-1.

409

Teguh (Karo agriculturalist),
94, 95, 98, 99.
Terada Kiichi, 115.
Terauchi Hisaichi, Marshall, 60,
63-4, 221, 342, 362.
Textile production, 248-9.
Timor, 144, 225, 231, 336, 338,
368.
Tjarda van Starkenborgh
Stachouwer, Jhr. A.W.L., 40,
43-9.
Tjokroadisoerjo, Ir. R.M. Pandji
Soerachman, 311.
Tjokroadisoerjo, Iskaq, 300.
TKR. See Indonesian Army.
Toba Bataks, 13, 16, 18, 20,
202.
Tobacco estates, 95, 102, 109.
Toihara, Gen., 237.
Tōjō Hideki, 29, 55, 56, 125,
129, 206, 221; Indonesian
petition to, 271-5;
statement on political
participation, 271, 279, 304.
Tōjō Katsuko, 273-4.
Tokyo: criticism of
administration in Java, 54-6;
16th Army liaison with, 48,
50, 60, 65, 70; visited by
Indonesian leaders, 124-5,
181. See also 'Centre'.
Tomigashi Takeomi, 220.
Tominaga Kyōji, 56, 57-8.
Tominaga Shōzō, Rear-Adm., 149,
151.
Tribunal, 65-7, 214, 275.
Trimurti, S.K. 312-13.
'Triple-A' movement (Gerakan
Tiga A), 71, 235, 278.
Tsuchihashi Division, 33, 37,
48, 49.
Tsuchiya Masanari, 163-5, 171.
Tsukada, Lt.-Gen., 63.
25th Army: and independence
issue, 270, 292-6, 304; in
Malaya, 117; policy for
Sumatra, 3-4, 27, 59, 84-5,
177, 198, 289, 290-2.
21st Special Base Force, 347,
354, 355, 357-8, 361, 370.

Ueda Mitsuko, 161, 162.
Uehara Yūsaku, Marshall, 64.
Ugaki Kazushige, Gen., 50-2.
Ujongrimba, Teungku Haji, 188.
Ujung Labuhan, 102-4.

Ujung Pandang. See Makasar.
Ulama, 9, 29, 182, 184, 185,
188.
Uleebalang (Aceh): collaborate
with Dutch, 9, 14, 26;
conflict with PUSA, 381-95;
anti-Japanese propaganda of,
29; opposition to judicial
reform, 177-90; situation of
under Japanese, 376-8.
Ushiyama Mitsuo, 375-95.

Violence: anti-Dutch, 351;
anti-Japanese, 351-69, 373,
379, 381.

Wakaf, 189.
Wakamatsu Mitsunori, Maj., 41.
Wakataka, 366, 367.
Watabe Iwao, 244.
Wavell, Gen. Sir Archibald,
44-5, 48.
Westerling, Raymond ('Turk'),
210, 211-12, 213, 214.
Wikana (Sunoto), 306-8, 315,
316-17, 318.
Wilopo, R., 114-15.
Women: in KTT, 204, 205; rela-
tionships with Japanese men;
348; in workforce, 157;
POWs, 334.
Women's Associations (Fujinkai),
235.

Yamachi, 282.
Yamamoto Gombei, Adm., 138, 150.
Yamamoto Isoroku, 131.
Yamamoto Moichirō, 313, 316,
320.
Yamamoto Seiji, 138.
Yamashita, Capt., 41, 42.
Yamashita Tomoyuki, Gen., 59,
79.
Yamazaki Guntarō, 138.
Yamazaki Hajime, Capt., 227,
228.
Yamazaki Iwao, 129, 130, 152.
Yamazaki (né Sumiya), 76-7.
Yamazaki, Sgt.-Maj., 382.
Yamin, Muhammad, 252.
Yanagawa Motoshige, 220-1, 222,
227-8, 232.
Yanagihara Masuzo, Capt., 280.
Yani Achmad, 330.
Yano, 164, 166.
Yasuoka Masahiro, 125.

410

Yogyakarta, 37, 336, 342;
    Sultan of, 116, 118, 120.
Yokōji Shun'ichi, 150.
Yōsei Juku, 305-6.
Yoshizumi Tomegoro ('Arif'), 80,
    269, 270, 279-81, 302, 305-8,
    316, 319, 321.
Youth activists, Indonesian
    (pemuda), 212, 300, 303, 306,
    328, 336-7, 369; abduction
    of Sukarno & Hatta, 315-19;
    and independence proclama-
    tion, 319-24. **See also**
    Seinendan.
Youth Training Centres, 221,
    236.
Yugawa Morio, 135.
Yugawa Mototake, 133.
Yuzawa Michio, 129.
Yūgeki Butai, 198-9.

MONOGRAPHS IN INTERNATIONAL STUDIES

ISBN Prefix 0-89680-

Africa Series

16. Weisfelder, Richard F. THE BASOTHO MONARCHY: A Spent Force or
    Dynamic Political Factor? 1972. 106 pp.
    049-0   (82-91676) $ 7.00*

19. Huntsberger, Paul E., compiler. HIGHLAND MOSAIC: A
    Critical Anthology of Ethiopian Literature in English.
    1973. 122 pp.
    052-0   (82-91700) $ 7.00*

21. Silberfein, Marilyn. CONSTRAINTS ON THE EXPANSION OF
    COMMERICAL AGRICULTURE: Iringa District, Tanzania.
    1974. 51 pp.
    054-7   (82-91726) $ 4.50*

22. Pieterse, Cosmo. ECHO AND CHORUSES: "Ballad of the Cells"
    and Selected Shorter Poems. 1974. 66 pp.
    055-5   (82-91734) $ 5.00*

23. Thom, Derrick J. THE NIGER-NIGERIA BOUNDARY: A
    Study of Ethnic Frontiers and a Colonial Boundary.
    1975. 50 pp.
    056-3   (82-91742) $ 4.75*

24. Baum, Edward compiler. A COMPREHENSIVE PERIODICAL BIBLIO-
    GRAPHY OF NIGERIA, 1960-1970. 1975. 250 pp.
    057-1   (82-91759) $13.00*

25. Kircherr, Eugene C. ABYSSINIA TO ZIMBABWE: A Guide to the
    Political Units of Africa in the Period 1947-1978. 1979,
    3rd Ed. 80 pp.
    100-4   (82-91908) $ 8.00*

27. Fadiman, Jeffrey A. MOUNTAIN WARRIORS: The Pre-Colonial
    Meru of Mt. Kenya. 1976. 82 pp.
    060-1   (82-91783) $ 4.75*

32. Wright, Donald R. THE EARLY HISTORY OF THE NIUMI: Settle-
    ment and Foundation of a Mandinka State on the Gambia River.
    1977. 122 pp.
    064-4   (82-91833) $ 8.00*

36. Fadiman, Jeffrey A. THE MOMENT OF CONQUEST: Meru, Kenya,
    1907. 1979. 70 pp.
    081-4   (82-91874) $ 5.50*

37. Wright, Donald R. ORAL TRADITIONS FROM THE GAMBIA: Volume
    I, Mandinka Griots. 1979. 176 pp.
    083-0   (82-91882) $12.00*

38. Wright, Doanld R. ORAL TRADITIONS FROM THE GAMBIA: Volume II, Family Elders. 1980. 200 pp.
084-9   (82-91890) $15.00*

39. Reining, Priscilla. CHALLENGING DESERTIFICATION IN WEST AFRICA: Insights from Landsat into Carrying Capacity, Cultivation and Settlement Site Identification in Upper Volta and Niger. 1979. 180 pp., illus.
102-0   (82-91916) $12.00*

41. Lindfors, Bernth. MAZUNGUMZO: Interviews with East African Writers, Publishers, Editors, and Scholars. 1981. 179 pp.
108-X   (82-91932) $13.00*

42. Spear, Thomas J. TRADITIONS OF ORIGIN AND THEIR INTERPRET-ATION: The Mijikenda of Kenya. 1982. xii, 163 pp.
109-8   (82-91940) $13.50*

43. Harik, Elsa M. and Donald G. Schilling. THE POLITICS OF EDUCATION IN COLONIAL ALGERIA AND KENYA. 1984. 102 pp.
117-9   (82-91957) $11.50*

44. Smith, Daniel R. THE INFLUENCE OF THE FABIAN COLONIAL BUREAU ON THE INDEPENDENCE MOVEMENT IN TANGANYIKA. 1985. x, 98 pp.
125-X   (82-91965) $ 9.00*

45. Keto, C. Tsehloane. AMERICAN-SOUTH AFRICAN RELATIONS 1784-1980: Review and Select Bibliography. 1985. c. 174 pp.
128-4   (82-91973) $11.00*

46. Burness, Don, and Mary-Lou Burness, ed. WANASEMA: Conversations with African Writers. 1985. c. 108 pp.
129-2   (82-91981) $ 9.00*

47. Switzer, Les. MEDIA AND DEPENDENCY IN SOUTH AFRICA: A Case Study of the Press and the Ciskei "Homeland". 1985. c. 97 pp.
130-6   (82-91999) $ 9.00*

Latin America Series

1. Frei M., Eduardo. THE MANDATE OF HISTORY AND CHILE'S FUTURE. Tr. by Miguel d'Escoto. Intro. by Thomas Walker. 1977. 79 pp.
066-0   (82-92526) $ 8.00*

2. Irish, Donald P., ed. MULTINATIONAL CORPORATIONS IN LATIN AMERICA: Private Rights--Public Responsibilities. 1978. 135 pp.
067-9   (82-92534) $ 9.00*

4. Martz, Mary Jeanne Reid. THE CENTRAL AMERICAN SOCCER WAR:
    Historical Patterns and Internal Dynamics of OAS Settlement
    Procedures. 1979. 118 pp.
    077-6   (82-92559) $ 8.00*

5. Wiarda, Howard J. CRITICAL ELECTIONS AND CRITICAL COUPS:
    State, Society, and the Military in the Processes of Latin
    American Development. 1979. 83 pp.
    082-2   (82-92567) $ 7.00*

6. Dietz, Henry A. and Richard Moore. POLITICAL PARTICIPATION
    IN A NON-ELECTORAL SETTING: The Urban Poor in Lima, Peru.
    1979. viii, 102 pp.
    085-7   (82-92575) $ 9.00*

7. Hopgood, James F. SETTLERS OF BAJAVISTA: Social and
    Economic Adaptation in a Mexican Squatter Settlement. 1979.
    xii, 145 pp.
    101-2   (82-92583) $11.00*

8. Clayton, Lawrence A. CAULKERS AND CARPENTERS IN A NEW WORLD:
    The Shipyards of Colonial Guayaquil. 1980. 189 pp., illus.
    103-9   (82-92591) $15.00*

9. Tata, Robert J. STRUCTURAL CHANGES IN PUERTO RICO'S ECONOMY:
    1947-1976. 1981. xiv, 104 pp.
    107-1   (82-92609) $11.75*

10. McCreery, David. DEVELOPMENT AND THE STATE IN REFORMA
    GUATEMALA, 1871-1885. 1983. viii, 120 pp.
    113-6   (82-92617) $ 8.50*

11. O'Shaughnessy, Laura N. and Serra, Luis H. CHURCH AND
    REVOLUTION IN NICARAGUA. 1986. 118 pp.
    126-8   (82-92625) $11.00*

Southeast Asia Series

31. Nash, Manning. PEASANT CITIZENS: Politics, Religion, and
    Modernization in Kelantan, Malaysia. 1974. 181 pp.
    018-0   (82-90322) $12.00*

44. Collier, William L., et al. INCOME, EMPLOYMENT AND FOOD
    SYSTEMS IN JAVANESE COASTAL VILLAGES. 1977. 160 pp.
    031-8   (82-90454) $10.00*

47. Wessing, Robert. COSMOLOGY AND SOCIAL BEHAVIOR IN A WEST
    JAVANESE SETTLEMENT. 1978. 200 pp.
    072-5   (82-90488) $12.00*

48. Willer, Thomas F., ed. SOUTHEAST ASIAN REFERENCES IN THE
    BRITISH PARLIAMENTARY PAPERS, 1801-1972/73: An Index.
    1977. 110 pp.
    033-4   (82-90496) $ 8.50*

50. Echauz, Robustiano. SKETCHES OF THE ISLAND OF NEGROS.
    1978. 174 pp.
    070-9   (82-90512) $10.00*

51. Krannich, Ronald L. MAYORS AND MANAGERS IN THAILAND: The
    Struggle for Political Life in Administrative Settings.
    1978. 139 pp.
    073-3   (82-90520) $ 9.00*

52. Davis, Glora, ed. WHAT IS MODERN INDONESIAN CULTURE? 1978.
    300 pp.
    075-X   (82-90538) $18.00*

54. Ayal, Eliezar B., ed. THE STUDY OF THAILAND: Analyses of
    Knowledge, Approaches, and Prospects in Anthropology, Art
    History, Economics, History and Political Science. 1979.
    257 pp.
    079-2   (82-90553) $13.50*

56. Duiker, William J. VIETNAM SINCE THE FALL OF SAIGON.
    Second Edition, Revised and Enlarged. 1985.   281 pp.
    133-0   (82-90744) $12.00*

57. Siregar, Susan Rodgers. ADAT, ISLAM, AND CHRISTIANITY IN A
    BATAK HOMELAND. 1981. 108 pp.
    110-1   (82-90587) $10.00*

58. Van Esterik, Penny. COGNITION AND DESIGN PRODUCTION IN BAN
    CHIANG POTTERY. 1981. 90 pp.
    078-4   (82-90595) $12.00*

59. Foster, Brian L. COMMERCE AND ETHNIC DIFFERENCES: The Case
    of the Mons in Thailand. 1982. x, 93 pp.
    112-8   (82-90603) $10.00*

60. Frederick, William H. and John H. McGlynn. REFLECTIONS ON
    REBELLION: Stories from the Indonesian Upheavals of 1948
    and 1965. 1983. vi, 168 pp.
    111-X   (82-90611) $ 9.00*

61. Cady, John F. CONTACTS WITH BURMA, 1935-1949: A Personal
    Account. 1983. x, 117 pp.
    114-4   (82-90629) $ 9.00*

62. Kipp, Rita Smith and Richard D. Kipp, eds. BEYOND SAMOSIR:
    Recent Studies of the Batak Peoples of Sumatra. 1983.
    viii, 155 pp.
    115-2   (82-90637) $ 9.00*

63. Carstens, Sharon, ed. CULTURAL IDENTITY IN NORTHERN
    PENINSULAR MALAYSIA. 1985. c. 109 pp.
    116-0   (82-90645) $ 9.00*

64. Dardjowidjojo, Soenjono. VOCABULARY BUILDING IN INDONESIAN:
    An Advanced Reader. 1984. xviii, 256 pp.
    118-7   (82-90652) $18.00*

65. Errington, J. Joseph. LANGUAGE AND SOCIAL CHANGE IN JAVA:
    Linguistic Reflexes of Modernization in a Traditional Royal
    Polity. 1985. xiv, 198 pp.
    120-9   (82-90660) $12.00*

66. Binh, Tran Tu. THE RED EARTH: A Vietnamese Memoir of Life
    on a Colonial Rubber Plantation. Tr. by John Spragens.
    Ed. by David Marr. 1985. xii, 98 pp.
    119-5   (82-90678) $ 9.00*

67. Pane, Armijn. SHACKLES. Tr. by John McGlynn. Intro. by
    William H. Frederick. 1985. xvi, 108 pp.
    122-5   (82-90686) $ 9.00*

68. Syukri, Ibrahim. HISTORY OF THE MALAY KINDGOM OF PATANI.
    Tr. by Conner Bailey and John N. Miksic. 1985. xx, 98 pp.
    123-3   (82-90694) $10.50*

69. Keeler, Ward. JAVANESE: A Cultural Approach. 1984.
    xxxvi, 523 pp.
    121-7   (82-90702) $18.00*

70. Wilson, Constance M. and Lucien M. Hanks. BURMA-THAILAND
    FRONTIER OVER SIXTEEN DECADES: Three Descriptive Documents.
    1985. x, 128 pp.
    124-1   (82-90710) $10.50*

71. Thomas, Lynn L. and Franz von Benda-Beckmann, eds. CHANGE
    AND CONTINUITY IN MINANGKABAU: Local, Regional, and
    Historical Perspectives on West Sumatra. 1985.   363 pp.
    127-6   (82-90728) $14.00*

72. Reid, Anthony and Oki Akira, eds. THE JAPANESE EXPERIENCE
    IN INDONESIA: Selected Memoirs of 1942-1945. 1985.
    c. 450 pp., 20 illus.
    132-2   (82-90736) $18.00*

ORDERING INFORMATION

Orders for titles in the Monographs in International Studies
series should be placed through the Ohio University Press/Scott
Quadrangle/Athens, Ohio, 45701-2979. Individuals must remit
prepayment via check, VISA, MasterCard, CHOICE, or American
Express. Individuals ordering from outside of the U.S. please

remit in U.S. funds by either International Money Order or check
drawn on a U.S. bank. Residents of Ohio and Missouri please add
sales tax. Postage and handling is $2.00 for the first book and
$.50 for each additional book. Prices and availability are
subject to change without notice.